POLITICAL TRADITIO

Political Traditions in Modern France

SUDHIR HAZAREESINGH

OXFORD UNIVERSITY PRESS

1994

Oxford University Press, Walton Street, Oxford OX2 6DP
Oxford New York Toronto
Delhi Bombay Calcutta Madras Karachi
Kuala Lumpur Singapore Hong Kong Tokyo
Nairobi Dar es Salaam Cape Town
Melbourne Auckland Madrid
and associated companies in
Berlin Ibadan

Oxford is a trade mark of Oxford University Press

Published in the United States
by Oxford University Press Inc., New York

British Library Cataloguing in Publication Data
Data available

Library of Congress Cataloging in Publication Data
Hazareesingh, Sudhir.
Political traditions in modern France / Sudhir Hazareesingh.
Includes bibliographical references and index.
1. France—Politics and government—19the century. 2. France-
-Politics and government—20th century. I. Title.
JN2451.H39 1994 320.944—dc20 93-39461
ISBN 0-19-878074-5 — ISBN 0-19-878075-3 (pbk.)

1 3 5 7 9 10 8 6 4 2

Typeset by Rowland Phototypesetting Ltd.
Printed in Great Britain on acid-free paper by
Bookcraft (Bath) Ltd., Midsomer Norton, Avon

To Kissoonsingh Hazareesingh (1909–1993)
In loving memory

ACKNOWLEDGEMENTS

The idea of writing a historical and conceptual account of French political traditions was suggested to me by Vincent Wright in April 1990. I am greatly indebted to him in three respects: for encouraging this project over the past three years, for his extremely generous and stimulating assistance in criticizing early drafts of the work, and for providing an admirable example of intellectual rigour and scholastic excellence.

Individual chapters of the book were inflicted upon several colleagues in Oxford and I wish to thank Martin Ceadel, Michael Freeden, Benedict Kingsbury, and Adam Swift for offering their most valuable comments. In addition, three anonymous readers for Oxford University Press took the time to make a number of helpful suggestions about both the substance and presentation of the material, for which I am very grateful. Conversations with Byron Shafer over the years continue to be a welcome source of intellectual sustenance. We can both rejoice in the fact that this book is in many respects a tribute to Gallic exceptionalism, and should confirm the French view that, whatever the Americans can accomplish, they can do just as well. I would also like to thank Tim Barton, my editor at the Press, for welcoming and supporting the publication of this book, and responding to queries and occasional demands with unfailing diligence and courtesy. Furthermore, I am obliged to the Master and Fellows of Balliol for granting me sabbatical leave in Michaelmas term 1992, during which the final draft of this work was completed. I am also very pleased to acknowledge the support given by the Oxford University Research and Equipment Committee, whose generosity enabled the purchase of computing and printing equipment which greatly facilitated the writing of this book. While researching in Paris I was again reminded of the great debt owed to those whose devotion and professionalism enables the preservation of primary sources for posterity. I am therefore glad to take this opportunity to thank the library staff of the Institut des Études Politiques, the Bibliothèque Nationale, the Archives Nationales, and the Bibliothèque Historique de la Ville de Paris for assisting my endeavours over the past three years.

Also in Paris (but not, she would submit, of it) is Michéle le Doueff, whose friendship and generosity have been much appreciated. While this book has little to say about the philosophical themes she pursues with such distinction, it has benefitted in many ways from stimulating discussions about the practice of politics in France. It was also her inspiration which helped to locate the illustrative material which adorns the paperbound cover of the book. In this context, I am very grateful to Monsieur Jean Mathelin for permission to reproduce the work of his father Lucien Mathelin.

Finally, my deepest appreciation goes to Karma Nabulsi, whose challenging criticisms prompted a reconsideration of several complacent assumptions about the relationship between ideology and political practice in France, and whose love and friendship provided an invaluable source of moral support throughout the production of this book.

Sudhir Hazareesingh,
Balliol College, Oxford,
April 1993

CONTENTS

Introduction

This book aims to introduce its readers to the underlying structure of political and intellectual life in modern France in a way which differs slightly from the narratives of conventional textbooks. Its focus is thematic rather than chronological but, at the same time, considerable weight is assigned to examining the formative impact of history on French public life. The analysis is also distinctive in that it takes political groups and movements as its principal subjects rather than the institutions of central government (with the exception of Chapter 6) or such other forms of organized public activity as trade unions and interest groups. Furthermore, it highlights the importance of ideology but stresses the role of ideological concepts in creating elements of consensus and accommodation between competing political forces, rather than division and fragmentation. This account thus concentrates on three interrelated aspects of the French public realm: the character of political movements, the role performed by ideological concepts, and the significance of historical continuities in shaping lines of political division. The relationship between these three features is explored through the overarching concept of a political tradition, a term whose substance and analytical value is examined in depth in the first chapter. This account is then followed by separate chapters on the political roles of intellectuals; the ideologies of republicanism, religion and clericalism, and nationalism; and the functions and underpinnings of the state. These chapters provide the broad setting for concluding accounts of peace movements, and the political traditions of liberalism, socialism, Gaullism, and communism. Each chapter is followed by a brief chronology; short bibliographies are provided at the end of the book as a guide for further reading.

The approach adopted in analysing these political traditions makes no particular claim to originality. Indeed, its central assumptions about the nature of politics are in many respects old-fashioned. Every chapter suggests that the substance of political ideas cannot be appreciated unless they are given an adequate context; that the character of public life in modern France remains deeply marked by the imprint of history, and often cannot be understood without reference to the formative influences of the past; and finally, that the study of political practice requires the integration of historical, sociological, institutional, and conceptual analysis. These assumptions are not meant to challenge those accounts of French politics which adopt any one of these approaches to the exclusion of the others. Indeed, this book presumes that the reader is already armed with a modest amount of historical and institutional knowledge about French politics, and it is appreciated that such information can be gleaned only from specialized textbooks on modern French history, government, politics, and society. On the other hand, the principal ambition of this work is to provide an integrated introductory account of the principal features of political and intellectual life in France, and to do so in a way which shows that a proper understanding of its political system cannot be acquired without substantial historical knowledge. This book also proceeds on the assumption that political ideas should be rendered intelligible first in terms of their subjective social meanings: specifically, what such ideas evoke in the minds of those who deploy them, and what these concepts come to signify to its recipients in society. This focus on the subjective dimension of ideological utterances leaves little room, regrettably, for a proper philosophical account of their meaning. Thus there will be no systematic exploration of the extent to which these ideological propositions can be given a philosophical justification. For example, it will be shown that different political traditions rest on contrasting assumptions about human nature; however, no attempt will be made to evaluate whether any of these conceptions of human nature are 'true'. This is in part because such an analysis would entail writing an altogether different book, but also because it is not at all clear whether, strictly from the point of view of successful outcomes, the truth and rationality of an ideological proposition has any measurable bearing on the fortunes of those political groups which advocate it. If pushed further on this issue, this author would in fact contend that many core propositions of ideological systems are grounded on intuitions rather than philosophically justifiable propositions. In this sense it is no accident that, in their public discourse, French political movements and groups (and, for that matter, those of all advanced industrial societies) make little attempt to demonstrate the truth of the underlying principles on which their programmatic objectives are framed. Political forces compete with each other by using ideological concepts which rest primarily on intuitions, and the business of politics consists essentially in convincing the wider public that a political movement's core intuitions correspond to their own. Of course, this exercise in public persuasion often requires intellectual sophistication and political skill, but this, as the French say, is a different problematic.

Fortunately, this argument does not have to be developed here. This book sets out to explain how and on what basis the principal lines of political division have been constituted in France over the past two centuries; the question of the philosophical significance of the ideas themselves can be left for further thought and discussion. Indeed, this book will be deemed to have succeeded if it prompts the reader not only to seek further acquaintance with the rich treasures of French political thought and practice, but also to reflect about the broader application of its conceptual framework. As a further encouragement in the latter direction, it should be stated that this book does not aim to provide a comprehensive account of modern French political traditions. For example, the political, social, economic, and cultural relationships between Paris and the provinces have provided enduring sources of tension which transcended traditional lines of party divisions. Unfortunately, considerations of space prevented the inclusion of a chapter on the intellectual articulations of these conflicts. Similar constraints precluded the systematic examination of the ideologies of such political movements as feminism, environmentalism, and anti-racism, which have acquired considerable public prominence in recent decades. Finally, there have been growing political divisions in France over the construction of European unity; most of these were starkly displayed during the 1992 referendum on the ratification of the Maastricht treaty. These cleavages would have amply justified the inclusion of a chapter on the different ways in which 'Europe' has been intellectually represented in modern French political writings. Suffice it to say that the author will be more than delighted if this modest contribution to the study of French political traditions induces his readers to explore some of these avenues in the years to come.

CHAPTER 1

Political Traditions in Modern France

This book aims to highlight three essential features of political practice in France: the multiplicity of the lines of division among political movements and groups, the sheer longevity of many of these cleavages, and the central role performed by ideological concepts in the political process. It is essentially an attempt to show that these numerous French social and political cleavages have a long history, and that the legacy of the past played a significant role in maintaining their salience in public life. It will also suggest that these elements of continuity in many ways still shape the contours of political argument in modern France. As its title makes clear, the explanatory framework of the book is ordered around the notion of a political tradition. This introductory chapter will begin by defining what is meant by such a notion, and then examine the implications of adopting it as an instrument for explaining and understanding the political process in France.

A tradition is characteristically defined as the transmission of a relatively coherent body of knowledge or thought from one generation to the next. A political tradition may be deemed to exist when that body of knowledge or thought is concerned with defining the good life for society, and serves as the principal basis for argument and action by organized political groups and movements. The inclusion of this collective institutional element distinguishes this type of tradition from the intellectual enquiries conducted within traditions of political and moral philosophy, which do not typically fulfil such a formative function.[1] As will be seen throughout this book, philosophers and intellectuals played a critical role in formulating the core principles and objectives of particular political traditions and redefining them for new generations. Many French thinkers also took an active part in

[1] For a discussion of the concept of tradition in moral philosophy see Alasdair Mac-intyre, *After Virtue* (London: Duckworth, 1981), 190–209; and *Whose Justice? Which Rationality?* (London: Duckworth, 1988), esp. 326–88. On Quentin Skinner's related notion of 'intertextuality' in the history of ideas see James Tully (ed.), *Meaning and Context: Quentin Skinner and his Critics* (Oxford: Polity Press, 1988), 29–132, 231–88.

public life, and indeed the following chapter examines the underlying sources and political significance of this distinctive feature of French public life. However, the aim here is not to assess critically the intellectual creations of specific thinkers but to examine the wider political ensemble to which they were attached. Political thinkers often operated within an institutional framework, where they encountered the values (and imperatives) of a wide variety of organizations, ranging from state structures and parties to political movements and pressure groups. The ideological output of French intellectuals could sometimes influence directly the activities of these institutions, but the reverse was more often true. Indeed, the questions posed by political philosophers and thinkers, and the answers they produced at different moments in modern French history, were often centrally related to the specific concerns of political groups and movements. Thus one of the basic objectives of the ensuing chapters will be to explore the relationship between the ideological and institutional domains of political traditions, and situate the writings of French thinkers in their specific contexts. In sum, this is a book which is as much concerned with the practical dimension of politics as with its theoretical and conceptual underpinnings.

The basic components of the political traditions surveyed in this book consist of the following: a set of ideological principles, the identification of a particular relationship between past and present, and an institutional dimension. Each of these components will be examined in turn.

THE FORMAL PROPERTIES OF IDEOLOGIES

Although there is no universally accepted definition of the term, there is general agreement that an ideology is an interpretive frame of reference which seeks to describe social, economic, and moral conditions in society in order to direct and mobilize groups towards specific political ends. This being accepted, there is little scholarly consensus on the sufficient conditions for defining a political end as ideological and much discussion of whether ideologies are essentially normative or descriptive in character; a strong variant of the former regards ideologies as distinctive precisely in that their basic claims cannot be upheld or invalidated by rational argument.[2] The philosophical

[2] D. D. Raphael, *Problems of Political Philosophy* (London: Macmillan, 1976), 17.

question of whether ideological propositions can be given rational justifications is important, but it will not be addressed directly in this introductory chapter or indeed in the rest of the book. Pursuing this line of enquiry would have involved writing a different account of political traditions, essentially focusing on their intellectual content in order to provide an analytical reconstruction of their philosophical properties (or the lack of them). This would have meant concentrating on the ideological components of the traditions at the expense of their sociological and institutional dimensions, but also to some extent abandoning the subjectivity of the values and beliefs embedded in these political traditions. This analysis, therefore, will primarily be concerned with the extent to which various political traditions embraced different ideological propositions or assigned different meanings to similar ideological concepts (such as freedom and equality).

The prime focus of this account of ideologies being thus established, the next step in the analysis involves ascertaining more precisely what the internal and external properties of an ideology are. All the ideologies treated in this book possess a particular formal structure, based on a relatively coherent ordering of their basic principles. In this context a number of common misconceptions about the internal properties of ideologies need to be dispelled: first, the tendency to see each component of an ideology as a rigid injunction, a principle to be applied irrespective of judgement or circumstance; second, the belief that all the internal concepts of an ideological system are equal in importance; and finally, the view that social and political movements could be influenced by an ideology only to the extent that they are guided in equal measure by *all* its principles. But ideologies are not necessarily (or even typically) inflexible constructs whose scope of application has to be comprehensive; their morphology may be understood better through a closer inspection of their internal structure. In addition to describing the world in a particular way, every ideology provides a set of responses to a number of basic political and philosophical questions about human nature and society. In everyday political discourse the range of such questions is of course immense; ideologies do not profess to provide answers to very specific questions, such as the precise level of taxation which could be compatible with the preservation of individual liberty or what might constitute an appropriate political response to the practice of euthanasia. The function of ideologies is to define the intellectual parameters within which such specific questions may be discussed critically, both within and between political traditions. In this sense, the principles embodied in ideologies are always pitched at a relatively high level of generality. Some of the basic questions which ideologies address would thus include the following: what can be construed as the defining characteristic of being human (rationality, sociability, aggression, creativity, the ability to experience religious fervour, or even sexuality); what it means to be free and, conversely, to be deprived of freedom; in what sense (if at all) human beings can be regarded as equal; what might be deemed the appropriate criteria for treating members of a society (and other societies) with justice; what type of political institutions can best guarantee social order and good government; and what should be the conditions for membership of a national community?

Ideologies differ not only in the responses they provide to these fundamental questions, but also in the ordering and presentation of their internal concepts. A French conservative and a member of the French Communist Party (PCF) might provide radically different definitions of the concept of liberty: the latter could see freedom as the opportunity for everyone to develop his creative capacities, whereas the former might define freedom as the capacity to own property and enjoy the fruits of capitalist entrepreneurship. But both ideological systems might also attribute a different place to 'freedom' in their internal hierarchy of values. A conservative might regard his type of freedom as being a central principle in his cluster of ideological values, whereas for a Communist the notion of equality might be deemed more important. In other words, ideologies assign different weights to their internal components, because different values are privileged in their overall conception of the good life. Thus within each ideological system a distinction can be drawn between core concepts and those which occupy a less central position within the ensemble. In the words of Michael Freeden, 'ideologies may be seen as a set of concentric circles with a core cluster of concepts and ideas, an adjacent band, and a peripheral one.'[3] Each of these circles performs different functions in the political tradition within which it operates. The core of an ideology typically defines the essence of what the political tradition represents. This might include law-based government, social order, and economic freedom for the liberal; the affirmation of the overriding importance

---

[3] Michael Freeden, *Liberalism Divided: A Study in British Political Thought 1914–1939* (Oxford: Oxford University Press, 1986), 4.

of shared cultural and historical affinities within a specific community for the nationalist; the rejection of state violence and the promotion of social co-operation for the pacifist; the imperatives of enhancing mass participation and promoting social reform through evolutionary change for the socialist; the recognition of divinity in both spiritual and temporal arrangements for the clericalist; and the transcendence of the capitalist system of social and economic exploitation for the Communist. A core ideological principle, it should be noted, may be shared by different organizations within the same political tradition (as in the attachment of all republican groups to the notions of popular sovereignty and representative government), and even altogether different political traditions (like the common identification of Gaullists, Socialists, and Communists with a distinctive conception of nationalism). In sum, few ideologies have exclusive claims to a particular concept or principle; ideologies are less distinctive in their core components than in the manner in which they are internally arranged. To quote Freeden again, 'it is the morphology of the ideology—the ordering, the patterning, the interplay among concepts—that determines its unique nature.'[4]

The adjacent and peripheral bands of an ideological system tend to express different types of concern from the core concepts. If the latter define the basic characteristics of the ideology, the adjacent concepts highlight its broader features, often by relating its basic principles to the wider range of questions which ideologies typically address. Peripheral concepts are, on the other hand, only loosely related to the central elements of an ideology, and often tend to express conjunctural or circumstantial preoccupations within it. To illustrate the significance of this distinction between adjacent and peripheral concepts the case of French liberalism may be cited. As will be seen in Chapter 8, the liberal tradition in France subsumed a number of ideological undercurrents during the nineteenth and twentieth centuries. These undercurrents shared certain core principles but diverged considerably in the nature and ordering of their adjacent and peripheral concepts. All liberals identified with such notions as law-based government, social order, and economic freedom, but conservative liberals regarded the principle of popular sovereignty (and its republican corollary, democratic political institutions) as a peripheral concept, both because of their fear of its destabilizing political consequences and because of

---

[4] Ibid. 5.

their intrinsic belief that government should be kept in the hands of an enlightened minority. On the other hand, the social Catholic undercurrent accorded greater weight to participatory approaches to politics, as seen in its emphasis on the value of social solidarity and the promotion of decentralization as an organizational principle of government.

This different position accorded to the same concept by various liberal undercurrents underlines one of the important heuristic functions of the distinction between core and adjacent concepts: to allow the identification of elements of convergence and divergence within ideological systems. But this distinction can also be used to isolate patterns of convergence between political movements. For example, throughout the modern political history of France, a distinction was drawn between forces of 'order' and forces of 'movement'. In broad terms, the former consisted of conservative social groups and political movements which rejected the values and aspirations embodied in the French Revolution (notably civil and political equality, and secularism) and sought to promote a political order based on hierarchical and religious principles. The forces of 'movement', in contrast, identified with the central tenets of 1789, and often united under the umbrella of republicanism to further their objectives of widening mass participation in public life, reducing economic and cultural differences between different sections of society, and establishing a form of government based on secularism, respect for legality, and the sanctity of individual rights. Neither 'order' nor 'movement' could properly be regarded as complete ideologies; indeed, both categories consisted of social and political groups which came from markedly different ideological horizons. Forces of 'order' included supporters of the monarchy and advocates of empire, religious zealots and agnostic notables, and paternalistic conservatives and dogmatic sponsors of a minimalist state. While their core ideological principles were different (sometimes markedly so), the adjacent concepts to which they subscribed were sufficiently compatible to allow for elements of convergence and political co-operation. The same pattern could be discerned within the constellation of groups which constituted the forces of 'movement', typically including reformists and revolutionaries, centralists and decentralists, nationalists and internationalists, and finally, class-based movements and groups which appealed to a wide variety of social forces. But again, while these movements took different ideological precepts as their core values, their adjacent and peripheral concerns

overlapped sufficiently to enable the formation of wider political agreements and alliances.

It is worth noting that the relationship between core, adjacent, and
peripheral elements of an ideology was not immutable, and indeed
often changed over time. As will be seen throughout this analysis,
political movements were constantly rearranging the ordering of their
principles to meet changing internal requirements and external circumstances. For example, as will be noted in Chapter 11, the PCF
regarded nationalism as a peripheral principle in its hierarchy of values
before 1935; if anything, the party denounced the way in which nationalist concepts were used by the 'bourgeoisie' to prevent the French
working class from recognizing their common interests with fellow-
workers from other countries. In the wake of the Popular Front strategy
of republican unity against 'fascism', however, the Communists discovered the benefits of appealing to the patriotic instincts of the Left.
By 1945, in the aftermath of the party's successful role in organizing
popular resistance against foreign occupation, nationalism had been
incorporated as a core ideological concept of the PCF.[5] Another
example of such a rearrangement was the ideological change which
occurred within the French Right after the Second World War. Core
republican principles such as civil and political equality were always
regarded with suspicion by many groups on the Right, who traditionally
expressed a preference for a political order based on clearly demarcated lines of hierarchy and frequently advocated the exclusion of
certain social and political groups from the national community. With
the defeat of the anti-republican forces harboured by the Vichy regime
(1940–4), and the concomitant rise of socially and politically progressive groups such as Gaullists and Christian democrats, mainstream
groups within the French Right internalized many basic republican
values, including the principles of civil and political equality. As will
be seen in Chapter 10, Gaullist ideology represented a successful
attempt to reconcile the traditions of the Right with the legacy of
French republicanism; this reconciliation was achieved in part through
the reordering of some of the Right's core ideological values.[6]

---

[5] For an excellent analysis of the transformation of the French Communist value
system during this period see Stéphane Courtois, *Le PCF dans la Guerre* (Paris: Ramsay,
1980); and Bernard Pudal, *Prendre parti: pour une sociologie historique du PCF* (Paris:
Presses de la Fondation Nationale des Sciences Politiques, 1989).

[6] On the changes within the Right during this period see S. Berstein and O. Rudelle
(eds.), *Le Modèle républicain* (Paris: Presses Universitaires de France, 1992), 357–81.

THE FUNCTIONS AND SIGNIFICANCE
OF IDEOLOGIES

The two examples cited above illustrate the central role which ideological concepts could play in representing (and redefining) the identity of political traditions. This raises the broader question of the varying functions of ideological concepts in French political discourse, which will be examined briefly in this section.

In the classical Marxist tradition an ideology is regarded as a coherent and comprehensive system of social and economic norms about the good life. These values typically express the world-view of a dominant class and are used by the latter to maintain their hegemony over other social forces. As Antonio Gramsci stated, 'one of the most important characteristics of every class which develops towards power is its struggle to assimilate and conquer "ideologically" the traditional intellectuals. Assimilations and conquests are the more rapid and effective the more the given social class puts forward simultaneously its own organic intellectuals.'[7] In their description of the world, it is thus claimed, ideologues deploy ideas and values for the manipulative purposes of dominant social groups.

The notion of ideology adopted in this book takes seriously the Marxian proposition that ideologies have a socially expressive dimension, and indeed that they are more interesting in terms of what they reveal about the present (and past) than in what they aspire to create in the future. But this narrative resists adopting the postulate that ideologies are illusory constructs, exclusively shaped and deployed by political elites for oppressive purposes. This book will show that ideological systems constantly responded to the yearnings and demands of social forces, and these groups often played a significant role in formulating the content of ideologies. In highlighting the role performed by ideological concepts within their respective political traditions, this analysis will endeavour to demonstrate that ideologies always depended for their existence (and survival) on the adhesion of particular social groups. Of course, it will not be denied that many French ideologies were consciously devised for deceptive purposes by certain political forces. It will also be accepted that groups in society

---

[7] Antonio Gramsci, 'The Formation of Intellectuals', *in The Modern Prince and Other Writings*, translated and edited by Louis Marks (London: Lawrence and Wishart, 1957), 122.

could often adhere to values and beliefs through ideological manipulation, but this will rarely appear as the principal basis for social identification with ideological systems. Furthermore, although this book shares the Marxist assumption that ideologies are expressive of social values, it rejects the tendency within the Marxist tradition to restrict the scope of enquiry to social classes. As will be seen in this analysis, ideological principles were indeed upheld by classes (as seen in working-class support for the PCF) but also functional groups within and outside the state (schoolteachers and lawyers), religious and secular communities, individuals who shared a common affiliation to a political movement (as with Gaullism), and also social forces which had different partisan attachments (as, for example, in the institutionally fragmented liberal and pacifist traditions). This book will seek, wherever possible, to connect the articulation of ideological principles with the social and political aspirations of specific groups and movements in society.

What did these ideologies signify to these different social groups? A distinction may be drawn here between the expressive and teleological dimension of an ideology. In the nineteenth century, for example, republican and Catholic ideologies posited clear (and sharply divergent) visions of an ideal society, whose emergence they hoped to facilitate through political activity and social mobilization. But these ideologies were also social constructs in that they expressed the preoccupations and anxieties of specific social groups (urban middle-class groups in the case of republicanism, and aristocratic and peasant communities in that of Catholicism). Ideologies thus represented ideas and values which expressed the experiences and concrete aspirations of particular sections of French society at a given time in its history. It is the basic assumption of this book that an ideology cannot be understood without reference to the historical context of its expression, as well as the social identities of its bearers. Once this context is identified, it becomes possible to take a closer look at the varying functions of ideological discourse in the political system. As will be made clear throughout this analysis, ideological concepts could be put to different uses by groups operating within distinct political traditions in France. Ideology could be deployed by groups who aspired to exercise state power, as well as those whose ambition was merely to influence state policy (for example, pacifists). It could express the aspiration of a group or community towards greater social and economic integration (as with the middle-class groups which identified with republicanism), or alternatively crystallize a particular group's rejection of existing society (like extreme forms of clericalism, anarcho-syndicalism, and anarcho-communism, or, more recently, 'deep' environmentalism). It could be used as a means of including groups within the community, often by appealing to notions of common interest (as with some strands of liberal ideology), or designating certain sections of society for exclusion (as with extreme forms of nationalism and fascism). Ideology could be deployed to justify particular actions or mobilize sections of society towards institutional goals (for example, the establishment of a new regime). It could provide the impetus for initiating specific public policies (as in creating a secular system of education or launching a programme of privatization) or alternatively it could inhibit (and even foreclose) the adoption of policies (hence, for example, the disinclination of the Communist Party to seek support from social groups other than the working class). Finally, at a higher level of generality, ideological concepts could contribute towards the legitimation of political institutions, as will be seen in the chapters dealing with the Republic, nationalism, and the State. Political ideologies were therefore eminently pliable constructs, whose articulation and use was always bound by other variables in the tradition within which they operated. This is not, of course, a particularly novel conception of ideology: reputable historians of ideas have always regarded it as an indispensable component of their intellectual tool-kit. In the words of Michael Oakeshott:

So far from a political ideology being the quasi-divine parent of political activity, it turns out to be its earthly stepchild. Instead of an independently premeditated scheme of ends to be pursued, it is a system of ideas abstracted from the manner in which people have been accustomed to go about the business of attending to the arrangements of their societies. The pedigree of every political ideology shows it to be the creature, not of premeditation in advance of political activity, but of meditation upon a manner of politics.[8]

The content of these 'meditations' varied considerably among the different political traditions which are discussed in this book. All traditions, however, saw themselves as expressing a particular form of continuity between past and present. The varying representations of these elements of continuity will be outlined in the following section.

---

[8] Michael Oakeshott, *Political Education* (Cambridge: Bowes and Bowes, 1951), 14.

POLITICAL TRADITIONS AND THE
ORDERING OF THE PAST

The political traditions analysed in this book consciously articulated a distinct relationship between past and present, in that they deemed themselves to be the bearers of a specific element of continuity in the social and political history of France. Every tradition, in other words, saw itself as representing a distinct set of ideas, principles, and values which had been upheld by earlier generations; indeed, their historical pedigree was regarded as an important (and, in some cases, sufficient) condition of their appeal. But this 'history' was always a particular intellectual construct, a narrative which consciously blended imaginary elements with objective events in order to posit a precise relationship between past and present. This historical dimension of political traditions could take a variety of forms. To begin with, many traditions identified with a founding myth, a particular turning-point in the past which was regarded as providing the initial impetus for their development. This founding event could be construed as a specific moment (the Revolution of 1789 for republicans or Hugues Capet's founding of the French monarchy in 987); the political legacy of a charismatic figure (Napoleon and the Bonapartist tradition in the nineteenth century; de Gaulle and modern Gaullism); or the fusion of interlinked but distinct episodes (the Communist Party identifying itself as the political expression of the October Revolution of 1917, the radicalization of the French Left after 1920, and the emergence of working-class consciousness in France).

Once its founding moment was identified, a political tradition's relationship with its past could also assume different forms. Some traditions posited a direct filiation between their founding moment and the present (as in the case of republicanism and the 1789 Revolution), while others regarded themselves as the inheritors of the principles and values of a broad range of movements, which were none the less united by common ideological principles (as with the modern Socialist Party and its nineteenth- and twentieth-century antecedents). The establishment of these lines of continuity invariably led to the creative reconstruction of the past. This mythological[9] dimension of French history came into full view with certain traditions which posited

---

[9] For further discussion of the role of myths in modern French political history see Raoul Girardet, *Mythes et Mythologies politiques* (Paris: Seuil, 1986), 9–24.

the existence of a golden age, the return to which was seen as the primary purpose of political action. Golden ages assumed different properties. Clericalists and monarchists presented France before 1789 as a political community embodying their primary virtues (religious piety, acceptance of a hierarchical society governed by the dynastic principle). Pacifists and some liberals went even further back in time to the period when social relations were allegedly governed by the peaceful interaction of small communities. At the other end of this spectrum, some political traditions saw the past as a condition from which to escape: an era of oppression and injustice (for Communists and the extreme Left), a succession of national betrayals, manipulation of governments by occult forces, and sinister conspiracies (the nationalist Right's view of the modern history of the Republic), or an enduring and tragic collection of mistakes and human failings, which should serve as a warning for present and future generations (the Gaullist vision of the past).

Another way in which political traditions differed in their conception of the past was in the extent to which sense and meaning could be attributed to the workings of history. For Communists and republican idealists, the past was seen as a succession of staging-posts in the emergence of the social and political order to which they aspired. In the Communist reconstruction of French history since 1789 there was a clear equation of historical succession with the notion of progress. With this almost linear conception of the past came a distinct ordering of its key stages. The proclamation of the Jacobin Republic in 1792, the overthrow of monarchies and empire in 1830, 1848, and 1870, the election of the Paris Commune in 1871, the creation of the first labour parties and associations under the Third Republic, and the October Revolution of 1917 were presented as distinct phases in the development of modern society towards the Communist ideal. In contrast, other political traditions saw the events of the past as merely fluctuating and contingent occurrences, with little underlying sense of positive direction or purpose. Rejection of the progressive meaning of history could take a variety of forms. In extreme cases (such as the conservative liberal strand) recent history was seen to be dominated by forces of chaos and destruction: there were few safe generalizations that could be offered about the future, except that tragedy and disaster would loom large on its horizon. The implicit elements of determinism embedded in this approach were made explicit in the clericalist vision of the past, in which calamitous occurrences (such as the military defeats of 1871 and 1940) were consciously identified as acts of divine retribution for the errors and follies of mankind. This contrast between progressive and regressive (or cyclical) conceptions of the past was further mirrored in the dichotomy between participatory approaches to politics on one hand and elitist and quasi-deterministic conceptions on the other. For those who believed that history had a positive sense of direction, political mobilization was seen as an important contributory factor to the process of social and political change. Hence, for example, the French Left's emphasis on the principle of popular sovereignty and the promotion of greater mass participation in public life. This was accompanied, however, by sharp differences between centralist and decentralist undercurrents over precisely how this participation should be directed. In the case of the Communists the emphasis on mass participation was rather awkwardly juxtaposed with a strong element of centralization and an underlying philosophy of history which exhibited strong elements of determinism. But, at least at the level of principle, the Communist tradition was committed to the view that wider public participation in politics was beneficial for society. For traditions which regarded the past as the reign of contingency and tragedy, however, this wider public involvement in political life was always held to be problematic. Human nature was governed by greed and passion, and the violent forces which it persistently unleashed could be controlled only by strong and decisive leadership, and a form of politics in which hierarchical lines of authority were clearly demarcated. In other words (and this is where these pessimists parted company with the equally centralizing aspirations of the Communists), if any lesson could be drawn from the past, it was the simple proposition that the habitual instincts of the 'people' were self-destructive as well as dangerous for social order.

THE BEARERS OF POLITICAL TRADITIONS

This reference to the participatory dimension of politics directly raises the broader question of the institutional parameters of these political traditions. Two dimensions of the latter have been highlighted so far: their ideological components, and the different ways in which they purported to reaffirm certain formal patterns in the relationship between past and present. Equally significant for the perpetuation of a political tradition in France, however, was the continued presence of enabling institutional forms which facilitated (or, at the very least, did not consistently and significantly frustrate) its existence, organized movements which directly identified with its central ideological tenets and specific social groups which could act as its primary bearers.

A hospitable institutional environment was a necessary but not sufficient condition for the development (and survival over time) of any organized expression of ideological activity. The ensemble of institutions which constituted the French State could influence the parameters of political activity within society in numerous ways, as will be seen throughout this book. Furthermore, a specific chapter is devoted to the different ways in which the State itself was regarded as a political tradition, with a distinct ideology and institutional vocation, a particular type of elite, and a consistent set of social and economic priorities. With regard to other political traditions, however, the enabling (or inhibiting) dimension of State activity could assume a variety of forms. A regime could encourage the institutionalization of a political tradition by directly sponsoring its development: hence, for example, the almost inextricable relationship between Gaullism as a political and ideological movement and the political system which was established in France after 1958. Conversely, a regime could use its institutions systematically to frustrate and undermine the organization of a political tradition. The panoply of powers available to State institutions was often used to these ends in France during the nineteenth and twentieth centuries. Radical republicanism was stifled in the nineteenth century by the effectiveness of the repressive measures taken by monarchical, imperial, and republican governments against its various organized undercurrents. It was this success which essentially accounted for the reputation of such figures as Auguste Blanqui (1805–81), a radical republican conspirator who owed his notoriety more to the frequency and duration of his incarcerations than to the intrinsic appeal of his ideas.[10] Following the emergence of the Republic after 1870, and its progressive stabilization in the decades which followed, the regime often used its coercive powers against groups which it regarded as subversive of the values it sought to promote. Thus the electoral system was frequently manipulated during the Third, Fourth, and Fifth Republics to promote certain types of political movement

---

[10] Blanqui's ideas and political career are evaluated in Jack Hayward, *After the French Revolution: Six Critics of Democracy and Nationalism* (London: Harvester, 1991), 222–65.

into the mainstream and marginalize and exclude others.[11] Political groups could also be discriminated against through the patterns of recruitment into the administration. At different times in the modern history of France Catholics and Communists found themselves ostracized from high administrative office on the grounds that their values were fundamentally incompatible with the deontological principles of the republican state. In the longer term a dynamic set of political institutions could even contribute towards the stifling of a political tradition altogether. As will be seen in Chapters 3 and 4, the swift disintegration of the monarchical and Bonapartist traditions in the twentieth century was partly caused by endogenous factors. However, the rapidity with which their institutional paradigms were marginalized was also a tribute to the success of republicanism, most notably its ability to deliver relative political stability, guarantee the preservation of social order, and promote a significant measure of economic prosperity.

Political traditions come in a variety of sizes and shapes: as will rapidly become clear, the institutional continuities surveyed in this book were extremely diverse in structure and character. The republican and state 'traditions' were examples of ideological and institutional continuities which operated at a high level of generality, subsuming the actions of a wide variety of groups and movements. On the other hand, many of the explicitly ideological traditions identified in these narratives were the specific preserve of parties and political associations. Some traditions were central to the political process, as in the case of the State and the Republic, whereas others operated at the margins of the political community—a fate which befell both Communist and Catholic groups for much of the modern era. The tradition of intellectual intervention in the public realm was self-evidently the preserve of a particular social stratum; on the other hand, the banner of clericalism was commonly waved by a number of different social and institutional groups. The traditions embodied in political organizations such as Gaullism, Socialism, and Communism were expressions of distinct ideologies, whereas nationalist discourse often transcended partisan ideological divisions (a situation which often encouraged the appropriation of nationalist concepts by particular groups, as will be

---

[11] For a demonstration of the negative effects of the electoral system of the Fifth Republic on the Communist Party see Vincent Wright, *The Government and Politics of France*, 3rd ed. (London: Unwin Hyman, 1989), 165–8.

seen in the case of the National Front). A number of traditions centred around political organizations (Gaullism, Socialism, Communism), whereas others were defined in terms of their relationship with social institutions (such as the Catholic Church). On the other hand, one of the distinctive characteristics of the French liberal tradition was that it was never to be represented exclusively by a social or political institution. In this respect French liberals shared the fortunes of pacifist undercurrents, which were scattered in a wide range of organizations and groups. The diverse forms assumed by the institutional components of political traditions point to the varying patterns which could be discerned in the relationships between ideologies and organized groups. An ideological ensemble could be the exclusive preserve of one political movement, but this was by no means the only possible (or even typical) configuration of relations, especially if it is remembered that core and adjacent ideological concepts could be shared by a wide range of social and political forces.

Finally, a few remarks may be offered with respect to the social and cultural identities embedded in political traditions. As already noted in the above paragraph, political movements were always based on the support of a distinct array of social forces. The identification of these elements of sociological support for political organizations, and their continuities over time, has been one of the mainstays of French political science in the twentieth century. But the study of political traditions amounts to more than the mere analysis of patterns of social alignment in French politics. It is useful to make a distinction between the social actors which actually identified with political movements, and the social groups which were assigned a privileged status within distinct political traditions. Successful political movements tended to attract support from a wide range of social forces, but those groups which were celebrated as the effective bearers of the political tradition occupied a distinctive position within it. These groups served a dual purpose within their respective tradition: to reinforce its internal cohesion by clearly spelling out the terms on which individuals and groups could rally to it, and to present the outside world with a living and concrete embodiment of the good life. As with the institutional components of political traditions, there were significant variations in the character of these emblematic groups. These bearers of the identities of political traditions could assume the form of classes (as in the PCF's glorification of the working class, or conservative nationalists' idealization of the peasantry); a specific social stratum (the ideals, values, and lifestyle of the Parisian intellectual); a way of life common to a range of social groups (the lower middle-class aspirations embodied in the Poujadist movement, or the religious values promoted by the clericalists); or even a public institution such as the Army (venerated by generations of authoritarian nationalists as the true symbol of the French martial spirit).

CREATIVITY AS A CONDITION OF SUCCESS

The political traditions examined in this book experienced contrasting fortunes. 'Success' is not always easy to define, particularly in the context of political movements which were often strikingly dissimilar, both in their aspirations and in their forms of organization. None the less, a number of criteria can be formulated to appraise the different traditions depicted in this analysis. The first (and arguably most important) condition of success of a tradition was its ability to retain and reproduce its essential ideological and institutional characteristics over time. If self-perpetuation of this type is taken as a first broad measure of achievement, it is clear that some of the traditions surveyed in this book were markedly more successful than others. The political fortunes of Socialists, for example, ebbed and flowed considerably between the late nineteenth and late twentieth centuries, but the various components of the tradition remained sufficiently vibrant to allow the transmission of the Socialist heritage from one generation to the next. At the other end of the political spectrum, the adversarial nationalist tradition maintained its presence on the French political scene for much of the modern era, and its revival through the activities of the National Front in the 1980s and early 1990s showed that a tradition could be perpetuated despite operating under inimical institutional conditions. On the other hand, the clericalist undercurrent signally failed to maintain itself as a mainstream political and intellectual force in the twentieth century; a similar fate appears to await the French Communists, whose ideology and organization suffered severe (and quite possibly fatal) blows between the late 1970s and the early 1990s. But success can also be attributed to a tradition on the basis of its consistent ability to inspire and promote intellectual arguments about the good life from within itself. Dynamic traditions did not merely preserve a given political heritage: they continually sought answers to basic political questions, and in so doing redefined their internal concepts to respond to changing circumstances and new challenges. Thus the status of republicanism as a political movement changed dramatically between the mid-nineteenth and the late twentieth centuries, but republican intellectual groups continued to argue about the meaning of such core concepts as liberty, equality, and fraternity throughout this period, and these debates ensured that republicanism retained a conceptual vitality which was often found wanting in its institutional embodiments. Intellectual success of this kind could be inversely proportional to institutional achievements; although French Socialists maintained their institutional and ideological heritage, they made few significant advances in their cogitations about the good life (as will be noted in Chapter 9).

Finally, a third measure of the success of a political tradition was the extent of its ability to influence social and political outcomes. Three factors are worth distinguishing under this heading: the practice of state power, the implementation of basic programmatic objectives, and the capacity to exercise ideological influence over other political traditions. These factors were not always conjoined. The achievement of public office could (but did not necessarily) lead to the implementation of a predetermined set of programmatic objectives; at the same time, the exercise of power was often inversely proportional to the capacity to retain ideological appeal. Gaullist parties were more successful in assuming political office than their liberal rivals between 1958 and 1993, but it is arguable that during the same period Gaullism came under (and eventually succumbed to) the increasing ideological influence of liberal undercurrents. Ideological factors could thus play a subtle role in shaping the success of political traditions; this point will be examined further towards the end of this chapter.

Just as success for a political tradition could be manifested in a variety of forms, so its prerequisites were equally numerous. Political traditions needed favourable institutional and sociological conditions to flourish, as has already been made clear. The decline of Catholic and Communist political cultures in France after 1945 was partly a function of the transformation of the social and economic structure of French society, resulting in a fall in religious observance and an erosion of class consciousness.[12] But these sociological and institutional factors were variables in a broader equation. Political traditions suffered vary-

---

[12] See Henri Mendras, *La Seconde Révolution française 1965–1984* (Paris: Gallimard, 1988).

ing fortunes over time partly because they were subjected to specific social and institutional influences, and were often forced to respond to events over which they had no direct control. Yet within these broad parameters, groups and movements which acted as the bearers of these political traditions were almost invariably faced with a range of choices and possibilities, and their ultimate success or failure often depended critically on their ability to work creatively within the environment they inherited. Creativity may be defined here as the ability to use both imagination and technical skill as an effective means of achieving a set of desired political ends. This attribute, for example, was often at the heart of the transformation of a given historical and ideological legacy into a successful founding myth. In this way the republican tradition reconstituted the destructive and somewhat shambolic experiences of the 1790s into the dawning of a new age for modern societies. The Communists fashioned their identity as the latter-day bearers of the radical (and internationalist) revolutionary tradition, and the Gaullists presented themselves as the modern embodiment of the social and cultural values of 'eternal France'.

The successful articulation of a founding myth in each of these three cases played an important role in strengthening the internal cohesiveness of each tradition, appealing to wider social constituencies, and adding to the political movement's sense of legitimacy. But not all myths were successfully made to operate in this manner. Some founding myths were unable to rise to positions of intellectual prominence because they were pre-empted by existing ideological currents. As will be argued in Chapter 8, the liberal tradition in France floundered on the republicans' violent and panoptic imagery of the French Revolution. Liberals sought to appropriate what they regarded as the positive phase of the revolutionary period (the abolition of feudal dues, and the proclamation of civil and political rights) and deny any legitimacy to the ensuing period of regicide, civil war, and terror. But the republican tradition rejected the very possibility of a distinction within the revolutionary totality, and strongly emphasized the legitimacy of its egalitarian ideals. To this extent, the continuing historical legacy of 1789 was a significant contributory factor to the ideological weakness of liberalism in France. But even established myths could be vulnerable to changing social and political circumstances. For example, the possibility of an alternative to the Republic (monarchical, imperial, or even clerical) was entertained by a variety of political undercurrents within the Right between 1870 and 1940. However, after the negative experience of the Vichy regime (1940–4), the notion of a possible return to a political order based on hierarchical and religious principles was almost irreversibly discredited. In the case of the Communists during the 1980s and 1990s, loss of legitimacy was partly a function of the collapse of the external component of the founding myth: the failure of the Leninist model in Eastern Europe and the disintegration of the Soviet Union.[13]

Creativity was also required in the exercise of political leadership, and this is another important variable in the assessment of the relative achievements of traditions. For political traditions which were explicitly founded on the legacy of a charismatic figure (as with Bonapartism in the nineteenth century and Gaullism in the twentieth) the quality of the leadership exercised by the founding figure was obviously a decisive contributory factor to success. Conversely, however, the fortunes of such political traditions after the demise of their founder could be significantly influenced by the quality of the leadership provided by the successors. In broader terms, the contrasting fate of political traditions which rested on classical ideological paradigms provided a good illustration of the effective (and often decisive) role of creative leadership. The contribution made by François Mitterrand to the fortunes of French Socialism after 1971 requires little elaboration,[14] particularly when contrasted with the ineptitude of the Communist leadership during the same period. Similarly, Jean-Marie Le Pen's role in the successful revival of the adversarial nationalist undercurrent in the 1980s and early 1990s cannot be overestimated.[15] In the case of some ideological undercurrents, effective leadership could almost constitute the principal defining characteristic. Conservative liberalism, for example, was rarely united as an organizational force in France during the nineteenth and twentieth centuries. Despite this organizational heterogeneity, this undercurrent succeeded in penetrating the highest levels of the French State, wielding a level of authority which was remarkably incommensurate with its strength as a political force. The

---

[13] A detailed account of the consequences of the failure of the Soviet model for French Communism is provided in my earlier work, *Intellectuals and the French Communist Party: Disillusion and Decline* (Oxford: Oxford University Press, 1991), esp. 265–96.

[14] For biographical details see Franz-Olivier Giesbert, *Le Président* (Paris: Seuil, 1990); on Mitterrand's role as Socialist leader see Alain Bergounioux and Gérard Grunberg, *Le Long Remords du pouvoir: le Parti Socialiste Français 1905–1992* (Paris: Fayard, 1992).

[15] The best (albeit slightly dated) academic study of the National Front is a collective work edited by Pascal Perrineau and Nonna Mayer, *Le Front National à découvert* (Paris: Presses de la Fondation Nationale des Sciences Politiques, 1989).

resilience of the conservative liberal undercurrent rested on its ability to provide a steady supply of technically competent, intellectually sober, and socially conservative elites, whose appeal was always high in a political system often characterized by instability, passion, and turmoil. On the other hand, the absence of decisive leadership could constitute a decisive handicap for the political tradition which suffered from it. The monarchist opposition to the Republic after 1870 rested on solid political and sociological foundations; one of the missing elements, however, was the presence of a figure who could unite these strands into a cohesive challenge to the new political order. Another example of decisive leadership failure, which will be discussed extensively in Chapter 7, was seen in the French pacifist tradition. Pacifist movements often operated in a highly favourable social and political environment during the twentieth century, but they consistently failed to produce leaders who could unite the disparate and often fractious undercurrents which subscribed to pacifist ideologies.

The exercise of leadership was particularly important in the articulation and ordering of ideological principles, and this was the third sense in which exploitation of the scope for creativity could be a critical factor in the achievements of political traditions. The first problem which should be considered under this heading might be termed the paradox of success. As suggested earlier, one of the measures of a successful political tradition was the extent to which it could transform its core objectives into public policy. The exercise of power, and the implementation of the basic programmatic aspirations of their institutional components, were clearly achievements which singled out the most successful political traditions from the rest. But comprehensive success of this type posed an obvious dilemma: if the primary objectives of a political tradition were achieved, on what ideological basis could it continue to justify its existence? The cases of the Radical movement under the Third Republic and the Gaullist tradition under the Fifth provided graphic illustrations of this quandary, and the attendant problems of political traditions which were unable to reformulate their basic principles in the wake of institutional successes. Like the Radicals, who lost their distinctive political identity when the essence of their political and economic programme was achieved by the early twentieth century, the Gaullists found themselves unable to articulate a new set of ideological principles after 'their' regime (the Fifth Republic) gained widespread political acceptance in France in the 1980s and 1990s. Of course, both of these movements continued to justify their existence on the basis of their record in office, during which they had clearly demonstrated their capacity to govern. But a dynamic political tradition does not merely rule, it governs for a purpose. As will be argued in Chapter 10, the Gaullist tradition became increasingly unsure of its ideological *raison d'être* in the decades which followed the death of its founder; in many respects the Socialist movement faced a similar dilemma in the 1990s, as it prepared to confront the prospect of existence without its supreme guide, François Mitterrand.

Ideological re-evaluation was thus a necessity for political movements which successfully implemented many of their core objectives in government, and the survival of these traditions often depended on the extent to which their leaders were able to reformulate their primary goals. But the imperative of re-evaluation was even more strongly experienced by political undercurrents which were excluded from the corridors of power. Here the impetus for reappraisal was a direct function of the need to survive and came essentially from two sources: the changing terms of political competition and the balance of forces inside the broader ideological community within which the specific undercurrent operated. To understand how these pressures worked, the contrasting fortunes of political movements which belonged to the same broad groupings ('order' and 'movement') may be evoked. When viewed from a broad historical perspective some undercurrents within each grouping clearly proved far more adept at survival than others, despite a common failure by most of them to hold high office for any length of time. Why, for example, did moderate Catholic undercurrents (such as social Catholicism) survive as dynamic forces until the end of the Fourth Republic, while clericalist groups became marginalized? Why did Communists maintain themselves as a mainstream movement on the extreme Left, while anarchists and anarchocommunists almost disappeared? Why were fascists and monarchists relatively isolated as institutional forces in France, whereas conservative nationalists enjoyed considerable successes? The common denominator in each of these cases was a readiness to accommodate changing political circumstances and show a considerable element of flexibility in the ordering of core ideological concepts. In the case of Catholicism the major turning-point in the modern history of France was the advent after 1870 of the Third Republic, whose elites were ideologically committed to the promotion of secular norms and values in society. This represented a direct threat to the entrenched position of the Church within the State and in society, and many Catholic groups rallied against this menace to their vested interests. However, as will be seen in Chapter 3, the republican regime showed considerable flexibility in applying its principles and was thus able to reach out to Catholic undercurrents which were prepared to compromise with the new regime. The compromise essentially took the form of a distinction between public retrenchment and private autonomy. The Church lost its status as a public institution but was allowed to retain much of its power and influence as a bearer of social and moral values. Catholic groups were able to accept this change by abandoning the core belief that religion should perform a public role in the arrangement of the temporal affairs of society. In restricting their activities to the private sphere, these Catholic groups were eventually able to adjust to the new conditions created by the advent of the republican regime. Similar elements of *aggiornamento* were carried out by Communists and conservative nationalists, both of which were able to respond to changing political parameters by reordering their core ideological principles. As already noted, the Communists transformed their place in the political system by affirming their commitment to nationalist and patriotic values. In the case of the conservative nationalists, the most significant element of ideological realignment was a willingness to accept the republican constitutional framework. Ideological flexibility was thus an important precondition for survival in a changing social and political environment.

THE VALUE OF STUDYING POLITICAL TRADITIONS

What does the study of political traditions contribute towards understanding the character of public life in France? The overarching theme of this book is that history exercised a vital influence in shaping the structure of political argument. Both the practice and the underlying concepts of French politics were deeply marked by the experiences of the past, and this imprint is perceptible in several ways. For example, this feature of political life partly explained the prominent role assumed by intellectuals in French public life. As will be made clear in the following chapter, one of the recognized functions of the intellectual in France was to provide the cognitive instruments needed to make the past accessible to present (and future) generations. The legacy of the past could also be noted in the tendency of political elites to refer consciously to France's historical experiences, sometimes spelling out in almost didactic form the pitfalls to be avoided and the lessons to be learnt from past tragedies. The institutions of the Fifth Republic were devised with the perceived inadequacies of its predecessor in mind; similarly, the failings and humiliations of the 1940–4 period were a direct source of (negative) inspiration for the founders of the Fourth Republic. But these historical discontinuities gave a profoundly ideological colouring to the presentation of the past, because few regimes in modern France could proudly recall the circumstances of their creation. The Fifth Republic was born out of a civil war; the Third Republic and the Vichy regime followed on the heels of a humiliating military defeat; even the Fourth Republic, which was formed in the wake of a successful act of resistance against foreign occupation, rapidly turned away from its founding myths because of the changing political alignments engendered by the Cold War. In the final analysis the weight of history in modern France was constantly evoked in its political vocabulary, and especially its vivid nomenclature. To this day an advocate of state sponsorship of industry and economic protectionism is designated as a Colbertiste, a believer in centralized government a Jacobin, and a leader with dictatorial tendencies a Bonapartist. Members of the leading party of the moderate Right still call themselves Gaullists; on the other hand, no Socialist would react passively to being described as a Molletiste,[16] and no self-respecting member of a mainstream right-wing party would appreciate being described as a Pétainiste. Thus the experiences of the past generations continue to colour the political dramas of the present.

The focus of this narrative on the underlying elements of continuity in the French political tradition also helps to posit a more discriminating relationship between tradition and innovation. Because the emphasis of this book lies on the notion of continuity, it should not be assumed that the political history of modern France is seamless in character. The central debates launched by the French Revolution were continued by subsequent generations throughout the nineteenth century (and for a considerable part of the twentieth); to this extent, modern political movements wrestled with a range of questions and problems similar to those which had exercised the attentions of their forebears. But the specific nature of these political and ideological

---

[16] Guy Mollet (1905–75) was the General Secretary of the French Socialist Party between 1946 and 1969, a period which witnessed a social, political, and ideological decline in the party's fortunes.

elements of continuity needs to be defined precisely. All political systems contain elements of inter-generational continuity in the ideological realm, and it is not being suggested here that France was exceptional in this respect. Even less is it being claimed that successive political generations were concerned with the *same* set of problems, and that there were no significant differences between de Gaulle's political philosophy and nineteenth-century Bonapartism; between the liberals of the UDF and their Orleanist ancestors; between modern Socialists and the generation of Louis Blanc; and between the Communists and late nineteenth-century French Marxists. Elements of ideological continuity of this type can be emphasized only by attaching similar meanings to terms and concepts often devised in strikingly dissimilar circumstances. Such an account could be provided only at the cost of impoverishing the analysis of political argument, especially with respect to its capacity to reflect the conjunctural preoccupations of the particular generation which conducted it. But at the same time the basic (and, admittedly, ambitious) aim of this book is not to allow specific circumstances and proper attention to historical detail to impede the identification of clear elements of continuity over time. If the danger of ahistoricism remains potent, in the final analysis it has to be accepted as an inevitable corollary to any enterprise of this nature.

But ahistoricism should not be eschewed by resorting to historicism. Indeed, the other serious danger in exaggerating the significance of the legacy of the past is to neglect the importance of discontinuities. The centrality of the notion of rupture in French political discourse attests to the turbulent and centrifugal character of its public life since 1789. Again, it is worth repeating that there is no teleological design lurking in these pages. The focus of this book on continuities in French political culture does not betray any leanings towards a particular philosophy of history; nor is there any attempt to undervalue the significance of sudden accelerations in the historical process. At the same time, however, every effort will be made to identify elements of continuity which were reasserted even in moments of great change. The momentous events of 1789 represented in many ways a break from the absolutist past, but within a decade Napoleon had succeeded in bringing together many of the contradictory impulses of the *ancien régime* and the Revolution. A concrete example of 'continuity in change' from the recent past may make this approach clearer. Soon after the election of François Mitterrand to the presidency in 1981 the Socialists proclaimed their conversion to the principles of free enterprise, thus reconciling themselves to an economic system (market capitalism) which they had vowed to reform radically ever since their reconstitution at the Epinay congress in 1971. Under the successive presidencies of Mitterrand, however, the Socialists' strategy of transcending capitalism gave way to a process of political accommodation with the principles of the free market. For most observers of modern French politics, the ideological realignment of the Socialists after 1982 represented a fundamental departure from the strategic objectives pursued by the party since the early 1970s, and there was an element of truth in the characterization of this process as a rupture. But it was no less accurate to regard the principles which eventually guided the Socialists in government in the 1980s and early 1990s (economic realism, political pragmatism, and social conservatism) as a return to the social and economic priorities of the party *before* the 1970s. Indeed, as will be claimed in Chapter 9, it was arguably the Epinay period (1971–81) which represented an aberration from the vantage point of the twentieth century. For most of the century the Socialists' record in government was characterized by incrementalism and prudence in the political sphere, and a high degree of caution in economic and social policy—precisely the features which were 'revived' by the Socialist leaders during the 1980s. Thus the important realignments of the Mitterrand decade were essentially consistent with the principles which had guided earlier generations of French Socialists in government; rather paradoxically, what appeared as rupture from a short-term perspective essentially amounted to a reassertion of earlier elements of political and ideological continuity.

Paradoxical elements of this kind figure prominently in the French political experience, and this is particularly evident in the conclusions offered in this book concerning the role of ideology in the political process. Indeed, a rather different view of the fundamental character of French politics emerges if the basic claims of this account are accepted. First, a general examination of the relationships within and between political traditions highlights the centrality of the notions of compromise and accommodation in the political process. Political traditions were held together because of their capacity to synthesize different and often radically divergent interests; at the same time, their dealings with each other were often marked by attempts to find a common ground between ideological positions. In this context the distinction between core, adjacent, and peripheral ideological concepts helps to explain how political groups could relate to each other on different levels and find areas of convergence which did not require compromise with their core principles. Under the Third Republic, republican and anti-republican groups could oppose each other fiercely over a range of fundamental issues, yet still agree that the claims of the extreme monarchists were fundamentally unacceptable (most notably and symbolically over the question of the colours of the national flag). Similarly, moderate republicans and moderate Catholics found common values in their joint struggle against the activities of extreme clericalist groups, while retaining core ideological positions which were often diametrically divergent. Communists and Socialists retained largely separate core identities throughout the twentieth century, but found ways of co-operating on the basis of shared assumptions about politics and society. In sum, many groups and movements were able to deploy ideological concepts to accommodate changing political conditions and imperatives, and reach agreements over a specific range of questions.

The argument of this book is therefore not only that compromise played a significant role in the French political process, but also that these various forms of accommodation were based on the flexible handling of ideological concepts. It is recognized that both of these claims are somewhat paradoxical concerning a political system which has always been depicted as unrelentingly fractious, with ideologies often being seen to play a catalysing role in the accentuation of existing divisions. Indeed, the relative abatement of ideological disputes in France since the 1980s has been widely welcomed as heralding a more consensual type of politics, thus ending the legacy of two centuries of political conflict. Whether these intimations of consensus prove accurate remains to be seen; it is not uninteresting to note, however, that strong elements of continuity may be found even in respect of this claim. The end of ideology, for example, was announced in France with great fanfare in the early 1960s, after Daniel Bell's pamphlet[17] had excited the appetites of technocratic elites on both sides of the ideological divide. The claim that the left-right division had become 'obsolete'[18] was asserted with great authority by the journalist (and later editor of *Le Monde*) Jacques Fauvet in 1947. The decline of intellectual intervention in the public realm was intoned by Julien Benda in 1927.

---

[17] Daniel Bell, *The End of Ideology* (New York: Free Press, 1960).
[18] Jacques Fauvet, *Les Partis politiques dans la France actuelle* (1947), quoted in Eugene Weber, *My France: Politics, Culture, Myth* (Cambridge, Mass: Harvard University Press, 1991), 42.

To go even further back, few believed that Socialism could recover from the terrible blow it received during the Great War. There can be no better testimony to the traditional character of French politics than the sheer persistence with which assertions of discontinuity and ideological decline have been proclaimed. Thus France remains marked by tradition even in its strident assertion of change and innovation.

CHAPTER 2
The Political Roles of Intellectuals

During the summer of 1983 the fortunes of the ruling Socialist administration were at a low ebb. Their economic policy was in tatters, many of their social objectives were unfulfilled, and their popularity was sinking rapidly. As many of the traditional constituencies of the Left voiced their disenchantment with the government, a debate was launched in the inside pages of the newspaper *Le Monde* over the apparent absence of enthusiasm shown by French intellectuals for the Socialist government. The Left had been in power for two years, and its traditionally large cohorts of intellectual supporters had fallen silent. Some did not hesitate to lay the blame for the strategic inadequacies of the new administration squarely on the intellectuals. The Left was deemed to be in crisis essentially because its intellectuals had failed in their appointed mission of defining a vision of the future for their political elites.

These were indeed troubled times for the French Left (and there was worse to come). But demoralization was not a condition unique to left-wing intellectuals: the French intellectual community as a whole had begun to undergo a rather turbulent phase from the mid-1970s. At this juncture the intoxicating effects of the ideological upheavals of 1968 had begun to dissipate, and many erstwhile radicals burned the revolutionary idols they formerly worshipped in a typically Parisian blaze of well-orchestrated publicity. A notable feature of this process of self-flagellation was the abandonment of the intellectuals' rose-tinted conception of the Soviet Union. Long after the rest of the Western world had seen through the pompous veneer of Soviet-style socialism, French intellectuals had remained fascinated by the Leninist experience. Their awakening was brought about by the publication of Alexander Solzhenitsyn's *Gulag Archipelago* in 1974; within a matter of months even the staunchly Leninist French Communist Party (PCF) began to criticize the 'imperfections' of the Soviet system. But the traumatic experiences of the 1970s and early 1980s were not limited to the domain of ideas. Many leading figures of the post-war generation

(Jean-Paul Sartre, Raymond Aron, Louis Althusser, to name but a few) departed from the worldly scene at this juncture, and the sense of loss experienced by the intellectual community was further accentuated by the premature disappearance of such luminaries as Jacques Lacan, Roland Barthes, and Michel Foucault. There was worse to come: the Socialist administration, elected in 1981 amid high expectations of social and economic change, rapidly accommodated itself to the harsh realities of office, and by the mid-1980s had decisively abandoned all plans to transform French society radically. By the end of the decade the continuing 'silence' of French intellectuals suggested to many that a stratum which had occupied a prominent role in French public life throughout the twentieth century had entered a phase of terminal decline.

The contention that intellectuals had declined, which was advanced with increasing frequency by observers of the French political scene in the early 1990s, rested on the conflation of three distinct claims about political conditions in modern France. First, as in the example cited above, it was argued that intellectuals had lost the capacity to influence political outcomes; in this sense their decline was an expression of their failure to articulate positive ideological goals for the country's political elites. Second, it was claimed that the moral and philosophical outlook of the intellectuals had degenerated, and that they had lost public respect because they had chosen to betray their vocation to act as guardians of the sacred temples of Truth and Justice. Finally, it was also suggested that intellectuals had lost their pre-eminent status because their hegemonic role in society had been successfully challenged by new forms of mass culture. It is important to begin by noting that these claims differed not only in their character, but also in their epistemological status. Decline in political influence and social status is (to a significant extent) a matter which can be objectively measured, whereas the charge of moral depravity is a normative claim, whose veracity can be conclusively established only if prior agreement can be reached about the conditions and objectives of intellectual intervention in public life. This was in itself a highly contentious issue, over which the intellectuals themselves could never quite agree. Furthermore, it should also be apparent that the different claims about the decline of intellectuals could not all be true at the same time. If these individuals were betraying their moral vocation, for example, it was hardly plausible to suggest that they were no longer influencing political outcomes (the nature of this influence could be questioned, but this was a separate issue). Indeed, it will be suggested at the end of this chapter that the terms of the debate of the early 1980s about the 'silence' of French intellectuals were misconceived; and that the questions raised about their continued existence as a political and sociocultural phenomenon arose only out of a misunderstanding of the roles they actually performed in the public sphere.

INTELLECTUALS IN FRANCE: DEFINITIONS AND ORIGINS

Before the argument can proceed further its principal subjects need to be defined precisely. Who were these 'intellectuals' and how did they come to be designated by this term? In modern European societies the definition of an intellectual varies considerably, both across countries and in academic disciplines. In its broadest possible sense, any person engaging consistently in abstract reflection about questions of truth and morality can be described as an intellectual. For the philosopher Alan Montefiore, an intellectual is 'anyone who takes a committed interest in the validity and truth of ideas for their own sake, i.e. for the sake of their truth and validity rather than for that of their causal relationships to whatever other ends'. A rather more restrictive definition takes the possession of a certain level of culture as the sufficient condition of intellectual activity. From this perspective artists, academics, schoolteachers, higher and middle-ranking administrative cadres, as well as members of liberal professions such as lawyers, doctors, and architects, can be broadly regarded as members of an 'intellectual community' by virtue of their educational and cultural endowments. A more precise definition is given by the sociologist John Goldthorpe, who sees intellectuals as

thinkers and writers who feel a close personal concern with questions of the human condition, and who aim to treat such questions in more than a purely scientific or scholarly manner: in particular, by 'situating' them ... within some wider context of meaning in order to bring out their significance beyond the immediate experience and interests of the individuals directly involved.

In this case it is neither exclusively the tendency to think in detached academic categories nor merely the possession of certain cultural endowments which defines the intellectual, but a particular cognitive tendency (the contextualization of thought) which tends to be exercised by a specific group of people (thinkers and writers).

In France the concept of the *intellectuel* had affinities with some of these above approaches, but was none the less distinctive in a number of respects. In the first instance, while the activities of culturally proficient groups were always held in good esteem, engaging in higher forms of cognitive activity was not in itself regarded as a sufficient condition for being designated as an intellectual. There were two essential prerequisites for being identified by this term. A true intellectual could first be detected by his educational background: a person who had frequented a prestigious Parisian *lycée* and then entered one of the capital's grand institutions of higher learning (such as the Institut des Études Politiques, the École Normale Supérieure, or the École Nationale d'Administration). But intellectuals, as mentioned above, did not merely exercise certain forms of cognitive activity: they also occupied positions of power and authority in society. Intellectuals tended to be found in large numbers among the specific range of occupations reserved for France's politico-cultural elites: the higher civil service, 'high' politics, the mass media, the artistic and literary world, and, of course, the apex of the (rigidly hierarchical) Parisian higher-education system. The same individual, it should be noted, frequently occupied significant positions within several of these occupational categories at the same time. The term *intellectuel* was reserved for those creative agents who assumed positions of power and authority in the political and cultural establishment, and thus defined norms and values for the rest of society. In French political and cultural discourse, it was therefore open to anyone to exercise intellectual activity but not everyone could be an *intellectuel*. For this accolade to be merited an individual had to be a recognized member of a highly visible group of political and cultural creators, who intervened constantly in national debates about major issues of public life.

This conception was largely inherited from modern French political history. The specific context which gave birth to the concept of the *intellectuel* in France in the late nineteenth century included public participation in political life as a defining characteristic of the phenomenon. Thus, from the very outset, productive intellectual practice was conceived as an activity which went beyond the pursuit of narrow scholastic aims. In this sense, the conditions of intellectual activity were almost invariably defined in relation to the political and ideological context of the time: to be a French intellectual required the endorsement (or rejection) of a wider set of public practices and values. In the course of the twentieth century this conception crystallized into a distinct tradition, of which a central element was later reflected in the Sartrian notion of commitment (*engagement*). The notion of the *intellectuel* was established in France in the late nineteenth century and popularized during the Dreyfus Affair. This episode was in many respects a turning-point in the modern history of France, notably in that its outcome strengthened the social and political legitimacy of the Republic. In itself the Affair involved a Jewish officer in the French Army, who was convicted of spying for Germany despite the signal absence of incriminating evidence against him. Gradually, however, his case was brought to public attention by a devoted group of intellectual campaigners. This eventually set the scene for the battle between the Dreyfusards, who argued for judicial revision on the grounds that an innocent man had been unjustly condemned, and the anti-Dreyfusards, who refused (for a variety of reasons) to entertain the thought that the Army could have erred in this way.

This emergence of the *intellectuel* as a distinctive semantic category at this juncture was not accidental. If the Dreyfus Affair was a 'victory of intellectuals', in the words of the historian Albert Thibaudet, this was true not only in terms of the leading role played by the Dreyfusard campaigners, but also from a wider social and political perspective. Refining Thibaudet's conclusion, it may be argued that the Affair was the political expression of the ascendancy of a new social stratum within the French intellectual world. In a functional sense, intellectual groups had operated in France long before the Dreyfus Affair. The writings of François Voltaire (1694–1778) and Jean-Jacques Rousseau (1712–78) played an important role in undermining the legitimacy of the old order during the decades which preceded the 1789 Revolution. At the other end of the political spectrum, prestigious scholastic and literary institutions such as the Collège de France and the Académies bore witness to the critical function accorded to cultural creators by the *ancien régime*. The social and political outlook of the scholars and writers who frequented these elite institutions was essentially tradition-alist, and in the late nineteenth century the dominant mood within this *milieu* was anti-republican. During the Dreyfus Affair the great names of French art, science, and letters were overwhelmingly opposed to the reopening of the case. Writers such as Emile Zola (1840–1902) and Charles Péguy (1873–1914) were exceptions to this rule, and they made few converts to the cause of Captain Dreyfus in the circles of the Académie Française. The underlying strength of the Dreyfusard campaigners was based on the unflinching support of large cohorts of republican schoolteachers and their disciples. The bourgeois intellectual stratum which came of age in the Third Republic was in the process of asserting its control over the principal levers of political command: in an important sense, therefore, the Dreyfus Affair confirmed the rise of this new generation, which was already beginning to challenge the orthodoxies of the cultural establishment.

This ascendancy was not restricted to the relatively narrow confines of the Parisian intellectual world. As mentioned above, the Dreyfus Affair also saw the triumph of a political system (the Republic) over an array of conservative and reactionary forces which was spearheaded by the intellectual establishment, but also included the Army, the Church, the nobility, and sections of the *haute bourgeoisie*. This fierce political battle forged an enduring alliance between the republican regime and the emerging intellectual strata. It was by no means the case that all French intellectuals became republican, or even politically active, as a result of the dramatic events at the turn of the century. The principal legacy of this period lay in the establishment of a paradigm of action. The strength and durability of this paradigm of intellectual practice could not be measured by the extent to which it was universally observed. Its historical significance lay in the fact that it provided a fixed point of reference, recognized and (often furiously) debated by subsequent generations of intellectuals. In this sense the Dreyfus Affair laid the foundations of a distinctive tradition of intellectual activity. Its basic features included a tendency towards generalization and abstraction on the part of intellectuals, a specific conception of political practice, the production of a particular type of polemical literature, and a strong identification with the basic goals and values of the republican regime. In order to understand the level at which this empathy operated, it should be noted that classical French republicanism was always a relatively fluid movement, which represented (at least) three contradictory aspirations: a belief in an ideal government, a radical opposition to the very principle of centralized power, and a relentless quest for political office. Thus nineteenth-century republicanism was already divided between revolutionists, radicals, and opportunists. But, as long as the cleavage between republicans and anti-republicans retained its political saliency, political circumstances always favoured tactical alliances between republican groups. Although separated by social, ideological, and institutional differences, their shared values brought them together whenever the survival of the Republic itself was at stake, as demonstrated most emphatically by the Dreyfus Affair. The tactical and highly circumspect conception of republican unity was well described in the memoirs of Jules Simon (1814–96), one of the great figures of nineteenth-century republicanism:

The republicans found themselves on the same side as the socialists and communists whenever fundamental issues were at stake. This was not an alliance, merely a temporary convergence. We fought for a brief moment under the same banner, still bearing our mutual animosities . . . Nothing brings men together as effectively as the hatred of a common enemy.

In addition to the loose ideological framework provided by republicanism, geography was also an important determinant of the conditions in which intellectual activity was exercised in France. It was no accident that the Dreyfus Affair was launched from Paris by a group of writers and artists who lived and worked in the cultural environment furnished by the capital. But, as was the case during the Dreyfus campaign, the definition of the precise social and political vocation of intellectuals was always fraught with controversy. The contrasting representations of Paris in French literary culture mirrored strikingly different conceptions of the role of intellectuals. For many Paris was both a symbol and a source of the cultural splendour of France. In the words of the literary critic and essayist Paul de Saint-Victor (1827–81), Paris was 'not only a seat of ideas, a workshop of progress, the foyer of peoples, the heart of Europe . . . Paris was also an immense museum, a vast collection of libraries, the receptacle of the masterpieces of human thought and creativity'. Against this view there was a strong tradition of outright hostility to Paris, which was often articulated in expressions of resentment against the city's intellectual and cultural pretensions. Commenting on the unfavourable outcome of the Franco-Prussian war of 1870–1, the writer Emile Leclercq denounced Paris as the source of French 'decadence'; in his view, Paris had been defeated 'because it is obsessed with pleasure, glittering spectacles, and stylistic artifice'.

There were thus several cleavages which became apparent in discussions of the role of intellectuals in French public life. There was the opposition between republicans and anti-republicans, as well as the cultural clash between Parisians and provincials. But intellectuals also expressed the social and political aspirations of secular groups

against the forces of organized religion; the hopes and fears of bourgeois France against the subversive threats of the extreme Right and
extreme Left; the growth in confidence of urban elites against the
traditional aristocratic powers of rural France; and the promotion of
domestic peace and national unity against the militaristic and chauvinist outpourings of bellicose groups. Intellectual groups in France had
articulated some of these concerns before the late nineteenth century,
but the parameters of their intervention in politics changed dramatically with the advent of the Third Republic. In the following sections,
an attempt will be made to identify the underlying reasons for the
modern tradition of intellectual involvement in the public realm. As
with many aspects of political life in France, the analysis begins with
the role of the State.

INTELLECTUALS AND THE FRENCH STATE

The definition of intellectuals, and the roles they performed in the
public arena, were always intricately linked to the conditions in which
political power was exercised in France. Indeed, intellectuals were
drawn into public life in the twentieth century partly as a result of a
process of direct encouragement and sponsorship of their activities by
the state. The development of centralized state institutions, which will
be analysed extensively in Chapter 6, had significant ramifications in
the social and material conditions of intellectual production. From a
broad historical perspective, the concentration of power and wealth in
Paris determined the very definition of cultural value. Since the market
for cultural goods was primarily located in the French capital, any
intellectual activity which operated outside the central channels of
cultural legitimation was eventually condemned to a parochial status.
This was best illustrated by the fate of one of the central vehicles of
a cultural system: language. The universalization of the French language was achieved through the decimation of local and regional dialects, which gradually alienated peripheral conceptions of culture from
the mainstream. This was a long, arduous and often fractious process,
which was accelerated by the French Revolution but effectively completed only in the early twentieth century. Thus it was by no means
accidental that the triumph of French idiom at this stage coincided with
the development of the concept of the intellectual. Social institutions
require secure cultural foundations: the Parisian intellectual could

become a model for the rest of educated society only after the conditions which allowed competing cultural conceptions to flourish had been superseded. The prominence of literary figures (including great writers such as Victor Hugo, Émile Zola, Charles Péguy, and Maurice Barrès) among the first generation of modern intellectuals in the late nineteenth and early twentieth centuries reflected the completion of an important stage in this overt process of cultural centralization. Paraphrasing Marx, it might be concluded that the new cultural order emerged only after the material conditions of its existence had matured in the womb of the old.

This formative influence of public authority in determining the normative parameters of intellectual activity was complemented by an active tradition of state involvement in the process of cultural creation. This practice was already prevalent under the *ancien régime*. The central place attributed to cultural creation by the French State was already fully displayed in the elaborate hierarchy of the absolutist monarchs: in this sense the palace of Versailles was itself a potent symbol of the perceived relationship between cultural splendour and political authority. The legacy of absolutism deeply influenced the manner in which political authority was exercised and perceived in France. As will be noted in the following chapter, the republican tradition perpetuated, and in many ways accentuated, this symbolic link between cultural production and political identity. The creation of a participant, undogmatic, and enlightened polity was a central feature of the republican conception of citizenship. Indeed, politics and culture presupposed each other: cultural activity was part of the wider pedagogical process which would nurture and consolidate the republican character of French public institutions. For the republican historian and pamphleteer Edgar Quinet (1803–75), education and culture were social goods which were indispensable for the preservation of French civilization. In his work *La République* (1873), he stated that 'as long as a nation retains within itself the power to produce and create great things, no fatal blow could strike it down . . . Death is powerless against a people which continues to create useful and beautiful objects for the benefit of all.'

But this active intervention of the state in educational and cultural matters was not always welcomed by French intellectuals. Throughout the twentieth century their relationship with the republican State was characterized by an almost schizophrenic alternation between strong support for the regime and opposition to many of its specific policies.

It is true that some intellectual groups remained unconditionally opposed to the Republic, but these were progressively marginalized as the regime gained widespread support from political groups of the Left and Right. Those who were broadly supportive of the regime, however, were often critical of particular attributes of the French State. One strand of critical intellectual opposition to the State was directed at curtailing its encroachment upon the individual liberties of citizens. Given its inherent obsession with the effective control of State power, liberalism was ideally suited to providing an ideological conduit for this concern. In the modern era this dimension of French liberal discourse was reflected in an essentially moralistic approach to the sphere of politics. The political writings of Émile Chartier (Alain) (1868–1951), Simone Weil (1909–43), and Albert Camus (1913–60) illustrated (from a variety of perspectives) the central French liberal contention that the state could not be entirely trusted to guarantee basic social and political freedoms. During the 1980s and early 1990s this moralizing posture was assumed by the philosopher Bernard-Henri Lévy, who urged his fellow-intellectuals to revert to the traditions of excellence which had been maintained by earlier generations. In his *Éloge des Intellectuels* (1987) Lévy went so far as to argue that intellectuals had spearheaded all the great battles against despotism in France throughout the twentieth century, often in direct opposition to the inclinations (and interests) of the State.

This intellectual opposition to the overbearing presence of the State also stemmed from the concerns of specific occupational groups. The active role of the French State in intellectual and cultural matters developed in the framework of a complex and often antagonistic relationship with particular groups. As with pressure groups more generally, the intricate connections between the State and the intellectual professions cannot be captured in a single formula. A sectoral approach would reveal a range of different attitudes adopted by public authorities which, in turn, could trigger a variety of responses from groups within distinct occupational categories. In some areas, such as the liberal professions, the element of confrontation was almost entirely excluded. The State's role in these areas was essentially limited to the ratification of corporate arrangements. As shown in Ezra Suleiman's study of the notarial profession (*The Notaires and the French State*, 1987), notaries entrenched their position so successfully that no French government was able to undermine seriously the enclosed and self-regulated character of the profession. In the field of education the modern republican State settled into a variety of roles. In the domains of primary and secondary education its basic function was mediatory, attempting to placate the divergent and often irreconcilable interests of secular and religious lobbies. In the field of higher education, on the other hand, the State attempted to play a more directive role, even though its efforts were consistently frustrated by entrenched institutional interests. Indeed, the passions generated by debates over the nature of the education system left few governments unscathed. In 1984 and 1986 Socialist and right-wing administrations helplessly witnessed the depths of resentment which could be triggered by relatively minor attempts to adjust the *status quo* in the fields of secondary and higher education. In some areas, however, the State was considerably more successful in determining the parameters of intellectual activity. But such successes often provoked an equally enduring legacy of resentment and opposition in intellectual quarters. The relationship between the French State and the mass media after 1944 provided clear examples of hostile intellectual attitudes generated by the heavy-handed behaviour of public authorities. After the Liberation the republican State maintained a keen interest in shaping the contours of professional activity in both the public and private sectors of the information industry. This was achieved through ownership of the means of producing information, by setting the standards of what could legally be published, intervening (formally and informally) to influence journalistic output, and finally, abetting private concentrations of resources in the hands of politically sympathetic industrial groups. This heavy-handed approach of the State was based on two equally compelling considerations: an almost pathological sense of its own vulnerability and an uncompromising belief in the strategic value of the control and dissemination of information. In other words, the State was aware that the social and political conditions of its existence were often precarious, and that specific intellectual groups could perform a critical role in buttressing (or undermining) the legitimacy of its institutions.

But the negative disposition of many French intellectuals towards the state ran deeper than the one-dimensional representations sketched above. Ideological and sectoral factors could often play a central role in determining approaches towards the state, but the ambiguous association between intellectuals and the republican regime can be understood adequately only if the different factors which impinged upon the relationship are considered cumulatively. The tendency of French intellectuals to be involved (both theoretically and in practice) in concerns which were often far removed from their areas of immediate specialization naturally resulted in varied forms of interaction with other social and institutional groups. It is from this perspective that the State loomed large on the horizon of the French intellectual. The persistence of the State tradition in France ensured that intellectual and cultural activities often intersected with the interests and concerns of the public authorities. In other words, the French intellectual and the State were never far removed from each other. The extent of this proximity varied in accordance with the intensity of the state's presence in particular domains of cultural endeavour. Members of the teaching profession, for example, are state functionaries in France: in the early days of the Third Republic many schoolteachers actively promoted the basic goals and values of the regime. This initial link between the republican State and the teaching profession provided the basis for a tradition of political militancy among the *instituteurs* which was sustained throughout the twentieth century. Schoolteachers were not overwhelmingly militant, but they displayed a greater tendency to become involved in political activity than other middle-class occupations. Thus, even in the 1980s, the proportion of schoolteachers returned to the National Assembly ranged between a third and a quarter, most of them elected on the Socialist slate.

The relationship between intellectuals and the State was also determined by the latter's interests. For example, the activities of the journalistic and legal professions were much more directly influenced by the proclivities of the state than those of the artistic and literary communities. Yet even the latter groups could not be said to operate in a context of relative autonomy. Writers and film producers could be materially independent but public authorities retained the power to facilitate cultural production (and thus influence the parameters of creativity) through different institutional forms of sponsorship. This patronage was reflected in the fact that the French State itself was a producer of culture on a scale unparalleled in any other Western advanced industrial nation during the modern era. This centrality of the State ultimately explained the paradox that French producers of intellectual goods regularly railed against the encroachment of the State, but none the less often turned towards public authorities to solve their professional problems. Writers petitioning to preserve the French language, film producers urging the adoption of measures to protect the local industry against foreign (i.e. American) influence, intellectuals generally yearning for a more vigorous defence of the cultural patrimony—each of these different approaches was under-pinned by a common set of normative assumptions about the symbiotic relationship between the producers of culture and the public authorities. This phenomenon of group dependence on the State was by no means confined to intellectual and cultural groups: it was an inherent feature of the relationship between the State and civil society in a country where associational activity was traditionally relatively weak. Intellectuals, however, were most sensitive to the attentions of the State, partly because their consciousness of the intrinsic value of their autonomy was greater than that of other occupational groups in French society, and partly because they were increasingly co-opted into the political elite during the twentieth century.

This co-optation constituted another significant illustration of the growing presence and stature of intellectuals in France during the twentieth century. The recruitment of intellectuals into the political elite rested on a number of shared cultural and ideological affinities. As noted earlier, French republicans passionately believed in the intrinsic value of knowledge. Thus, from a very early stage, the political elites of the Third Republic were imbued with a positivistic ideology of science and learning which was almost religious in character. In the long term this convergence underlay the penetration of the French State and its political institutions by elements of the new intellectual stratum. One of the earliest examples of overlap between scholastic and political success was provided by the itinerary of Auguste Burdeau (1851–94), a leading political figure in late nineteenth-century French public life. Despite his modest social origins, this graduate of the École Normale Supérieure (the most prestigious tertiary establishment in France during the Third Republic) rose through the ranks of the French political system to become the President of the National Assembly. The regime's recruitment of the brightest minds of its time included such laureates of the *concours général* as Paul Bert (1833–86), a physiologist who played a leading role in formulating educational policy in the early days of the Third Republic. His itinerary was followed in subsequent generations by Édouard Herriot (1872–1957), the immutable mayor of Lyons and leader of the Radical Party, whose success was a testimony to the regime's enduring ability to draw men of modest social origins into positions of power and responsibility. Herriot was also a graduate of the École Normale Supérieure, which constituted the principal source of intellectual recruitment into the political elite during the first half of the twentieth century. Leading *normaliens* included the Socialist leaders Jean Jaurès (1859–1914) and Léon Blum (1872–1950), the modernizing conservative André Tardieu (1876–1945), and the Gaullist Prime Minister (and later President) Georges Pompidou (1911–74). This intellectualization of the public domain was further accentuated after 1945 by the creation of the École Nationale d'Administration (ENA), which in some respects supplanted the École Normale as the privileged training centre for French political and administrative elites. The consequences of this process of elite formation (for the character of both political and intellectual life) will be examined in the concluding section of this chapter.

THE INTERPENETRATION OF THE POLITICAL AND INTELLECTUAL REALMS

In sum, the relationship between French intellectuals and the State may be characterized as one of interpenetration. In a nation repeatedly scarred by social strife and profoundly shaken by institutional instability after 1789, those who wielded power were always aware of the ideological value of intellectuals as creators (or destroyers) of political legitimacy. The strategies adopted by different regimes to cope with this influential and potentially subversive social stratum varied significantly. The July Monarchy (1830–48) successfully co-opted intellectual elites from the academic world, while the Second Empire (especially during the 1850s) and the Vichy administration (1940–4) were united in their hatred of intellectuals. These regimes deployed a battery of coercive methods to maintain political conformism among creative intellectuals, and often achieved the opposite result. The Third Republic witnessed, and in part sponsored, the development of an intellectual stratum which challenged the dominant positions of the cultural establishment. As will be noted later in this chapter, the Dreyfus Affair provided a striking demonstration of the growing convergence between the rising generation of republican intellectuals and the core political values of the new order.

Despite these conjunctural variations there was a basic continuity of concern on the part of the public authorities. This disposition was reflected in the fact that the State itself took an active part in the process of intellectual creation, thus establishing the promotion of cultural value as one of its defining attributes. Nowhere was this interdependence of politics and culture better illustrated than in the consistent interest shown by public authorities in controlling the establishment of academic disciplines in French universities. During the Second Empire the State's awareness of the political implications of intellectual activity was prominently demonstrated by the education minister, Victor Duruy, sponsoring the discipline of political economy in the 1860s as a means of preventing the diffusion of revolutionary ideas. Similar considerations underlay the establishment of sociology as an academic discipline in the early 1890s. This persistent interest of the State in the cultural domain was mirrored by an enduring intellectual fascination with the central institutions of political authority. In a political system in which education and culture were accorded high status it was not surprising that intellectuals were increasingly drawn into active participation in public life. One of the most visible signs of this presence was the growing recruitment of intellectuals into the French political elite during the twentieth century. The occupation of leadership positions by intellectuals was initiated during the earliest stages of the development of mass parties in France. The first modern French political party, the Parti Radical et Radical Socialiste, was established in 1901 as an attempt to unite the different strands of the republican movement. From its very inception this organization was dominated by middle-class urban professionals whose rise to social prominence had coincided with the consolidation of republican institutions in France: political philosophers, a new generation of professional activists, but also local associations, Masonic groups, journalists, freethinkers, and anticlerical education lobbies. Four years later the unity congress of the Section Française de l'Internationale Ouvrière (SFIO) led to the establishment of a Socialist Party whose basic ethos was equally marked by the rising generation of bourgeois republican intellectuals (typified in the person of Jean Jaurès). Even the formation of the Communist Party in 1920 did not initially alter this preponderance of intellectuals in the leadership positions of mainstream republican organizations. Two early party leaders, Louis-Oscar Frossard (1889–1946) and Albert Treint (1889–1971), were both schoolteachers by profession, and the Executive Committee elected at the founding congress of the party contained a small minority of members of working-class origin. Only in the late 1920s did the Communist International definitely transform the sociological character of the new party organization by instituting the Bolshevization programme, which stipulated that all Communist cadres should be of proletarian origin. None the less, Albert Thibaudet's general (if somewhat polemical) depiction of the regime established in 1875 as a 'Republic of Professors' contained more than a grain of truth.

This presentation of the successful co-optation of intellectual groups into the public realm should not ignore important shifts in the distribution of power within the Republic's political elites after the 1880s. The Third Republic consecrated the ascendancy of social strata which had hitherto been excluded from high political office. Parliamentary and ministerial offices alike were dominated by the liberal professions (medicine, law, journalism) and a considerable brigade of primary and secondary schoolteachers. Higher civil servants and industrialists were essentially excluded from the centres of decision-making, and the configuration of the system was well reflected in the leadership of the Radical Party, which typified the socio-professional characteristics of the new middle-class political elite. Under the Fourth Republic, however, the political centrality of these occupational groups began to be eroded, and this decline was accelerated decisively with the advent of the Fifth Republic. The Gaullist executive, armed with a firm resolve to sweep away the power of traditional political elites, recruited an increasing proportion of higher civil servants into the political arena. These bureaucrats were trained in such institutions as the ENA and the École Polytechnique, and their emergence coincided with the relative decline of the École Normale Supérieure as the privileged recruiting ground for the French political elite. With the progressive adoption of the institutional parameters of the Fifth Republic by mainstream political groups, this tendency facilitated the emergence of a new social stratum within the political elite, which in many ways supplanted the dominant positions occupied by traditional socio-professional groups. By the early 1990s it was even being suggested that the preponderance of higher civil servants in the leadership of the parties of the moderate Right and Left was one of many illustrations of the increasing primacy of technocratic values in the political system. But what had essentially occurred was a shift in the source of recruitment of French political elites from one type of intellectual institution to another. Indeed, the existence of the network of Grandes Écoles, and the continuing recruitment of political leaders from these institutions, revealed a profound element of continuity in the French political tradition during the twentieth century: the belief that political and administrative leadership required a rigorous and comprehensive intellectual formation, which could be provided only in specialized institutions.

THE CULTURAL FOUNDATIONS OF
INTELLECTUAL PRACTICES

It should be clear by now that intellectuals always evolved in relatively close proximity to the seat of political and administrative power in France. This proximity has been characterized in a number of dimensions: the occupation of the same physical space, the recruitment of political elites from intellectual strata, and the intervention of public authorities in the cultural endeavours of intellectual groups. Indeed, so close was the relationship between these groups and the French State that it spawned a distinct tradition, in which the parameters of intellectual intervention in public life were clearly demarcated. But, before evaluating the effects of this tradition on French public life, one of the claims about the causes of intellectual decline in modern France should be examined more closely. It will be remembered that the 'silence' of French intellectuals was explained by some as the result of profound transformations in the French social and cultural landscape in the twentieth century. If the logical implication of this argument is accepted, the political roles of intellectuals declined because the agents themselves came to be submerged by the appearance of new cultural forms in France. It is therefore important to establish whether one could meaningfully posit the existence of an 'intellectual tradition' in France throughout the twentieth century, and a good way of ascertaining this is to examine the claims of those who dispute its continued existence during this era.

No attempt will be made here to deny the intrinsic scale of the changes in the structure and content of intellectual activity in France since the Dreyfus Affair. There was a remarkable expansion in each of the principal intellectual occupational categories (artistic, scientific, literary, and pedagogic). It is hardly necessary to provide quantitative evidence of this expansion: it was reflected in the sheer growth of institutions of higher education in France during the twentieth century. In 1876 there were 13,000 university students in the whole of France (from a total population of 37 million). A century later the estimated figure was 1.1 million (out of a total population of 56 million). After the Liberation this expansion produced a cultural inflation, reflected in a sharp rise in the demand for intellectual goods. Within this wider market for cultural artefacts the impact of technological changes on traditional forms of intellectual production was dramatic. The mass media, particularly the television industry, played an increasingly central role in bestowing status on intellectual goods, thereby influencing the parameters of cultural activity in an unprecedented manner. Furthermore, the mass media became intellectual producers in their own right, generating a form of popular culture which competed with (and threatened to submerge) the traditional high culture of the classical republican period. In the gloomy assessment of Alain Finkielkraut: 'Barbarity has finally triumphed over high culture. In the shadow of this once great concept, intolerance has grown, as well as infantilism . . . And life, together with all forms of creative thought, yields slowly to the terrible and derisory confrontation of the fanatic and the zombie.' But, although the character and scale of these cultural changes are not open to question, their effects on the political behaviour of intellectuals require careful analysis. As previously suggested, the rise of a technocratic stream of political leaders in France during the Fifth Republic was partly a cause (as well as a reflection) of changes in the nature and scope of intellectual occupations. But the effects of greater specialization on the general political disposition of intellectual groups cannot be deduced readily. It has been argued by some that the emergence of an increasingly professionalized community of cultural producers after the 1950s totally destroyed the classical Dreyfusard paradigm of intellectual activity in France. For example, George Ross put forward a radical explanation for the withdrawal of left-wing intellectuals from the political scene in the 1980s, which was noted at the beginning of this chapter. In his view this eclipse was triggered by political and ideological factors, but was essentially a product of changes in the structure of the demand for intellectual goods. The advent of mass culture had consecrated the domination of 'large culture marketing organizations', and completely altered the very nature of an intellectual product. In short, there were no longer any left-wing intellectuals because the market for their products had vanished, and the institutions which distributed high cultural goods were no longer in a position to exercise a hegemonic influence over society. Once spellbound by the writings of Zola and Sartre, France had succumbed to the numbing strains of Madonna, soft pornography, and television game shows.

The underlying assumption in Ross's argument was the existence of an inherent link between the circulation of an intellectual product in society and its creator's disposition to become involved in political activity. But the origins of intellectual intervention in the political realm were not immediately connected to the existence of a cultural market;

the underlying self-justifications for intellectual involvement in public life were of a different order. From the Dreyfusards to contemporary public figures in the literary, philosophical, and scientific worlds, the identity of French intellectuals was always a composite of several roles: they were producers of a certain type of culture, figures of distinction in their respective fields, and bearers of a particular moral and philosophical outlook. The authority of their intervention in the affairs of the temporal world rested on the general recognition bestowed upon each of these roles. The wider market for the goods produced by the intellectuals, it will be noted, was relevant only to the first of these factors. In the case of the second the competence of a cultural producer was essentially determined by peer (as opposed to mass) evaluation. The reception of a particular intellectual's moral statement about the political sphere depended, in part, on the status of the wider philosophical system from which his position was derived. But what traditionally gave an intellectual the authority to make general statements about the political world was his status within his cultural and professional community, rather than the extent of his wider audience in society. Indeed, it has been one of the claims of this chapter that French intellectuals always operated in something of a microcosm (geographical, cultural, and ideological): the standards they set were regarded as authoritative, but only within those sections of society which regarded the possession of high culture as a valuable good. From this perspective, modern trends towards greater specialization and professionalization in the occupational structure of the intellectual community could not have had a determinant impact on the status of particular individuals within the collectivity. In fact the reverse was more likely to be the case: the greater the compartmentalization of intellectual activity, the wider the scope for establishing positions of competence (and prestige) within each domain of endeavour.

Thus the undeniable changes in the structure of intellectual professions in the modern era did little to alter the essential parameters of intellectual intervention in politics. A key prerequisite for such political activism was a concern with abstract moral principles: this determined the content of the intellectuals' intervention in the public realm. What made this intervention possible, however, were the qualifications of intellectuals in their specific fields of endeavour. In 1898 Émile Zola wrote his open letter over the Dreyfus case on the basis of his belief in universal principles of justice and morality. But what gave him the authority and confidence to intervene in the political realm was his recognized competence in his particular field of creativity. The same basic pattern underlay the involvement of intellectuals in public affairs throughout the modern era. The 1970s and 1980s witnessed a decline of the radical tradition of republican intervention in the political arena and a resurgence of the liberal variant. But the assumptions of the liberal and neo-liberal intellectuals who dominated the ideological scene for much of the 1980s were marked by the same sense of self-assurance as those of their radical and revolutionist predecessors. Evidently this sense of confidence arose in part from their belief that the ideological tide was turning to their advantage. But the basic belief that professional competence in any field of cultural endeavour entitled an intellectual to intervene in the public arena was not substantively different from that of earlier generations of intellectuals.

The republican intellectual tradition was, accordingly, predicated upon the existence of a set of core political beliefs and values, but also on a generalized belief that the possession of a certain level of professional authority in a given cultural field was in itself a sufficient qualification for public intervention in the political world. This was, and indeed remains, one of the distinctive features of the structure of political life in France.

IDEALISM AND MILITANCY

The tradition of intellectual practice which dominated the political horizon for most of the modern era in France rested on two pillars. The first was a moralistic concern with abstract principles of truth and justice, which was ultimately derived from classical republican philosophical concerns. The second was a conception of the universality of reason, which regarded the possession of a certain level of cultural authority (not merely competence) as a sufficient qualification for intervention in the political arena. The mutually reinforcing effects of these principles produced a tradition of intellectual universalism. On one hand, French intellectuals were persistently drawn outside the circle of their specialized knowledge as a result of their disposition to view the political sphere through the prism of general moral principles. On the other hand, their authority for making evaluative judgements about the temporal world rested on an underlying appreciation of the interdependence of the worlds of culture and politics. The net result was a fluid conception of the socio-professional identity of the intellectual, who could simultaneously perform the role of a thinker, a producer of culture, an adviser to the prince, and a political activist.

As already suggested, however, this universalist tradition did not produce a monolithic conception of the nature of intellectual involvement in political life. Although moral principles consistently underlay the concerns of republican intellectuals, the ethical systems from which these principles were derived were not necessarily compatible. Concerns about justice, for example, could be based on Marxian, socialist, Christian, or liberal individualist approaches. Each of these ideologies was universalist in scope, but the specific political conclusions reached by respective intellectual groups would often differ. Furthermore, there was no substantive agreement on the circumstances which called for the intellectual's political intervention. The Dreyfusard paradigm was interpreted in two ways by subsequent generations of republican intellectuals. On one hand, it was believed that intellectuals could retain their integrity as guardians of basic moral principles only if they refrained from consistent partisan activity. On the other hand a more militant conception emerged, which stressed that intellectuals had to become directly involved in the political world if the principles which they professed to defend were to be upheld. The idealistic and militant paradigms further reflected the cleavage between the liberal and revolutionist variants of the republican tradition. The classic version of the idealistic conception of the intellectual's role was expounded in Julien Benda's *La Trahison des clercs*, a pamphlet published in 1927. In his view the First World War and its aftermath had provoked a significant distortion of the basic paradigm established during the Dreyfus Affair. Instead of remaining aloof from the passions of daily political life, intellectuals were increasingly taking sides in the great ideological cleavage between nationalism and socialism. In his view the function of intellectuals was to ensure respect for the foundational values of society, and not become involved in the squalid practices of political partisanship. Throughout the modern era this idealistic conception of intellectual practice remained counterposed to the passions of the militant intellectuals. Until the 1980s, however, this approach tended to be adopted only by a minority of intellectuals. During the interwar period the philosopher Alain (Émile Chartier, 1868–1951) typified Benda's vision of a politically conscious publicist who none the less remained relatively distant from partisan activity. Alain was affiliated to the Radical Party, but he never ceased to preach the virtues of vigilance and detachment to his fellow party members. After the Liberation this tradition was continued by the small stream of intellectuals who sought to distance themselves from the ideological battles of the Cold War. The novelist Albert Camus perfectly embodied this idealistic spirit during the late 1940s and 1950s. In the 1980s, with the accentuation of the decline of left-wing ideology, this underlying conception became dominant among intellectuals; it was no accident that the sceptical realism embedded in Raymond Aron's writings finally met with critical acclaim at this juncture.

The militant conception of intellectual *engagement*, against which the idealistic tradition developed in the 1920s, initially grew out of the ideological polarization of French political life in the turbulent aftermath of the First World War. The creation of the French Communist Party in 1920 provided a focal point of attraction for radical intellectuals who sought to undermine the foundations of bourgeois society. Thus pacifists, surrealist writers, materialist philosophers, and radical Marxists converged towards the organization in the hope of furthering their political objectives. Although many were rapidly disillusioned by the endemic dogmatism and rampant anti-intellectualism in the party, enough remained to constitute the first generation of a new breed in the cultural community: the Stalinist intellectual. In the Popular Front era, and especially in the aftermath of the resistance, this militant conception of intellectual practice became dominant on the Left. But it would be inaccurate to suggest that partisan attachment was the distinctive feature of the radical intellectual tradition. Its principal defining characteristic was the attachment of intellectuals to a political cause: membership of a political organization was a necessary but by no means sufficient condition for intellectual militancy. Thus it was appropriate that the epitome of the new breed of intellectual was never a member of the Communist Party, even though, as for all left-wing intellectuals of his generation, the organization stood as the cardinal point of reference in his political universe until the early 1960s. Throughout his life Jean-Paul Sartre (1905–80) typified the characteristics of the committed intellectual (*intellectuel engagé*). His conception of the intellectual's role emphasized the values of political radicalism and universalism. Demarcating himself from the standard occupational view of the intellectual, he argued that intellectual activity was defined exclusively in the context of a specific political project: the overthrow of bourgeois society. Thus the ultimate function of the intellectual was to reveal the class tensions inherent in capitalist society and prepare the ground for its destruction. As he stated in his *Plaidoyer pour les Intellectuels* (1972) in his characteristically emphatic and opaque prose:

The intellectual is the person who becomes conscious of the opposition, within himself and in society at large, between the search for practical truth (with all the norms that this implies) and the dominant ideology (with its system of traditional values). This awakening of the intellectual's consciousness . . . is nothing other than the unveiling of the fundamental contradictions in society, in other words the class struggle, and, within the dominant class itself, an organic struggle between the truth which it demands for its purposes and its mythologies, and the myths, values, and traditions which it maintains and with which it seeks to infect other classes in order to perpetuate its hegemony.

The militant tradition typified by Sartre clearly served as a model for emulation in French intellectual circles until the mid-1970s. There were two basic characteristics of this type of intellectual. First, unlike the idealistic Dreyfusard tradition, which was essentially concerned with defending republican institutions and values, the militants were more inclined to challenge the existing social and political order. Although Communist intellectuals belonged to the same ideological tradition, the true spirit of intellectual militancy in the 1960s and 1970s was embodied in individuals and groups which operated outside the framework of conventional institutions. In the early 1960s these dissident intellectuals directed their support towards the struggle for national liberation in Algeria. Later in the decade the same underlying spirit of radical protest underlay the emergence of the student movement. In the 1970s the rise of alternative social movements such as feminism, regionalism, and environmentalism further attested to the growing ideological diversity of the French Left, and the equally inexorable intellectual decline of classical Marxism (which closely followed the withering away of the Communist Party). The second dominant characteristic of the militant tradition was expressed in the method and style used to convey its political messages. During the Dreyfus Affair the use of the manifesto by intellectuals introduced a new mode of political expression: the public petition. This could take the form of an open letter written by an individual (as in the case of Émile Zola's *J'Accuse*, published by the newspaper *l'Aurore* in 1898) or, more generally, a declaration signed by a large group of intellectuals. These forms of political discourse were by no means the exclusive preserve of the Dreyfusards. During the Affair, and throughout the modern era, nationalist and conservative intellectuals also intervened in the political arena by appending their names to general or specific political declarations, which would then be published in the Parisian press. But the frequency with which this method was used ultimately depended upon the intellectual's conception of his role as a political actor. For those who believed that the intellectual should intervene in politics only in relatively serious circumstances, the manifesto was an instrument for occasional use. For the *intellectuel engagé*, however, politics was the essence of life. Thus the petition became a privileged mechanism for expressing the passions of the militants, and it was no accident that one of its most consistent users between the late 1940s and the late 1970s was Jean-Paul Sartre.

THE SIGNIFICANCE OF INTELLECTUAL ACTIVISM

At the end of this general survey of the place of intellectuals in French politics and society, it may be affirmed that the parameters of their intervention in public affairs during the modern era were determined by trends in three key areas. The first determinant was contextual, but its intrinsic significance should not be undervalued. The Parisian microcosm constituted the sphere within which intellectual and cultural creation flourished, and this geographical concentration undoubtedly influenced the morphology of the intellectual community. Physical proximity facilitated substantial interaction between different intellectual groups and occupations; this concentration was amplified by the presence of the principal institutions of public authority and the increasing weight of the State tradition during the twentieth century. More precisely, the character of the French State reinforced the tendency for cultural activity to be centred within a remarkably small network of institutions, thus contributing to the strikingly incestuous nature of the Parisian intellectual community. The rise of the modern democratic Leviathan also had a direct impact on the social and political conditions of intellectual production. Always conscious of the legitimating and potentially subversive role of intellectuals in a society deeply scarred by social divisions and institutional discontinuities, the French State often sought to influence the parameters of cultural activity to serve its particular political and ideological concerns. This pervasive character of the presence of the state in the French cultural universe had profound consequences on the intellectuals' perception of the nature of public authority. On one hand, the very nature of the

Republican regime facilitated the penetration of public institutions by intellectual groups. But the French State's attempts to intervene in the process of intellectual and cultural creation also generated strong feelings of hostility. These structural factors ultimately explained why many French intellectuals' relationship with the State often assumed a fraught and almost schizophrenic character. Yet the overall thrust of the analysis in this chapter has shown the limitations of some of the claims about the decline of intellectuals in modern France. Far from eroding their influence on political elites, the transformations witnessed in recent decades strengthened the grip of intellectual groups on centres of decision-making in France. Furthermore, the significant technological changes which brought about a revolution in cultural forms did not fundamentally alter the foundations of intellectual intervention in public life.

The final dimension of intellectual decline highlighted in the introduction to this chapter was philosophical. It was claimed that intellectuals had betrayed their vocation to uphold basic principles of truth and justice, and this perversion of their appointed role had contributed to the declining moral standards of the French nation. This raises the wider question of the justifications invoked for intellectual participation in politics, and the effects of this phenomenon on public life in general. What difference did the presence of intellectuals make to the character of political life in France? Furthermore, was the apparent decline of intellectual intervention in public life in the 1980s simply a conjunctural phenomenon or a symptom of a far deeper ideological crisis? The two questions are related, in that the answer to the second very much depends on the dimension of public intellectual activity which is highlighted. Some of the public roles performed by creative intellectuals were essentially cosmetic. The signing of public petitions to promote particular political causes is a case in point. It might be of interest to a cultural historian that the artist Pablo Picasso regularly urged French voters to support the Communist Party, or that the actress Catherine Deneuve pledged her full support for the Maastricht treaty, or even that the novelist Albert Camus chose to remain silent over the war in Algeria; but the wider political significance of these individual alignments was relatively limited. Yet although the positions taken by creative intellectuals rarely (if ever) caused fundamental shifts in public opinion, they could provoke great ructions within localized communities, often because they tackled issues which politicians were reluctant to confront openly. Thus the most vigorous opposition to the Algerian war (expressed in the *Manifeste des 121* of September 1960) came from a group of radical intellectuals with no partisan attachments, who publicly denounced the French State for waging an unjust war with unjust means. Similarly, Catherine Deneuve's signature of a petition advocating the legalization of abortion in April 1971 was a courageous political stance for a woman to adopt in a Catholic country, independently of its actual impact on public opinion at the time. From a comparative perspective, however, what remained interesting about the phenomenon of intellectual petitions in France throughout the twentieth century was not so much the nature of the opinions expressed by the signatories, but what the practice itself implied about the close relationship between politics and high culture. There is no doubt that one could always have found creative intellectuals in Britain who held (and would willingly express) forthright views on just wars and the rights of women. The difference, however, was that a petition of British intellectuals on such major public issues would have been greeted with a mixture of derision and contempt, whereas in Republican France it was always deemed legitimate that men and women of culture should publicize their views about greater (and lesser) matters of State.

Next it may be asked whether the prominence of intellectuals in the political arena made a critical difference to the manner in which major public issues were aired and confronted. For example, did the intervention of intellectuals help to clarify arguments between different ideological world-views, as might be expected of a social stratum which had a professional interest in identifying logical relationships between propositions? This takes the argument back to earlier controversies over the precise role of intellectuals in public life. Julien Benda's view, subsequently propounded by Raymond Aron, was that intellectuals should remain aloof from partisan passions and seek to influence opinion by constructive argument and debate; their direct involvement in political action was required only when the foundational principles of social order were at stake. As against this view, the notion of *engagement* claimed that intellectuals had a duty constantly to be present on all political fronts, and indeed that failure to do so would represent a betrayal of their fundamental vocation to challenge the existing order of things. The Aronian intellectual, in sum, was essentially a liberal sceptic; the committed intellectual, on the other hand, was a revolutionist with a natural inclination towards dogmatism. During the twentieth century, as noted earlier, the dominant tendency among

French intellectuals was undoubtedly closer to the paradigm of *engagement*. This was even more the case if one included under this heading not only the left-wing radicalism typified by Sartre and the Communist intellectual tradition, but also the revolutionism of the authoritarian nationalist Right, which shared almost all the formal attributes of intellectual commitment. Indeed, if the voluminous political output of French intellectuals is studied closely, what emerges immediately is the striking absence of real debate between the different ideological camps. A revealing indicator of this lack of genuine ideological interchange is the fundamental continuity in the underlying arguments advanced by successive generations of intellectuals within their respective camps. The world-view of the Algérie Française intellectuals was an almost direct replica of the ideas and values promoted by the anti-republican publicists of the late nineteenth century; similarly, there was remarkably little change in the vision of the world propounded by left-wing intellectuals between the 1930s and the early 1980s. To a large extent this was because the propositions of each camp were essentially a matter for ritualistic assertion rather than rational argument, and this preponderance of dogmatism and rhetoric over careful debate had two particularly negative consequences in the output of the French intellectual community. First, it bred a tendency towards abstraction, self-congratulation, and superficiality. This partly explained why the overwhelming majority of French intellectuals remained fixated by the Leninist experience for so long: they were always willing to have the grimness of everyday Soviet experience translated into transcendental categories of meaning by ingenious sophists. This tendency also accounted in part for the relative poverty of French social and political thought during the twentieth century. In other words, there was a major cost to the close alignment of French intellectuals on the priorities of the political elites: a gradual atrophy of the creative and critical dimension of intellectual activity. This was nowhere better displayed than in the profound weakness of French theoretical and philosophical thinking in the domain of mainstream political ideologies such as Marxism, socialism, and liberalism. In the latter case, the French 'discovery' of liberalism in the 1980s took the form of a revival of its classical paradigm; until the early 1990s, for example, few French intellectuals had even heard of the work of John Rawls. As for the ideological categories of the Left, there is no more damning indictment of the French Marxist tradition in the twentieth century than that Louis Althusser should have come to be regarded as the one of its most creative figures. For their part, the Socialists failed consistently to give a theoretical response to the emergence of communism in France, and even their complete political triumph during the 1980s was not accompanied by a redefinition of the strategic aims of socialism in the era of economic rigour and complex interdependence—a failing which contributed significantly to their humiliating defeat in the 1993 legislative elections.

But although the association of intellectuals with the political elites of the Republic proved damaging to the real interests of the former, it arguably made a positive contribution to the quality of the latter. As noted earlier, the recruitment of political leaders from intellectual strata was closely associated with the consolidation of Republican institutions; the public education system (and particularly the focal point of French humanist endeavours, the École Normale Supérieure) provided the Republic with several generations of distinguished leaders. With the advent of the Fifth Republic there was a marked shift towards a more technocratic type of politics, and the principal institutional source of recruitment of the political elite became the administrative training schools, especially the École Nationale d'Administration. In both cases the quality of the political elites produced was not without its critics. The leadership of the Third Republic was pilloried for corrupting the ideals of the republican movement, lacking in decisiveness, and failing to prepare the country for the cataclysm of 1940. Despite their recognized intellectual qualities, the elites of the Fifth Republic were accused of excessive formalism and a tendency to reduce politics to discussions about means rather than ends. Some of these criticisms were certainly justified: the type of government produced by the Republic during the twentieth century was anything but perfect. But the continuing recruitment of its elites from the higher spheres of the intellectual community made for a political class which was (and remains) deeply cultivated, and which was well equipped to respond to the social and political problems with which it was confronted. To take the apex of the political system as an example, the successive presidents who held the reins of power under the Fifth Republic were men of remarkable ability and intellectual vigour, whose political and administrative talents could stand up well to any comparative test with their counterparts in other advanced industrial societies during the same era. For all their limitations, furthermore, the leaders of the modern Republic almost always found the intellectual resources to tackle the pressing social and economic problems with which they were faced, and resolve them in ways which were consistent with the preservation of the republican ideal of liberty.

But the achievements of the past will be of little help in facing up to France's social, political, and economic problems in the 1990s. As the country edged towards the end of President Mitterrand's second term, there was a widespread feeling of disillusionment with politics. Were intellectuals in any way responsible for the politicians' failure to mobilize society? To answer in the affirmative would be to give French intellectuals a form of power which they never really enjoyed. Indeed, if the argument of this chapter is accepted, the relative withdrawal of French intellectuals from the public scene since the early 1980s was only to be expected. The idea that intellectuals could lead the way out of the ideological predicaments of the 1980s was an illusion—partly entertained by the intellectuals themselves, of course, out of a mixture of vanity and wishful thinking. What this chapter has tried to show, however, is that intellectuals were never really able to lead opinion in France, and even less to determine the direction of political events. Their appointed role, which they discharged admirably (and often with great ingenuity) throughout the modern era, was to relay the message of their political masters to the wider public. The Dreyfus Affair was an expression of the republican tradition, not the other way round; similarly, the Sartrian concept of intellectual commitment in many ways constituted a philosophical representation of the activities of the French resistance. Intellectuals seized upon important social and political alignments and helped to mobilize opinion in their direction. But they never had the power to create these alignments. Thus two equally misleading generalizations about the effects of intellectual intervention in French public life should be avoided: the claim that intellectuals were always at the forefront of battles to preserve fundamental liberties and the view that intellectuals were always guilty of moral corruption and political depravity. As an example of the former, Bernard-Henri Lévy's claim that intellectuals spearheaded most of the major struggles for freedom and justice in twentieth-century France does not stand up to critical scrutiny. The Popular Front's creation may well have been helped by the activities of such organizations as the Comité de Vigilance des Intellectuels Antifascistes; the sufficient condition of its formation, however, was the determination (and flexibility) showed by the Communist leadership, as well as the fear induced in Socialist and Radical minds by the threat of 'fascism'. Similarly, the small band of dissident intellectuals who campaigned against the Algerian war in the early 1960s displayed great honour and personal courage, but their actions had no perceptible effect on the course of the conflict itself (or on French public opinion). The war ended in 1962 because de Gaulle believed that a negotiated settlement (paving the way to Algerian independence) was the only way to release France from the burden of a bitter and destructive conflict; his opinion would not have been any different had the dissident intellectuals never existed. At the same time, the existence of these moralistic groups, together with the overall subordination of intellectuals to the ideological orthodoxies of the time, forces a qualification of the claim that intellectuals consistently betrayed their vocation to uphold fundamental principles of truth and justice. In the latest version of the Benda thesis on the treason of clerks, *Un Passé imparfait* (1992), Tony Judt lambasts the intellectual generation of the postwar era for falling prey to the ideological sophistries of Stalinist communism. In essence, however, they did nothing but follow the lead given by political elites; to expect them to have acted otherwise is in a sense to fall into the classic trap of attributing to intellectuals more power and autonomy than they ever actually wielded in France.

It was only natural, therefore, that the intellectuals should have gone silent in the 1980s when their political masters found that they had nothing to say. Faced with a political situation in which traditional lines of ideological conflict abated significantly, men and women of culture took refuge in the brilliant extrapolations of Michel Foucault and Jacques Derrida, whose works questioned the very foundations of intellectual, social, and moral activity in modern societies. But the retrenchment of intellectuals was hardly a departure from tradition: the history of French intellectual involvement in public life since the mid-nineteenth century was consistently marked by temporary retreats of this kind. In the early 1850s the Second Empire's repressive approach towards intellectuals prompted the writer Gustave Flaubert (1821–80) to advocate a tactical withdrawal from the material world: 'Let us ascend to the heights of our ivory tower, on the ledge which is closest to the sky. It may be a bit cold up there at times, but what of it? At least we can see the stars shining, and no longer have to suffer the turkeys gobbling.'

Chronology

1898   January. Émile Zola's *J'Accuse* launches public debate about Dreyfus Affair.

       September. Formation of Comité de l'Action Française.

1920   December. Socialist Congress split; majority later forms Communist Party (PCF).

1927   December Publication of Julien Benda's *La Trahison des clercs*.

1932   October. First issue of *Esprit*.

1934   March. Formation of the Comité de Vigilance des Intellectuels Antifascistes, the intellectual wing of the Popular Front.

1936   May. Election of Popular Front government, headed by Léon Blum.

1942   September. Foundation (by leadership of the Communist Party) of *Les Lettres françaises clandestines*, the most widely read journal of intellectual resistance.

1945   June. Creation of the École Nationale d'Administration.

1947   May. Expulsion of Communists from government; beginning of the Cold War.

1950   March. Stockholm appeal against nuclear weapons raises 9.5 million signatures in France.

1956   November. Soviet intervention in Hungary leads many intellectuals (including Jean-Paul Sartre) to distance themselves from the PCF.

1960   April. Establishment of Parti Socialiste Unifié, a breakaway group from the Socialist Party.

       September. Manifesto of 121 intellectuals against the Algerian war.

1968   May. Student movement launches wave of protest.

1971   April. Petition advocating legalization of abortion signed by group of 343 women.

       June. Epinay congress of Socialist Party; François Mitterrand elected First Secretary.

1972   June. Joint programme of government signed by Socialists and PCF.

1973   January. First issue of *Libération*.

       December. Publication of Alexander Solzhenitsyn's *Gulag Archipelago*.

1978   March. After defeat of Left in legislative elections, intellectual revolt in Communist Party.

1980   April. Death of Jean-Paul Sartre; funeral procession followed by 20,000 mourners.

1981   May. Election of François Mitterrand to the presidency, with overwhelming support from French intellectuals.

1983   October. Death of Raymond Aron; tributes from leaders of all major parties.

1984   June. One million protesters in Paris march to defend principle of private education.

1985   February. PCF abandons traditional reference to alliance with intellectuals.

1986   November. Widespread student protests against education reforms proposed by Chirac government.

1988   May. Re-election of Mitterrand as President; despite absence of mobilization, considerable intellectual support for Socialist candidate.

1992   September. Referendum on Maastricht treaty approved by slender majority, after wide-ranging public debate in which intellectuals figured prominently.

CHAPTER 3
The Republican Tradition

Throughout the summer of 1989 the bicentenary of the French Revolution was lavishly celebrated across France. This commemoration provoked a wide-ranging debate about the legacy of the momentous events of the late eighteenth century in the character of political life in modern France. One of the central issues raised in the course of this discussion was the latter-day significance of republicanism, a political conception of State and society which rose to prominence on the coat-tails of the Revolution. Was the fact that France was a Republic still a matter of any political significance?

In contrast to the dominant view reached by most commentators and political analysts in 1989, this chapter will suggest that there were many important areas of French public life in which the legacy of republicanism was still potent. A specific characterization of republicanism will follow later; at this stage, it will be sufficient to note that the central tenets of classical republican ideology consisted of a basic commitment to the concepts of political liberty and equality of condition, and the foundation of a political order based upon representative institutions and the principle of popular sovereignty; these principles were reflected in the French Republic's motto of liberty, equality, and fraternity. By the time of the commemoration of the revolutionary bicentenary in 1989 France had lived under five Republican constitutions: the Jacobins had proclaimed the First Republic in 1792, while the latest (the Fifth) had been established in 1958, after the return to power of Charles de Gaulle. But republicanism was not a partisan phenomenon: despite being championed by specific groups in each of its successive manifestations after 1792, the republican tradition was never simply the preserve of a particular political formation. At the height of its ideological influence it expressed a vision of society and its basic institutions which appealed to a broad range of political organizations, ranging from progressive groups on the Left (forces of 'movement') to relatively conservative forces of the centre Right and even Right (forces of 'order'). This unity was based on converging approaches to a number of foundational principles and values: a belief in the centrality of reason, and the critical role of education in the development of human individuality; a deep attachment to the nation; an abiding commitment to the transformative value of good laws; and a quasi-mystical identification with the 'people', the defence of whose interests was deemed to be the rationale for the Republic's very existence.

But the way in which these precepts were interpreted and operated by different political groups allowed considerable room for flexibility. Republicanism was always an extremely elastic political concept, and this malleability was visible in two dimensions. First, its practice was not slavishly derived from its professed principles. For example, republican governments believed in the rule of law, and indeed gave lawyers an important role in the codification and supervision of State practice; the institution which performed both of the latter roles was the Council of State (Conseil d'État). Yet these same governments tended to regard the legal process merely as an instrument of State power, and French judges and magistrates were never granted the kind of autonomy which became an established feature of modern British and American juridical culture. Similarly, the belief in the superiority of reason suggested the possibility of determining the best interests of society *a priori*, and thus constructing a political order on the basis of a preconceived model of the good life. When in government, however, republican groups rarely followed their programmatic constructs in a systematic fashion, but instead allowed their policies to be guided by the search for social compromise and political accommodation. Indeed, there was a sense in which this flexibility was forced upon republican governments by the uncomfortable relationship between many of the different component principles of their ideology. Knowing what was best for society did not sit very well with proclamations of popular sovereignty; vibrant appeals to patriotic virtue clashed with affirmations of the universal brotherhood of man; and, most significantly of all, maintaining social order often conflicted with promises of a fairer and more equal distribution of economic goods. French republicanism was thus riven with ambiguities and internal contradictions, despite the appearance of cohesion and unity of purpose suggested by its ideological and programmatic constructs.

By 1989, as noted above, it was generally concluded that none of this historical baggage mattered very much. The public discussion of the republican legacy converged on two essential points: republicanism was no longer a dynamic ideological undercurrent, and the Republic itself was nothing more than a facade. At best, it continued to provide the framework for what the British constitutionalist Walter Bagehot would have described as the 'dignified' part of French political institutions: a historical source of their identity and legitimacy, providing a sense of continuity between the present regime and the constitutional tradition from which it originated. At worst the Republic was simply a limp relic of a bygone age, a political institution which had lost all the vitality it once possessed—a 'museum exhibit', in the scathing words of the historian Jean Petot. How and why had this process of ideological and institutional dissipation occurred? Several explanatory claims were proffered, both by those who deplored the apparent decline of republican institutions and values, and by those who saw in their passing an opportunity to transcend the deep-seated political divisions which they had engendered. Three principal dimensions of the disintegration of the republican tradition were noted: its failure to renew itself intellectually after the republican regime had achieved its initial programmatic objectives in the early twentieth century; the progressive endorsement of (or, at least, tacit acquiescence in) its basic institutions by the social and political minorities which had originally challenged its legitimacy; and the significant changes its classical institutional paradigm had undergone in the wake of the new Republic created by de Gaulle in 1958. Two further dimensions of the decline of the classical republican tradition were also noted (it was a matter of some debate as to whether these were contributory factors to or immediate effects of this decline): the abatement of ideological conflict during the 1980s and the concurrent movement towards European political and economic integration, both of which helped to shift the terms of public debate away from the question of the basic structure of the nation's political institutions. Two hundred years after the Revolution the Republic seemed to be a subject of public indifference; even worse, its elites appeared to be engulfed by a wave of general disillusionment with politics which many believed could threaten the legitimacy of the system as a whole.

It will be argued in this chapter that these claims of ideological and institutional dilution of the republican tradition in France were overstated, essentially because they rested on a misunderstanding of its real character. Republicanism was not a rigid ideological construct: its real essence lay in its capacity to accommodate different political groups on the basis of an appeal to a limited range of common interests.

These common interests were derived from the bedrock of republican principles outlined above, but their specific interpretation was almost always open to bargains and compromises. Indeed, it will be suggested at the end of this chapter that it would be a mistake to evaluate the phenomenon of French republicanism by taking its ideological declarations as the benchmark of analysis. What was always much more important to republican elites were the circumstances in which power had to be exercised, and thus the need to confront their ideological principles with the exigencies of political survival. This complexity of the republican tradition is best captured by a detailed investigation of its historical development, and this account will begin by examining the roots of French republicanism. These origins will be viewed first in the context of the revolutionary experience of 1789, then the struggle against imperial and monarchical conceptions of political order throughout the nineteenth century. The implementation of these principles (as well as some of the modifications they underwent) will next be examined in relation to the political system established under the Third Republic, which in many ways represented the apogee of the classical republican tradition in France. Finally, the impact of the political and constitutional changes introduced under the Fifth Republic will be examined, and the extent to which these modifications represented fundamental departures from the practices and norms of the classical era of French republicanism will be assessed. It will then be seen that the modern republican system in France still bears a strong imprint of the ideological and institutional characteristics it inherited from its founding fathers.

THE LEGACY OF THE FRENCH REVOLUTION

As noted earlier, the French republican movement was born of the revolutionary experience of 1789. The Revolution influenced the political and intellectual parameters of republicanism in five ways: it established the principle of popular sovereignty (and specifically linked its application to the exercise of critical reason), affirmed both the possibility and desirability of constructing a rational political order, emphasized the universality of the principles and values created by this new political order, projected a new conception of patriotism and nationalism, and finally, highlighted the notion that political structures could be used to promote greater equality (of outcome) and social justice.

Participationism, perfectionism, universalism, nationalism, and revolutionism: each of these dimensions of the formative character of the revolutionary experience in the development of French republicanism will be illustrated briefly.

Although the 1789 Revolution and the republican movement were closely connected, the Republic was not proclaimed in the immediate aftermath of the Revolution. None of the central figures of the revolution was a self-confessed republican, and France was declared a Republic only in September 1792, after the experiment of a constitutional monarchy had been deemed a failure. The proclamation of the Republic was itself accelerated by popular pressure, emanating particularly from such grass-roots organizations as the anti-monarchical *clubs de quartiers*. These popular groups were dominated by the poorer elements of Parisian society, which eventually developed into an autonomous movement of *sans-culottes* (literally 'those without knee-breeches', a vestimentary condition characteristic of men of humble origins). The role of the *sans-culottes* in the dynamic process which swept away the French monarchy in August 1792 was preponderant. Thus the emergence of the Republic gave a new dimension to the concept of popular participation in French public life—a turning-point which was given legal grounding in the adoption of universal suffrage in the Jacobin Constitution of 1793. During the nineteenth century this aspiration towards wider public participation in political life lay at the heart of the republican movement's struggle to re-establish Republican institutions in France. This continuity of purpose was reflected in the Second Republic's adoption of (male) universal suffrage in 1848, and the Third Republic's proclamation of the same principle during the 1870s (women were granted the right to vote only in 1944). This participationist strand was thus directly inspired by the revolutionary practice of drawing wider sections of society into the political arena.

But, as already noted, the internal inconsistencies of republicanism often forced its advocates to juggle with conflicting imperatives. While the value of greater public participation was accepted, it was also acknowledged that mass involvement in political life could not be effective unless the public was educated in the principles of good citizenship; hence the pivotal role accorded to education in the republican movement's hierarchy of values. In the *ancien régime* social origins and wealth were the exclusive determinants of status and power. The Revolution rejected these principles of social organization, and the emerging republican polity in many ways supplanted these criteria by insisting on the value of education and intellectual formation. Although they were never organized as a separate group, thinkers and philosophers figured prominently in the *dramatis personae* of the Revolution. As noted in the previous chapter, the writings of François Voltaire and Jean-Jacques Rousseau played a significant role in undermining the legitimacy of the *ancien régime*. Voltaire denounced the pernicious character of the absolutist system of government, and his caustic prose savaged the moral corruption of the clerical establishment. Rousseau's writings offered a philosophical justification for the foundation of a new social order, even though his explicit political prescriptions were often deeply pessimistic about the possibility of ever creating it. The influence of these ideological changes was reflected in the leading role taken by intellectuals during the Revolution itself. In keeping with its fundamental objective of bringing enlightenment and learning to the French people, the revolutionary government drew up a blueprint for introducing a universal and secular system of primary education in France—a project which was to a large extent conceived by the republican philosopher Marie de Condorcet (1743–94). This approach was based on the belief that ignorance and illiteracy were the greatest obstacles to the development of a stable political community. Given the short life of the First Republic, there was little time to implement this ambitious programme for mass literacy; a century later, however, the governments of the Third Republic introduced wide-ranging education reforms which were directly inspired by the plans drawn up by their republican predecessors.

The promotion of education and mass literacy was a specific aspect of the wider legacy of the Enlightenment to the first generation of French republicans. Condorcet summed up the optimistic philosophy which underpinned the construction of the post-revolutionary political order in his *Esquisse d'un tableau historique des progrès de l'esprit humain* (1793), where he stated that 'the perfectibility of man is really infinite and that the progress of this perfectibility will last as long as the globe endures.' The First Republic was deeply imbued with this perfectionist spirit, which sought to turn France away from the ignorance and servility of its past and promote a conception of the good life based on the flowering of human 'reason'. The attempt to cut loose from the past was graphically illustrated by the introduction of a new 'revolutionary' calendar in 1792, which sought to transform popular conceptions of the present by establishing a new configuration of space and time. Most significantly, the Revolution rested on the assumption that political institutions did not evolve organically. This traditionalist conception of the State was powerfully articulated in Britain and France after 1789 by counter-revolutionary thinkers such as Edmund Burke (1729–97), Joseph de Maistre (1753–1821), and Louis de Bonald (1754–1840).

The French Revolution established the principle (which was also rooted in Enlightenment thinking) that the constitution of a State was not simply a passive legacy from one political generation to another: it was a political construct which could (and, indeed, had to) be moulded by constant human intervention. This emphasis on the 'constructed' character of State institutions was a second important feature of the legacy of the French Revolution to the republican tradition. It was reflected in the creation of the École Polytechnique in 1794, a state training school for French technical administrators, and in plans to set up a training school for higher civil servants (an objective which was fully achieved only in 1945). These ambitions would directly inspire the practices of Napoleon Bonaparte (1769–1821), who retrieved and consolidated this aspect of the revolutionary legacy by creating the centralized administrative structure which the Revolution failed to engender. A similar inspiration would later lead to the revival of positivist ideas, which were centrally informed by the postulate that political institutions should be used to promote a social order based on the principles of science, progress, and rationality. But again, the perfectionist strand in the republican tradition was always circumscribed by other imperatives. Particularly after 1870, republican elites were always aware that imposing their conception of the good on a recalcitrant society was not a good recipe for political longevity; this realization led to the search for compromise, even in areas (such as religion) where the objective scope for accommodation seemed extremely limited. There was also a clear element of tension between the first and second aspect of the revolutionary legacy. The perfectionist strand tended towards an elitist conception of politics, in that it regarded the definition of the good life (and the practical means of attaining it) as being the exclusive preserve of the political and intellectual elite. But this elitism always had to be reconciled with the Republican State's need to be attentive to the subjective interests and aspirations of its citizens; a 'sovereign' people could not be governed by constantly being told what was in its best interests.

The first generation of republicans also shared a profound belief in the universality of the values affirmed by the French Revolution. This sense of universality was projected in two distinct directions: in the domestic sphere it informed the nature and scope of much of the legislation enacted by the republican regime; in the external context it inspired a messianic attempt to spread the principles of the Revolution to the rest of the world. In the former sense, the notion of universality was most directly reflected in the 1789 *Declaration of the Rights of Man*, which proclaimed principles of social and political organization which were deemed to be valid at all times and under all circumstances. In its benign form the application of this principle of universality brought about the abolition of all privileges based on rank and birth (on the famous 'night of 4 August'), and generated an inclusive rather than exclusive conception of citizenship; it was in this spirit that Jews were granted full civic rights after 1789. But this belief in the universality of the principles of good government instituted by the Revolution also produced actions which rapidly negated the libertarian thrust of 1789. A few years after the Revolution the principle of universality was more forcibly expressed in the Jacobin principle that the laws, norms, and values of the new political order had to be applied in all corners of French territory, without any undue regard for particular circumstances (be they regional, social, cultural, religious, or political). This highly centralizing and authoritarian dimension of the principle of universality rapidly degenerated into violence: the Terror (1793–4) and the murderous conflict between the revolutionary government and the Catholic territory of Vendée (1793–5) were two of the most destructive manifestations of the Jacobin revolutionaries' belief that no derogation could be allowed from the values of the new political system. There were similarly contradictory tendencies at work in the external dimension of the principle of universality. On one hand, many French republicans believed that the emancipation of their society from the bonds of servitude was simply the prelude to a general transformation of the entire world. Thus the revolution's principles of *liberté, égalité, fraternité* were regarded as qualities which were not for promotion within the boundaries of the French nation alone. The First Republic reflected this universalist approach by proclaiming the abolition of slavery in its colonies (in February 1794): this was probably the most genial expression of the revolution's messianic quest to liberate the world. In the same breath, however, the new political order sought to spread the message of the Revolution by force of arms after 1791. Almost invariably, the 'liberation' of neighbouring territories from absolutist political domination simply provided a disguise for the pursuit of traditional French imperialist ambitions. In this respect as well, Napoleon consolidated the legacy of his revolutionary predecessors.

After 1789 one of the central concerns of the revolutionaries was to constitute a social basis for the country's new political institutions. This task was a matter of some urgency by the time the Republic was proclaimed in 1792, given that the three principal institutional foundations of the *ancien régime* (the monarchy, the Church, and the nobility) had been swept away by the Revolution. In order to bring this task to fruition the new rulers needed to create an alternative focus of identification for society, an integrative concept which could provide a basis for rallying the different sections of the community to the new order. The concept which served this function was that of the *patrie*, which was used to telling effect by the revolutionary governments during the 1790s, particularly when France was threatened by invading troops. The immediate social and cultural consequences of this process should not be overstated. The Republic's patriotic rhetoric was not sufficient in itself to establish a sense of national identity across France; in this substantive sociological sense, nationalism was not 'created' by the French Revolution. None the less, the appeal to patriotism succeeded in filling some of the emotional and affective void created by the destruction of the old institutional order. The regime's appropriation of nationalist discourse fed into the revolutionary principle of universalism in both its domestic and external manifestations. As noted above, the postulate that French material and spiritual values were superior to those of other nations inevitably yielded the belief that these values had to be exported to the rest of the world. Thus nationalist considerations played an integral part in the Republic's efforts to spread the message of the Revolution beyond French borders. Hence the paradoxical conflation, in the justificatory language of the French military adventures of the 1790s, of the principle of nationality with that of political liberation. The messianic message of the Republic assumed both a universalistic and a nationalist character—a symbiosis which was most tellingly illustrated a century later in the Third Republic's ideological justification of its policy of colonial expansion.

Finally, the experiences of the 1790s provided a direct source of inspiration for subsequent generations of revolutionaries in France and in Europe. Outside France, the spirit of the French Revolution haunted the capitals of Europe for much of the nineteenth century:

thus the myths of 1789 were often invoked by the radical protest movements which inflamed the European political scene in 1848–9. In France the legacy of 1789 in the revolutionary political tradition was rather complex. This tradition accommodated several strands, all of which were direct descendants of movements which were prominent during the 1790s. The Jacobin ideals of radical democracy and social virtue (typified by Maximilien de Robespierre (1758–94), the 'incorruptible' revolutionary leader who instigated the Terror) were remembered in later campaigns to extend the franchise to all sections of society; similarly, the underground activities of Gracchus Babeuf (1760–97) spawned an insurrectionary tradition, which was continued by the secret societies of the 1830s, most notably by Auguste Blanqui. Later anarchist, socialist, and communist conceptions of the revolutionary heritage were to emerge. All these different radical strands proposed (sometimes strikingly) different visions of the future but had three basic features in common: the view that politics was essentially about the conflict between the haves and the have-nots; the belief that the Revolution did not end in the 1790s, but marked the beginning of a new epoch, which would culminate in the liberation of mankind; and finally, a deeply ambiguous relationship with the constitutionalist republican movement. Up to the demise of the Second Empire in 1870, many of these revolutionary currents regarded the republican movement as an ally in the common struggle against imperial and monarchical conceptions of political order. This tentative sense of solidarity was bruised severely during the Second Republic, when workers' revolts were suppressed by the fledgling republican regime. The proclamation of the Second Empire in 1852 re-established the conditions for (at least tactical) co-operation between radical groups and the republican movement. However, after the suppression of the Paris Commune in 1871 and the consolidation of the 'bourgeois' Republic in subsequent decades, a clear division over the status of the Republic emerged within the radical revolutionary tradition. Some groups regarded the new political order as a mere instrument of class domination (a view taken by anarchists and revolutionary socialists); others, while noting its imperfections, came to see the Republic as providing the political and legal framework within which the battle for greater equality and social justice could be conducted most effectively. In broad terms, the history of the French Left during the twentieth century witnessed the (slow and extremely painful) assertion of the latter tendency over the former. But it was a testimony to the com-

plexity of republicanism that violent revolutionaries and moderate con-
stitutionalists could derive their ideological genealogy from the same
cluster of historical events, and indeed sometimes form tactical alliances over specific political issues, even though the extreme revolutionaries did not really regard themselves as constituent members of the
republican family.

WHY A REPUBLICAN TRADITION?

Despite the benevolent aspirations of the first generation of French
republicans, the immediate legacy of the First Republic was far from
impressive. In fact, even a cursory survey of the condition of France
in the early nineteenth century, after a decade of republican rule,
would raise the question of how subsequent generations could have
derived any inspiration at all from such a legacy. The Revolution
further damaged France's already weakened economic infrastructure,
destroyed the bases of traditional order without creating any stable
alternative institutions, replaced the crumbling administrative structure
of the *ancien régime* with an equally chaotic bureaucracy, exhausted
the nation's creative energies by engaging in costly military adventures
abroad, and perhaps most important, instituted a reign of terror which
acquired such a momentum that it swept away many of the Revolution's own leaders. In terms of its practical achievements the First
Republic was a social and institutional calamity, and few mourned its
passing when it was officially abolished by Napoleon in May 1804.

How did this disastrous social and political experiment come to
provide the original point of reference for the French republican tradition? As mentioned earlier, part of the explanation lay in the achievement of the 'Republican Emperor', as Napoleon sometimes liked to
call himself: the incorporation of some of the Republic's programmatic
aspirations into the imperial system established after 1804. Objective
political circumstances also helped a great deal, for the restoration of
the monarchy after 1815 turned the Republican experience into the
only available ideological framework for expressing political opposition
to the existing order. The idealism of the young generation of anti-
monarchist activists did the rest: the sordid legacy of the 1790s was
effectively transformed into the dawning of a new era. This ideological
sleight of hand was achieved by essentially focusing on the grandiose
aspirations of the Revolution, rather than the disasters which attended

the implementation of most of its schemes. In the same way as apologists for the October Revolution of 1917 later explained away Stalinism as a contingent feature of the Leninist heritage, the Terror was presented as a largely conjunctural response to internal and external pressures. Golden ages also needed their ideologues. During the nineteenth century the events of the revolutionary era found theirs in the highly romanticized writings of a new generation of historians, notably Adolphe Thiers (1797–1877) and François Guizot (1787–1874), two academics who eventually assumed high political office. The historian who arguably did most to glorify the memory of the French Revolution in the nineteenth century was Jules Michelet (1798–1874), an idealist who saw the events of 1789 as the point of departure for a new age of human civilization. For much of the twentieth century this idealist historical interpretation of the Revolution was complemented by the Jacobin-Marxist tradition. Its leading adepts (Alphonse Aulard, Albert Soboul, and Michel Vovelle) presented the events of 1789 as the first expression of the modern struggle for democratic socialism, setting the scene for the upheavals which would culminate in the 1917 revolution in Russia.

However, the Revolution did not survive purely as a golden legend. Another way in which the experience of the 1790s was perpetuated was through the collective memories of those groups and institutions which suffered directly at the hands of the revolutionaries. In this sense probably the most significant negative image associated with the First Republic was its execution of King Louis XVI in January 1793. The Republic instantly became associated with the practice of regicide and, because the King was the anointed representative of God, his execution was also construed by many French Catholics as a declaration of war against the Christian faith. This proved to be the source of one of the most enduring cleavages in French politics, characteristically expressed in the highly antagonistic relationship between French republicans and traditionalist sections of the Catholic community. During the nineteenth century, for example, ultramontane Catholics (i.e. those who accepted the doctrine of papal infallibility and regarded the Vatican as the essential source of guidance) were considered by most republicans to have alienated themselves from French society because they gave their ultimate allegiance (both spiritually and temporally) to the papacy in Rome. This emphasis on the principle of intellectual autonomy was a distinctive feature of republican ideology. The belief in the value of autonomy did not mean that transnational ideologies were necessarily excluded from the republican fold: one could be a Catholic (and, in the twentieth century, a Marxist, and even a European supranationalist) and still be deemed a good republican, as long as one's religious and political beliefs were freely subscribed to. Alienation of thought to a foreign institution, however, was always considered incompatible with the spirit of republicanism. This subtle distinction enabled republican politicians to accommodate some groups and exclude others from the political mainstream: on one hand, to build bridges with those whose principles conflicted with their own but were prepared to compromise (for example, Gallican Catholics, who advocated relative autonomy from Rome); on the other hand, to exclude groups on the Right (such as ultramontane Catholics and extreme monarchists) whose positions were not negotiable under any circumstances.

Violence was a central part of the revolutionary experience of the 1790s and its place in the republican tradition was somewhat controversial. The painful memories of regicide and mass violence (typified by the Terror and the murderous expedition against the Vendée) helped to sustain anti-republican feelings in many quarters. These sentiments were reinforced by the reluctance of most republicans even to acknowledge (let alone dwell on) the negative aspects of the legacy of the First Republic. Indeed, few nineteenth-century republicans were prepared publicly to condemn the violence which had accompanied the triumph of the new political order after 1792. For at least 150 years after the event, embracing the republican tradition required accepting (and thus justifying) the entire revolutionary experience. Georges Clemenceau (1841–1929), the fiery Radical politician who later became (a very conservative) Prime Minister, described the French Revolution as a 'bloc' from which no particular events could be detached. At the same time, the negative images associated with the Terror were not unduly celebrated: violence had been necessary, and its apologists did their best to explain why. But the Terror was not presented as the central feature of the Revolution; even after the Third Republic was securely established, and up to the present day, no public statue of Robespierre was erected in France, not even in his home town of Arras. If republicans celebrated violent acts at all, they were more inclined to commemorate the heroic virtue of the French revolutionary armies which successfully confronted the invading Austrian and Prussian forces at the battle of Valmy in September 1792; this proved to be the first victory of the Republic in the war

against its monarchical enemies. This affinity with nationalist sentiment constituted a vital component of republican ideology for most of
the nineteenth century, and remained an important element thereafter.
The history of the French national anthem, *La Marseillaise*, provides
a good illustration of the conflation of republican and nationalist
values. This battle-cry of the Republic was composed by Claude
Rouget de Lisle (1760–1836), a captain in the French Army which
fought gallantly against the invading forces of the King of Bavaria.
Like the Republican doctrine which it subsequently came to symbolize,
La Marseillaise was profoundly nationalistic in character. Although
banned by Napoleon III during the Second Empire, it re-emerged as
the battle-cry of his Imperial Army in 1870, at the height of the conflict
against Prussia. After its proclamation as the national hymn under the
Third Republic, it became the accepted symbol of French national
unity. The Communist Party adopted it during the Popular Front as
a token of its patriotic commitment. It became the battle-cry of resistance groups between 1940 and 1944 (while groups favourable to the
Vichy regime sang the Pétainist hymn, *Naréchal nous voilà*. In 1968 the
immense crowd which rallied to support de Gaulle after the events
of May repeatedly sang the national anthem to demonstrate its attachment to the republican system of government. The history of the
Marseillaise illustrates an important (and perhaps critical) condition of
the success of republican tradition: its ability to convey, through specific and highly evocative imagery, the substance of French national
character.

As noted earlier, the revolutionary experience established the principle of popular sovereignty, which most republican ideologists
regarded as valuable only if exercised under the guidance of critical
reason. Most republicans did not wish to promote political participation for its own sake, but rather sought to foster a form of public
involvement based on informed judgements and a sense of civic responsibility. The political turbulence of nineteenth-century France
further accentuated the republicans' awareness of the dangers inherent
in uncontrolled mass involvement in the political process. In December
1848 Louis Napoleon was triumphantly elected President of the
Second Republic; four years later he abolished the Republic. After
the proclamation of the Empire, furthermore, Bonaparte's nephew
made effective use of the plebiscite as a means of consolidating his
political support in the country at the expense of the republican opposition. Even as late as May 1870 electoral returns showed overwhelm-

ing public support for the Empire. These experiences had three lasting consequences in the republicans' conception of representation. Conservative republicans like Adolphe Thiers openly expressed their contempt for the 'vile multitude', which had easily been manipulated by the Empire, and elements of which would rise in revolt during the Paris Commune. More generally, the events of the late 1840s and early 1850s severely damaged the republicans' optimistic faith in the essential goodness of their fellow-countrymen. Second, the circumstances of the failure of the Second Republic introduced a lasting fear of the principle of direct presidential election. The spectre of Bonaparte's slide towards authoritarian rule after 1848 was repeatedly invoked over the next century whenever there emerged the possibility of power being concentrated in the hands of one individual; thus de Gaulle's centralization of power in presidential hands after 1958 drew accusations of 'Bonapartism' from the centre Left opposition. Finally, and somewhat in contrast to the previous fear of political centralization, the events of the nineteenth century confirmed the problematic character of the representative process. It was remembered that the conservative majority elected in 1849 rapidly proceeded to restrict the principle of universal suffrage; the majority of monarchists returned in 1871 similarly opposed the principle of mass democracy; lastly, it was the chamber elected with a Popular Front majority in 1936 which voted to suspend the Republic and grant full powers to Marshal Pétain in 1940. The proposition that representatives of the people could not be entirely trusted with the powers they exercised became embedded in the republican tradition, hence the feeling (articulated among others by the philosopher Alain) that elected representatives needed to be constantly watched, because they were often inclined to succumb to the vulgar charms of charismatic figures. The classical republican philosophy of representation was thus profoundly dualistic: on one hand it emphasized the importance of mass participation in public life through regular electoral consultations, thus according a central role to the representative of the people (the *député*) in the mediation of political interests. At the same time, however, the republican postulate that too much power should not be entrusted to one institution alone (a founding principle of the American constitution) was also applied to elected representatives; hence the guarded suspicion with which the *député* was viewed in the French republican tradition.

THE APOGEE OF REPUBLICANISM

The development and consolidation of the Third Republic after 1875 laid bare the deep divisions which were always latent in the republican camp. Although this chapter has been primarily concerned with the historical continuities in the republican tradition, enough has already been said to suggest the existence of important social and ideological cleavages. During the Third Republic these differences were accentuated by the institutionalization of the republican regime, which immediately established a dichotomy between the so-called 'opportunist' politicians, who rapidly emerged as the new ruling elite of the system, and more radical groups (both inside and outside the National Assembly), who constantly reminded government elites that the Republic was the inheritor of the Revolution of 1789. These cleavages between the forces of 'order' and 'movement' within the republican camp were further enhanced by the greater saliency of such doctrines as socialism and anarchism, the aggravation of social cleavages between peasants, workers, and the middle classes, and finally, the international context of the late nineteenth and early twentieth centuries, which saw the Third Republic's acquisition of a colonial empire which turned France into the second largest imperial power in Europe. Ultimately these political cleavages expressed contrasting conceptions of the three foundational precepts of the classical republican tradition: liberty, equality, and fraternity. These different conceptions could be seen in two dimensions: first, in the definition given to each concept by different political groups, and second, in the relative ordering of the three principles in these groups' respective hierarchy of values.

The forces of 'order' tended to define liberty in negative and procedural terms: the emphasis was on keeping the state from imposing its conception of the good life on society, and confining its role to the regulation of competition between different social and economic interests. Hence the strong attachment of these conservative republican forces to the universality of the rule of law and the principle of private property. On the other hand, the forces of 'movement' saw liberty as a substantive concept, embodying a broad range of 'positive' social and political attributes, ranging from the acquisition of education and culture to the eradication of class oppression. For the groups which subscribed to this approach, the achievement of greater freedom in French society required significant changes to the existing distribution of social and economic goods. In this sense liberty was itself an expression of a particular conception of equality, in that greater freedom was conditional upon the achievement of greater equality of outcome. Thus, at the risk of crude oversimplification, it may be suggested that the forces of 'order' regarded their conception of liberty as the *summum bonum* of the republican trinity of values, whereas the forces of 'movement' tended to see equality (of outcome) as the most important principle in the republican hierarchy. But, as always in the republican context, elements of ambiguity remained. For much of the Third Republic, the Radical Party saw itself as a party of 'movement' solely because of its commitment to secularism and anticlericalism; it had no serious aspiration to reduce economic inequalities, and indeed tended to side with the forces of 'order' whenever the issue of economic and social justice had to be confronted.

The differences which emerged within the republican camp during the Third Republic may best be illustrated by highlighting the varied (and often conflicting) ways in which the foundational principles of republicanism were interpreted and acted upon by its successive elites after 1875. Three political figures played a decisive role in the process which led to the consolidation of republican politics and government in the 1870s and 1880s: Adolphe Thiers, the historian turned statesman, whose conservatism rallied those who feared that the Republic would challenge propertied interests by introducing extensive social reforms; Léon Gambetta (1838–82), who campaigned tirelessly for the establishment of the Republic in the 1860s and 1870s, and fought to secure its social base in the country; and Jules Ferry (1832–93), at whose initiative many of the fundamental legislative reforms of the early Third Republic were enacted.

The first important feature which was enshrined in both the theory and practice of the Republic was procedural: the centrality of democratic institutions in the political process. This was an expression of the classical republican commitment to the principle of popular sovereignty. The Third Republic created the basis for modern political participation in France by enshrining freedom of association in the constitution and according a central role to representative institutions (both locally and at the national level). The importance given to the principle of representation has already been noted; another indication of its significance was the vitality of local political life in the Third Republic. Democracy revitalized municipal politics, and this set the scene for one of the distinctive (and enduring) features of republican politics: the close interpenetration of local and national political elites, typically reflected in the practice of multiple office-holding (*cumul des mandats*). Thus it was no accident that most mainstream parties began their lives as local associations. Radical politicians, for example, were first elected to the municipal council of Paris in the 1880s, before sweeping into the National Assembly a decade later. Similarly, local elections provided Socialist politicians with their first elected offices. After the creation of the French Communist Party in 1920, the new party also made its mark first in the suburban municipalities of the Parisian region; the PCF became an effective parliamentary force only after 1936. Local political life was therefore an effective laboratory for socializing groups and institutions into the values of the Republic. The only major exception to this trend in modern French politics was the Gaullist party, which swept into national office after 1958 despite the absence of a supportive network at local level. At the same time the forces of 'order' and 'movement' differed in the substantive significance they attached to the principle of popular sovereignty. For the former (up to 1945), democratic institutions were simply a means of reinforcing the stability of the social and economic order. If electoral outcomes appeared to threaten this status quo, for example, as seemed to be the case with the election of the Popular Front government in 1936, these forces were often tempted to dispense with the formal trappings of democracy altogether; this did indeed happen under the Vichy regime between 1940 and 1944. The forces of 'movement', on the other hand, regarded democratic institutions as a vital component of republican politics, partly because mass participation was seen to be an essential prerequisite of an active and enlightened citizenry, but also because (as will be seen below) representative institutions were regarded as the most effective safeguard against authoritarian government.

The centrality of representative institutions was also reflected in the key role accorded to the National Assembly and the Senate in the political process. The upper house was indirectly elected, and its basic purpose was to give voice to the conservative aspirations of rural France (a function which it continues to discharge with quiet efficiency to this day). At the same time the powers of the president were emasculated to prevent these aspirations from being exploited by a charismatic figure. Indeed, part of the reason why the National Assembly emerged as the pivotal political institution was the fear of the past: many republicans were haunted by the experience of the Second Republic, which, as noted earlier, had seen the subversion of the political process by a demagogue.

The Third Republic shied away from entrusting high office to such individuals for any length of time; in this sense it has been rightly maintained that classical republican political culture was profoundly distrustful of strong individual leadership. Thus Jules Ferry was the object of violent attacks from the republican camp throughout his political career because of his (perceived) attempts to concentrate power in his own hands. In the early days of the Fourth Republic Charles de Gaulle's efforts to establish a strong executive were effectively countered by a coalition of 'republican' parties and groups. A few years later the reforming zeal of Pierre Mendès-France (1907–82) was similarly stymied by the unwillingness of his parliamentary colleagues to countenance the emergence of a powerful leader. But this resistance to the exercise of strong individual leadership should not be confused with weak government. The Republic was capable of decisive action against its internal enemies, as the experiences of Catholics, authoritarian nationalists, Gaullists, and Communists bore out during the Third and Fourth Republics. The collapse of the Third Republic in 1940 was often presented as a symptom of the exhaustion of the republican political and ideological dynamic; yet there was no doubt that a common identification with republican values was an essential underpinning of the formation of the resistance, as well as its victorious struggle against the German occupation forces and their Vichy allies between 1940 and 1944. In the economic sphere, although republican governments were hardly a model of dynamism and entrepreneurship, the State was always willing to use its resources to secure the adhesion of important socio-economic groups to the Republic. In the late nineteenth century, for example, Prime Minister Jules Meline's promise of order, stability, and a guaranteed market for agricultural commodities through rigid protectionism made a decisive contribution to the overwhelming legitimation of the Republic in rural France. The Republic was thus eminently capable of firm government and even decisive leadership, provided these attributes were expressions of the interests and objectives of collective groups in the National Assembly, rather than those of a strong individual leader.

The second basic feature of republicanism was also typified by Jules Ferry: the creation of a system of free, compulsory, and secular primary education. This was promoted in part for intrinsic reasons (because the wider dissemination of knowledge was seen by the regime as inherently valuable), but also to encourage such ideals of republican citizenship as individualism and secularism. These militant ideals were derived from the classical republican principle of fraternity and were the exclusive preserve of the forces of 'movement'. These goals were predicated upon a vision of the nation's social and cultural condition which was essentially monolithic, in that only the values promoted by the republican system of education were regarded as legitimate. Education remained an essential instrument for the pursuit of republican social and cultural objectives, and this association provided the new regime with some of its most militant advocates. The promotion of these social values was seen as an essential condition of the fulfilment of the principle of fraternity: it was believed that society would be more cohesive if its members saw themselves as individuals with clearly defined social and historical identities, free from the retrograde ideological influence of the Church. The latter was decried as the principal agent of traditionalism, and the social and cultural objectives of the republicans predictably brought the regime into direct conflict with the ecclesiastical hierarchy. As mentioned earlier, the conflict between these two groups dated back to the Revolution; further sources of conflict emerged during the Second Empire. From the 1860s republicans pressed for the suppression of the ecclesiastical budget, which provided extensive state subsidies to the Church. This arrangement gave the State an element of control over the Church (for example, through the nomination of bishops), but also had the effect of turning Catholicism into a quasi-official religion of the State, and legitimizing the Church's ideological influence over the education system. The republicans' plans to institute a comprehensive system of free (and compulsory) secular education met with considerable resistance from the Church, and the fierce struggle which ensued ended with the proclamation of the separation of the two institutions in 1905. The legislators of the First Republic had sought to promote comprehensive education reforms, but were unable to bring their objectives to fruition because of the tempestuous and unstable character of the post-revolutionary order. Under the leadership of Ferry, however, the Third Republic instituted the educational reforms conceived by its predecessors. After 1880 French local life was transformed by the appearance of the *école républicaine* (often housed in the same building as the municipality). In many communes of France the schoolteacher (the *instituteur*) and the mayor became the principal agents of republicanism, inculcating its basic values in local communities which remained profoundly marked by traditional ideas and customs. But the image of the republican *instituteur* transforming the social and cultural attitudes of his locality by pedagogical indoctrination has been much exaggerated. As with other aspects of republican ideology, education was a matter for compromise; the school-teacher could not operate without at least the tacit acquiescence of his local community, and this imperative often necessitated a prudent and accommodating approach towards the social and religious hierarchies with which he was confronted.

Third, there was a distinctive social dimension to the republican movement. This was reflected in the social origins of its governing elites, the social values promoted by the regime, and (as noted in the previous chapter) the particular role accorded to intellectuals in the republican tradition. In the early 1870s Léon Gambetta hailed the advent of a new social force, the *couches nouvelles*, which he believed were destined to occupy positions of power and authority in the newly established political system. Gambetta never gave a precise definition of this social stratum, but it was clear that he was referring to the middle classes, elements of which did indeed come to play a privileged role in the new political order. From a sociological perspective the political elites of the Third Republic were relatively homogeneous, and their common social origins provided an essential underpinning of the inner cohesiveness of French governments between 1879 and 1940. Throughout this period the National Assembly became the preserve of the French bourgeoisie: for example, liberal professions were sig-nificantly over-represented, and the working classes had to wait for the election of a sizeable Communist contingent in 1936 to find an effective voice in Parliament. The bourgeoisie also provided an explicit social model for the rest of the community under the Third Republic. On such questions as the importance of private property, the privileged role of the family, the value of education, the acquisition of knowledge and culture, and even the merits of the urban way of life, there was a clear sense in which the bourgeoisie was held up as an example to the rest of society. The economic underpinnings of this social hegemony should not be overstated: bourgeois financial interests had been more than adequately defended by the Second Empire, and even the July Monarchy's reign (1830–48) was well remembered for its repeated and undisguised appeals to bourgeois self-interest. Furthermore, the French middle classes did not constitute an entirely cohesive social group, for the objective interests of small businessmen were by no means always similar to those of the financial bourgeoisie. Similarly, the interests of civil servants, barristers, doctors, and journalists did not always converge. But these groups undeniably had more in common with each other than with other social and occupational groups, such as peasants and industrial workers, who always remained institutionally under-represented throughout the Third Republic (although the interests of the former were much more effectively promoted by the Republic than those of the latter).

But there was one social group whose fortunes were directly promoted by the Republic after 1870: the intellectuals. Whereas economically privileged groups had survived (and even prospered) under imperial and monarchical regimes, intellectual groups had been alienated by them. As noted in the previous chapter, intellectuals were far from homogeneous as a social stratum: it was clear that the status, material circumstances, and lifestyles of provincial schoolteachers and Parisian intellectuals diverged considerably. What united them, however, was a common attachment to the principles and values enshrined in the Republican State (most particularly its guarantee of freedom of expression, and the importance it attached to promoting secular education). As shown in Chapter 2, this common identification with the regime was translated into effective mobilization in its defence whenever the Republic appeared to be threatened by its enemies. At the turn of the century the Dreyfus Affair provided a characteristic example of such mobilization. In 1894 a Jewish officer of the French Army, Captain Alfred Dreyfus, was convicted of spying for Germany. Over the next four years doubts emerged as to the validity of his conviction, and a campaign for a retrial was launched. In 1898 the writer Émile Zola denounced the military authorities for fabricating all the evidence against Dreyfus, in an open letter to the President of the Republic (*J'Accuse*). The case was reopened and Dreyfus was eventually pardoned in 1906. The Affair thus stretched over a period of twelve years, but its most intense and passionate moments came after 1898, when France was radically divided between two camps: the Dreyfusards, who argued for revision of the case, in the firm belief that Dreyfus had been unjustly convicted; and the anti-Dreyfusards, who stood by the verdict reached by the military court in 1894. The Dreyfusard intellectuals entered the fray initially only to defend an innocent individual; by the time the Affair had ended, however, it had become a battle between advocates and opponents of the Republic itself. In this sense, the Dreyfus Affair was the first modern example of a pattern which was repeated on several occasions during the twentieth century: the involvement of intellectuals in public life as a means of protecting (and, where possible, consolidating) the political and cultural achievements of the Republic.

The Dreyfus Affair also provided a significant illustration of the fourth important feature of the modern republican tradition: its emphasis on citizenship rather than race or ethnicity as the defining condition of membership of the national community. This feature was derived from the classical republican principles of equality and fraternity: all members of society were entitled to the same rights and privileges, and had to be treated in accordance with the same universal principles of justice. Throughout the Dreyfus Affair the nationalist and anti-republican camp invoked the Jewish origins of the defendant as its principal argument against judicial revision. In their eyes the cosmopolitan character of Jews made them inherently treacherous, and therefore unworthy of full membership of the French nation. The same principle was invoked *a fortiori* against all foreigners who applied for French nationality. In contrast the Republic's principle of equal citizenship rested on an 'open' conception of national identity. Membership of the national community was available not only to those who had been born in France (or had lived there for several generations), but also to those who had elected to make France their *patrie*: for example, citizens of its colonies and immigrants. Membership was not granted automatically: alien groups were required to demonstrate their willingness to integrate into their new motherland by undergoing a process of cultural assimilation. But it was an essential feature of the republican tradition that such a process of integration was held to be necessary (for the purposes of civil peace), desirable (to enable immigrants to receive the benefits of French civilization), possible (there were no inherent obstacles to the successful integration of minority groups), and, finally, irreversible (once awarded, French nationality could not be taken away by the state). During the Third Republic immigrants from southern, central, and eastern Europe were assimilated into French society in this way; during the Fifth Republic a similar process of integration was initiated with regard to North African immigrants. In contrast the anti-republican conception of nationality was founded not on citizenship but on race: it therefore denied the possibility of cultural integration, and also consistently advocated the withdrawal of citizenship from individuals and groups whose loyalty to the nation was deemed suspect. The nationalist writer and polemicist Charles Maurras (1868–1952) characterized as 'anti-France' such groups as republicans, Jews, Protestants, and Freemasons. It was in a similar spirit that the Vichy regime promulgated a special statute for Jews and reviewed the naturalization policies of the Third Republic.

In the modern era a similar approach has been taken by the National Front, whose leaders have consistently suggested that membership of a Semitic culture is incompatible with the values of French nationhood. As will be noted in Chapter 5, the adversarial nationalism of Jean Marie Le Pen's movement is deeply rooted in the exclusionary tradition of anti-republicanism.

The fifth dimension of the classical republican tradition was reflected in the pursuit of greater social justice through institutional means. This feature was derived from the principle of equality and was the essential (but not exclusive) preserve of the forces of 'movement' within the republican camp. Their reformist aspirations were first outlined systematically in the Belleville Manifesto of the Radical movement in 1869. As noted earlier, however, the social policy of the first generation of 'opportunist' republican elites was deeply conservative. As early as 1876 the cleavage in social objectives between Radicals and opportunists had been highlighted by Georges Clemenceau, who declared that 'we, the *radical* republicans, want the Republic because of its results: the great and fundamental social reforms to which it leads. Our proposed aim is the fulfilment of the great metamorphosis of 1789, launched by the French bourgeoisie but abandoned before it had been completed.' (Clemenceau really meant 'because of the Republic's promise', since he seemed to be suggesting that the Republic had yet to complete its social programme.) Many republicans of 'movement' became increasingly dissatisfied with the relative social conservatism of their governments, and they also sought to meet the political challenge of socialism, which began to establish itself as the doctrine of the underprivileged in the 1880s and 1890s. These strategic and tactical concerns resulted in the proclamation of the doctrine of solidarism. This concept was coined by the Radical Prime Minister Léon Bourgeois (1851–1925), who defined the principles of this philosophy in a work published in 1896, *La Solidarité*. Bourgeois believed that classical republican social philosophy had been excessively individualistic. Its emphasis, for example, on the *Declaration of the Rights of Man* had rested on the unduly narrow view that the state's social obligations were limited to the protection of individual rights. While accepting that the protection of these rights was a necessary condition of a modern republican society, however, Léon Bourgeois also emphasized that the state had duties towards its citizens: 'The Republic is not merely the name of a political institution, but the instrument of moral and social progress, a permanent means of reducing inequality and increasing solidarity between men.' The political programme of the solidarists thus contained an extensive range of social reforms, including the shortening of the working day, the provision of pensions and public assistance, and the introduction of progressive income tax.

The emergence of the doctrine of solidarism reflected the dilemmas faced by the forces of 'movement' within the republican tradition in the wake of the institutionalization of the Third Republic. Intellectually convinced of the need for greater social and economic justice, reformist groups fought to make the Republic live up to the ideals of *liberté, egalité fraternité*. But they also discovered that these principles were not fully compatible with one another. Equality of outcome was an ideal which could be attained only by substantively altering the existing distribution of economic and social goods in society, whereas the classical republican conception of liberty (which was championed by the forces of 'order') was based on allowing individuals to pursue their conception(s) of the good without external regulation—a state of affairs which presupposed that the existing order was just. This tension expressed the problems inherent in any attempt to reconcile competing claims about justice and order. When in government these republicans (particularly the Radicals) were necessarily concerned with political stability, social cohesion, and economic development, all of which depended critically on the preservation of order. At the same time they sometimes remembered, like Léon Bourgeois, that the Republic historically symbolized the hopes of those who wanted to transform the existing order, in the name of the same ideals which had impelled their ancestors to overthrow the old regime in 1789. This tension between preserving social stability and promoting social justice was later inherited by the socialist tradition, which also shared many of the reformist ideals of the solidarists. The life and work of such figures as Jean Jaurès, Léon Blum, Pierre Mendès-France, and François Mitterrand represented a continuing attempt to bring about a synthesis of the classical republican concerns with freedom and democracy with the socialist objectives of reducing social inequalities and enhancing social solidarity. How far the years of Socialist rule after 1981 contributed towards the advancement of this synthesis will be discussed at greater length in Chapter 9.

MODERN FRENCH POLITICS AND THE
CLASSICAL REPUBLICAN LEGACY

The different features of classical republican ideology outlined in the preceding section amounted to a distinct way of life, complete with its state institutions, political movements and secondary associations, social intermediaries, and moral and cultural value system. As has been emphasized throughout this narrative, however, republicanism was also an extremely flexible political construct; much of its force rested on its ability to cut across many of the traditional cleavages in French politics. In its consensual dimension (which was most tellingly demonstrated in times of direct challenge to the republican regime itself) this underlying convergence brought together political groups from different social and ideological horizons. In this sense core republican ideas and values were a source of unity and cohesion in French public life. But this unity was not synonymous with uniformity; as has been shown, republican political groups had different conceptions of the substantive significance of the concepts of liberty, equality, and fraternity, and these conflicting approaches were expressed in enduring battles between the forces of 'order' and 'movement'.

At this juncture the question posed at the beginning of the chapter may be restated: what remains of the legacy of the republican tradition in modern France? After considerable public reflection during the commemoration of the bicentenary of the French Revolution in 1989, most political analysts concluded that little survived of the original heritage. However, if the claim that republicanism has lost its political and ideological significance in modern France is to be made good, it has to be demonstrated not only that the regime created by de Gaulle in 1958 (the Fifth Republic) transformed the character of the country's political institutions beyond recognition, but also that the social and ideological underpinnings of republicanism were undermined irreversibly by these transformations. In what follows it will not be denied that the political and social architecture of the Republican State has undergone several important changes under the Fifth Republic; at the same time, the claim that these changes amount to a transcendence of the classical republican paradigm will be resisted. Furthermore, the survival of republican values will be demonstrated in the widespread public support for the Republican regime in France, as well as a general attachment to many of the social and cultural values embedded in the classical republican tradition.

The contention that the political institutions of the Fifth Republic represent a fundamental departure from the classical republican conception of the State is most frequently supported by invoking significant changes in the distribution of power at the apex of the political system since 1958. The centralization of power in the hands of the presidency has been accompanied by a dramatic decline in the status and functions of the National Assembly. This was an almost exact inversion of the classical republican institutional configuration which, it will be remembered, vested effective policy-making powers with the representatives of the people and was expressly hostile to the exercise of strong individual leadership. A further element of evidence which is cited is the emergence of the Constitutional Council as a relatively autonomous actor in the process of judicial review in France during the 1980s and early 1990s. The increasingly prominent role of the Court in controlling and often challenging the legislative output of the National Assembly is seen as a fundamental departure from classical republican legal philosophy, which was founded on the principle of the unconditional supremacy of the representatives of the people in the determination of legal norms. That there have been significant changes in the distribution of power within the political elite since 1958 is beyond dispute; however, it is far from clear that they are sufficient to support the claim that the political and administrative institutions of the Fifth Republic are fundamentally different in nature from those of its predecessors. Indeed, most contrasts between the institutions of the Fifth Republic and its ancestors tend to exaggerate the salient characteristics of each regime, as well as undervaluing the strong elements of continuity between them.

As noted earlier, the classical Republican State was often capable of firm and decisive leadership, and the formal powers enjoyed by the *député* were always an object of suspicion. At a more fundamental level all republican regimes have been inspired by a strong sense of purpose. Even the governing elites of the Fourth Republic, who are generally lampooned for presiding over a chronically unstable regime, were strongly committed to the preservation of the republican form of government against the powerful onslaught of Gaullist and Communist revisionism. Indeed, even their failure to resolve the Algerian issue in the late 1950s was an expression of a cohesive—albeit anachronistic and ultimately self-destructive—world-view of France's civilizing mission in the colonies. The Third Republic's institutional vocation was the promotion of republican social and political values through education and mass culture; the founders of the Fifth Republic were driven by the objective of modernizing the country's economic and political institutions. Thus the discontinuities between different republican regimes were not as great as might initially be believed: each of them shared a common political and ideological ancestry, a commitment to a well-defined set of social and economic objectives, and accommodated significant (but different) elements of centralization in their midst. In the latter context it is particularly important not to exaggerate the distinctiveness of the Fifth Republic: the trend since the late 1970s has been clearly moving away from the hyper-centralization of the Gaullist era. The powers of the president have been exercised under increasingly compelling political and economic constraints, in both the domestic and external spheres. For example, the decentralization reforms of the Mitterrand presidency were a response to the perceived incapacity of the French State to manage its territorial relations optimally. The reforms in many ways merely gave legal form to an already existing distribution of power at local level, and served particularly well the interests of the *notables* who governed France's large cities. But they also sanctioned the emergence of counterweights to the centralized institutions of government and thus placed a new limitation on the powers of the French executive. In the international sphere the movement towards European integration (despite the problems encountered by the project to create a single European currency) has provided opportunities for the assertion of French political influence, but also significantly reduced the scope for autonomous presidential action in the field of economic (and especially monetary) policy. The net effects of these constraints has been to make the contemporary French state even less dissimilar to its republican forebears; indeed, from the vantage point of the late 1990s, the highly centralized political structure of the early Fifth Republic may well appear as a (conjunctural) deviation from a relatively continuous institutional pattern.

If the regime which to-day governs France is clearly the product of a recognizable institutional paradigm, what of the social and ideological aspects of the legacy of the republican tradition? It would be foolish to assert that all the basic components of classical republican ideology continue to occupy the centre of the political stage. For example, the titanic battles over education seem to have given way to a guarded but generally respected truce, occasionally broken only when the government of the day attempts (or, as in 1984 and 1993, appears to seek) to upset the delicate balance of power between secular and religious groups. From a wider perspective the ideological gulf between the two camps is no longer as deep as in the late nineteenth century, partly because both communities have witnessed significant internal realignments. Despite the antics of French fundamentalist zealots, the Catholic Church in France has become much more forward-looking, tolerant, and heterogeneous. At the same time, its overall influence as a purveyor of social values has receded significantly; indeed, its metamorphosis appears to have done little to arrest the relentless trend towards secularization in French society.

With the ebbing of the confrontational character of French politics by the mid-1980s, and the discrediting of grand schemes for comprehensive social change, in what sense could it be argued that classical republican values continued to inform the practice of politics in modern France? The concise answer is that the foundational principles of republicanism had become firmly embedded in the fabric of French politics and society, and that the process of ideological convergence in the 1980s significantly narrowed political disagreements over the substantive definition and relative ordering of these principles. The erosion of the traditional divide between the forces of 'order' and 'movement' made possible a broad consensus over the meaning and substance of the concepts of equality, fraternity, and liberty. The overwhelming public attachment to the country's democratic institutions represents a vindication of the republican ideal of individual liberty, of which the regime is now almost universally seen to be the best guarantee of protection. From a broad historical perspective the Republic's faith in (and strength in defending) democratic values was an essential condition of its eventual triumph over its various enemies (monarchy, empire, right- and left-wing authoritarian movements) at critical moments in the history of modern France. Equally significant (although rather less celebrated) was the republican regime's success in influencing the political culture of parties and movements whose attachment to the value of democratic institutions was less than fulsome. Until the middle of the twentieth century, as noted earlier, most parliamentary parties of the Right regarded the democratic heritage of the Republic as (at best) a conditional good or (at worst) the antechamber of a communist revolution. The 'republicanization' of the Right was essentially a product of the resistance, which brought together social and political groups from widely differing ideological horizons on the basis of a common identification with core republican values. The integration of the parliamentary Right into the democratic institutions of the Republic was almost complete by the end of the Fourth Republic; indeed, this process was a necessary condition of de Gaulle's success in preventing the Algerian crisis from degenerating into a civil war in France, and ultimately destroying the democratic legacy of the Republic.

In the domain of equality the Socialist experiment of the 1980s put paid to the Left's aspirations to use political institutions to engender greater equality of outcome; to this extent, one of the direct ideological legacies of the French Revolution was forsaken (whether irreversibly so is, however, far from evident). By the early 1990s the French Left as a whole was in an advanced state of decomposition. Neither of its two principal components had been able to devise an effective response to the intellectual failures of the 1980s. Indeed, the only significant link which survived the halcyon days of Left unity between Socialists and Communists was strictly procedural: the electoral agreement known as the *discipline républicaine*, by virtue of which each party agreed to stand down if the other party's candidate was in a better position to defeat the representative of the Right. As might be expected, the disintegration of the radical Left's intellectual armoury shifted the parameters of equality towards the definition traditionally favoured by the forces of 'order'. For the latter, equality was always an essentially procedural and juridical concept, expressing the principle that every member of society should be entitled to the same rights and privileges, irrespective of social, religious, and political conditions. Yet the forces of 'order' were not left untouched by the classical republican concern for social equality. In fact, it is arguable that one of the most significant long-term achievements of the republican tradition was the decisive influence its core principles exercised on the social philosophy of the French Right.

The provision of assistance to underprivileged sections of the community had some historical pedigree on the Right as an expression of (aristocratic) paternalism; but it was always seen as an act of charity, rather than a necessary feature of the state's social obligation to its citizens. The conversion of the forces of 'order' to the principle of state provision of welfare functions came after the Liberation, when right-wing elites were dominated by Gaullist and Christian democratic influences. Under the Fifth Republic the parties of the Right were united in agreement over the essential characteristics of the welfare state, and this consensus was reflected in the consistent social dimension of the presidencies of de Gaulle, Pompidou, and Giscard d'Estaing. This underlying sense that the state had an obligation to protect and enhance the quality of life of its citizens went somewhat further than the traditional commitment of forces of 'order' to the principle of equality of condition. It expressed the characteristically republican view that the promotion of solidarity in French society required an element of state intervention to correct social inequalities acquired at birth (and accentuated by the market). The conversion of the Right to the value of social solidarity may have been initiated out of expediency, but it eventually assumed an intrinsic character. Again, it could be argued that this conversion had important consequences for public policy. Thus it was partly the legacy of these republican values which blunted the radical edges of the neo-liberal experiment of 1986–8 in France, insulating the Right from the frontal assault on the social principles of the welfare state which was witnessed in Britain and the United States during the 1980s. Thus France's forces of 'order' fully internalized the republican notion that the State was not simply a legal construct, but also (and perhaps especially) an institution with a sense of moral purpose: to safeguard the interests of those too weak to defend themselves against the contingencies of the human condition.

To conclude, there are many ways in which the republican character of French public institutions continues to matter. Even the widespread sense of disillusionment with French political elites is (paradoxically) a symptom of the continuing vibrance of republican principles. The standards by which politicians are judged (and increasingly found wanting) are still defined by republican parameters: it is because they are deemed to be insufficiently principled, financially scrupulous, idealistic, and concerned with the public good that confidence in French elites has declined over the last decade. In other words, public expectations as to what politics should be about continue to be informed by republican ideals. But this survival of republicanism is not limited to the sphere of public expectations. As has been seen throughout this chapter, the republican regime has also provided a means of socializing political groups into the mainstream and excluding others from it. Republicanism has not been exclusively (and, perhaps, not even predominantly) a cohesive ideology whose goals have been implemented by successive regimes since 1870. It has also provided a means of brokering political conflict and defining areas of common interest between groups whose primary objectives were not necessarily convergent. This is perhaps the sense in which the republican (institutional) tradition has been most successful. Since the 1970s social and political relations in France have been clearly less confrontational in character and, by the time of the commemoration of the bicentenary of the French Revolution in 1989, there were very few areas over which mainstream political groups disagreed fundamentally. This absence of ideological dissonance was not, as political commentators concluded rather hastily, a symptom of the demise of republicanism; indeed, it constituted a triumph of the eminently republican notions of accommodation and compromise. In one significant respect, however, the modern Republic has failed to promote social and political consensus. The rise of the National Front, and its successful articulation of racist and xenophobic discourse, has seriously undermined the stability of the political system in the 1980s and 1990s. Despite their weak response to the Front's public discourse on issues of race and immigration, however, republican politicians (of the Left and Right) continued to share a common bedrock of values which could provide a basis for a substantive reaction against the poisonous ideological influence of the extreme Right. That this struggle has yet to be waged effectively is evidence only of the lack of dynamism of France's rather jaded political elites. Opinion polls clearly suggest that their reluctance to engage with the National Front is not shared by the overwhelming majority of the French electorate, which remains firmly attached to the solidaristic and egalitarian heritage of republicanism on the issues of race and citizenship.

Republicanism was thus not a purely opportunistic phenomenon. There were (and remain) a number of core questions over which republicans were never prepared to compromise: the principle of popular sovereignty, the sanctity of democratic institutions, and the notion of civil equality. This is why French republicans refused to countenance the restoration of the monarchy in the 1870s or condone the Vichy regime's abandonment of the democratic heritage of the Third Republic after 1940; and it is in a similar spirit that many republicans reject the National Front's calls for discrimination against French citizens on racial and cultural grounds. In a more limited way than a century ago, perhaps, but no less categorically, the principles and values of republicanism continue to define the limits of the acceptable—and the unacceptable—in French public life.

Chronology

1789   July. French Revolution begins: overthrow of the *ancien régime*.

1789   August. Abolition of privileges, and proclamation of the *Declaration of the Rights of Man* by the National Assembly.

1792   September. First Republic.

1793   September. Beginning of the Terror.

1794   February. Proclamation of the abolition of slavery in French colonies.

1804   May. Empire inaugurated by Napoleon.

1815   July. Second Bourbon restoration: return of Louis XVIII.

1830   July. July revolution: liberal monarchy of Louis-Philippe.

1848   February. Proclamation of Second Republic

1852   December. Napoleonic plebiscite sanctions birth of Second Empire.

1870   September. Fall of Second Empire after military defeat by Prussia.

1871   March. Paris Commune elected.

1875   February. Constitutional laws of Third Republic voted by National Assembly.

1877   October. Decisive republican victory in legislative elections.

1884   March. Legalization of trade unions.

1898   January. Émile Zola's *J'Accuse* launches Dreyfus Affair.

1905   December. Separation of Church and State.

1936   April–May. Electoral victory of Popular Front.

1940   July. After German military defeat of France, full powers voted to Marshal Pétain.

1944   August. Liberation of Paris.

1945   October. Referendum ends Third Republic.

1946   October. Adoption of constitution of Fourth Republic.

1958   September. Constitutional revision: proclamation of Fifth Republic.

1958   December. De Gaulle elected first President of Fifth Republic.

1962   October. Amendment to constitution: president to be elected by universal suffrage.

1981   May. Election of François Mitterrand to presidency; pledge to maintain constitutional order of Fifth Republic.

1989   July. Commemoration of bicentenary of French Revolution.

CHAPTER 4

Religion, Clericalism, and the Republican State

On a warm afternoon during the summer of 1984 immense crowds gathered in a number of major French cities to protest against recently enacted government legislation. In Paris alone, more than a million people marched through the streets chanting anti-government slogans. Since its liberation from German occupation in 1944, the capital had witnessed many similar protest marches, of course, but there was a distinctive character to this particular gathering: it was led by the Archbishop of Paris in person, Monseigneur Aaron Lustiger. In other French cities the Catholic clergy played an equally prominent public role in organizing anti-government rallies. What had brought Church men and women out into the political arena in such numbers?

The issue which had generated this high level of political mobilization was part of a recurrent problem, which had provoked passionate and occasionally violent confrontations in France ever since the middle of the nineteenth century. The problem was the relationship between the Catholic Church and the French State, and the issue over which this confrontation was typically articulated was education. What degree of freedom should be allowed to religious institutions in educational matters? How far did the duty of the State to ensure that its citizens received an acceptable standard of learning override the rights of religious groups to educate their offspring in the ways of God? It is in this general context that the problem of clericalism, which is the subject of this chapter, assumed a central place. The wider significance of the protests of July 1984, which led to the withdrawal of the offending piece of legislation (and the resignation of the Socialist Minister of Education, Alain Savary) can be understood adequately only if the historical roots of the confrontation between Church and State in France are examined. In a narrow sense, the 'clerical question' occupied the forefront of the French political scene during the Second Empire and much of the Third Republic. In 1905, however, the official separation of Churches from the State formally ended the conflict between the Republic and traditionalist Catholic forces over the place

of religion in French public life. But the clash between these institutions was the political expression of a more basic collision between
religious and secular conceptions of life, and this conflict continued
to inform social relations in France for many decades. For example,
the legacy of the clerical question was still felt during the interwar
period, when the Radical Prime Minister, Edouard Herriot, tried to
use the issue to unite his left-wing Cartel des Gauches coalition against
conservative opposition to his government. During the Vichy administration (1940–4) the Catholic Church was given a relatively privileged
position in the hierarchy of public institutions, and conscious attempts
were made to devise social policies under the guidance of clerical
doctrines. After 1945, furthermore, the debate over the status of private schools periodically resurfaced: in this sense the events of 1984
simply represented a further episode in the long tradition of confrontation between secular and religious forces in France. But this chapter
will also show that there were always groups on both sides who were
willing to reach a compromise, and indeed, that part of the reason
why the clericalist challenge to the Republic failed so decisively was
that it rejected all efforts to come to terms with the social and institutional changes introduced by the new regime.

DEFINITIONS AND PARAMETERS

To define precisely the notion of clericalism is a hazardous exercise.
In modern France the term 'clericalist' is purely descriptive, simply
denoting an action, attitude, or belief emanating from the clergy. In
its original form, however, the term was first used in 1866 to express
the attitudes of those individuals, groups, and institutions who advocated an active role for the French clergy in public life. In this ideological form, therefore, clericalism represented an assertion of the
authority of the Church in spiritual and temporal affairs. However,
this doctrinal dimension does not provide a satisfactory basis for understanding what is conventionally defined as the 'clerical question' in
French politics. Like republicanism, clericalism is best seen not as a
narrow doctrine, but rather as a cluster of socio-political attitudes,
beliefs, and values which emerged during a specific phase of the conflict between the Church and the State in France. Clericalist views
were not exclusively defended by a single group or institution: 'clerical'
positions could be taken by a variety of social actors who did not

necessarily espouse the same core ideological principles. Thus there were imperial, monarchist, nationalist, and conservative clericalists, in the same way as there were liberal, radical, socialist, and (later) communist forms of republicanism. The working definition which will be used throughout this chapter, therefore, will consider clericalism as the political expression of those groups and movements which believed that religious institutions should play a significant role in determining standards of public and private life. Clericalism was a cry of political anger and religious despair in the face of the perceived decadence of French society; it was no accident that its strongest articulations came during periods of intense national crisis (most notably after the military defeats of France in 1871 and 1940). The following exhortation from a pamphlet entitled *Faith and Fatherland*, compiled by a churchman from Limoges shortly after the humiliation of Napoleon's troops at Sedan in 1870, provides a graphic insight into the clericalist world-view:

We could never be victorious in battle! We, the French, have too many flaws. We are boastful, lazy, languid, disciples of immorality and luxury; we lack energy, vigour, and honesty. This is why we have been defeated, why we shall be conquered, and why we have to yield. We must eliminate our arrogance, our excitement, our agitation, our lies. Our women must become chaste, they must abandon their wild dresses and their loose morals.

We must break with licentious literature, especially with licentious plays. We must put an end to our detestable mundane customs, which corrupt our spirit and our habits, and we must abandon our abominably frivolous lifestyle, the cause of so many of our vices. We must become industrious, sober, honest, faithful to our wives, and spend our leisure with our families, instead of wasting our time in cafés, clubs, and even worse places. We must become a different people, before we can hope to recover from our terrible calamities. We have lost our valiant spirit through our own fault; let us endeavour to regain it through our regeneration.

Clericalism thus stood for a number of simple precepts: order, temperance, humility, and above all, subservience to the teachings of God (as revealed by the Church). It was strongly reactive, first and foremost against what was deemed to be the disintegration of the fabric of French society. But the origins of this collapse were ultimately traced back to the eighteenth century: to the French Revolution, which was regarded as an unmitigated disaster; the Enlightenment, whose leading intellectual figures (such as Voltaire) were regarded as the creatures of Satan; and the republican tradition, which was held responsible for the corruption of the social fabric and the degradation of public and private morality. These beliefs were translated into an obsessive concern with questions of ethics and civic conduct, but also more basic social issues such as how and where people should be buried, and whether Sunday work should be allowed. The institutional component of clericalism must also be emphasized, because the clerical question was *sensu stricto* a dispute over the role of the Catholic Church in French society. But clericalism also had an international dimension. The Church was closely associated with the fate of the Vatican, and indeed constantly pressed the French State to defend and protect the interests of the Holy See. During the process of Italian unification, for example, the Pope became a viutal prisoner of the new Republic, and the ultramontane wing of French Catholicism advocated the use of force by France to help the Vatican restore its temporal powers. Ultramontane clericalists urged their compatriots to follow closely the teachings of the Pope, whose dogmatic and illiberal *Syllabus* (1864) constituted a point of reference for intransigent Catholicism throughout the rest of the nineteenth century.

Returning to the question of definition, a word must be said about the denominational specificity of clericalism. France in the late nineteenth century was overwhelmingly Catholic: 90 per cent of the population was baptized, and other religious groups (such as Protestants) constituted only a small proportion of the adult population. What was the social and political significance of the fact that Catholicism was the dominant religious denomination in France? First, its treatment of other social and religious groups mattered, since its pre-eminent position allowed it to exercise a powerful influence over the ways in which these minorities were perceived by society. The Church essentially used this influence to reinforce the negative image of these groups within the Catholic community. For example, Catholics and Protestants had a long record of intense animosity, which dated back to the persecutions of the Reformation era. Protestants were still considered as schismatics by large sections of the Catholic community, and this conception was strengthened further after 1870 by the perceived prominence of Protestants among the political, administrative, economic, and intellectual elites of the new Republic. Clerical groups regularly denounced the pernicious influence of Protestants in public life, and this process of denominational hatred was typically expressed during the Dreyfus Affair in the late nineteenth century, when the clerical newspaper *La Croix* denounced 'the Protestant' as one of the four enemies of the French nation (the other three being the Jew, the Freemason, and the Socialist). Jews were the object of equally fierce hostility, and the intensity of public expressions of anti-Semitism throughout the Catholic community during this period is worthy of note. Edouard Drumont's *La France juive* (1886), a crude and extravagant account of the alleged power wielded by the Jewish community in France, went through 200 editions within the first fifteen years of its publication. For much of the twentieth century relations between the Church and the French Jewish community remained haunted by these memories; after the Liberation a further source of contention was the failure of the Church publicly to denounce the persecution of French Jews by the Vichy regime. The survival of an anti-Semitic streak within Catholic culture in France seemed to be borne out by the network of clericalist support provided to the notorious war criminal Paul Touvier, a leading member of the Vichy militia in Lyons, who organized the systematic murder of Jewish civilians during the Second World War. Sentenced to death in 1946 and 1947 for his criminal activities during the war, Touvier escaped from his detention centre and went into hiding, and for the next forty years (until his arrest in May 1989) was granted extensive material and spiritual assistance from the highest authorities in the French Catholic Church.

Whether taken in the narrow sense of the specific conflict between the Catholic Church and the Republican State between 1870 and 1905, or in the wider context of the role of religious forces in the public life of the nation in the twentieth century, three important parameters of clericalism are worthy of note. First, the saliency of clerical ideas and values was directly linked to the extent, form, and content of religious practices in French society. It was no accident that sharp surges in clericalist sentiment corresponded to periods of high religious feeling in French society. The last three decades of the nineteenth century, and also the period immediately following the occupation of France in 1940, witnessed a remarkable rise in religious fervour. In both cases this phenomenon was primarily a reaction against the defeat and humiliation suffered by the nation at the hands of the German invader. For Louis Veuillot (1813–83), the leading Catholic intellectual of the Second Empire and early Third Republic, the defeat of France in 1871 was nothing less than an act of Providence. As he declared in an article written in *l'Univers*, in his characteristically forceful language: 'As the doctor who uses poison, divine Providence resorts to plagues for curative purposes. And this is why poisons and plagues exist. *If God did not wish to heal, he would not strike*. . . Every war is the expression of his compassion and the decree of his justice.' Clericalism thus bred on the terrain of social and political despair: the themes of penitence and retribution were central to its appeal to large sections of the community. Between 1870 and the early twentieth century another important factor underlay the emergence of clericalism: a change in the social expressions of popular piety, best reflected in the proliferation of prophecies, visions, and miracles during this period (for example, the cult of Mary, the bleeding heart, and mass pilgrimages to the Lourdes shrine). The Assumptionist Order played a vital role in providing these forms of popular superstition with a political outlet. This militant clerical group controlled the Catholic newspaper *La Croix*, which, as already noted, firmly established itself as the voice of anti-republican France (it was banned by the Waldeck-Rousseau government in 1900). There was a strange contrast between the sophistication deployed by many clericalist groups to disseminate their message, and the crudeness and extreme simplicity of its content. The Assumptionists realized from a very early stage that newspapers were a highly effective means of propagating their views; they were also one of the first Catholic groups to organize support committees for candidates who espoused clericalist causes (notably in the elections of 1898). At the same time, however, the message itself rested on a bleak vision of human existence, which had little to offer by way of appeal except the prospect of salvation in the next world.

If the level and expressions of religious sentiment are important parameters to be considered in analysing the development of clericalism, it is also relevant to remember that clerical forces in the Third Republic (and this is true of French Catholicism more generally in the twentieth century) were members of a transnational community whose widely acknowledged source of authority was based in Rome. As noted earlier, the history of clericalism (and Catholicism more generally) in France cannot be understood without taking into account the central and often determinant influence of the Vatican on the French religious community. Although by no means all clericalist groups recognized the spiritual and temporal authority of Rome (Gallicans, for example, refused to acknowledge the pre-eminence of the Vatican), the immense sense of reverence for the Pope in French Catholic society meant that every intervention of the Vatican in French affairs had significant repercussions on the religious community. Despite being one of the most authoritative figures of French Catholicism in the late 1860s and early 1870s, Louis Veuillot was subsequently marginalized because the Vatican did not believe that his extreme pronouncements were helpful to the Roman cause in France. Subsequently Pope Leo XIII (1810–1903) played a privileged role in the effort to forge a *modus vivendi* between the French Republic and the Catholic Church in the early 1890s (the *Ralliement*). This attempt to bring the two camps together did not succeed fully, but the Pope's intervention defined the terms of the political debate within the Catholic community during that period. Similarly, the condemnation by Pius XI of the heretical doctrines of the *Action Française*, and the insertion of its journal on the Vatican's *Index* of proscribed books in 1926, severely traumatized parts of the French Catholic community, and forced many clericalists to choose between their spiritual allegiance to Rome and their temporal affinities with the nationalistic political dogmas of the extreme Right.

The third point to remember—and this is already implicit in the previous section—is that clericalism was a political configuration emanating from a wider community of religious belief, and ought not to be regarded as expressing the social and political values of French Catholicism as a whole, even if clericalist sentiments were undoubtedly dominant during the first three decades of the Third Republic. French Catholicism was never entirely monolithic, and indeed contained many undercurrents which did not share the clericalists' dogmatic traditionalism and inveterate hostility to the Republic. As will be noted subsequently, the republican regime was eventually able to reach a compromise with some of these Catholic groups over the question of religious education. But even within the clericalist ensemble, there were clear nuances which could be identified between its different components. There were considerable variations in temperament and political emphasis (and little love lost) between, for example, agnostic defenders of the Church and the 'ultra' (fundamentalist) Catholics, between the sceptical Catholic notables in regions such as the west of France and the devout religious militants of clericalist associations, and finally, between the ecclesiastical hierarchy of the Catholic Church (most notably the Gallican bishops), who were often conscious of their institutional and diplomatic obligations towards the French State, and the local village *curé*, who tended to regard the Republic as the incarnation of Satan, State schools as the antechambers of Hell, and all government institutions as the sinister preserve of Jews, Protestants,

Freemasons, and Socialists. But this vertical opposition sometimes produced different types of division, particularly when the question of poverty and social deprivation was at stake. The local *curé* was often more acutely aware of the need for greater social justice than the distant ecclesiastical hierarchy, and this explained the appeal of a figure such as Albert de Mun (1841–1914), a fiery orator of the extreme Right who strongly advocated the pursuit of social reform. The persistence of this concern also explained the growing strength of social Catholicism during the first half of the twentieth century, as a progressively broader spectrum of opinion within the clergy became convinced that the Church needed to give greater prominence to its role as the protector of the underprivileged. In sum, Catholic opinion was diverse and indeed often divided, and this situation was eventually exploited by republican elites to marginalize the extremist clericalist groups who categorically refused to compromise with the regime on matters of common concern.

THE PHILOSOPHICAL ORIGINS OF CLERICALISM: DE MAISTRE AND DE BONALD

Although it has been seen that the concept of clericalism was devised only in the latter half of the nineteenth century, the intellectual challenge it posed during the Third Republic needs to be placed in its wider ideological context. As with republicanism, clericalist ideas were given a decisive impetus by the experiences of the 1790s. As noted in the preceding chapter, the Church hierarchy was almost totally alienated by the radicalization of the French Revolution, and became one of the staunchest advocates of monarchical restoration after 1792 (although the lower clergy, always closer to the reality of poverty and oppression under the *ancien régime*, was much less militant in its antirepublicanism). The prehistory of French clericalism was thus founded on this close link between royalist ideology and the Catholic establishment. It was no accident that the intellectual matrix within which clericalism emerged in the second half of the nineteenth century posited an almost theocratic vision of the world, in which the French monarchy and Church were the privileged executors of divine will. Politically expressed in the doctrine of legitimism, this approach was first articulated clearly in the writings of two political philosophers: Louis de Bonald (1754–1840), a political thinker and parliamentarian who served in the National Assembly after the Bourbon restoration in 1815; and Joseph de Maistre (1753–1821), a French *émigré* who lived in the kingdom of Sardinia.

Both these thinkers were primarily responding to the legacy of the French Revolution, which they regarded as the greatest calamity which ever befell the French nation. Bonald regarded the democratic politics introduced after 1789 as an 'organic disease of society', and warned that 'a Republic in France will eventually destroy the monarchy throughout Europe, and a republican Europe will mean the end of the civilized world.' If this was not apocalyptic enough, de Maistre added: 'What makes the French revolution a uniquely distinctive event in French history is its radically *evil* nature . . . it represents the highest degree of corruption known to man; it is impurity in its purest form.' De Maistre believed that the revolutionary experience was the divine punishment the French had invited for what he termed 'a century of blasphemy'. He proposed a political system which harked back not so much to the immediate pre-revolutionary era, but rather to the medieval Christian monarchies of Europe. In this idealized vision of the past a central role was assigned to religious institutions in spiritual and temporal matters, and the role of the family in sustaining a hierarchical political order was strongly highlighted. Both de Maistre and de Bonald completely rejected the Enlightenment, which had attempted to destroy the natural order of society by stressing the redemptive possibilities of political action supported by the critical use of human reason. In their eyes the very idea of human progress was a heresy. Man was born to sin, and only two things could prevent him from following his natural inclinations: the fear of God, and the even greater fear of the guillotine. The writings of de Maistre and de Bonald graphically anticipated many of the key ideas and themes of clericalist groups in France after 1870. Perhaps the most striking way in which this continuity was expressed was in the advocacy of penitence. In the strictly determinist vision of the world adopted by clericalists, no worldly occurrence, however destructive and painful, could be anything other than an act of Providence. The experiences of war, defeat, and humiliation therefore had to be seen as a divine message to those who had strayed from the path of God. Under these circumstances the only way to revert to the true path of faith was through atonement. Hence the collective repentance which was advocated in France after 1870, which was best illustrated by the building of the Sacré Coeur as an act of contrition. The same theme also resurfaced powerfully during the Vichy years, after France's humiliating defeat by Germany.

THE PRINCIPAL GOALS OF CLERICALISM

The counter-revolutionary intellectual origins of clericalism thus specified, attention can now be turned to the immediate context which conditioned the emergence of clericalist attitudes during the Third Republic. The definition of clericalism adopted initially, it will be remembered, identified these attitudes as expressing the belief that religious institutions should play a significant role in determining standards of public and private conduct. But what exactly were these standards of action and belief; why did they have to be defended, and against whom?

Nothing of the passion and fury which the clerical question generated between 1870 and the early twentieth century can be appreciated without a brief return to the late 1840s. In December 1848 Louis Napoleon was elected President of the Second Republic, and he rapidly set about granting a privileged role to the Church in educational matters (in the Falloux laws of 1850). This preferential treatment was enhanced after the proclamation of the Second Empire in 1852. Under the reign of Bonaparte's nephew the Church was restored to many of the privileged positions it enjoyed under the *ancien régime*. Catholicism became, to all intents and purposes, the religion of the French State: the Church enjoyed a virtual monopoly of public charity; Church officials were given places of honour at all State gatherings; censorship of the press made direct attacks on Catholicism impossible; finally, bishops could communicate with the Vatican without any interference by the State. The Empire was presented as a quintessentially Christian state, and Louis Napoleon was its benevolent patriarch. The benefits accorded to the Church by the Second Empire did not end there: the Napoleonic State granted Catholic authorities an unchallenged monopoly in the field of social indoctrination. Until 1860 clerical influence over education was dominant in all areas. Universities and secondary schools were governed by a 'Higher Council of Public Instruction', which was dominated by bishops; many primary schools were guarded by the parish clergy, who saw to the dismissal of teachers with anticlerical (or merely secular) views; and a climate of profound intolerance against all forms of secular humanist thought prevailed. In other words, the Church used its political influence to destroy what it saw as the illusory and dangerous beliefs propounded by the Enlightenment. The typical objects of clerical concern were idealists such as the republican historian Jules Michelet (1798–1874), who saw history as the triumphant march of reason against superstition, and rationalist thinkers such as Ernest Renan (1823–92), who believed that society could be organized on the basis of scientific principles. Under the pressing influence of conservative forces (within as well as outside the Church), Michelet's post at the Collège de France was suspended in 1851; Renan was similarly banned in 1862. It is true that, during the 1860s, this favourable disposition of the Church towards the Empire was undermined by Bonapartist support for Italian reunification (and thus France's *de facto* endorsement of the challenge to papal supremacy). The Church also did not find cause to rejoice in Napoleon's appointment of a secular academic (Victor Duruy) as Minister of Education. None the less, the overall balance sheet of relations between Church and Empire was undoubtedly positive.

This alliance between Church and Empire naturally assumed overtly political undertones. The Catholic authorities did not limit themselves to persecuting anticlerical academics in universities and schools; they often condoned the political persecution of the republican opposition to the Empire during the 1850s and 1860s. More generally, the Church turned its back on the liberal and social tradition of Catholicism which, until the late 1840s, kept open at least the possibility of an alliance between the clergy and the republican movement. During the Second Empire these hopes were irreversibly shattered: the Church threw itself entirely and unreservedly behind the most reactionary and repressive social and political forces which supported the new regime. This legacy went a long way towards explaining the virulence of expressions of anticlerical sentiments during the Third Republic. For the new republican elites the Church was a public institution which had exercised a powerful social and ideological influence during the Second Empire, and which could continue to do so if its powers remained unchecked. The battle fought by clericalists after 1860 represented an attempt to defend (at all costs) the material and intellectual privileges which the Catholic Church had acquired during the first decade of the imperial era. These immediate negative ends of the clericalists determined the adoption of a positive political strategy, which centred on providing unstinting support for all groups and parties which were committed to overthrowing the Republican regime. Indeed, the passions generated by the clerical question in the early days of the Third Republic would not have reached such heights if the Church and its supporters had limited themselves to the strictly negative objective of preserving their material and intellectual interests. What made clericalism such a dangerous force in the eyes of the republicans was the fact that it hurled itself into the political battle to destroy the Republic itself after 1875. When republican leader Léon Gambetta declared, in a speech in May 1877, that clericalism was the enemy, he was not identifying the Church as an institution which was seeking simply to protect its vested interests, but as a firm ally of those political forces which wanted to destroy the Republic itself. The struggle waged by the clericalists thus became a struggle against the political order, in the same way as the battle of anticlericalists was inextricably bound up with the wider conflict between pro- and anti-republican groups in French society. The Church stood staunchly behind every effort to undermine the Republic between 1870 and the early twentieth century: the proposed restoration of the Bourbon monarchy, the attempted coup of President MacMahon in 1877, the Boulangist challenge to the Republic in the late 1880s, and last but by no means least, the Dreyfus Affair at the turn of the century.

The outcome of the protracted struggle between clericalist forces and the republican elites over the preservation of the material and intellectual interests of the Church was never in serious doubt, despite strategic and tactical rifts within the anticlerical camp. There were at least five shades of opinion within the republican movement over the attitude to be taken towards the clerical question. First, there were those Socialists (like the followers of Jules Guesde) who, despite their profound atheism, argued that the struggle against clericalism was simply a red herring, a diversion from the only conflict which really mattered: the class struggle against capitalism. As Guesde declared in an article in *Le Socialiste* in December 1891: 'for a long time, as a means of alleviating proletarian hunger, you have been fed with priests. Let us henceforth concentrate all our efforts on the struggle against the capitalist order.' For others (including many in the Radical Party establishment, and Socialists such as Jean Jaurès) the primary goal was to ensure an institutional separation of the Church from the French State: once this objective was attained, they believed, the social and political relevance of the Church would gradually decline. Third, there were those moderate anticlericals who sought to preserve an element of state control over the Church, to ensure that the latter did not develop into a bastion of anti-republicanism. This position was taken by the so-called opportunists, who recognized the important social function of the Church in preserving order and stability in society. Fourth, there were positivists such as Paul Bert (Jules Ferry's successor as Minister of Education) who, despite their militant anti-clericalism, recognized the utility of the Church in the French drive towards colonial expansion in the 1880s. These statesmen drew a clear line of demarcation between anticlericalism in France, which was a necessary struggle, and anticlericalism outside France, which was detrimental to the pursuit of the Republic's national interests. Finally, there were the militant anticlericalists (such as the Radical Georges Clemenceau, and the Socialist Edouard Vaillant), who were passionately and obsessively committed to the struggle against clerical influence, and refused to rest until every single church in the country had been burnt down, and the ideological influence of the Church utterly obliterated. This, for example, is how French Catholicism was described by the Radical deputy Maurice Allard, during the parliamentary debate on the 1905 Act on the separation of Churches from the State: 'Christianity is an outrage to reason, an outrage to nature ... When Christianity left Rome and Greece, where it had stifled all civilization and left nothing but devastation and ruin, and reached France, our country was bereft of art, letters, and, especially, science.'

Two equally important points need to be made about these divisions within the republican camp on the question of anticlericalism. On one hand these cleavages were not sufficient to prevent the republicans from uniting against the clericalist challenge against their regime, and achieving their minimal objectives. Thus the law of December 1905 formally separated Churches from the State, officially ending the public patronage enjoyed by French Catholicism. The education reforms passed by Jules Ferry in the early 1880s, which were consolidated in further legislative acts adopted in subsequent decades, brought French schools and universities under the administrative tutelage of the State, while allowing a privately funded stream of *écoles libres*. The Church thus lost its monopolistic influence over the education of the young, and this minimal republican achievement proved irreversible. At the same time, however—and this is the second point—the tactical differences within the republican camp were sufficiently strong to prevent the adoption of the maximalist objectives of the militant anticlericalists (namely the eradication of all religious influences in French schools, and the creation of a unified and secular system of education). There was a sense in which the settlement reached in the early twentieth century represented a compromise between moderates within the religious and secular camps, both of whom were equally wary of the dangers posed by their own extremists. Moderate republicans saw no sense in destroying civil peace in pursuit of an ideological objective (comprehensive secularization) which many of them did not regard as a necessary (or even desirable) feature of the social order they wished to create. Indeed, many republicans were conscious of the positive role performed by the clergy in society, not only in providing a focus for the social needs of communities, but also in helping to propagate the French language at local level. In the Catholic camp there were also many forces (such as the Gallican bishops) who regarded the utterings of their own zealots as fundamentally damaging to the prospects of securing a *modus vivendi* with the new regime. Furthermore, many of these pragmatists were far from unhappy to see the state confront such congregations as the Jesuits, whose loyalties to the French nation were often regarded as suspect even within the Catholic community itself. The Vatican was equally reluctant to endorse the imprecations of these groups, because the interests of the Holy See became increasingly convergent with those of the Republic on the question of French colonial expansion. Clericalism was thus partly the victim of a compromise between conciliatory forces on both sides of the secular-religious divide; its defeat had important consequences for the changing balance of power within French Catholicism. In 1870 there was little question that the overwhelming majority of Catholics were sympathetic to the clericalist sirens of piety, tradition, and anti-republicanism; this was reflected in the authoritative position of such intellectuals as Veuillot, who commanded the attention and respect of the entire Catholic community. By 1919 the picture had become rather different, as increasingly larger groups within the Catholic community (both at the summit of the ecclesiastical hierarchy and at its base) came to accept the existence of the Republic.

SOCIAL AND IDEOLOGICAL DIMENSIONS OF THE FAILURE OF CLERICALISM

This wider political dimension of the clerical challenge to the Third Republic ultimately explained the movement's failure to achieve any of its negative objectives. The republicans rallied effectively against all groups which sought to undermine the social and political order they attempted to create after 1880. The fact that the clericalists were consistently on the losing side in each of these major battles between republicans and anti-republicans dealt a severe blow to the aspirations of the latter.

The question could, then, be taken one step back: why did these challenges to the Republic fail so decisively during this period? The effectiveness of the republican response was probably the most important single factor. Never completely united over positive socio-economic objectives, republican groups still had enough in common to mount effective defence campaigns whenever the political system they had created seemed to be in jeopardy. The threats to the integrity of the system united republican groups in the early days of the Third Republic, and this tradition was not forgotten when similar challenges to the regime were perceived in the 1930s (this mobilization gave rise to the Popular Front), the 1940s (the victorious struggle against German occupation), and the early 1960s (the defeat of the extreme Right's challenge to General de Gaulle). But the failure of the clericalist challenge was also a function of intrinsic weakness and divisions within the Catholic camp. For example, splits appeared very quickly after 1871 over the question of French support for the papacy. Despite their impeccable Catholic credentials, leading figures of the French monarchist Right such as the Duc Albert de Broglie (1821–1901) refused to follow the lead of clericalist extremists who advocated an unconditional French alignment on the positions of the Vatican. Furthermore, the charismatic quality of most of the political figures supported by the Church left a great deal to be desired. MacMahon, the spearhead of the clericalist cause in the 1877 elections, was a man of monumental denseness, even by the standards of the Napoleonic officer corps from which he emerged. Royalty provided no better alternative. Until his death in 1883 the Comte de Chambord (Henri V) was the principal contender for the French throne, and the Church hailed this aspiring monarch as the saviour of Christianity in France. The dogmatic intransigence of the legitimist pretender, however, scuttled all efforts to restore the French monarchy. Chambord refused, for instance, to compromise over the national flag, and insisted that he would return to power only if the tricolour (red, white, and blue flag) was abandoned in favour of the old royalist white emblem. This attitude was typical of a naïve and dim-witted figure, who regarded the whole nineteenth century as a tragic aberration, and never even learned how to tie his own shoelaces.

The clericalists were also weakened by their internal divisions. The interests of the Vatican became increasingly divergent from those of the French Church, for example, as it became apparent that the republican regime was happy to use (and, when necessary, defend) Catholic missionaries to extend and stabilize the boundaries of its empire after 1880. This diplomatic convergence made the Roman Church much more accommodating towards the atheistic elites of the Republic than its French branch. For example, the *Ralliement* was essentially an attempt by the Vatican to force the French Church to accept the irreversibility of the Republic. At the same time the Vatican also made clear its hostility to the constitution of a Catholic political party in France, thus helping to scuttle Albert de Mun's project in 1885. In any case, it is doubtful that a Catholic party would have been more successful in promoting the clericalist cause, given the considerable differences in outlook and interests within the Catholic fold. Ultimately, the failure of the clericalist challenge was a revealing indicator of the scope for political accommodation offered by the emerging regime. Clericalists regarded their conflict with the republican regime as an entirely non-negotiable exercise: there was no room for compromise over such basic social and political issues as the nature of the State and the role of the Church. Clericalist attitudes and beliefs were expressions of an intransigent vision of society, which was projected in the writings of de Maistre and de Bonald. For these thinkers the laws which governed human affairs were divinely ordained: any attempt to tamper with the natural order of things was bound to lead to catastrophe. The republican elites, on the other hand, believed that political institutions could be used to promote perfectionist ends: human intervention could thus improve upon existing forms of social order. But they did not believe that this change could be carried out exclusively on the basis of *a priori* principles, and without taking some account of the beliefs and interests of different groups in society. Thus they were always willing to reach out towards social groups who were prepared to recognize the irreversibility of Republican government. The result, as noted above, was that the religious question was settled through compromise between pragmatists, leaving the clericalists to continue their obsessive and ultimately futile battle against modern society.

RELIGION AND THE CLERICALIST
LEGACY AFTER 1919

In its pure form traditional French clericalism was already moribund by the end of the First World War. The attitudes, beliefs, and values it encapsulated were undercut by a number of developments within the Catholic community and French society at large, and accelerated by the effects of social and political change in subsequent decades.

The first point to note, as suggested earlier, is that the official separation of Churches from the French State had beneficial long-term consequences in the institution's receptiveness to social concerns. The intellectually dogmatic and socially reactionary strand of Catholicism which had been expressed in French clericalism was gradually supplanted by a greater diversity of concerns, and many of these led the Church to rediscover the progressive traditions it had embodied before 1848. During the second half of the nineteenth century the Vatican encouraged the development of Catholic approaches to social problems. This change was reflected in the papal encyclical *Rerum Novarum* (1891), which urged Catholics to seek legislative solutions to questions of poverty and social deprivation. Social Catholicism, which was represented even at the height of the clericalist phase by Marc Sangnier's *Sillon* movement, was given a considerable boost during the interwar period by such organizations as the Association Catholique de la Jeunesse Française and the Jeunesse Ouvrière Chrétienne, both of which based their appeal on principles of co-operation, solidarity, and social justice. During the Second World War many Catholics fought on the side of the resistance, and the emergence of the Mouvement Républicain Populaire (MRP) during the Fourth Republic bore witness to important changes in the social and political values of the French Catholic community. But these transformations did not entirely obliterate the legacy of the past. Indeed, the MRP reflected fully the contradictions of French Catholicism in the era of social and economic modernization. Its elites were often highly progressive, as might be expected of political leaders who had sided with the resistance against the German occupiers and their Vichy allies. The MRP electorate, however, was on the whole rather less enlightened, a condition which was accentuated after 1947 when the party came to be perceived by the ex-collaborationist Right as a bulwark against Communism (hence the MRP's depiction by the Left as a *Machine à Ramasser des Pétainistes*—a Pétainist collecting agency). The MRP was the closest approximation to a mass Christian Democratic party ever to have emerged in France: its disappearance in the mid-1960s pointed, among other things, to the declining saliency of religion as a political issue.

Clericalism was also undermined by the spirit of national reconciliation which emerged during the First World War. In the late nineteenth and early twentieth century French Catholics had the sensation (which was constantly reinforced by their Church) that they were part of a community which was distinct from civil society, and clericalist attitudes were clearly predicated upon this sense of particularism. The solidarity which French citizens acquired in the trenches and on the home front made such cleavages appear increasingly irrelevant: religion became less divisive as a constitutive dimension of human identity. Georges Clemenceau, one of the great scourges of French clericalism during the early stages of his political career, attested to this evolution during his tenure of office as Prime Minister during the Great War. Presenting the Legion of Honour to an Army priest who had distinguished himself on the front, he remarked that he had never thought that he would come to present the highest commendation of the Republic to a practising Catholic. (The priest retorted that he never would have thought it possible that a man of god could receive such an award from Clemenceau.) In the decades which followed the end of the Second World War, furthermore, the number of practising Catholics also declined steadily in France, and religious values ceased to exercise a significant influence on social practices. In 1958, 92 per cent of the French population was baptized; this figure had fallen to 65 per cent in 1983. To take another indicator, 24 per cent of the French population attended religious services in 1955; in 1988 this figure had been reduced to 12 per cent. Traditional rituals which were associated with these religious practices correspondingly declined: confession, for example, became virtually extinct.

This declining significance of religion in French private life during the twentieth century also transformed the relationship between religion and the political realm. Clericalism was given its clearest political expression in the struggle between republican and anti-republican groups after 1870. After 1919, and even more so after 1945, the Republic was accepted as the legitimate form of government by an increasingly wider proportion of French society, including the overwhelming majority of Catholics. Religious belief long remained one of the most accurate indicators of political affiliation in French politics: practising Catholics almost systematically voted for the Right, committed atheists for the Left. Even on the second ballot of the 1988 presidential election, twice as many practising Catholics voted for the Gaullist candidate, Jacques Chirac, as for the Socialist candidate, François Mitterrand. Conversely, 74 per cent of those who did not belong to any religious denomination voted for Mitterrand, and only 26 per cent for Chirac. But these old cleavages began to break down, and the best illustration came from observation of French electoral geography. The staunchest bastions of clericalism in the early days of the Third Republic were also the strongholds of the French forces of 'order': the west (especially the departments of Vendée, Basse-Normandie, and Bretagne), the Cévennes, and such departments of the east as Meurthe-et-Moselle and the Vosges. In the 1980s, however, the forces of 'movement' made considerable inroads into these areas: Socialist deputies were elected in Brittany in 1981, and a Socialist mayor was returned in 1989 at Strasburg, the historical bastion of liberal Catholicism. It is true that these inroads were made only in parts of these departments which had already become secularized, and appeared further threatened by the collapse of the Socialist vote in the 1993 legislative elections. None the less, religion undoubtedly became less of an issue in politics, and this further undermined one of the necessary conditions of the emergence of clericalist attitudes and values in French society.

THE GHOST OF CLERICALISM:
THE POLITICS OF EDUCATION

Although clericalism was essentially overcome (in its traditional form) by the end of the First World War, its legacy continued to affect the character of French politics in specific policy areas throughout the twentieth century. The changing nature of Church–State relations after the official separation of 1905 meant that the problem of clericalism could no longer be posed in the same terms as during the first four decades of the Third Republic. The objectives of militant Catholics remained, to an essential extent, unchanged: to preserve the material and intellectual interests of the Church. Since these interests were transformed as a result of separation, and since the Church itself withdrew from active involvement in public political life, the legacy of clericalism became increasingly identified with social issues. For example, the adoption of the French law on abortion in January 1975 provoked a temporary realignment of political forces which seemed to hark back to the cleavages of the early days of the Third Republic: on one hand the inheritors of the republican tradition (which by then also included groups which supported President Valéry Giscard d'Estaing), and on the other an array of conservative clerical forces, joined by a lobby of 'natalists' who were obsessed with France's (alleged) declining birth rate.

The social issue which constantly reproduced religious-based cleavages in French society after the end of the First World War was education. This can be explained by returning to the notion of vested interests: it will be remembered that, under the terms of the compromise worked out during the Third Republic between the State and the Catholic Church, the latter was able to retain control over a stream of private schools, the *écoles libres*. After 1919 the terms (and, at times, the very nature) of this compromise were a frequent object of political discord, and behind these political differences continued to lurk the spectre of clericalism. The most serious attempt to revert to the *status quo ante* 1870 occurred during the Vichy administration (1940–4). Marshal Pétain's regime could not be defined as a clerical state, but its emphasis on the values of *travail*, *famille*, and *patrie* (a substitute for the republican trinity of liberty, equality, and fraternity) was directly inspired by traditionalist Catholic thinking. In particular, the thrust of the regime's legislation in the field of education appeared as a conscious effort to wipe out the secularizing influences of the previous sixty years. Catechism, for example, was reintroduced in the State-school curriculum; and a law of October 1941 granted State financial assistance to religious schools. This policy appeared to many republicans as the long-awaited revenge of the clericalists, and was promptly abandoned at the Liberation, even though it should be stressed that by no means all the French clergy's aspirations were met by the Vichy administration. It is only fair to add that the clergy's undeniable sympathy for the Vichy regime (and particularly for its leader, Marshal Pétain) did not extend to the German occupant, and even less to Nazi ideology. There were small groups of clerics (led by Cardinal Baudrillart, the rector of the Catholic Institute in Paris) who consistently advocated a policy of collaboration with Germany. On the whole, however, this approach was rejected by the majority of the French clergy, despite its undeniably conservative political leanings.

During the Fourth Republic the issue of State funding of private schools reappeared briefly during the early 1950s, when conservative governments, under the strong influence of clerical associations, introduced legislation to provide State funding for private schools. The bill which introduced this measure was passed by a conservative majority and opposed by a coalition of forces which was impeccably 'republican': Communists, Socialists, and left-wing Radicals. Under the Fifth Republic the Debré law of 1959 created the basic framework for the compromise which is still essentially in force to-day. Private schools were offered two types of contract (*contrat simple* and *contrat d'association*). The first provided State funding for staff salaries and national insurance, while the second went further, supplying public funds for maintenance of school buildings and equipment, in exchange for some degree of State control over staff appointments. As noted earlier, Socialist efforts to tinker with these arrangements in 1984 came to a sticky end. But this political protest did not herald a return to the clericalist practices of the Third Republic. After the private education issue had been settled in 1984, the Church reverted to its pastoral concerns: there was never any question of attempting to seek a more prominent role for religion in French education, even less to force the French state to recognize Catholicism as the official religion of the Republic. What the private-school controversy of 1984 demonstrated, in other words, was not that clericalism was re-emerging from the ashes of the past, but more simply that French parents were fundamentally attached to the principle of freedom of *choice* in educational matters.

THE END OF A WAY OF LIFE

As a historical phenomenon, clericalism was the political expression of Catholic anxiety in the face of the republican challenge to the material and intellectual interests of the Church in France. The strident claim that the Church should play a significant role in determining the standards of public and private life amounted, in essence, to a negative demand. Clericalism expressed the desire of the Church to preserve its entrenched positions in society, and this was politically translated into active support for groups and movements which sought to destroy the republican political system after 1880. But perhaps more important than its political manifestations were the social dynamics which made possible the rise of clericalism. Like the core of the republican movement, which (at the height of its ideological influence in French society) represented a distinct way of life, clericalist ideas and values expressed a set of social practices which centred around the traditional institutions of Catholicism. From the cradle to the grave these institutions articulated a way of life which provided individuals with clear standards of public and private conduct, and these norms and values were disseminated through the influence of schools, convents, newspapers, and parish bulletins. Above all, this influence was diffused by the army of devoted servants of the Church, from the most powerful archbishop to the humblest village *curé*. As noted from the outset, clericalism was a cry of despair against what seemed to be the irreversible decadence of French society; its core values were in many respects diametrically opposed to those of the republicans. The clericalist vision of the future was pessimistic and highly fatalistic, whereas republicans were optimistic voluntarists, who believed that social and political conditions could be improved by human intervention. Clericalists regarded the unbounded claims of human reason as an arrogant attempt to question the ways of Providence, whereas republicans saw the dissemination of education and culture as a critical means of founding a well-ordered society. Clericalists responded to all situations in public and private life by returning to their immutable principles, whereas republicans were pragmatists, whose first instinct was to take stock of a situation, and only then ascertain whether it was conducive to the implementation of their objectives. Clericalists often emphasized the duty of obedience to the Pope; republicans were profoundly attached to the nation, and remained deeply suspicious of all groups (whether religious or secular) which seemed beholden to a foreign institution. Clericalists espoused a hierarchical view of the world, in which clear distinctions were made between leaders and followers, and between the elective community and the godless hordes; republicans were committed to the principles of the civil and political equality of all citizens (social equality, as noted in the previous chapter, was a different matter). Clericalists were finally communitarians, who believed that social norms and moral values should be determined by the wider group of which the individual was a member; republicans, in contrast, were committed to the notion that these norms and values were acceptable only if they were discovered through individual reason.

But although the clericalist value system was opposed in many ways to the core precepts of republicanism, there were none the less some significant areas of convergence between republicanism and Catholicism. To be a good Catholic involved believing in the importance of the family, cultivating a sense of dedication to work, striving for the preservation of social order, despising the cult of materialism and the pursuit of pleasure for its own sake, and ultimately recognizing that an element of spirituality was necessary for the good ordering of society. No self-respecting republican could disagree with these precepts, and this common bedrock of 'adjacent' values provided the foundations for the compromise which enabled secular and religious groups to coexist in France during the twentieth century. By the same token, this common ground was insufficiently broad to appeal to the clericalists, who were not prepared to accept anything less than a wholesale republican endorsement of their agenda—which was tantamount to expecting a complete repudiation of all the basic principles they stood for. As France moved into the modern era these clericalist groups became increasingly marginalized, and the political significance of religion ceased to be a matter of great debate. The Church retreated from public life, and only occasionally broke this vow when, as in 1984, it believed (many would argue mistakenly) that its vital interests were at stake. As regards private life, the moral authority of the French Catholic Church was undermined by three general developments in and after the 1960s: the absolute decline in religious practice, which has already been discussed; the effects of the Second Vatican Council, which recognized the moral autonomy of the individual, and thus reduced the need for an intermediate institution between the believer and God; and finally, the institutional fragmentation of French Catholicism, illustrated in the 1980s by the rise of fundamentalist Catholic groups, and the Vatican's excommunication of Monseigneur Lefebvre's fundamentalist (intégriste) community from the fold.

Indeed, Catholic intégriste communities (and those fundamentalist groups which still remain inside the Church) undoubtedly constitute the most faithful descendants of the clericalist tradition in modern France. There are important differences between these latter-day clericalists and their nineteenth-century forebears, the most obvious being that the modern variants operate in the margins of (and in many cases in direct opposition to) the Catholic Church, whereas earlier clericalist groups occupied a much more central position within the Catholic establishment. But the intellectual and theological filiation of these small intégriste communities is, none the less, unmistakable. This is perceptible in three ways. First, contemporary Catholic fundamentalism is dogmatic in the literal sense of the term: its theology is inflexible, and its emphasis on traditional rituals (for example, the Tridentine Mass) harks back to the mass gatherings of the Assumptionist Order between 1870 and 1900. The *intégristes* are remarkably sectarian: the Abbé Georges of Nantes, for example, took such exception to the pronouncements of the Second Vatican Council that he denounced Pope Paul VI as a heretic. The social concerns of Catholic fundamentalists also provide clear echoes of the golden age of clericalism. A typical example may be found in the programme advocated by the Chrétienté-Solidarité committees, a neo-clericalist network which calls for the consolidation of the family as the basic unit of a hierarchical society, a return to Church control of education, the banning of pornography, and the repeal of abortion laws. Finally, the *intégriste* networks often have a symbiotic relationship with political groups and associations on the extreme Right. The Chrétienté-Solidarité groups officially merged with the National Front in 1984, and there are perceptible intellectual affinities between the party newspaper *National-Hebdo* and fundamentalist Catholic groups (most particularly, the themes of material decline, moral corruption, and the search for purification). During national and local elections, furthermore, the Front's candidates can often rely on the mobilization of local fundamentalist associations, in the same way as their anti-republican predecessors in the late nineteenth century organized their campaigns through clericalist organizations.

But the significance of these activities should not be exaggerated. These vestiges of religious traditionalism in society do not suggest that France is about to experience a clericalist revival. Fundamentalist groups experienced more remarkable growth during the 1980s in Protestant communities such as those in the United States. In France the *intégriste* sects remained small and relatively isolated from mainstream Catholic opinion, and there was clearly a sense in which the noise they made was inversely proportional to the social and political influence they wielded. Religious fundamentalism also showed some signs of revival in French Islamic communities, but even there the role of *intégriste* groups was considerably exaggerated. Léon Gambetta could rest in peace: the clericalist enemy, whose menace to the Republic he identified so dramatically a little over a century ago, remained well and truly buried. The fact that its ghost has continued to haunt the French political stage for much of the twentieth century should be interpreted not so much in terms of the survival of the same cleavages which gave rise to clericalism in the early days of the Third Republic, but rather as a testimony to the enduring ability of French politicians (and their captive public) to fence with historical shadows.

Chronology

1789   November. Nationalization of Church property: beginning of conflict with the revolutionary state.

1790   July. Legislature votes civilian constitution of clergy: priests to be elected by local assemblies.

1797   Publication of de Maistre's *Considérations Sur la France*.

1848   December. Crushing defeat of liberal Catholic candidate Lamartine in presidential elections.

1851–5   Church granted extensive privileges by Second Empire.

1871   July. Bishops urge National Assembly to help restore temporal powers of the Pope.

1877   October. Defeat of clericalist forces in legislative elections, after Gambetta denounces clericalism as 'the enemy'.

(1879–82)   Educational reforms of Jules Ferry.

1883   February. Death of the Comte de Chambord (Henri V).

1885   November. Albert de Mun abandons scheme to set up French Catholic party after Vatican opposition.

1885   December. Publication of Edouard Drumont's *La France juive*.

1889   September. Boulanger electoral challenge overcome: further defeat for clerical forces.

1890   November. Initiation of *Ralliement* by Cardinal Lavigerie.

1891   May. Papal encyclical *Rerum Novarum*.

1899   June. Government of republican defence under Waldeck-Rousseau overcomes strong anti-republican challenge.

1901   July. Law on congregations.

1905   December. Law on separation of Churches and State passed.

1910   November. Pope denounces social Catholic movement *Le Sillon*.

1927   January. Vatican announces indexing of *Action Française*.

1941   October. Vichy regime restores state funding to private schools.

1944   November. Founding congress of Mouvement Républicain Populaire.

1959   December. Church school bill proposed by Debré government.

1963   Second Vatican Council.

1975   January. Abortion law voted by National Assembly.

1984   June. Church mobilizes successfully to protest against government bill on education reform.

CHAPTER 5
The Two Faces of French Nationalism

The French readily confess their attachment to their nation. Whether this Gallic self-obsession is more intense than other expressions of nationalism in advanced industrial societies is a moot point. However, the French variant has enriched our stock of concepts not only with the term 'nationalism', but also with such notions as 'patriotism' and 'chauvinism' (derived from Nicolas Chauvin, a typically enthusiastic soldier of the First Empire). Discussions of the underlying character of nationalism almost invariably tend to stimulate French rhetorical glands. Some take refuge in mysticism, as for example the philosopher Ernest Renan in his often quoted (but not immensely edifying) definition of a nation as 'a daily plebiscite'. Others allow their grandiloquence to flow without inhibition, as seen in the opening of Charles de Gaulle's *Memoirs of Hope*:

France comes from the depths of time. She changes . . . yet remains herself throughout the ages. She is inhabited by peoples who have been marked by adversity during the course of History, but have none the less been moulded into one nation by nature and politics.

For all their pomp, both the mystical and the grandiloquent conceptions highlight the importance of shared historical experiences in the formation of French national character. The basic thrust of this chapter will underscore this approach by advancing three claims: first, that nationalist themes pervade French social and political discourse, and this diffusion rests to an important extent on common historical experiences; but second, that this unity of French nationalist discourse is only apparent, and that behind a common stock of concepts lurked two radically different visions of the constitutive features of French national character; finally, that both these conceptions of the nation continue to be articulated by different parties and groups in modern France, and that the National Front is the inheritor of a distinct type of adversarial nationalism which harks back to the early days of the Third Republic.

As mentioned above, the introduction of the concept of nationalism into French political discourse occurred during the revolutionary period. It was preceded by the concept of *patriotisme* (which could roughly be translated as 'public-spiritedness'), which gained wide currency in intellectual circles during the final decades of the *ancien régime* between the 1760s and the late 1780s. As noted in Chapter 3, the concepts of the nation and the *patrie* were used during the early days of the Revolution as a means of buttressing the legitimacy of the new political order by pointing to its radical philosophical underpinnings. Thus the third article of the 1789 *Declaration of the Rights of Man* stated emphatically that 'the principle of sovereignty resides essentially in the nation.' This overturned the *ancien régime* precept that sovereign power was vested in the monarch, and underscored the emergence of a radically different conception of the relationship between the State and the national community. When events took a disobliging turn after 1790, however, another dimension of the concept of nationalism emerged: it became an ideological instrument of state power, deployed as a means of rallying mass support to the regime and attacking its enemies (both within and without). This more aggressive brand of nationalism was expressed in the patriotic appeals to French national consciousness launched by Jacobin governments during the revolutionary wars. As with the Republic, the association of nationalism with the Revolution initially had the effect of alienating the supporters of the *ancien régime*. Since the very concept of nationhood was promoted by the revolutionary camp, nationalism clearly implied the endorsement of Jacobin objectives. This made it extremely difficult for monarchists and Catholics to identify with the essentially republican postulate that France was a nation. (It was only if this premiss was accepted that the notion of popular sovereignty made any sense.) Thus it took the partial reconciliation of the monarchy with some of the principles of 1789 to make possible a wider political dissemination of the concept of nationalism. This began to occur under the constitutional monarchy of Louis-Philippe (1830–48, commonly known as the July Monarchy); only then did the concept of nationalism begin to express basic values and a sense of identity which were widely recognized by political elites. But this common recognition of the substance of national identity was not widely shared throughout French society in the middle of the nineteenth century. Indeed, it will be argued elsewhere that this *popular* sense of nationhood did not emerge fully until the second half of the nineteenth century, and was as much an ideological construct of the

Republican State as a genuine recognition (and affirmation) of shared cultural values by diverse sections of the community.

THE UNDERPINNINGS OF NATIONALISM

Before examining these differences in the expression of nationalist ideas and values, the social and political conditions which facilitated their emergence during the nineteenth century will first be outlined. The pervasiveness of nationalism in modern French political discourse and practice was a function of five broad historical factors, each of which served to preserve and reinforce the saliency of the phenomenon.

First, the urgency of the national question was fuelled by repeated experiences of war and military occupation in the nineteenth and twentieth centuries. As early as 1814 French territory was occupied by Russian and Prussian troops, as the Tsar of Russia and the King of Prussia marched into Paris after the capitulation of Napoleonic armies. After the Franco–Prussian war of 1870–1 the French were subjected to the humiliation of occupation, but also the spectacle of the Prussian King being proclaimed German Emperor in the Hall of Mirrors at Versailles. The indignity of occupation was repeated on a more modest scale in 1914, but more thoroughly in 1940, after the embarrassing collapse of French troops in the face of the superiority of the *Wehrmacht*. From this angle the Second World War represented the ultimate dishonour: by late 1942 the whole of French territory was occupied by German and Italian forces.

Furthermore, the absence of secure borders on the east kept the question of national identity at the centre of French political debate after 1870. As the European state-system became increasingly fractured along nationalist lines, borders assumed a central position in demarcating the national identity of groups. The status of the departments of Alsace and Lorraine thus directly became a question of national identity, rather than simply a quarrel over a piece of territory. Lost to the German Empire after 1870, won back after the First World War, annexed by the Germans again in 1940, and liberated by French troops in 1944, the fate of these two departments was never far removed from the minds and hearts of their countrymen throughout this period.

Third, national identity became the concern of local groups which felt threatened by the arrival of immigrants on French soil. Modern French racism, which is commonly directed at North African and Indochinese communities, has a long if sordid ancestry: similar expressions of xenophobia greeted the first generations of Polish, Italian, Belgian, Spanish, and Portuguese migrant workers who came to France in the late nineteenth and twentieth centuries in search of better living conditions. *La France aux Français* ('Keep France French') has been the slogan used to exclude others from the national community, even though the underlying conception of Frenchness which informed these assertions was never very clear. The issue becomes even more confusing in a diachronical perspective; it is rather ironical that current members of the National Front who are of Italian and Spanish extraction, for example, would have been denounced as *métèques* ('foreign scum') by extreme right-wing militants during the interwar period.

French nationalism was also encouraged by a typically Gallic obsession with material and especially intellectual decline. From a broad historical perspective, this concern arguably evolved as a consequence of the collapse of French power in Europe by the early nineteenth century. The future of the French nation became a source of enduring anxiety to politicians and intellectuals alike: this fixation was expressed in three recurrent themes. Economic decline, triggered by a relatively backward infrastructure and late industrialization; demographic decline, caused by a falling birth rate and the destructive effects of wars (particularly the Great War, which wiped out 10.5 per cent of the active male population); and cultural decline, illustrated most graphically by the regression of the French language in the world. These experiences tended to provoke sharp nationalist reactions in France. Unlike Britain, which on the whole adjusted quite contentedly to its more modest status in world politics after 1945, the French took every challenge to their condition as an opportunity to restate the greatness of their national character. This contrasting response to decline was due in part to the strong element of cultural universalism which was embedded in French elite discourse about the nation. The belief in the inherent superiority of its cultural values was a distinct feature of French nationalism, which had no strict equivalent in Britain.

Finally, the national question was maintained at the centre of political debate as a result of the fragmentation and polarization of French society, and its reflection in the ideological character of its political discourse. The more divided a political community, the greater the political appeal of the idea of unity; the greater the appeal of unity, the more urgent the need to find a normative language in which this goal could be formulated. Nationalist ideologies performed this function throughout the process of national and cultural integration in France, which was conducted through the development of centralized state institutions. The tension between centralism and localism remained an interesting feature of the French social and political fabric during the modern era. The Republic was often accused of insensitivity and outright brutality in its treatment of local and regional cultures. There was no doubt that some of these accusations were justified: for example, local dialects were given short shrift by the educational establishments of the Republic. At the same time, however, republican governments were always aware of the dangers of over-centralization. Thus, after the return of the departments of Alsace and Lorraine to France in 1919, the 1905 regime of separation of Church from State was not imposed on these overwhelmingly Catholic populations. The Republic's cultural centralism, carried out in the name of the ideal of national unity, was often tempered by practical and prudential considerations.

It will already be clear from the remarks above that nationalist concepts were used by a wide range of groups and movements in France, not all of which agreed entirely on its underlying characteristics. Behind the façade of conceptual unity, contrasting conceptions of the good life were put forward by different social and political forces throughout the modern era, and nationalist concepts and themes provided a vehicle for the articulation of these values. In the following sections these contrasts will be outlined in a series of oppositions, ultimately suggesting the existence of two basic undercurrents in French nationalism. The first will be seen to be moderate, cautiously expansive, optimistic, favouring the economic *status quo*, and thus essentially the preserve of republican elites. The second undercurrent, in contrast, will emerge as authoritarian, retreating, obsessively suspicious, opposed to the economic *status quo*, pessimistic, highly adversarial in character, and in sum, fundamentally anti-republican.

MODERATION AND AUTHORITARIANISM

French nationalist themes were adopted and articulated by both moderate and authoritarian political groups. On one hand the republican tradition self-consciously developed as the expression of the basic values and ideals of the French nation. All the historical symbols of the Republic (the principle of popular sovereignty, the celebration of the taking of the Bastille on 14 July, the national anthem *La Marseillaise*, the red, white, and blue tricolour flag, and the culturally unifying education system) were established (or recreated) as paradigms of French nationhood during the Third Republic, and subsequently retained this symbolic importance in the minds of republican politicians. But this view was not the exclusive preserve of French political elites. One of the immediate causes of the perceived illegitimacy of the Vichy regime after 1940 was its decision to abandon such central Republican symbols of French nationhood as the principles of popular sovereignty and equality (supplanted by a return to the notions of individual leadership and hierarchy) and the *Marseillaise* (alongside which emerged the Pétainist hymn *Maréchal, nous voilà*). The French Army's relations with the Republic were often tempestuous after 1870 (most notably during the Dreyfus Affair in the late nineteenth century), but the regime eventually convinced the majority of its members that the Republic could be counted on to defend and protect the integrity of national territory. It was the Republic, under the frenetic leadership of Léon Gambetta, which pursued the war against Prussia until the bitter end after September 1870; it was also the Republic which recaptured the lost territories of Alsace-Lorraine from Germany after the Great War, and eventually liberated the entire territory from foreign occupation in 1944. The regime was thus able to retain the allegiance of the French Army—a critical factor in its successful handling of the major crises which pitted the military establishments against the State between 1940 and 1962.

On the other hand, nationalist sentiments and doctrines also became specific attributes of a distinctively anti-republican and anti-democratic political tradition, which regarded the public institutions of the French Republic as perversions of the real ideals and spirit of the nation. Charles Maurras (1868–1952), the leader of the monarchist movement Action Française (a significant force in French politics for much of the Third Republic) captured the essence of this sentiment when he distinguished between 'legal France' (*pays légal*) and 'real

France' (*pays réel*). The official institutions of the Republic, according to this view, represented the negation of the essential values of French society. Authoritarian right-wing groups differed in their characterization of the social identity of the 'real' France. The Action Française presented the monarchy as the emblem of traditional social and political values, while paramilitary organizations of the interwar period (the Ligues) looked to the Army as the institution which typified the virtues of the French nation. Marshal Pétain (and traditionalists in the Catholic Church) held up the peasant community as the uncorrupted paradigm of national excellence. During the Fourth Republic the populist Poujadist movement presented the lower-middle classes as the embodiment of the traditional French way of life. In modern France the National Front seeks to define French citizenship in racial and cultural terms, essentially on the basis of European ancestry (both the Poujadist movement and the National Front will be discussed in greater detail at a later stage). Despite these different representations of national excellence, this basic distinction between the nominal and real essence of French national character remained one of the distinctive underpinnings of authoritarian nationalist undercurrents.

CONSERVATION AND REVOLUTION

Second, French nationalism assumed both a conservative and a revolutionary character. Conservatism, in a strict sense, is a backward-looking political doctrine, which seeks to preserve the heritage of the past from the intemperate effects of change. A particular conception of the nation's heritage often serves as a natural focus for this enterprise of preservation. Again, conservative conceptions of the particular aspect(s) of the national patrimony which needed to be defended varied over time. As noted in the preceding chapter, the clericalist groups of the second half of the nineteenth century were conservative nationalists who sought to preserve the material and intellectual interests of the Church by fending off the resurgence of the atheistic and regicide Republic. In the interwar period republican conservative nationalists such as Raymond Poincaré (1860–1934) were principally inspired by the fear of social revolution in France and national resurgence in Germany. After 1945 there was a distinct streak of cultural nationalism which ran through the entire French intellectual community, and was founded on a common apprehension of the consequences for French culture of the rising tide of American cultural barbarity. The conservative character of the National Front is expressed fully in its efforts to preserve French racial and cultural purity from noxious foreign influences. Revolutionary nationalism, on the other hand, was teleological. It regarded the past not as a frozen representation of an ideal order which needed to be preserved (or recreated), but rather as a necessary foundation of a future order which could emerge only through the destruction of present society. This revolutionary conception was not exclusively championed by the extreme left. As will be noted later, the few genuinely Fascist groups which emerged in France during the interwar period were radical authoritarian nationalists who despised what they saw as the rampant intellectual mediocrity, social degeneration, and political corruption which attended the final years of the Third Republic. Capitalism, in their view, was as great an evil as Communism (which they tended to described as *judeo*-Bolshevism, because they were convinced that Communism was nothing more than the modern version of the international Jewish conspiracy); and the influence of the Church was equally as pernicious as that of the trade union. It was immensely ironical, from this point of view, that many of these extreme French nationalists ended up wearing German uniforms during the Second World War. On the extreme left the marriage of nationalism with revolutionary principles can be traced back to the Jacobin Republic, as noted earlier. During the nineteenth century the spirit of Jacobin nationalism was maintained by Auguste Blanqui, a revolutionary socialist who devoted his entire life to conspiratorial activities against the State (and, as noted in Chapter 1, ended up with unrivalled personal experience of the French prison system); in the modern era, and especially after 1945, the French Communist Party resolutely waved the flag of French patriotism while also proclaiming its objectives to be both internationalist and revolutionary.

EXPANSION AND RETREAT

Third, nationalist ideas and values informed the vision of groups advocating expansion, but also retreat. The universalism which was one of the principal intellectual legacies of the Enlightenment was blended after 1789 into a messianic vision which portrayed French political and cultural values as paradigms of excellence. It was this form of reasoning which led the German mystic Anacharsis Cloots (1755–94) to proclaim revolutionary Paris as 'the Vatican of Reason' (the Committee of Public Safety proved him right by having him decapitated during the Terror). That which was in the best interests of France thus became necessary and beneficial for the whole of humanity. The wars of the revolutionary era were undertaken to 'liberate' Europe from absolutist despotism, and led to the establishment of a constellation of fraternal republics in neighbouring territories. Like all forms of internationalism, however, this elevated universalism was essentially a cloak for the pursuit of an expansionist strategy: the reunification of the 'great French nation'—a mythical entity which happened to include Belgium and the Rhineland, and was based on the equally fanciful concept of 'natural frontiers'.

Almost a century later, under the Third Republic, a similarly messianic form of nationalism underlay the movement towards French colonial expansion. It should be stressed that this universalism could be dressed very comfortably in both spiritualist or materialist garbs. For the sanctimonious Catholic missionaries France was conveying the Christian message of moral regeneration to the lands of Eternal Darkness; for the positivist republican elites the French nation was providing the less fortunate with the essential benefits of Science and Progress. Stripped of their metaphysical pomp, both visions were essentially instruments of French domination. From this angle it was rather paradoxical that, precisely at the moment when the Catholic Church and the Republican state were locked in conflict in metropolitan France, the two institutions marched hand in hand into the remote corners of Africa, Asia, and the Near East. This Church–State alliance proceeded forcibly to turn local populations into rootless and confused pseudo-Europeans, who were ruthlessly indoctrinated about their 'ancestors the Gauls' in schools run by Catholic expatriates.

But this brand of French nationalism could also be given a particularist expression. This sentiment was especially marked when domestic and external circumstances forced French political elites into a defensive and retreating posture. During the Third Republic's phase of colonial expansion many inflexible French nationalists refused to support the principle of expansion outside Europe, on the grounds that such a policy would divert attention from the essential task of recapturing the territories of Alsace and Lorraine (lost to the Germans in 1871). The siege mentality which accompanied this defensive form of nationalism was essentially at variance with any project of territorial aggrandizement. The moral and physical essence of the nation had been sullied: only the return of the conquered departments, and the exemplary punishment of the aggressor, could restore the status and dignity of the French nation. A variant of this form of defensive nationalism also prevailed during the Algerian conflict (1954–62). For the doctrinaire supporters of *Algérie Française*, granting independence to Algeria was tantamount to dismembering the French nation. For many years after the end of the war the nostalgics of French Algeria could not bring themselves to forgive President de Gaulle for taking the only logical and reasonable way out of the conflict: recognizing that France had to accede to Algerian demands for national self-determination.

THE ENEMY WITHIN AND THE ENEMY WITHOUT

Fourth, French nationalists identified various external and internal threats to the sovereignty and integrity of their nation. The principal candidate for the position of the enemy without was Germany, for reasons which are so evident (territorial contiguity, military conflict, cultural and religious opposition, economic rivalry, and ideological cleavages) that they need not be explained in detail. Anti-German sentiment is so profoundly rooted in French history since 1870 that it is almost tempting to regard it as a constitutive feature of French national character. Since the Franco–German reconciliation sponsored by de Gaulle in 1963, it is undeniable that this feeling has receded from the immediate political horizon. But old traditions die hard. It was striking to note that some sections of the French Left were not averse to rekindling crude forms of anti-Germanic sentiment in the 1970s (on the question of the West German state's response to terrorism). In the late 1970s both Communists and Gaullists resurrected the image of German domination in Europe to rally the support of those who felt threatened by the process of European integration. After the reunification of Germany, and especially during the campaign for the referendum on the Maastricht treaty in 1992, the PCF (by now joined on this issue by the National Front) underlined the point even further, raising the spectre of the German occupation of France in 1940 to rally public support against President Mitterrand's policy of Franco–German co-operation. A slightly different variant of French nationalism aspired to represent the superior values of the Latin peoples of Europe against both superpowers. During the 1960s de

Gaulle articulated this cultural conception of French 'Europeanhood' (or, to be more accurate, European Frenchness). This ensemble was deemed to be constituted by a community which was distinct both from the Saxons of Western Europe, the compliant stooges of the American *imperium*, and the Slavic peoples of the East, eternally condemned to live under the shadow of the Great Russian state. Gaullism also subsumed a narrower tradition of Anglophobia based on a long history of mutual enmity, which was particularly marked among groups and institutions which had historical cause to regard the British as rivals and competitors rather than mere neighbours. The French Navy never forgave the British for sinking its fleet at Mers-el-Kébir during the Second World War. On a less elevated note, the Catholic writer François Mauriac (1885–1970) recalled that his father used to demonstrate his intense loathing of the old enemy by turning his face towards Britain whenever he relieved himself.

These varying conceptions of the external threat were accompanied by a strong focus of French nationalists on the enemy within. In one sense this internal threat was simply seen to emanate from the local agents of the outside enemy. Thus Socialists of the Second International were decried as German agents; ultramontane Catholics were lambasted as proxies of the Vatican; Communists were regarded as Soviet stooges; the Alsace-born Robert Schuman (1886–1963), one of the leading figures in the politics of European integration after 1945, was sometimes heckled as a *Boche* (the French equivalent of 'Kraut') by Communist deputies; more generally, European integrationists were denounced as lackeys of Anglo–American imperialism by Jacobins of the Left and Right. In each of these cases the underlying appeal to a sentiment of patriotism was unmistakable. But this vision was almost always complemented by targeting specific social and institutional groups in French society. Nationalists, often but not always of the Right, demonstrated an enduring capacity to deny membership of the national community to certain sections of society on a variety of grounds. Traditional groups which typified *l'anti-France* in the eyes of the nationalist Right included Jews, Protestants, immigrants (*métèques*), Freemasons, and republicans. During the interwar period immigrants from southern and eastern Europe were the object of racialist taunts for failing to conform to the stereotypes of French nationalism. Thus the culinary customs of the Italians led to their widespread—and deeply resented—designation as *macars*. In the 1980s and 1990s this tradition of social exclusion was resurrected by the National Front, whose leaders defined Arabs and particularly their Islamic religion as the principal internal threat to French cultural cohesion.

SATISFIED AND DISCONTENTED NATIONALISM

Fifth, nationalist themes were expounded by social and political groups which were on both sides of the economic divide between 'haves' and 'have-nots'. Examples of satisfied nationalism included the anti-Americanism of the French intellectual community. This was (and remains) primarily an attempt by an elite to protect the rich treasures of its patrimony from the corrosive influence of an imported culture. More generally, as suggested earlier, the process of state-building in France (the construction and consolidation of central political institutions) often coincided with the rise to prominence of specific social and occupational strata. These 'ascending' groups (financial bourgeoisie under the July Monarchy; *couches nouvelles* of the Third Republic; managerial and technocratic elites of the Gaullian era) always sought to legitimize their institutional power by identifying their particular interests with those of the nation as a whole. Hence the production of a nationalist ideology which translated the particular goals of these social strata into expressions of national interest. The calculated nationalism of the governing elites of the July Monarchy was part of a political enterprise which sought to reconcile elements of the monarchical and revolutionary traditions. In the same way republican educational philosophy in the late nineteenth and early twentieth centuries was influenced by such pedagogues as Emile Littré (1801–81) and Ernest Lavisse (1842–1922). Their writings, emphasizing heavily the values of collective identity, civil peace, and political stability, played an important part in winning over the mass of the peasantry—the bulk of the French population—to the unitary ideals of the republican regime.

But nationalist values also appealed to social and occupational groups which could be described as 'descending'. The heterogeneous groups which constituted the anti-Dreyfusard coalition could not easily be classified in these terms: for example, the ecclesiastical authorities which unequivocally stood behind the anti-Republican challenge in the 1890s had suffered considerable loss of status under the Third Republic, but this was hardly the case with the military. More generally

the social origins, occupational backgrounds, and economic circumstances of the disparate individuals who followed such paramilitary
groups as the Croix-de-Feu differed from those of the supporters of
the monarchist Action Française. None the less, it is undeniable that
these authoritarian right-wing groups recruited many of their followers
from sections of society which were (both subjectively and objectively)
alienated from French society, and felt directly threatened by the success of its 'ascending' groups. Under the Fourth Republic precisely
such feelings of despair and anxiety gave rise to the Poujadist movement (named after its leader Pierre Poujade), which briefly rose to
public prominence between 1956 and 1958.

Poujadism was the perfect modern illustration of a nationalist ideology which expressed widespread social frustration and economic dis-
content. The 2.5 million French voters who supported Poujadist
candidates in 1956 essentially came from lower middle-class groups
such as artisans, office clerks, and shopkeepers. Their grievances were
telling representations of the plight suffered by those who felt left
behind by social and economic changes in France in an era of rapid
modernization. To be a Poujadist was to stand for the values of the
provinces against the artificial and cosmopolitan character of Paris; for
those who felt treated like objects by the State, against those parliamentarians who regarded the State as their privileged possession; for the
common sense and honesty of the small entrepreneur, against the
bogus ratiocinations and intrigues of intellectuals; for the preservation
of the European presence in Algeria, against the disintegration of
French territorial integrity; for the tried and tested ways of living *à la
française*, against the Americanization of modern life; and for the free
and unrestricted disposal of private earnings, against the principle of
taxation. Poujadism did not survive the return to power of General de
Gaulle in 1958, but its principal concerns in many ways harked back
to the themes of the nationalist and authoritarian Right of the Third
Republic. As will be seen later, the National Front is in many ways
the modern expression of the same type of nationalism, and this broad
historical continuity is reflected in the fact that its leader Jean-Marie
Le Pen began his political career as a Poujadist deputy in 1956.

OPTIMISTIC AND PESSIMISTIC THEMES

Sixth (and following from the previous point), French nationalism expressed an outlook on life which was informed by both optimistic and pessimistic visions. For much of the nineteenth century early ideologies of French nationalism were grafted on a romantic interpretation of the Jacobin heritage which was common to most republican groups, and they found their culminating point in the effusive sentimentalism of the Second Republic. At the level of practice nothing better symbolized these republicans' naïve conception of the nation than their adoption of the principle of (male) universal suffrage in 1848. Universal suffrage, according to the dreamy poets and writers who constituted the bulk of the Second Republic's elites, was not only a fair but also an expedient procedure, in that it would provide a mass base to the new institutions created by the Republic. (It was an article of faith of the classical liberal tradition that the 'people' embodied the virtues of human reason.) Unfortunately, the fallacy of this optimistic faith in the inherent rationality and goodness of human nature was soon exposed. This allegedly rational people first elected in 1848 a Bonapartist adventurer as President of the Republic, who then proceeded to abolish the Republic four years later. This brand of optimistic nationalism never really recovered from the mortal political and psychological blow of the collapse of the Second Republic, and the later defeat of the French Army at Sedan in 1870. There still remained echoes of this romantic nationalism in the late nineteenth century, but by the early 1890s the dominant strand of French nationalism was expressed by forces which almost entirely rejected the benevolent social and political assumptions of their forebears.

This pessimistic strain became the central feature of the French nationalist tradition as a result of growing concerns about the identity and future of the French nation. As noted earlier, this anxiety was articulated around the theme of decline, reflected in a weakening of the French martial spirit after 1870; the degeneration of ruling elites; the decline of population growth during the twentieth century; the collapse of France's role in the world; the debasement of national blood by noxious foreign admixtures; and the corruption of the nation's moral fibre. These concerns sprang partly from external shocks such as military defeat, retreat from empire, and the declining status of French culture in the world. But many sources of anxiety were internal: for example, the experience of political instability and economic stagnation during much of the Third Republic, and the loss of status and income suffered by 'descending' groups in society. This brand of nationalist pessimism was accelerated by the military defeat of 1871, and was deeply influenced by the doctrines of the Catholic Church. It first came to the fore with the attempt to restore the monarchy in the 1870s, and was also prominently displayed in the challenge mounted by General Boulanger (1837–91) to the Republic in the late 1880s and early 1890s. Its darkening clouds menacingly loomed over the passionate debates provoked by the Dreyfus Affair. During the twentieth century its most vocal expression came from the extreme Right. Intellectuals such as Maurice Barrès (1862–1923) and Charles Maurras (1868–1952), political movements such as the monarchist Action Française and the Poujadists, terrorist groups such as the Organization de l'Armée Secrète (which fought a desperate rearguard battle to maintain French rule in Algeria), and even the État François of Vichy echoed these visions of national decline and humiliation. But this bleak vision was by no means the exclusive preserve of the authoritarian Right. The Gaullist *Weltanschauung* was also informed by a tragic conception of history (based on de Gaulle's personal experiences of French humiliation); even the restitution of France's 'rank' in the 1960s did little to change de Gaulle's essentially sceptical, and often pessimistic, outlook on life. The common thread which united many of these different individuals and movements was their attachment to traditionalist Catholic values (even de Gaulle was deeply influenced in his youth by Charles Maurras), which thus constituted one of the underlying sources of this pessimistic strain of French nationalism.

ELITE NATIONALISM AND ADVERSARIAL NATIONALISM

As the above contrasts have made clear, nationalist themes transcended the very basic cleavage between State and civil society. As noted earlier, nationalism was an integral part of the ideology of state construction, and in this loose sense informed the official rhetoric of most French governments after 1789. This instrumental dimension of state nationalism should be distinguished from the regimes which accorded a central position to the promotion of nationalist values in France and abroad. De Gaulle springs to mind immediately, of course, but also the Jacobin advocates of wars of national liberation in 1793, who were similarly inspired by a mystical conception of national grandeur. Despite its official title, and the undeniable patriotism of its leading figure, it is arguable that the Vichy État François did not fall into the same category. Notwithstanding Marshal Pétain's frequent references to the traditional virtues of the French nation, the Vichy governments' *de facto* collaboration with the German occupant represented the very negation of a basic principle which was common to most mainstream nationalists of the Left and Right during the interwar period: Germanophobia. In this sense, Charles Maurras's utter contempt for German society and culture typified the beliefs of many conservative nationalists, even though most of them recognized the tactical value of an alliance with Nazi Germany against Bolshevism during the Second World War.

The essential spirit of French nationalism, however, was adversarial. It has often been remarked that the French have a tendency to rebel against established order—it was in this spirit that the political scientist, André Siegfried, once described his countrymen as 'a nation of riotous conservatives'. But negativity of this kind has to be grounded on firm social and cultural foundations if it is to serve any useful analytical purpose (even then, the dangers of circularity loom large). A sociological approach could express the adversarial dimension of French nationalism in a less deterministic way. As has been seen in this chapter, most mainstream political and intellectual movements which based their appeal on nationalist ideologies in the twentieth century found the bulk of their support in relatively vulnerable and increasingly marginalized social and occupational groups. It is revealing, for example, that the extreme Right-wing nationalist groups of the Third Republic consistently failed to find support in prosperous agricultural communities. Similarly, as already noted, the Poujadists expressed the tensions and anxieties of discontented sectors of provincial France. In the 1980s and 1990s both the Communist Party and the National Front tried to capitalize (with contrasting results) on social and cultural dislocations triggered by the important economic adjustments of the late 1970s and early 1980s. From a sociological perspective, a particular type of nationalism thus flourished in expressions of rejection of the social and political *status quo*.

This negative dimension is confirmed by a cursory glance at the political status of most mainstream nationalist groups since the Third Republic. French nationalism assumed an intransigent character which almost always resulted in its alienation from the institutions of public authority. This inflexibility was a constant feature of nationalist politics, from the challenge of General Boulanger to the anti-Dreyfusards, from the Action Française to the Ligues of the 1930s, and from the supporters of Algérie Française to the exclusionary politics of the National Front in contemporary France. While French nationalism should not be reduced to this adversarial aspect, the phenomenon was undeniably exemplified by social and political groups which opposed (always passionately, often radically, sometimes violently) the official institutions and values of the Republic. There was one sense in which the Vichy regime represented the triumph of precisely those groups which had couched their opposition to the Third Republic in the language of militant nationalism; Charles Maurras was right, from this perspective, to characterize the period between 1940 and 1944 as 'the revenge of the anti-Dreyfusard camp'. But, as argued earlier, the Vichy regime was not consistent in its nationalist practice: hence the disillusionment of many anti-Republican nationalists with its policy of collaboration with Nazi Germany.

ADVERSARIAL NATIONALISM AS DISTINCT FROM FASCISM

These undercurrents of conservative, authoritarian, retreating, pessimistic, and essentially adversarial attitudes and practices in many ways dominated the phenomenon of French nationalism after the advent of the Third Republic. They expressed a cluster of sentiments which were shared by a variety of social and occupational groups, but which typically included fear of social revolution, rejection of democratic and representative institutions, obsession with the idea of French decline, and radical opposition to the institutions of republican government. Their anti-republican character was manifested in their repudiation of the core values of civil and political equality; the former in their denial of full membership of French society to certain minority groups, and the latter in their rejection of the republican claim that all citizens had equal rights of participation in public life. In rejecting the notion of civil equality these anti-republican nationalist movements also directly challenged the principle of fraternity, in that they did not accept the postulate that the state had a vocation to integrate peoples of different racial and cultural origins into an artificially constructed 'national' community. The French nation, for these adversarial nationalist groups, was a fragile entity whose identity had to be nurtured and protected from the threat of invasion and debasement.

The complex relationship between this type of adversarial nationalism and the distinct ideological tradition of French fascism will now be explored. The Left in France often tended to tar this entire brand of intransigent nationalism, from Boulanger to the National Front, with the brush of 'fascism'. Yet few political epithets have been used with as little rigour and as much passion as the concept of 'fascism'. In a certain type of left-wing discourse fascism has been the permanent ideological condition of the authoritarian Right: the Ligues of the interwar period, the État François of Vichy, the Poujadists, and the National Front have been presented as the French epigones of Mussolini and Hitler. For example, the idea of a 'fascist threat' to Republican institutions underlay the formation of the Popular Front after 1934. This idea was effective in mobilizing left-wing opinion, but the substance of the alleged 'threat' was mystifying on two counts: the antiparliamentary groups which rioted outside the French Parliament on 6 January 1934 were not exclusively (or even predominantly) Fascist, and most did not really want to overthrow the Republic by force anyway.

This is not to deny the reality of French fascism during the interwar period. The groups which clearly and unambiguously identified with fascist principles, however, were politically and institutionally insignificant. For example, Georges Valois tried to set up a Fascist movement in France after Mussolini's successful march on Rome in 1922. His Faisceau was never anything more than a sect, and it folded up as early as 1925. Other Fascist groups included the Francistes led by Marcel Bucard, the Solidarité Française movement of Jean Renaud, and the Cagoule terrorist organization. None of these groups was supported by more than a handful of simple-minded thugs (assisted by recruits from the *milieu* of petty crime); the most they achieved was the disruption of public meetings and marches organized by parties of the Left. Two dominant figures to emerge from these movements, however, were Jacques Doriot (1898–1945) and Marcel Déat (1894–1955), an ex-Communist and Socialist respectively. Doriot established his political base in local politics in the Parisian suburb of Saint-Denis, and until his expulsion from the PCF in 1934 symbolized the emergence of a tough younger generation of Communist leaders. Déat was a prominent Socialist intellectual who advocated an ideological realignment of the SFIO, based on the creation of a wide anti-capitalist alliance of workers, peasants, and the middle class. After losing the argument inside the party, he was expelled from the SFIO in 1933. Doriot, founded the PPF in 1936, and this organization proved to be the most important Fascist group in France, although even there the element of ambiguity remains. At the height of its popularity in 1938 the PPF was probably the largest political organization in France. But it declined rapidly after Munich, and by 1940 had shrunk to the traditional size of Fascist organizations in France. The ambiguity about the PPF hinges on the fact that it openly defined itself as a Fascist movement only *after* 1940, in other words, after it had ceased to be a nationally significant political institution.

What makes only these few organizations worthy of the label 'Fascist', and not the other nationalist movements mentioned earlier on? What is recognizably fascist about the activities and beliefs of Doriot and his gang after 1940, which could not equally be applied to the practices and doctrines of patriotic paramilitary groups such as Colonel de la Rocque's Croix de Feu, or the nationalist ravings of Charles Maurras's Action Française? In brief, fascism was a much more precise and historically specific ideological doctrine than the ideas and themes articulated by the authoritarian nationalist Right. Fascist and right-wing authoritarian movements certainly *shared* several 'adjacent' ideological concerns, such as an intransigent conception of nationalism and a marked tendency towards anti-parliamentarianism, and this convergence in some ways facilitated the conflation of authoritarian nationalism with fascism. But at heart fascism represented a number of core ideological principles which were the negation of the traditional values of the authoritarian Right. Fascism was not conservative but revolutionary; the order it sought to create did not hark back either to the frozen social and economic hierarchies of the *ancien régime*, or the classless society to which Socialists and Communists aspired, but to a new social system which transcended capitalism and communism. The corporatist order which was advocated (but by no means consistently practised) in Mussolinian Italy was a good example of such a scheme. Furthermore, the intellectual origins of French fascism were rooted in Marxist revisionism, whereas authoritarian nationalist movements echoed the conceptions of counter-revolutionary and conservative political traditions. From this point of view, it is also worth noting that the social constituencies of Fascist groups were markedly more plebeian than those of parties and groups of the authoritarian Right. As in Germany, where the traditional aristocracy and bourgeoisie supported von Papen rather than Hitler before 1933, economically prosperous groups gave French Fascist organizations a wide berth for most of the 1920s and 1930s. On one hand their revolutionary objectives made them suspect in the eyes of social strata whose supreme political goal was the preservation of existing privileges. But Fascist movements were also deeply suspect because of their anti-religious and anticlerical sentiments—an important factor in the alienation of PPF support in France after 1940. Finally, Fascists worshipped their leader and celebrated the institution of 'the party' in a way which was alien to the traditions of the nationalist Right. This is not to deny that General Boulanger, Charles Maurras, Colonel de la Rocque, and Jean-Marie Le Pen were regarded as strong figures in their time. But they did not seek (nor did they generally receive) the same kind of adulation which was showered upon leaders of fascist groups in France and all over Europe. (The only leader who did receive such adulation was Marshal Pétain, but even his fiercest critics could not reasonably accuse him of having been a fascist.)

The lines of demarcation between French fascism and the wider tradition of authoritarian nationalism can therefore be drawn with some precision. To argue that French fascism was already established as a coherent doctrine in the principles and values of the authoritarian nationalist tradition by the turn of the century (as is suggested in Zeev Sternhell's *Ni droite ni gauche*) is to disregard and undervalue evident discontinuities between the two conceptions. But this reductionist approach should not be inverted. Just as it would be a fundamental error to present all adversarial nationalists as proto-fascists, it would be equally schematic to treat the adversarial nationalism of the authoritarian Right as a political tradition united by core ideological principles. For the analytical purposes of this presentation a number of elements of continuity have been identified. But there were also notable differences in the principles and objectives adopted by these adversarial nationalist groups. The Boulangistes and the Croix de Feu were disillusioned republican nationalists, while supporters of the Maurrassian Action Française regarded the monarchy as the only acceptable regime; the populist repertoire of the paramilitary *Ligueurs* included the systematic use of violence, whereas the populism of the Poujadists did not; the clans, factions, and assorted groups which vied for influence and power within the Vichy administration included technocrats,

traditionalists, fascists, and conservative republicans, whose core ideological principles were often strikingly different.

Ultimately, however, the question of the full extent of fascist influence in French politics during the interwar period cannot be answered
merely by rebutting the charge that all authoritarian nationalists were
fascists. The historian Raoul Girardet coined the concept of 'fascist
impregnation' to describe the ways in which fascist ideas, symbols,
and practices were appropriated by the forces of 'order' in France
during the 1930s, and this conception is worth retaining. Despite
differences between fascism and traditional French authoritarian
nationalism, there were perceptible affinities between the adjacent
ideological concerns of the two groups in the decade which preceded
the outbreak of the Second World War. The French Right espoused
many fascist themes, such as the cult of strong leadership, virulent
anti-Communism, and anti-Semitism; copied, or at least tried to imi-
tate, the pompous style adopted by Fascists in their marches and
mass gatherings, and watched with growing sympathy and interest as
Mussolini and especially Hitler made their presence felt on the European stage. But, to repeat, this did not mean that the Right as a whole
became fascist during the 1930s (or, for that matter, at any other
moment in French history). Even under the Vichy administration it is
clear that there were significant differences and open expressions of
hostility between the nationalist groups which gathered around Pétain
in Vichy and the doctrinally fascist *collabos* in Paris, who constantly
urged the regime to establish closer ties with Nazi Germany. In sum,
Fascist and authoritarian nationalist undercurrents shared many
common adjacent and peripheral ideological concepts, while retaining
distinct emphases on different core values.

THE NATIONAL FRONT AND THE PERSISTENCE
OF ADVERSARIAL NATIONALISM

These persistent manifestations of adversarial nationalism can be
further demonstrated by a closer examination of the origins and ideological affiliations of the National Front. This right-wing nationalist
organization, led by the former *Poujadiste* deputy Jean-Marie Le Pen,
first rose to public prominence in September 1983 by winning control
of the municipality of Dreux as part of a united right-wing coalition.
The Front made its first breakthrough in national politics in the Euro-

pean elections of 1984, with 11 per cent of the votes cast, and dramatically illustrated its strength by winning 35 seats in the Parliament
elected (by proportional representation) in March 1986. Although the
return to the majority voting system in June 1988 denied it a fair share
of seats, the movement's firm roots in national politics were confirmed
by Le Pen's remarkable electoral performance in the presidential elections of April 1988: with 14 per cent of the vote, the candidate of the
Front won more than twice the number of votes received by the official
Communist candidate, and around a quarter of the total right-wing
vote in the country. In the regional elections of 1992 the Front confirmed its entrenchment in national politics by winning 13.9 per cent
of the vote. By the early 1990s, accordingly, the movement had become
solidly established in the French political landscape, with an active
membership of around 100,000 (according to official 1990 figures),
strong and often strategic positions in regional and departmental
assemblies, a vibrant network of satellite organizations (ranging from
youth movements and Christian fundamentalist associations to the
Association for the Defence of Marshal Pétain's Memory), and a growing presence in the police and the Army.

The National Front is the modern expression of nationalist and
populist undercurrents of the French Right, which first emerged in
the activities of anti-republican groups after the 1870s, and were subsequently typified by the practices and beliefs of the anti-Dreyfusards,
the revolutionary nationalists, the *Ligueurs* of the interwar period, some
elements of the Vichy regime, and the Poujadist movement in the
1950s. It has, beyond any doubt, been the most successful articulation
of this brand of nationalism to date, both in terms of its capacity to
unite the different (and always fractious) strands of the nationalist
Right, as well as its wider impact on the political scene. It differs
from its ideological predecessors in one significant respect: it does not
question the legitimacy of the Republican form of government, and
indeed claims to accept the Revolution of 1789 as an integral part of
the French political heritage. But, while it may accept the Republic
as a system of government, the National Front is clearly at odds with
many of the basic values of the republican tradition. Like its predecessors, the National Front rejects the claim that the notions of fraternity and equality can serve as the foundational principles of the French
polity. For example, the republican concept of fraternity stresses the
importance of universality rather than particularism, and thus seeks to
promote unity and solidarity in French society on the basis of shared

social and cultural values. The National Front's value system denies the possibility of a common understanding between European and non-European cultures, and bases its conception of human relationships on particularist concerns. Its president, Jean-Marie Le Pen, defined national preference, the cornerstone of his movement's ideology, in the following terms: 'I like my brother more than my cousin, my cousin more than an acquaintance, an acquaintance more than a stranger, a stranger more than a foreigner.'

Jean-Marie Le Pen's movement also denounces the republican principle of equality as 'decadent', and underlines its pernicious social, economic, and moral consequences: the imposition of a sham form of parity between men and women, the destruction of the family as the basic unit of society, the undermining of popular belief in religion, the creation of disincentives to productivity and individual effort, and the imposition of alien racial and cultural values on French society. Also, like many of its forebears of the nationalist Right, the National Front stresses the importance of the values of order and hierarchy, the decadence and corruption of French political elites, and the need to found the social and political order on an entirely new philosophical basis (an aspiration which is somewhat inconsistent with the party's claim to accept the Republic). The decline of the French nation lies at the heart of the National Front's political message. It suggests that France's economic decline was caused by 'collectivist' public policies followed by both left- and right-wing governments since the 1970s; the decline of traditional social communities was caused by mass unemployment, itself occasioned by excessive immigration (in 1988 and 1989, one of the National Front's principal election slogans was 'two million unemployed, two million immigrants'). National Front leaders also stress such phenomena as racial decline, resulting from the Semitic corruption of the French nation (the Front's leaders are both profoundly anti-Arab and anti-Jewish); cultural decline, reflected in the collapse of the status of the French language; social decline, brought about by a loosening of public morals, permissive laws on abortion and divorce, and the legalization of pornography; and, last but not least, political decline, reflected in the corruption and incompetence of governments of both Right and Left.

Why did the 1980s and 1990s witness a revival of the adversarial dimension of French nationalism, and a commensurate decline of the moderate and cautiously expansive conception traditionally championed by the elites of the Republic? What did the emergence of the National Front reveal about the conditions which governed the prevalence of one form of nationalism over the other? Like most of its twentieth-century ancestors, the National Front is a child of despair and humiliation. It expressed the anxieties of groups which suffered as a result of the economic dislocations and readjustments of the 1970s and 1980s: the fears of urban communities which felt threatened by violence and insecurity, the defensiveness of white Europeans in the face of immigrant concentrations in inner-city areas, the anger and frustration of those who became disillusioned with traditional parties of the Left and Right, and finally, the hostility of social and occupational groups which felt vulnerable in the face of rapid moves towards European political and economic integration. The political discourse of the National Front effectively translated the social, economic, and cultural concerns of different groups in society into an appealing brand of populism. There were thus many necessary conditions for the emergence of the National Front: an economic crisis (or, at least, the experience of severe downward mobility by significant social strata), an external threat to French sovereignty (the process of European unification, closely linked to the political resurrection of a united Germany), a dramatic decline in public confidence in the country's political elites, a weakening of secondary institutions (both religious and secular) which could act as forces of social cohesion, the presence of an unpopular and ideologically confused left-wing government for much of the 1980s, and the fragmented and fractious nature of the Right. Yet many of these necessary conditions also obtained during previous upsurges of adversarial nationalism in France, without producing as strong, tenacious, and durable a political movement as the National Front. It is arguable that the critical difference was made by the availability of a charismatic leader whose strategic and tactical skills allowed the organization to exploit to the full the vacuum created by the strained circumstances of the 1980s. Indeed, the underlying cause of the National Front's ideological success was its ability to transform the social and political dislocations of the 1980s into a crisis of *national* identity. This capacity to focus the political debate on issues of race and immigration, and ensure that these discussions were conducted essentially on the National Front's terms, was a testimony to the resourcefulness of the movement's political strategy. More generally, it highlights the importance of leadership as a critical variable in the success of political movements. As noted in Chapter 1, the presence of strong and creative leadership can often constitute the sufficient

condition of a political organization's successful exploitation of propitious social and political circumstances.

In this sense the prevalence of the darker side of French nationalism
in the social and political conditions of the 1980s was no accident: it
was made possible by a fracture of significant proportions in the fabric
of French public and private life, which enabled a demagogic organization to manipulate to its advantage the fears created by the uncer-
tainties of the moment. How long will this adversarial form of
nationalism continue to dominate the political scene? Past political
experiences appear to provide a comforting answer: after all, every
previous surge of this type of chauvinism ultimately ran out of momentum. From the Boulangist challenge to the extreme nationalists of
French Algeria, each major resurgence of the adversarial nationalist
tradition was eventually defeated by the Republic. But these victories
were not inevitable: on each occasion, they occurred essentially
because the republican camp was able to respond positively (and creatively) to the political and ideological challenges posed by its enemies.
The aggressive and backward-looking nationalism of the anti-
Dreyfusards was overcome by the democratic and progressive nationalism of the republicans; the despondent and penitent nationalism which
culminated in the État Français was swept away by the optimistic
patriotism of the resistance; and the retreating and cramped chauvinism of the extreme Right over the Algerian question was defeated by
the realistic nationalism of de Gaulle. History thus seems to indicate
that the traumas and anxieties provoked by the adversarial form of
nationalism could readily be overcome, provided France's republican
elites were both able and willing to face up to the challenge it poses.

However, the response of these elites to the nationalist upsurges of
the 1980s and early 1990s was far from inspiring. The National Front
was allowed to capitalize on fears provoked by the presence of immigrant communities in France to convey its racialist message of conflict
and hatred. Even the process of European political and economic
integration, which should have been presented by French political
elites as an opportunity to improve the republican framework of
government by learning from the experiences of other European countries, became essentially an instrument of inter- and intra-party division during the 1992 referendum on the Maastricht treaty. The
predictable result was that extremist organizations such as the National
Front (flanked on this issue by a rag-tag assortment of neo-Gaullists,
dissident liberals, Jacobin Socialists, monarchists, hunters, *Gitanes-*

smokers, and Communists) were able to exploit deep-seated fears of Germany to oppose the process of European unity and reinforce expressions of adversarial nationalism in society. How these problems are eventually confronted in the 1990s will provide a stern test of the governing elites' sense of political leadership and moral integrity, and ultimately determine how long the adversarial form of nationalism paraded by the National Front will continue to occupy a prominent position on the contemporary political stage.

Chronology

1789 August. *Declaration of the Rights of Man* asserts the principle of popular sovereignty.

1792 April. Declaration of war against Austria.
October. Legislature votes decree promising French assistance to all peoples seeking liberation from oppression.

1814 March. Occupation of France by Russian and Prussian troops.

1830 July. Constitutional monarchy of Louis-Philippe.

1847–8 Nationalist upsurge in Europe; July Monarchy replaced by Second Republic in France.

1871 May. Treaty of Frankfurt confirms French loss of Alsace and Lorraine to Germany.

1881 May. Tunisian protectorate: beginning of Third Republic's colonial expansion.

1882 February. Foundation of Ligue des Patriotes.

1889 April. Boulanger challenge to Republic foiled.

1898 January. Beginning of Dreyfus Affair.
September. Formation of Comité de l'Action Française

1914 August. Union Sacrée as France enters war.

1923 January. Occupation of the Ruhr by French troops.

1934 February. Riots outside the National Assembly launch movement towards the Popular Front.

1936 June. Jacques Doriot sets up Parti Populaire Français. Colonel de la Rocque forms Parti Social Français, after dissolution of Croix de Feu.

1940 July. Constitutional laws of État Français.
Sinking of French fleet by Britain at Mers-el-Kébir.

1942   November. Total occupation of French territory by German and Italian troops.

1944   August. Liberation of Paris.

1947   May. Expulsion of Communists from government: beginning of Cold War political realignment.

1954   May. Fall of Dien Bien Phu heralds the end of French colonial presence in Indochina.
July. National Assembly rejects treaty on European Defence Community.

1956   January. Notable Poujadist success in parliamentary elections.

1957   March. Rome treaties for European Common Market ratified by National Assembly.

1961   April. Attempted coup by *Algérie Française* officers foiled by de Gaulle.

1962   July. Proclamation of Algerian independence.

1963   January. Franco-German treaty signed by de Gaulle and Adenauer.

1966   March. France withdraws from military wing of Atlantic Alliance.

1972   October. Foundation of National Front.

1979   June. First elections to European Parliament.

1983   September. National Front's first major electoral success at Dreux.

1986   November. Ratification of Single European Act by French National Assembly.

1988   April. Jean-Marie Le Pen wins 4.375 million votes in presidential elections.

1992   September. Referendum approves Maastricht treaty by slender margin.

CHAPTER 6

The Strengths and Limits of the Étatiste Tradition

Italians regard theirs as a haven of corruption and incompetence. British political discourse (rather misleadingly) appears to recognize its existence only with reference to the ceremonial aspects of government. Americans employ the term frequently, but only as a means of designating a unit of sub-central government. For older generations of Germans, finally, the concept evokes nothing but painful historical associations. Yet for the French the State is a prominent (and indeed obligatory) feature of the landscape of politics. It comes from the depths of time: in his classic study *l'Ancien Régime et la Révolution* (1856), Alexis de Tocqueville claimed that the institution of administrative centralization was a creation of the absolutist monarchs which transcended history. It survived the events of 1789, and indeed, was deemed by Tocqueville to have been a significant contributory factor to the Revolution itself. Menacing Leviathan for some, ineffectual agency for others, often an object of suspicion and distrust, the French State always remained a source of political controversy during the nineteenth and twentieth centuries. The arid tables of National Income statistics provide the first inkling of its distinctive presence: French government expenditure accounts for a considerably higher proportion of national income than its British or American counterparts. This state activism is translated into a high level of territorial penetration, resulting in the establishment of vast state networks throughout the land. It is also reflected in a high level of functional complexity, as seen in the extent of its historical involvement in such spheres as agriculture, education, health, and religion. Finally, the presence of the State is maintained through its self-image as the guardian of the long-term interests of the nation. This self-image is constantly projected to the population, reminding French citizens of the benevolent and paternalistic vocation of their State. Until recently, for example, a sign displayed prominently in the courtyard of the Louvre palace in

Paris asserted 'Ici, l'Etat veille à la sauveguarde de votre patrimoine culturel' ('Here the State watches over the preservation of your cultural patrimony'). Whether the French State has a more grandiose self-image than its counterparts in the Western world could be debated; after all, higher civil servants have a universal inclination towards pomposity and delusions of grandeur. But the French State is almost unique in the extent to which its public discourse reflects its inflated view of itself.

As might be expected, such expressions of vanity often provoked resentment and ill-feeling in society. Indeed, such was the hostility at the intrusive nature of some forms of state intervention that the concept of *étatisme* (statism) was coined to designate the quasi-monarchical power exercised by the French State over its citizens. But, while the idea of *étatisme* has become commonplace and its fundamental manifestations largely taken for granted, the precise ramifications of the phenomenon are rarely discussed in a systematic fashion. For observers of the French political scene, *étatisme* is sometimes viewed as a particular type of power exercised by the higher civil service; on other occasions it seems to denote an ideology shared by political elites; others still regard its manifestation as an epiphenomenon of conflicts between competing social forces. It has even been suggested that the *étatiste* tradition was simply an institutional consequence of the congenital disposition of the French to submit to authority. This chapter will attempt to explore these different representations of state power in France, and ultimately assess the heuristic potential of the concept of *étatisme*. It will be seen that this notion does indeed capture distinctive elements of the practice of politics in France; at the same time, however, some of its underlying assumptions about the role of the State will be disputed.

The normative controversy about the place of the State in society was matched by the absence of fundamental agreement over the locus of power within the institution as a whole. The French State always possessed a rather intangible quality, which was painfully apparent whenever attempts were made to identify its internal centre of power. Which forces controlled the direction of the ship of state? Its political leaders, particular social and economic groups, or its administrative elites? With respect to the latter alone, a wide range of views could be elicited. Like their British counterparts, French higher civil servants (*hauts fonctionnaires*) regarded themselves as embodying a particular institutional vocation: the defence of the public interest. According to these mandarins, political elites tended to be guided merely by immediate contingencies. Only a highly trained, disciplined, and efficient body of public servants could act as the guardians of the long-term interests of society, because only they had as their prime motivation an abiding attachment to the common good. This conception of the bureaucracy as the protector of the public interest was deeply ingrained in the ideology of the revolutionary elites after 1789; its spirit in many ways influenced the Napoleonic administrative reforms of the early nineteenth century. In the modern era this conception continued to be distilled in generations of graduates of the *Grandes Écoles*, the training institutions for the higher civil service; its spirit no doubt underlay the production of the sign outside the Louvre, which was quoted earlier. From this perspective the *étatiste* tradition appeared as an expression of the paternalistic concerns of the bureaucracy for a society suffering from the destructive effects of social conflict and political instability. Quite naturally, political elites tended to take a different view of the role of the state bureaucracy. In their eyes the good society was a matter for definition by politicians, not administrators: the role of civil servants in furthering its achievement was nothing more than instrumental. The institution which appeared to bear out this paradigm almost to perfection was the Conseil d'État (Council of State), which discreetly performed its advisory role in the sphere of legislative codification and administrative regulation without overtly impinging on the leadership functions of political elites. To support their instrumental view of the bureaucracy, political elites pointed to the ease with which they could purge the administration after their accession to high office. Indeed, rather like their absolutist predecessors, republican political elites seemed to regard the distribution of public offices to loyal subordinates as a natural right. Under the Fifth Republic, successive presidents used their extensive powers of appointment to place their political supporters at key posts in the public sector. This spoils system *à la française* seemed to provide modern governments with a secure means of controlling the higher civil service and highlighted the apparent vulnerability of the administration in the face of political contingencies.

More polemically, it was suggested that both political and administrative elites were merely the agents of occult socio-economic interests. Marxist and anarcho-syndicalist approaches to the relationship between the State and the political realm tended to stress the subordination of public authority to the interests of powerful economic groups.

The State's essential vocation was to serve the economic interests of dominant social forces; it followed, therefore, that the bureaucracy's role was simply to support financial oligarchies in their efforts to preserve their leading positions in society. At the other end of the political spectrum the extreme Right often claimed that republican governments were manipulated by a small coterie of speculators, Freemasons, and Jews. Common to these conspiratorial approaches was a firm belief that malevolent forces were constantly lurking behind the benign façade of the French State, subverting its universalist vocation to further the interests of specific groups. A more recent version of this sensationalist approach highlighted the technical formation of French political elites as the determining factor in identifying the locus of power within the State. In contrast to the conspiracy theories mentioned earlier, which took the outcomes of the state's actions as evidence of group control, this line of enquiry focused on the process by which decisions were made. If the social and occupational origins of the French political elite were examined, it was suggested that there had been a progressive colonization of the political system by higher civil servants. Thus, according to this view, the real influence of the bureaucracy was to be gauged not by the existing relationship between politicians and civil servants, but by examining the professional and occupational origins of the politicians themselves. Seen under this light, the French higher civil service appeared to have assumed an almost hegemonic position in society. Three of the four presidents of the Fifth Republic were graduates of a French *Grande École*; almost all prime ministers were, at some stage of their careers, members of the higher civil service; similarly, an average of one-third of all ministers appointed after 1958 had emerged from the upper echelons of the administration. The real power of the French State, in sum, was displayed in its ability to create a political elite in its own image, which shared its values and assumptions about the relationship between State and society.

Which of these different images captures the reality of state power in France? The answer, not surprisingly, is that these ambivalent images stem from conflicting features of the State itself. It is not easy to appreciate where power really lies within the State, because the institution often seems to be driven by contradictory impulses. For example, the French State was historically committed to the ideals of neutrality and civil equality. These principles stemmed from the Revolution of 1789, whose leaders attached a high priority to the abolition of such *ancien régime* practices as the unequal and often discriminatory treatment of subjects, restrictions on the access of social groups to high administrative positions, and the purchase of public office. But a neutral State could operate only in the context of a wider agreement over the basic features of the political order, and this was always a highly problematic question in France after 1789. Faced with strong and often violent remonstrations about its very existence, the French State's practice thus rapidly belied its commitment to the principle of neutrality. Similarly, the State was dedicated to the preservation of social order and attached a particular importance to the promotion of good laws. The notion that France was governed by a law-based State (*état de droit*) was central to the public discourse of successive regimes during the nineteenth and twentieth centuries. But the ideal of a law-based society also included the proposition that the State should be subject to independent (or, at least, autonomous) legal control. As will be noted later, the French State never applied this notion to itself. As a result its practice again flew in the face of its self-image: France was an *état de droit* in which the State always remained above the law. A third contradiction centred on the relationship between the administration and the political elite. Under the Republic the administration was designed to execute the goals of their political masters, who were accountable to the electors. Implicit in this instrumental role devolved to it was the assumption that the State did not involve itself in determining social and political ends. In other words, its role was to provide elected governments with the means of implementing decisions taken by politicians on the basis of their notion of the good life. The French State accepted this subordination of its role, but also retained its self-definition as a repository (*the* repository) of scientific and technical knowledge. In practice, this often resulted in blurring the distinction between means and ends, with its agents adopting postures which suggested that only they knew what was in society's best interests. To give a comparative example, British civil servants traditionally relied on the expertise of specialized interest groups in the framing of legislation over a wide range of social and economic issues. This process of consultation was conducted partly for political purposes, most notably to facilitate the endorsement of the eventual legislative Act by the interests concerned. But it also gave these groups a distinct status by recognizing the value of their professional and technical competence. The French State's dealings with organized groups often involved consultation for political ends, but the administration rarely (if ever) accorded these groups the sort of status and legitimacy which their British counterparts enjoyed. This obsession with the superiority of its knowledge engendered postures of assertiveness, aloofness, and stridency, none of which sat well with the State's claims to be merely responsive to the directives of political constituencies.

These contradictions suggest that the reality of State power in France can be understood adequately only if the conflicting pressures to which it has been subjected since 1789 are fully appreciated. This chapter will therefore begin by rehearsing the main stages in the development of State institutions in France. This will be followed by an attempt to suggest some of the underlying reasons for the State's pervasiveness in modern French political discourse. Only after these foundations are laid will it be possible to delineate the precise contours of State power and authority in France, and thus assess the explanatory value of the notion of *étatisme*.

THE TERRITORIAL DIMENSION OF THE STATE

One of the central dimensions of the existence of a state is its territorial aspect: the geographical area over which it exercises sovereign power. The current French state is the product of a protracted process of territorial expansion and stabilization which originated in the medieval era. The French obsession with the protection of its existing frontiers is a relatively recent phenomenon, derived mainly from the experiences of military defeat, war, and occupation in 1871, 1914–18, and 1940–4. Until the early nineteenth century, however, France was mainly concerned with territorial aggrandizement at the expense of her neighbours. As the historian Fernand Braudel has argued, this expansion was a natural consequence of the territorial location of an economically dynamic state which preyed on the weaker peripheral zones which bordered it. But this process of territorial growth was uneven and often accompanied by retreats. Many areas were brought under French control, only to be lost again through military defeat or political accommodation. The region of Alsace, for example, was acquired during the Thirty Years' War by Mazarin in 1648 (the Treaty of Westphalia). It was first lost to the Germans as a result of the Franco-Prussian war in 1871. It was then returned to France after the Treaty of Versailles in 1919 and annexed again by the Germans in 1940, before finally reverting to French rule in 1944. These setbacks were especially marked on the country's eastern frontiers; none the less, in the early modern era France generally continued to expand in a southward and north-easterly direction. By the end of the reign of Louis XIV (1643–1715), the territorial contours of the modern French state were essentially in place.

In fact the history of early modern and modern Europe until the beginning of the nineteenth century was dominated by attempts to contain French expansionary thrusts. Louis XIV, the revolutionary governments of 1792–4, and the Napoleonic regime all sought to extend French political and territorial influence beyond its existing boundaries. But these efforts were blocked by alliances of major European powers, with Britain often playing a leading role in opposing French designs. There were variations in the justificatory grounds for French expansion before 1815. Naked ambition played a central part, but it was often disguised by lofty nationalist rhetoric. For example, the Enlightenment conception of French *natural frontiers* stipulated that the limits of national territory had to be extended to include the Rhine, the Alps, and the Pyrenees. Similarly, the revolutionary messianism of the 1790s gave an ideological rationale for what was essentially a policy of territorial aggrandizement. The defeat of Napoleon's armies by 1815 ended attempts to extend Gallic influence in Europe by military means. French frontiers expanded slightly in 1860 as a result of the incorporation of Nice and the Savoie, but this gain was soon offset by the loss of the departments of Alsace and Lorraine to Germany after the Franco-Prussian war of 1870. By this time it was becoming apparent that France's days as an expanding continental power were numbered.

It was no accident that the French state began to press its territorial claims outside Europe precisely at the moment when its capacity for lateral expansion on the continent was undermined. The French acquisition of colonies occurred in three stages. The first came during the era of mercantilist conflicts in the seventeenth and eighteenth centuries, which yielded strategic and profitable enclaves such as Pondicherry and Saint-Domingue. Following her defeat in the Napoleonic wars, France lost many of these colonial possessions. But this deficit was soon compensated by a second wave of imperial expansion after 1830, enabling French colonists to gain footholds in North Africa and China. Finally, in the 1880s, the republican regime completed the imperial saga, thus ensuring that France controlled the world's second

largest empire by the end of the nineteenth century. After the deco-
lonization process of the 1950s and 1960s most of these prize possessions were lost, but a few outposts of French colonial rule still
subsisted: New Caledonia and Polynesia in the Pacific, Réunion and
Mayotte in the Indian Ocean, French Guyana and the islands of Saint-
Pierre et Miquelon in the Atlantic, and Guadeloupe and Martinique
in the Caribbean.

Although the acquisition and loss of colonial territories sometimes
provoked significant political storms in Paris, and certainly mattered
to French prestige, the impact of these territorial tribulations on the
character of the State itself was minimal. There was only one significant respect in which the development of the French empire under
the Third Republic had a tangible effect on the way in which State
power was exercised in the *métropole* (the colonial subjects' wistful
term for mainland France). As noted in Chapter 4, Catholic missionaries played a valuable role in the consolidation of French rule in its
newly acquired territories. This collaboration between State and
Church contributed in no small way to the search for (and eventual
achievement of) compromise between secular and religious groups in
France in the late nineteenth and early twentieth century. But this was
an exception which largely confirmed the rule: the internal configuration of the French State remained essentially unaffected by the acquisition of new territories. The main influences on the development of
the State were domestic: as will be seen next, these factors included the
social consequences of the Revolution, the centrality of the Napoleonic
heritage, the nature of the political and administrative system created
by the Republic, the normative goals of the State, and, finally, the
development of welfare functions.

THE DEVELOPMENT OF THE STATE

The French Revolution posed the problem of the constitution of the
State in acute terms. 1789 was not only a political upheaval marking
the transition from monarchy to Republic: it was also, and perhaps
especially, a social transformation of an unprecedented nature. The
ancien régime constituted a complete social order, which preserved its
political stability through an elaborate hierarchy of agents. The cataclysm of 1789 swept many of these pillars away: most particularly, the
nobility and the Church lost their privileged positions in the social

order. With the emaciation of these 'estates', however, the social and economic functions which they exercised ceased to be performed. Hence the obsessive concern shown in French early nineteenth-century political thought (from Joseph de Maistre to Benjamin Constant) with the reconstitution of the social fabric. After the end of the era of revolutionary upheavals, the reconstruction of the political order appeared indissociable from the problem of filling the void left by the old social institutions.

The French State responded to this problem by gradually attempting to assume the functions of the social institutions destroyed by the Revolution. The Napoleonic reforms of the early nineteenth century represented the most ambitious attempt to come to terms with the social and political legacy of the Revolution. There were many distinctive features of the Napoleonic State: an emphasis on power, authority, and technical competence, a strict system of hierarchy, a clearly delineated system of rules, which were applied in a uniform manner, and a scope of intervention in matters both public and private which was pervasive (in comparison with its predecessors). The most important and durable feature of the Napoleonic system was the principle of centralization, which Napoleon consciously adopted from the Jacobin heritage of the 1790s. From the apex of the administration to its lowest level, a firm chain of command was conceived within the State, locking all its agents into a rigidly centralized system. The proud symbol of this new structure of authority was the prefect, who theoretically represented the sovereign in the localities and acted upon his command. But the prefect was essentially a symbol of the centralizing aspirations of the French State; in practice his powers were always exercised under close and imperative constraints (both local and national in character).

It was against this background of social instability and the Napoleonic administrative legacy that the Republic was finally established after 1870. As argued above, both of these factors had been conducive to the development of state institutions in France, and the advent of the Republic gave a further fillip to the process. Not that it should be assumed that the administration's growth in the nineteenth century was smooth and unimpeded. The higher civil service was not insulated from the effects of the endemic political instability of nineteenth-century France. Each political earthquake experienced by the country, from the restoration of the Bourbons in 1815 to the effective triumph of the Republic in the late 1870s, was invariably accompanied by purges in the administration. The fate of the prefectoral corps was in this sense exemplary. The return of the Bourbons was followed by a purge of almost half of the Napoleonic prefects; the proclamation of the Second Empire in 1852 swept away around a third of the incumbents appointed by the previous regime. But this treatment appeared lenient when compared to the ruthlessness with which other regimes purged the administration: in 1848, 1870, and again after 1879, almost the entire prefectoral corps was replaced. It would appear that these discontinuities severely impaired the growth of administrative institutions in France, and that the endemic political instability of nineteenth-century France had a deleterious impact on the State. But such a conclusion would be excessive. For one thing, despite the radical nature of the purges, new incumbents were often drawn from a relatively restricted social group (many came from the prefectoral corps itself); this had the effect of ensuring a considerable element of administrative and sociological continuity. This was reinforced by the effects of the training offered by the specialized schools for higher civil servants (such as the École Polytechnique), which perpetuated a relatively strong sense of cohesion within the prefectoral corps. Under the July Monarchy and the Second Empire, furthermore, the higher civil service continued to constitute a reservoir from which the political elite was drawn. Above all, the formal structure of the administration remained essentially unaffected by the political turbulences of the nineteenth century. Thus the administration always remained institutionally subordinated to the political elites, but the latter continued to rely on civil servants to define and implement their objectives.

The consolidation of Republican institutions after 1880 introduced a new dimension to the growth of the French State: the accentuation of local power. Elected mayors and members of Parliament came to occupy a pivotal role in the political system. The mayor and the *député* (many of the latter also exercising the former functions) emerged as the key figures in a relatively decentralized political system, which allowed for local control of state institutions and the dispensation of social and economic patronage as a means of cultivating electoral support. From the point of view of the ordinary citizen, however, the democratization of local politics did not encourage a greater element of identification with the State. Opportunities for greater public participation in decision-making were often exploited by organized interests, which were able to exercise a powerful influence on political elites. Thus the importance of agricultural lobbies in the politics of the Third and Fourth Republics was enhanced by an electoral structure which granted disproportionate representation to rural areas (on the time-honoured principle that peasants prefer order and stability to revolutionary change). At the same time the local bias of the system ensured that a career in national politics could not be envisaged without strong local affiliations. It should be stressed, however, that the republican emphasis on decentralization and greater political participation at local levels was by no means a reflection of the State's lack of purpose. On the contrary, Republican governments often displayed a strong sense of direction in defining and executing their political objectives after the 1870s. The Republican State was faced with the fundamental problem which beset all its predecessors after the Revolution: the need to establish its legitimacy in the eyes of the majority of the population. No regime could achieve this durably if it was overwhelmingly perceived to defend narrow sectional interests or appeared to be grossly incompetent at managing the affairs of the State (both of which failings were particularly emphasized in the years which immediately preceded the downfall of the *ancien régime*). A third condition was also essential: the regime should not seem obsessed with the pursuit of military adventures abroad. Both the revolutionary and Napoleonic States collapsed partly as a result of exhausting the nation's human resources by protracted military conflicts in Europe; in 1870 the Second Empire was swept away after the humiliating defeat of the French Army at Sedan.

The Republican regime which emerged after the 1870s was not slow to learn these historical lessons. While guarding itself against the charge of weakness and indecision (particularly in its dealings with Wilhelminite Germany), the Republic clearly emphasized that its strategic objectives in Europe would be attained only through political means. The search for glory through military expeditions, a hallmark of the Napoleonic era, was thus abandoned. It is true that the Third Republic compensated for this relative quiescence in Europe by following an active policy of colonial expansion after the 1880s. But even this had to be presented to the country primarily as humanitarian and economic enterprises; Jules Ferry fell foul of his colleagues in 1885 essentially because his colonial policy was seen to have acquired an excessive military dimension. The sense of purpose which underlay the colonial policy of the French State during the 1880s is best captured by comparing the French approach to colonization with that of the British. At the risk of crude oversimplification, it could be suggested that material considerations were of primary importance in the British acquisition and cultivation of empire. The French, however, were also keen to extend and perpetuate their culture (in the broad sense of the term): the universality of French civilization was an essential under-pinning of the Third Republic's drive towards colonial expansion. Another illustration of the purposive character of the French State was its education policy. The reforms of the late nineteenth century were inspired by the basic objective of legitimizing the regime through the propagation of republican values in the classroom. Naturally, the implementation of this objective necessitated a firm policy of State intervention in the field of education: hence the separation of Church from State in 1905. But, as noted in Chapter 4, the anticlerical excesses of the revolutionary period were avoided. The State was able to reach a compromise with religious institutions, which allowed private schools to operate without undue interference from public authorities. At the same time many of the social constituencies of the Church were brought into partnership with the Republic. For example, the peasantry was provided with guaranteed markets through a policy of protection-ism, thus establishing a collusive relationship which helped to legi-timize the regime in the eyes of the rural world. The immediate rewards of this policy were social peace and economic prosperity, but its indirect consequence was again a strengthening of the attributes of the State.

The final feature in the historical growth of the French State which deserves to be highlighted is the development of welfare functions. The previous factors listed (the social void created by the revolution, the crystallization of the Jacobin model under Napoleon, the impact of local politics, and the ideological purposes of the State) were distinctive offshoots of the French political tradition, whereas the welfare state is commonly associated with the development of advanced industrial societies in the Western world. As in Britain, the Second World War played a central role in bringing about a new conception of the role of the State in economic and social affairs. Completing one of the basic objectives of the republican movement, the French State had instituted a scheme of social insurance in 1928 (much later, it should be noted, than in Germany, where provisions of a similar nature had been promulgated in the late nineteenth century). But a comprehensive system of social security was introduced in 1945–6; this was based on compulsory contributions from workers and employers and bore wit-ness to a radical transformation of elite attitudes towards the role of the State. Five factors were determinant in bringing about this transformation during the period 1940–4. First, the humiliating collapse of the French State in 1940 brought home to many the relative social weaknesses of the Republican system of government and encouraged some experiments of a neo-corporatist character during the Vichy period. While the political dimensions of these experiments were rapidly abandoned after the Liberation, many of the technocratic underpinnings of the État Français survived after 1944. Second, the political objectives of the resistance converged on the need to introduce a greater element of social welfare in France, thereby strengthening the place of the State in society. This agreement was partly based on tactical considerations, notably the need to provide an attractive set of alternatives to the paternalistic policies of the Vichy governments. But all the major components of the resistance were also ideologically committed to social change: this was true not only of left-wing groups such as the Communists and the Socialists, but also of Gaullist and Christian democratic elements of the resistance coalition. This basic consensus in the need to introduce significant social reforms was reflected in the charter of the Conseil National de la Résistance; most importantly, these agreements survived the onset of the Cold War in France, which in most other respects destroyed the political unity forged during the war.

Furthermore, the physical impact of the war on the French infrastructure (both human and material) required a radical change in approach on the part of policy-makers after 1944. The devastation inflicted upon the country's resources assumed such proportions that traditional forms of state action in the industrial sector needed to be complemented by new instruments. Hence the adoption of indicative planning by the French State after the Liberation, and the central role devolved to the State in the reconstruction (and redeployment) of French industrial capacity. In this context—and this is the fourth point—the objectives of the State were necessarily transformed by conjunctural requirements: for example, the nationalizations carried out after the Liberation constituted a response to the various challenges which confronted policy-makers after four years of war and occupation. In this sense the contrast between the reconstruction policies pursued by the French State after the First and Second World wars was instructive. After 1919 a high premium was placed on recreating the same physical environment which had been damaged by the war. As a result many opportunities were missed to capitalize on the destruction of outdated machinery in order to foster industrial regeneration. After the Liberation, however, the State was explicitly committed to the modernization of the economy, as illustrated by its adoption of indicative planning and the establishment of the Commissariat du Plan under the leadership of Jean Monnet (1888–1979). The pursuit of this objective of economic modernization ensured that the process of reconstruction would not be limited to a recreation of the past. Furthermore, the imposition of state control in the energy, transport, and credit sectors marked a decisive departure from the minimalist conception of state intervention which had been intellectually dominant in France until the late 1930s.

This reference to the change in the economic thinking of political elites provides an appropriate point of transition to the fifth factor which favoured the expansion of state functions after the Liberation: the Keynesian intellectual revolution in Western Europe. It would be insufficient to explain the transformation of French elite thinking on the question of the welfare state by internal factors alone. Throughout the Western world classical economic paradigms were being challenged by the Keynesian vision of the economy as a system of variables which could be manipulated in the pursuit of specific social and political objectives. The view that the economy was governed by 'natural' laws (which was maintained by both classical and Marxist economists) was abandoned in favour of a voluntarist approach which stressed the central role of government in regulating the economy for the purposes of greater efficiency, social justice, and social stability. The history of the reception and dissemination of Keynesianism in France is highly complex, because Keynesian ideas were used in the context of different political projects by various political figures, ranging from reformist liberals such as Pierre Mendès-France and Valéry Giscard d'Estaing to social democrats and Socialists such as Michel Rocard and François Mitterrand. At the same time the continuing force of internal intellectual influences (such as Jacobinism) prevented the incorporation of a number of features of the Keynesian model in France. Thus, for example, there were few explicit references in France to the principle of decentralization, which featured prominently in Keynes's own writings. French Keynesianism was thus a compound of endogenous and exogenous principles. But this dilution of some of its features did not detract from the role it performed in providing an additional impetus to the growth of the State in France after 1945.

THE UNDERLYING SOURCES OF STATE EXPANSION

From the above account of the historical development of the French State it may be seen that the process was influenced by a variety of factors, and that the structure of the modern French State was derived from a complex and often contradictory set of circumstances. Both across the entire chronological period surveyed in this narrative and within specific periods there were factors which stimulated the growth of the State and, at the same time, worked against its development. An example of structural tension within the administration was the tendency for bureaucratic agencies to seek to reinforce their control over public policy-making, which had the effect of fostering and perpetuating a sense of mutual animosity; this was expressed typically in the long tradition of the hostility of the *Grands Corps* (especially the Council of State, the finance inspectorate, diplomacy, and the prefectorate) towards each other. From a conjunctural perspective, tension resulted from clashes between the ideological objectives of political groups exercising power on one hand and considerations of self-interest on the other. During the 1980s, for example, both the Socialists and the right-wing coalition implemented policies which were explicitly designed to reduce the stranglehold of the State over society (decentralization in the case of the Mitterrand presidency, privatization in that of the Chirac government). But considerations of self-interest also led the two ruling coalitions to use the available resources of State power to further their own political objectives. The nationalizations carried out under the Mitterrand presidency were partly devised to bolster its economic power in a sphere of policy-making where left-wing governments in France had traditionally lacked resources. Similarly, the growth of the prime ministerial bureaucracy under the Chirac administration was a direct consequence of the Gaullist leader's (not entirely successful) efforts to usurp the presidential mantle between 1986 and 1988. Furthermore, appointments to key administrative posts during the 1980s were often made on a partisan basis, thus ensuring that the political struggle between Left and Right was also carried into the State structure.

In sum, the emergence of the modern French State was influenced by a complex range of factors; indeed, France was distinctive in the sheer range of contributory causes to the process of institutional development. First, the growth of the State was favoured by a relatively backward economic substructure, which frequently experienced long spells of recession. For much of the nineteenth century the French system of land tenure was dominated by scattered peasant holdings, which rested on inherently conservative methods of cultivation. Long phases of depression (as in the 1870s and 1880s) were characteristically met by strong State responses, thus establishing a dialectic which was repeatedly displayed during the industrial crises of the twentieth century. The depression of the early 1930s led to the Popular Front's attempts to extend public-sector control; similarly, the post oil-shock recession of the 1970s was met by a highly interventionist government strategy. Furthermore, the State expanded its activities in the course of the protracted process which led to the establishment of the French nation. During the nineteenth and early twentieth centuries the development of nationalist consciousness in Europe generally preceded the emergence of nation-states. Germany and Italy, for example, became nation-states after the basic contours of their respective national identities had been defined. In the French case the nation had little substantive existence in the late eighteenth century. As noted in Chapter 5, nation-building was an arduous product of social and political engineering, carried out by successive generations of French elites against the opposition of local social forces. For example, signs bearing the following injunction could still be seen in Brittany well into the twentieth century: 'Défense de parler breton et de cracher par terre' ('It is forbidden to speak breton and to spit on the ground'). The creation of a unified linguistic community was achieved throughout France only by the middle of the twentieth century; it was made possible through the use of effective State power to crush horizontal particularisms (such as regional dialects) as well as alternative institutional focuses of identification (most notably the Church).

The enhancement of State power was also buttressed by repeated experiences of war and military conflict on French territory after 1870. Political and economic rivalry with Germany was triggered by the defeat of 1871. This produced domestic tensions which often forced the French State to assert itself in the international arena, thus generating a foreign policy which was characterized by the aggressive pursuit of French national interests. Typical examples of this approach were the colonial expansion of the 1880s, Raymond Poincaré's harsh policies towards Germany in the 1920s, and de Gaulle's assertive foreign policy in the 1960s. This quest for status was particularly marked after the impact of defeat: it was no accident that the search for colonies was given a boost by the humiliation of 1871, and that de Gaulle's verbal acrobatics in the international arena followed close on the heels of France's painful withdrawal from Algeria. It was the frequency with which France found herself in such troubled circumstances which provided the justificatory grounds for the ideologies of State domination, which both reflected and further contributed to the expansion of executive power in France. As noted earlier, the idea of an all-powerful State was firmly embedded in the intellectual landscape of the *ancien régime*. The apotheosis of monarchical centralization was in many ways provided by Louis XIV. But the Jacobin tradition continued to celebrate the virtues of centralized authority throughout the nineteenth and twentieth centuries, occupying a hegemonic position in French intellectual approaches to the question of the relationship between State and civil society. This intellectual domination generated a set of normative assumptions about the nature of the State which were widely shared by leading political and economic actors, and cut across ideological divisions between forces of 'order' and 'movement'.

Finally, it is clear that the profoundly ideological character of French political discourse, which produced a highly conflictual approach to public affairs, also directly contributed to the development of State power. The ideological polarities of French politics after 1789 were often a reflection of bitter conflicts for power between competing social groups. The triumph of a political elite in these circumstances of heightened ideological oppositions was invariably accompanied by attempts to preclude a return to the *status quo ante*. This would be best achieved, it was quite naturally believed, by the dual process of political colonization of the State and the ever wider extension of its tentacles into French society. Most major political revolutions in France were accompanied by further additions to the territorial and functional attributes of the State. The State thus became an essential instrument for the fulfilment of the ideological objectives of ruling groups, from the revolutionaries of 1789 to Napoleon, from the Second Empire to the Third Republic, and from the Vichy État Français to the Gaullist founders of the Fifth Republic. As noted in the introduction to this chapter, this association of the State with the goals of particular elites fundamentally subverted the institution's professions of neutrality and impartiality; it also had the effect of increasing the saliency of State institutions in French society.

A STATE TRADITION?

After this outline of the growth of State power in modern France since the early nineteenth century, the issues arising from the question of *étatisme* can be formulated more precisely. It will be remembered that *étatisme* is something of a movable feast. It has variously been taken to refer to a specific form of administrative power, a common ideology of governing elites, an expression of class conflict between competing social forces, and even an institutional by-product of a widespread yearning in French society to submit to higher forms of authority. The latter claim is hardly worth taking seriously: there is little evidence to suggest that the French are any more masochistic about their State institutions than their European counterparts. If anything, the evidence points in the opposite direction. French public institutions have long suffered from a problem of legitimacy, partly triggered by the sense that they are unrepresentative of 'local' interests. Similarly, the conspiratorial claims concerning the subversion of State power by occult forces (advanced by the extreme Left and the extreme Right) are often more revealing about their proponents than the object of their investigations. For example, Marxist and neo-Marxist conceptions of the State are singularly unenlightening about the processes through which decisions are reached by its internal structures, because their object of interest lies essentially in the consequences of State actions. Furthermore, despite the useful reminder that the social consequences of State actions are rarely neutral, these approaches are too one-dimensional to capture the sheer complexity of the process by which public policy is made. There is no denying that the French State has sometimes acted on the impulse of occult forces; the sinking by French secret agents of the Greenpeace ship *Rainbow Warrior* in New Zealand in 1985 was but one example of the way in which the policy-making process can be subverted to suit the interests of unaccountable groups within the State structure. Conspiracy theories are thus occasionally accurate, but they rarely reveal anything useful about the operations of the machinery of the State in general.

This effectively leaves two dimensions worth pursuing in the notion of *étatisme*: the idea of a particular type of administrative power and the continuities in the ideological aspirations of political elites. But it is essential to formulate propositions concerning these features of the state tradition with precision and rigour. Such influence as is exercised by the administration is not based on the existence of a unified and cohesive structure. It should by now be clear that the French State is a fragmented and often incoherent institution, within which certain units none the less exercise significant forms of power. In the modern era, furthermore, public policy has tended to suffer from a process of fragmentation, essentially because the State has lost its capacity to control and direct the process of policy formation. Agricultural policy, for example, is typically a product of the interaction of a wide range of public and private groups within France. These in turn respond to the parameters of the Common Agricultural Policy, which are determined in the final instance by the European Community. Similarly, the common aspirations of a wide range of political groups for a strong centralized State should not be taken as an expression of ideological convergence; in fact, it was because political groups disagreed so violently over fundamental aspects of public life that the need for a powerful State was articulated with such consistency. It is also important to remember that the historical challenges faced by the French State have varied to a considerable extent since the early nineteenth century, and that the modernization of society has presented the institution with a bewildering range of problems which its forebears could not even have imagined. Thus the internationalization of financial markets and the growth of computer technology have ended the State's relative ability to exercise control over capital movements into and out of the country. In effect, the exchange level of the national currency is determined by international flows over which the French State has precious little control—a deeply humbling experience for the descendants of Colbert.

Ultimately, the heuristic value of the concept of *étatisme* depends on the boundaries within which the State is located. If, for example, the paradigm of the State was to be limited to the powers of the executive (and their distribution between its different branches), it would be hard to vindicate the claim that France has developed a powerful state tradition. From a comparative perspective French political experience since 1789 shows no obvious tendency to favour strong governments and powerful leaders. In this respect the recent experience of the Fifth Republic should not be construed as the norm. As a general rule republican government (this was especially true of the Second, Third, and Fourth Republics) was characterized by a relative fragmentation of power at the summit. Part of the reason for this diffusion of power was the deep-seated fear that strong rulers would develop authoritarian and anti-republican tendencies. Louis Napoleon and Marshal Pétain were good examples of conservative leaders brought in by the Republic who rapidly dispensed with the ponderous formalities of representative democracy. Thus the only generalization about executive power which appears to be supported by modern experience is the cyclical nature of strong centralized government and individual leadership. As Stanley Hoffmann pointed out long ago, classical republican political culture was characterized by a yearning for strong leadership but, at the same time, a tendency to curtail the powers of strong governments when they were in office. Examples abound, from Georges Clemenceau to Pierre Mendès-France, of charismatic republican leaders whose careers were abruptly halted by the hostility generated by their activism. The Fifth Republic saw a reassertion of strong individual leadership under the president, but even in this sphere a number of qualifications need to be made. First, the president could exercise his powers only if he enjoyed majority support in the National Assembly. When such support was lacking, as happened between 1986 and 1988 and again after 1993, the president's substantive powers were sharply curtailed. In sum, the presidency is likely to remain the dominant source of political power and patronage, but the range of internal and external restrictions on the exercise of these attributes will continue to grow—particularly if moves towards greater European political and economic co-operation are accelerated in the 1990s.

If the 'horizontal' powers of the State appear to offer little comfort to the *étatiste* thesis, a more promising avenue seems to be opened by an examination of the 'vertical' structure of the State in France. It is not contentious to suggest that the legacy of the Jacobin-Napoleonic model was especially powerful in shaping the French administrative structure during the past two centuries. But again, the case should not be overstated. As argued earlier, the administration was always internally fragmented; in this sense, even the Napoleonic State was never 'truly' Napoleonic. Furthermore, its lack of internal cohesiveness was accentuated by the effects of the endemic political instability which the country suffered after the Revolution. More recently the administration saw many of its formal powers transferred to locally elected assemblies, and the fragmentation of the policy-making process is likely to be enhanced during the 1990s with the development of the constraining powers of the European Commission. Perhaps the most visible impact of the administration on the political process in recent times was the penetration of the political elite by the personnel of the higher civil service. The *Grandes Écoles* thus emerged not only as training schools for the bureaucracy, but as the breeding ground for current and ensuing generations of political leaders. This institutionalization of the process of elite formation remains significant (especially from a comparative perspective) in that France is one of the few advanced industrial societies which effectively recruits and trains its political elites to exercise power. But the functions of these institutions should not be misunderstood. A graduate of a *Grande École* may, of course, eventually choose not to enter the political stream; furthermore, it should not be assumed that the ideological consequences of the intellectual formation received in these institutions are monolithic. To take examples from contemporary politics, the Gaullist Jacques Chirac, the Socialist Michel Rocard, the liberal Valéry Giscard d'Estaing, and the Communist Philippe Herzog all attended a *Grande École*, but this did not prevent them from embracing distinct ideological and partisan attachments and differing significantly over major areas of public policy. Yet these politicians share certain formal characteristics which transcend the lines of party division: a high (indeed, remarkable) level of intellectual ability; an intuitive sense that a distinction can be drawn between ideological and technical problems, and that politicians can find solutions to the latter; and a deep faith in the enabling function of State institutions, in both economic and social policy.

So far it would seem that neither from the perspective of executive power, nor even from that of administrative cohesiveness, is it evidently the case that the French political tradition has been distinctively *étatiste*. But scepticism about the attributes of public authority should not blind the observer to the very real dimensions of State power. Perhaps the most persistent manifestation of this phenomenon was the French State's dismissive (not to say contemptuous) treatment of the principle of judicial autonomy. Unlike Britain and the United States, post-revolutionary France evolved no tradition of sanctifying the practice of independent judicial control over the administration. In 1790 the revolutionary authorities promulgated a law which explicitly denied the courts' jurisprudence over actions taken by the State. In fact, what followed was the development of a purely subordinate relationship between the State and its legal institutions. Napoleon abolished the democratic heritage of the Revolution (for example, the election of magistrates) and formalized the internal divisions of the French judiciary. Thus already by 1810 the two basic features of the judicial system were established: its fragmentary character and its almost complete subordination to political authority. These divisions have survived to this day. Administrative justice is rendered under the guidance of the supreme administrative court, the Conseil d'État. Its verdicts often lead to the overturning of administrative regulations, but its effectiveness as a controlling agency is limited by its close (not to say collusive) relationship with the State. Furthermore, the Conseil d'État has been forced to concede that Community laws and norms take precedence over French laws—in effect, recognizing the limits on national sovereignty imposed upon France by membership of the European Economic Community. The legal scrutiny of the legislative process suffers from different but equally crippling problems. In 1958 provisions were made for the creation of a Constitutional Council, an independent body which could determine the constitutionality of laws. But even this departure from precedent was conceived essentially as a means of shielding the executive from the encroachments of the legislature, by preventing the National Assembly from overstepping the constitutionally defined bounds of its legislative powers. During the 1970s the Council widened its scope of intervention and in the following decade overturned around forty-five laws passed by the legislature. But the weaknesses of French judicial institutions remained deeply entrenched, primarily due to the historical legacy of State control. When taken in conjunction with the high level of political instability experienced by the country during the nineteenth and twentieth centuries, this legacy has produced a weak and demoralized judiciary, which has been constantly vulnerable to external political pressures. As mentioned earlier, every major change in the French political system was accompanied by sweeping purges of the administration, and the higher levels of the judiciary were rarely spared. At the same time, judges and magistrates who were not purged often remained tainted for having passively sanctioned the legal improprieties of previous administrations. For example, many of the judges who presided over the trials of the most notorious figures of the Vichy administration after the Liberation had themselves served the regime between 1940 and 1944 without demurring. At the trial in 1945 when he was sentenced to death former Vichy Prime Minister Pierre Laval challenged the right of his prosecutors to sit in judgement over him, given that they, like him, had previously sworn an oath of allegiance to Marshal Pétain.

Thus the modern French judicial system continued to provide a shining example of the subordination of law to the interests of the State. The limitations of the Constitutional Council and the Conseil d'État were, from this perspective, symptoms of a more general malaise. When the French State protected and even sanctioned the criminal actions of its own agents at home and abroad (as with the sinking of the *Rainbow Warrior* in 1985, which was mentioned earlier) it demonstrated that international law was just as expedient a precept as domestic law. The French State's contempt for the law was borne out by repeated instances of blatant executive interference in the judicial process, ranging from discreet telephone calls to the appropriate agent of the Ministry of Justice to the wholesale reappraisal of legal statutes to serve the political ends of particular governments. A few years after the end of the Algerian war, for example, the Gaullist regime passed a law which shielded all participants who were guilty of atrocities from prosecution. But two decades later the French State appealed to the notion of 'crimes against humanity' in the prosecution of the Nazi war criminal, Klaus Barbie. In his celebrated defence of the latter Maître Jacques Vergès pointed out that a State which had whitewashed the atrocities perpetrated by its own soldiers against civilian populations in Algeria had no moral right to judge the criminality of others. Furthermore, almost every government of the Fifth Republic was tainted with political and financial 'scandals' involving its members; sanctions were never anything other than minimal. Thus the notion that *fiat iustitia pereat mundus* was supplanted by the principle that laws were valuable only to the extent that they protected the French State's conception of the national interest.

There is a second, more subjective sense in which the French political tradition has been marked by *étatisme*: at the level of general perceptions of the outcomes of State actions. Seen from the perspective of the apex of the political system, or alternatively, from that of the different levels of government, the French State often appeared as a fragmented and differentiated entity, with little sense of collective identity or purpose. As has been shown in this chapter, this image can be misleading, even though it bears witness to the complex nature of the structure of public authority in France. But the very presence of the image (and its persistence over time) clearly showed that the institutional consequences of State actions continued to generate considerable social passions. It is true that the days of unqualified enthusiasm for the virtues of State action appear to be numbered. The Jacobin model, once the hegemonic conception of State organization with Left and Right alike (or at least with the Gaullist and Communist wings of each), has now been relegated to the museum of political history, alongside its progenitor, the French Revolution. Indeed, many of the orthodox assumptions about the role of the State came under increasing critical scrutiny in France during the 1980s and early 1990s. The Napoleonic conception of a unified administration serving the national interest was questioned by critics who stressed the impersonal and irrational character of the French bureaucracy; the *Grandes Écoles* were accused of producing a self-perpetuating ruling elite which was divorced from the social realities of its time; the traditional practice of State intervention in the economy as a means of regulating key industrial sectors was almost universally decried as the principal source of inflation, unemployment, and technological backwardness. However, to interpret these challenges as symptoms of a terminal decline of the French State would be premature. In this sense, a comparative examination of arguments levelled against the State from conservative and neo-liberal quarters in Britain and the United States during the same period shows how resilient the State tradition remained in France. There was some talk of 'rolling back the frontiers of the State' among mainstream parties of the Right between 1986 and 1988, but the principles of the welfare state continued to be the object of widespread political consensus. So why the attacks against the State? In truth, as was made clear at the beginning of this argument, the actions of the State in France were always a source of controversy. But the institution always adapted itself to changes in the social and intellectual environment, and there is little doubt that the current challenges will provoke a number of qualitative readjustments over the next decades. After all, the creation of the welfare state and the proclamation of decentralization were, in an important sense, responses of political and administrative elites to social and intellectual pressures from outside. In this respect the development of European political and economic co-operation, in the context of the creation of a single market in 1993, will certainly require important alterations to the policy-making process. What all this implies is that the State has been, and is set to continue to be, the principal arena within which major social and political debates are aired and, where possible, resolved. In this respect the classic weakness of French political parties (and, more generally, of intermediate associations) is not fortuitous: it is precisely because political associations are generally seen as mere instruments of executive power that parties have acquired an image of weakness and futility in the eyes of the public.

This provides an ideal transition to the third distinctive dimension of the *étatiste* tradition in France: the extent to which 'statist' ideas, values, and practices have penetrated into the public domain. As has already been made clear, the development of the French State has often played a key role in shaping the contours of social and political institutions. Thus the ideology of the republican movement was centrally informed by the objective of capturing State power; once this was achieved on a relatively durable basis after the 1870s, the implementation of basic republican aims led to the reformulation of several aspects of the doctrine. The institutions of French Catholicism were part of the state until the early twentieth century. Even after their separation from it, however, they continued to look towards the State to maintain the terms of the compromise reached between secular and religious elites in 1905. In a similar vein, the status of social groups in France was intimately bound up with the sociological underpinnings of the State. As seen in Chapter 2, the privileged place of intellectuals in French society could not be divorced from the deeply ambiguous relationship which this social stratum developed with the holders of public authority ever since the Dreyfus Affair. Furthermore, as will emerge later, the message which lay at the heart of the Gaullian design was the imperative of re-establishing the grandeur of the French State. Even a revolutionary organization such as the French Communist Party was crucially affected by the organization's embrace of the republican tradition after 1934.

In sum, there appears to be ample evidence that the State has left a durable mark on the practice of politics in France. But, as is often the case, there is a considerable gap between popular imagery and political reality. French *étatisme* evolved without a durable experience of a 'strong' executive and in spite of the absence of a consistently and comprehensively Napoleonic administrative structure. The visibility of the State was partly accentuated by the depth of social and political divisions, which forced its entry into spheres of life (such as education and religion) from which public authorities tended to be excluded in other advanced industrial societies. Despite its weaknesses, however, the French State showed considerable resilience and imagination in adapting to changing social and political circumstances during the modern era. Those who have trumpeted its demise with the advent of European unity and complex interdependence would do well to

remember the simple truth that, even in France, institutions generally
tend to outlive their critics.

Chronology

1789   July. Beginning of the French Revolution.

1799   November. Coup d'état of Napoleon, who initiated administrative
reforms in an attempt to recreate centralized state institutions.

1804   May. Napoleon proclaims First Empire.

1815   June. Restoration of Bourbon monarchy after battle of Waterloo.

1830   July. Louis-Philippe monarchy (July Monarchy).

1848   February. Second Republic established after overthrow of July
Monarchy.

1851   December. Coup d'état of Louis Napoleon.

1852   December. Proclamation of Second Empire.

1870   September. End of Second Empire after French defeat at Sedan:
Republic established.

1871   May. Treaty of Frankfurt cedes Alsace and Lorraine to Prussia.

1884   Law on elections for municipal government.

1892   Méline tariff establishes system of agricultural protection.

1905   December. Separation of Churches from State.

1914   August. Outbreak of First World War.

1919   June. Versailles treaty; return of Alsace and Lorraine to France.

1928   April. Legislation on social insurance (completed by 1930 law).

1940   June. German troops overwhelm French forces; Pétain becomes head
of government.

1944   September. De Gaulle government; birth of modern welfare state in
France.

1945   June. Creation of École Nationale d'Administration.

1958   September. Referendum overwhelmingly endorses creation of Fifth
Republic.

1962   April. Ratification of Evian agreements; Algerian independence
proclaimed.

1982   March. Defferre law on decentralization voted by National Assembly.

1985   August. *Rainbow Warrior* affair: Greenpeace ship sunk in New
Zealand by French secret service.

1986   March. Right-wing government under Chirac announces
       privatization programme.

       November. Ratification of 1985 Single European Act by French
       National Assembly.

1992   September. Maastricht treaty ratified by narrow majority in
       referendum.

CHAPTER 7
Why No Peace Movement in France?

The operational involvement of French troops in the Gulf war in the early months of 1991 was overwhelmingly endorsed by public opinion in France. This spirit of national unity was by no means unprecedented; indeed, it expressed a sense of patriotic fervour which generally surfaced when French forces had to be deployed in overseas military engagements. Although the Gulf intervention provoked some opposition from the leaderships of some political groups, notably the Communist Party and the National Front, opinion polls showed high levels of public enthusiasm for the President's policy. Throughout the course of the war (between 17 January and 27 February 1991) more than two-thirds of the public stood firmly behind France's participation in the international effort to liberate Kuwait from Iraqi control; this figure included a majority of National Front sympathizers. In addition to the Communists, passionate opposition to the war was articulated by pacifist groups (accompanied by a rather colourful assortment of deep environmentalists, dissident Socialists, Christian devotees, and middle-aged relics of May 1968). But, as with all previous instances of French military engagement abroad during the twentieth century, these groups did not wield enough power and authority in society to constitute a serious threat to government policy. In fact, France was never blessed with a unified mass movement campaigning for 'peace'. In Britain, for example, the Campaign for Nuclear Disarmament (CND) was a powerful force in the country's political and intellectual life between its foundation in 1958 and the end of the Cold War. During the Vietnam war American peace protesters succeeded in focusing public attention on the conflict, and forced the Johnson and Nixon administrations into defensive postures over the issue. It could even be argued that the success of the anti-war movement drove American presidents into a vortex of deception and secrecy which eventually exploded in the face of the hapless Richard Nixon, forcing his resignation from office in 1974.

In contrast, the activities of French peace movements rarely troubled the attention of their countrymen during this period. It is the purpose of this chapter to offer an explanation for the apparent weakness of organized pacifism in France. The existing literature on peace movements tends to highlight a number of factors: the inherently nationalistic character of the French, the conservatism of the Roman Catholic hierarchy (and thus its reluctance to endorse pacifist activities), the conformism of the young, and the traditional weakness of associational activity in France (the latter is merely a restatement of the problem). When necessary, these propositions are underscored by references to the violent legacy of the Jacobin revolutionary tradition: its penchant for grandiose imagery and heroic action, and the spilling of impure blood which is chillingly celebrated in the *Marseillaise*. Yet the explanatory force of these propositions is far from compelling. Strong peace movements flourished in the United States and Britain during the twentieth century despite the existence of powerful nationalist undercurrents in their midst; in fact, peace movements in the United States were able to capture a mass audience during the Vietnam war precisely because their political objectives were seen as articulations of 'American' ideas and values. Similarly, the Labour Party sometimes acted as the institutional vehicle for many of CND's fundamental objectives (most significantly, between 1979 and 1989), but this was consistent with the entrenchment of the party's political platform in a vision of Britain as an isolated and almost self-sufficient political community. This world-view was shared by most of its members, to say nothing of the Labour electorate, which was (and arguably remains) deeply marked by parochial tendencies. In other words, the prevalence of internationalist sentiments is by no means a sufficient condition for the emergence of peace movements. The British and American cases demonstrate that the yearning for peace could effectively rest on semi-detached and even isolationist world-views.

What about the conservatism of the religious hierarchy? It is true that French Roman Catholic authorities gave little encouragement to the propagation of irenic themes within their fold either during or after the Cold War, but this disposition was not necessarily reflected at lower levels of the Church organization. For example, many of the lower clergy and members of Catholic trade unions often supported political campaigns in favour of peace and disarmament (despite the fact that, as will be noted later, the driving force behind many of these campaigns was the French Communist Party). In other words, the political authority of the ecclesiastical establishment on such a sensitive issue as peace was not universally accepted within the Catholic community. Furthermore, the increasing secularization of French society after the 1960s enhanced the political marginality of the Roman Catholic hierarchy. Thus it was not simply that lines of communication between higher and lower levels of the Catholic community were being undermined, but there was also a steady decline in the absolute number of French men and women who believed that spiritual ideas and values could have overriding claims over the arrangement of the temporal world.

Equally problematic is the claim that French youth showed little inclination to depart from the canons of social and political convention over the past thirty years. It is arguable that an 'alternative culture' did not emerge in as fully structured a form in France as, for example, in Germany (or Italy) between the 1960s and the 1980s. It might even be suggested that the existence of a system of military service might have had the effect of neutering nonconformist tendencies among the young. But President de Gaulle legalized the practice of conscientious objection in the 1960s, thus further limiting the socializing potential of military service (which, in any event, was never very strong). More fundamentally, however, there is much evidence since the mid-1960s to suggest that social and political attitudes among French youth showed little respect for established orthodoxies. The events of May 1968 represented a clear statement of the collective disillusionment of French youth with existing social and political institutions, of both the Left and the Right. Patterns of social interaction changed significantly after the 1960s, and these transformations were reflected in the breakdown of traditional structures of authority across a wide range of political and social institutions (including the family). During the 1970s and 1980s these challenges to established order were given political expression in such movements as feminism, regionalism, environmentalism, and anti-racism, many (if not all) of which derived their support disproportionately from lower age-groups. It is hard to see how this pattern could be consistent with the claim that French youth was socially and politically passive. The appropriate question therefore seems to be not whether younger generations of French men and women were quiescent, but rather why strong tendencies towards anti-conformist behaviour failed to be translated into organized political activity in favour of peace.

This leaves the contention that the relative political eclipse of French peace movements in the modern era should be explained by the vitality of the revolutionary tradition. This proposition has a ring of plausibility: as shown in Chapter 3, the events of 1789 played a central role in the formation of the political culture of the republican movement. In the aftermath of 1789 French 'wars of liberation' were enthusiastically supported by the revolutionary camp (with the exception, on the Left, of a small group led by Maximilien Robespierre and Jean-Paul Marat). Furthermore, the nineteenth-century republican movement proudly recalled the military exploits of the Jacobins, and was strongly influenced by the Revolution's messianic aspiration to liberate mankind from the clutches of absolutist tyranny. But on the whole, these generations of republicans sought primarily to emphasize the democratic and solidaristic principles of the French Revolution, rather than its egalitarian and revolutionist dimension. During the second half of the nineteenth century republican groups struggled to establish their preferred political system in the face of strong opposition from imperial and monarchical quarters. In the course of this political struggle the spirit of the French Revolution was invoked repeatedly as a means of countering the powerful political myths which underlay the popular appeal of the empire (and, after 1870, the monarchy). At a rhetorical level, this often led republican politicians to invoke and even justify the brutal excesses of the revolutionary period. In this sense, Georges Clemenceau's famous depiction of the French Revolution as a *bloc* typified the refusal of moderate republican groups to abjure their political heritage. But this invocation of the past was essentially ritualistic: it was more a means of shoring up their political and intellectual legitimacy than a serious attempt to derive specific prescriptions from the events of the revolutionary period. Thus, when the Republic was established after 1875, its leaders displayed considerable pragmatism and flexibility in securing the social base of the new political system. This 'opportunism' of republican elites was always consistent with the retention of the violent imagery of the French Revolution. This tendency was continued by subsequent republican generations. For a small but highly symbolic example, the experience of the Radical politician Gaston Monnerville (1897–1991) may be considered. When he joined the resistance after 1940 he chose Saint-Just as his pseudonym. Louis de Saint-Just (1767–94) had been one of the leading advocates of the Terror, and his name figured prominently in the demonology of the French Revolution. Monnerville, on the other hand, remained the epitome of political moderation throughout his political career (ranging across the Third, Fourth, and Fifth

Republics), which culminated in the presidency of the Senate. Yet he saw no contradiction between his passionate commitment to representative institutions and law-based government and his identification with a revolutionary figure whose actions often represented the negation of those very principles.

In other words, there was a considerable gap between the rhetoric and the practice of moderate republican groups, and this disparity became even greater with the institutionalization of the Republic after 1875. It could be suggested that the egalitarian principles of the French Revolution continued to be upheld under the Third Republic by the extreme Left (anarcho-communists and syndicalists, socialists, and, after 1920, Communists), and that the sustained commitment of these groups to revolutionary change ensured that violence remained an integral part of the political culture of the Republic. Again, however, this would be an overstatement of the case. Many of these groups (especially anarchists) rejected some of the central tenets of republican ideology, particularly its emphasis on the virtues of knowledge and representative government. Their conception of social and political change did not seek to accommodate existing institutions, but to change them fundamentally. In this sense these movements were never really part of the republican tradition. On the other hand, those republican groups which explicitly embraced the egalitarian intellectual legacy of 1789 often made the same distinction as the moderate republicans between rhetoric and political practice. After 1905 the socialist SFIO's programme consistently advocated radical change, but the substance of this commitment was increasingly eroded by the party leadership's quest for exercising power within the existing institutional framework of the Republic. As will be observed in Chapter 11, a similar process occurred with the PCF during and after the Popular Front. It retained its core identity as a revolutionary movement, but also acquired a republican dimension which increasingly emphasized the tactical (and arguably, after the 1960s, strategic) necessity of compromise and co-operation with other social and political groups on the Left. These considerations are not meant to deny the possibility of *any* connection between the dominant political culture and the absence of organized campaigns in favour of peace. Indeed, at a later stage of the argument, it will be seen that the existence of a powerful Communist organization in France was a significant impediment to the development of peace movements. What the above considerations do suggest, however, is that it would be misleading to generalize about the inhibiting consequences of republican political culture merely on the basis of its rhetorical component. Generations of moderate and even extreme left-wing politicians invoked the taking of the Bastille as a means of establishing the authenticity of their political credentials. But this exercise of legitimation had little direct bearing on their immediate political preoccupations; in fact, it might be argued that the aggressive images and symbols of the revolutionary period survived merely as a veneer, under which developed the compromises and bargains which were the essence of political life in the republican polity.

Given the limitations of many standard accounts of the relative weakness of peace movements in France, how should the problem be approached? The first step is not to conflate the organizational dimension of peace campaigning with the issue of 'pacifism'. One of the basic claims of this chapter is that the weakness of peace movements was not a function of the absence of anti-war (and anti-force) sentiments in French society; paradoxically, there was a sense in which the strength and diversity of these sentiments was a direct obstacle to the emergence of a unified peace movement. For the purpose of this argument, pacifism should be taken to include not only the unconditional expression of opposition to war (which the French describe as *pacifisme intégral*), but also the attitudes of those with deeply held inclinations to oppose force, who none the less remained committed to its use under circumstances of self-defence (a conception defined by Martin Ceadel as pacificist). A typology of the different manifestations of French pacifism would thus begin with 'integral' pacifism, which was highly moralistic and individualistic, and deeply disdainful of any consequentialist advocacy of force. But French pacifist concepts also occupied adjacent and even peripheral positions within the ideological concerns of a broad range of social and political movements. In this specific and rather more selective sense, pacifist concepts were present in the discourse of some religious groups, which emphasized the universality of the idea of Christian brotherhood. One could further identify an economic form of pacifism, which was based on the classical liberal view that the development of commercial relations between states would bring about peace and social harmony; a legalistic conception, highlighting the promotion of pacific ideals through international institutions such as the League of Nations and the European communities; the class-based approach of the labour movement, which suggested that peace within and between nations would emerge only when capitalist exploitation was abolished; a middle-class brand of pacifist internationalism, which pointed to the global affinities of bourgeois culture, and underlined the common interests of all social groups; and, finally, the instinctive pacifism of the rural world, which was grounded in a self-interested and essentially parochial conception of the world (as expressed typically in the anti-nuclear campaigns of the 1970s).

Pacifism thus constituted a fully fledged ideology in the case of a small number of secondary associations and movements, but its influence also lay in the appropriation of some of its principles and concepts by a broader range of political groups. The rejection of war and violence was one such principle, which was advocated by parties and groups which occupied radically different positions on the ideological spectrum. This accounted for the sheer diversity of pacifist discourse in France during the nineteenth and twentieth centuries, as will be shown in the following section.

THE DIVERSE INSPIRATIONS FOR PEACE

Before illustrating the profusion of pacifist undercurrents in France, it should be remembered that, until at least the early nineteenth century, the French State had a generally well-deserved reputation for aggressive behaviour in the European arena. But the expansionism of Louis XIV, the revolutionary governments of the 1790s, and Napoleon Bonaparte could hardly be taken to represent more general bellicose tendencies in early modern French society. For example, the wars of the absolutist era provoked strong reactions within leading sections of the educated community. As the eighteenth century progressed, a range of arguments was put forward, to the effect that social and political trends would soon bring an end to traditional patterns of conflict between states. The Abbé de Saint-Pierre (1658–1743) believed that peace could emerge from a (French-led) confederation of European states; François Voltaire (1694–1778), on the other hand, held that wars were caused by the intemperate ambitions of absolutist monarchs. In other words, if absolutism was ended, peace would spread rapidly throughout the world. In a broader sense there was an assumption (which was embedded in the Enlightenment's conception of human development) that the dissemination of science and learning would bring forth a new age of harmony within societies, thus enhancing the prospects for peaceful co-operation between states. In different ways the republican philosopher Condorcet (1743–94), the political economist Henri Saint-Simon (1760–1825), and even the utopian socialist Charles Fourier (1772–1837) shared this faith in the pacificatory attributes of modern society. Of course, none of these thinkers could be described as pacifists *sensu stricto*, but they shared the fundamental irenic postulate that traditional forms of conflict in society would be transcended by the advent of new modes of social and political organization.

Until the outbreak of the First World War these various philosophical aspirations towards greater social harmony reflected widespread French sentiments about both the desirability and actuality of peaceful interaction in society (and also in relations between states). These aspirations were often indirectly expressed in the course of promoting more general conceptions of the good life. It should be mentioned that not all these visions accepted the basic premise that modern society would be increasingly pacific. The Catholic Church, for example, regarded the advent of industrial society with great foreboding, and propagated a vision of social order which essentially rejected its materialist and individualistic trappings. Although this was the prime focus of religious doctrine, the basic social themes of the Catholic hierarchy throughout the nineteenth century (the importance of traditional social values, the pernicious effects of competition, and the redemptive character of man's relationship to the soil) were predicated upon the belief that a return to traditional patterns of interaction between groups would better serve the prospects for social harmony in France. This amounted to saying that the 'natural' condition of man was peaceful: the perversion of his spirit was produced by the corrupting influence of modern society. There were times, of course, when this emphasis on the value of order and rural tranquillity was undercut by the particular political interests of the Church. The sufferings of Catholics during the revolutionary period were not forgotten by subsequent generations. Furthermore, when anticlerical republican lobbies attempted to undermine the ideological influence of the Church on the education system after 1880, many Catholic groups believed that this sacrilegious intrusion of the State provided justificatory grounds for confrontational (and even violent) political action. Similarly, the just war tradition was invoked by ultramontane groups in the 1860s to urge the French government to use its troops in the Vatican to defend the Pope, who had become a virtual prisoner in the hands of Risorgimento nationalists. But the fact that Catholic groups were sometimes prepared to advocate violence to promote (or protect) their social and political interests did not negate the Church's basic aspiration towards social peace and harmony. In sum, Catholics were pacificists rather than pacifists: in this sense it could be argued that Catholic culture remained profoundly marked by irenist ideas and values, despite the turbulent political trajectory of the Church during the second half of the nineteenth century. As noted in Chapter 4, republican and Catholic elites eventually reached a *modus vivendi* over the question of Church-State relations, and this compromise rested in no small way on the strong elements of convergence in the social and moral value systems of republicanism and Catholicism.

Pacific ideals also exercised a strong appeal in the republican camp during the nineteenth century. During the short-lived Second Republic, despite the fleeting revival of the notion of wars of liberation, the basic aspiration of most republican leaders was pacific, and this was based on their (ill-founded) belief that a new age of fraternity was about to dawn. After the brutal suppression of these aspirations by Louis Napoleon, many republicans became committed to pacifist ideas during the 1850s and 1860s. In 1869 the Belleville Manifesto of the Radical movement explicitly advocated the abolition of standing armies, and the pacifist wing of the party later exercised a significant ideological influence over the movement. During the Third Republic, Socialists consistently opposed the use of force as a means of settling international disputes, and campaigned against the bellicose rhetoric of nationalist groups. Anti-militarist sentiments were widely expressed by different Socialist groups in France during the second half of the nineteenth century, and this tradition was upheld after the unification of the Socialist movement in 1905. Jean Jaurès attempted to argue that his fellow-comrades were not unconditionally opposed to the use of force, and advocated a reorganization of the French Army as a token of the defencist credentials of his party. But his arguments failed to convince the French State that Socialists were not potentially treacherous, and when the Ministry of the Interior drew up a list of pacifist agitators to be arrested in the event of a declaration of war (the famous *Carnet B*), Socialists (and trade-unionists) were over-whelmingly singled out.

But it would be misleading to suggest that these pacific principles were expounded exclusively by such social and political institutions as the Church and the Socialist movement. In fact, these sentiments were aired by these organizations precisely because they corresponded to widespread social aspirations towards peace. France remained a country of peasants until well into the twentieth century, and the essential objective of this social class (or, rather, the diverse groups of which it was constituted) was to live in tranquillity. Memories of physical losses suffered by peasant communities during the Napoleonic wars of the early nineteenth century were sustained by oral traditions. Furthermore, the nationalist rhetoric which several regimes (e.g. the Second Empire) used to rally popular support found little resonance in peasant communities. Their political allegiance to the Empire was based on two fundamental considerations: the satisfaction of their immediate material interests and their fear of social revolution. In fact, as has been argued elsewhere, for much of the nineteenth century the mass of peasants had little consciousness of even belonging to a national community. Their social and political horizons tended to be strictly limited by the boundaries of their *pays* (a term which originally described a particular locality, rather than a territorial entity as a whole). Thus the parochial character of rural life bred an instinctive form of pacifism, which was deeply suspicious of any interaction with groups which were external to the locality (including, for these purposes, agents of the State).

These aspirations towards social peace were equally prevalent in working-class communities. The development of a sizeable proletariat did not occur in France until the early twentieth century. Until this time the working class consisted essentially of artisans and workers employed in small-scale industries. Their living conditions were often extremely precarious, and these strained circumstances produced widespread feelings of alienation and apathy. The low level of class-consciousness prevented effective political mobilization, and this was an important factor in inhibiting the development of Socialist and trade-union organizations in France. A number of factors encouraged the convergence of working-class communities towards pacific ideas after 1870. The first was the memory of the atrocities which followed the suppression of the Paris Commune. The massacres of 1871 had a traumatic effect on working-class communities and encouraged the development of anti-militarist tendencies; these sentiments were exacerbated in subsequent decades by the State's not infrequent use of the Army to quell political disturbances by workers. More generally, the early decades of the Third Republic witnessed a widespread feeling of working-class alienation from parliamentary politics. This gave rise to the phenomenon of *ouvriérisme*: an affirmation of the distinct social and political interests of workers, and their refusal to allow their future to be determined by 'bourgeois' politicians. As will be noted in Chapter 11, this sense of working-class separateness was later perpetuated in the labour movement through the influence of the Communist Party. It is true that *ouvriériste* feelings of exclusion (or marginalization) from the public sphere led some workers to embrace the violent ideals of the anarchists and anarcho-syndicalists, but a considerably larger number sought refuge in pacifism. In any event, large sections of the working class rejected the nationalist and occasionally bellicose discourse of the bourgeois republican elites after the 1880s.

In sum, there was a wide variety of pacifistic undercurrents in French politics and society for much of the nineteenth century: intellectuals, members of religious organizations, left-wing groups, peasants, and workers aspired (for different reasons and with varying degrees of intensity) to the ideals of social peace and international co-operation. In this sense it could be argued that, after the First World War, social and political conditions were just as propitious for the development of peace movements in France as in Britain and the United States. If anything, France should have led the way: after all, she lost a considerably greater proportion of her adult population between 1914 and 1918 than either of these two countries, and the damage to her infrastructure (particularly in those departments which had been close to the battle front) was also of a vastly higher magnitude. Every commune erected a war memorial after 1918, and these grim relics seemed to underscore the survivors' determination to avoid a repetition of what had passed. Yet the 1920s and 1930s saw little in France to match the activities of Dick Sheppard's Peace Pledge Union in Britain. To understand why peace movements of a similar nature did not develop in France after 1918, it is first necessary to return to the second half of the nineteenth century; more specifically, to the event which transformed the character of French politics in several important respects: the defeat of France by Prussia in 1871.

THE IMPACT OF THE FRANCO-PRUSSIAN WAR

The defeat of France by Wilhelminite troops had many critical consequences in the character of French politics in the late nineteenth and early twentieth centuries. The most significant impact of the humiliating defeat suffered by the French Army was the collapse of Napoleon's Second Empire and the eventual emergence of the Republic after 1875. But the Franco-Prussian war also durably transformed many of the central parameters of the intellectual debate in France about war and peace. Three aspects are particularly worthy of mention. First, the Army became a focus of national pride and popular mobilization, in ways which had not been witnessed under previous regimes. Nationalists in the Ligue des Patriotes looked forward to the day when the lost territories of Alsace-Lorraine would be returned to the motherland, and these revanchist feelings were shared by many politicians. Republicans hoped that the Army would contribute to the levelling of social hierarchies by forcing men of different classes (and regions) to live together within the same institution. Textbooks in State schools presented glowing images of French soldiers and officers, not only in the context of the imperative of recapturing Alsace-Lorraine, but also as a means of glorifying the exploits of French troops in the acquisition of colonies in Africa and Asia. It is true that, during the 1880s and 1890s, many high-ranking Army officers (such as General Boulanger) were actively involved in attempts to destabilize the Republic, and this naturally provoked hostile responses within the republican camp. But a distinction should be drawn between republican attitudes towards the military establishment and their conception of the Army as a public institution. The Dreyfus Affair confirmed republican suspicions that the military elite was still markedly hostile to the existing political system, but this did not drive republican politicians towards anti-militarism. On the contrary, the Army continued to be regarded as a valuable public institution, and indeed the military establishment was pilloried precisely because it was seen to have diverted the Army from its proper social and national role.

The second important consequence of the 1871 defeat was to make Germany one of the central subjects of internal political debates about national security. After the Franco-Prussian war French concerns about the security of her borders were no longer expressed in abstract terms: she now had a clearly defined continental enemy, whose diplomatic objectives (both within and beyond Europe) were regarded as potentially injurious to French interests. The defeat of 1871 led to the development of anti-German sentiments throughout French society, but these did not necessarily culminate in a yearning for military confrontation with Germany. If anything, the display of German military and political superiority inspired intellectuals and politicians to emulate

German successes. The historian Hippolyte Taine (1828–93) explored the past to find the possible cultural causes of German superiority; the writer Ernest Renan (1823–92) gazed enviously at the place accorded to science and learning in Prussia; and the sociologist Emile Durkheim (1858–1917) derived many of his key concepts from categories of German social thought. French Socialists continued to regard Germany as the country of Marx and the Second International, where the SPD enjoyed political and institutional advantages which the fragmented Socialist movement in France could only envy. It was true that most Frenchmen yearned for the return of the lost territories of Alsace-Lorraine, but there was little agreement on the means of achieving this objective. A minority of aggressive nationalists (such as Paul Déroulède and his Ligue des Patriotes) believed in using force if necessary, but most simply hoped that the matter would be resolved through diplomatic methods. None the less, Germany provided the focus for French debates about her future and security after 1871. Britain had long been regarded as the country which was most hostile to French interests, and the incidence of Anglophobia did not disappear entirely during the late nineteenth and early twentieth centuries, despite the signing of the Entente Cordiale in 1904. But Germany appeared increasingly as the immediate menace. Its status as a permanent threat to French national integrity was enhanced after the First World War, and further reinforced by the events of 1940–4.

The third lasting consequence of the Franco-Prussian war was to compel forces of 'movement' in France to re-evaluate the importance of nationalism. As has been seen in Chapter 5, the pervasiveness of nationalism in France was reflected in the capacity of different institutional and ideological groups to adapt nationalist ideas and concepts to their particular world-views. For much of the nineteenth century politicians and intellectuals took an optimistic and expansive view of nationalism. The forces of 'movement', in particular, continued in the universalist tradition of 1789 by equating the interests of the French nation with those of the international community. During the Second Empire most republicans supported the principle of national self-determination for Italy because they saw no contradiction between the interests of different national communities. Following in the tradition of Voltaire and Condorcet, they believed that wars were caused by corrupt and autocratic rulers. As soon as political institutions became genuinely representative (of national character), international conflicts would end, because the *volonté générale* was inherently paci-fistic. The Franco-Prussian war effected a fundamental change in traditional modes of thought on the question of nationalism. On the whole, nationalism in France became more strident, pessimistic, and at times even aggressive. This was particularly true of the forces of 'order', but the phenomenon was so powerful that the republican camp could not afford to ignore it. This was particularly the case, given that the final defeat of French troops in early 1871 occurred under the republican government of National Defence. In consequence, the pro-nouncements of French forces of 'movement' on nationalism became much more defensive: the republican movement came under increas-ing pressure to demonstrate its practical commitment to the interests of the French nation. Socialists remembered their Jacobin ancestry, and politicians such as Jules Guesde proclaimed their dual attachment to the universalist ideals of Marxism and the particularist interests of the French nation. (It was, in this sense, no accident that Guesde rallied his party to the Union Sacrée in 1914.) But the group which was most critically affected by the change in mood on the national question was the Radical movement. Its urban social constituency (especially the rising middle classes) was particularly receptive to the sirens of nationalism, and Radical politicians always did their best to echo the popular sentiments of their electorate. The result was that they often played up their nationalist credentials for the sake of their local audiences (as noted before, the images and symbols of 1789 were of immense value in this respect) even if the governments they formed (and supported) almost invariably refused to be led down the path of bellicism.

In sum, the defeat of 1871 revived the country's attachment to its Army, gradually turned Germany into France's main continental enemy, and made the French forces of movement (especially their Radical component) more attentive to the question of nationalism. The effect of the Great War was merely to accentuate these tenden-cies. The long and bitter conflict with Germany sealed the reconcili-ation of France with its Army: only then did it become possible for Philippe Pétain to emerge as a national republican hero after 1918. Germany remained an object of fascination and distrust, despite grow-ing disagreements during the 1930s (both within and between parties) over how Nazi expansionism should be contained. These factors clearly militated against the development of peace organizations of a scale comparable to the British and American movements. But these were not the only considerations which limited the growth of peace organizations in France between 1919 and 1940. As will be argued in the next section, a number of important changes in the structure of domestic politics also had a critical impact on the parameters of the debate about war and peace. These modifications were brought about by institutional transformations on the Left, changing attitudes towards Germany on the Right, and, perhaps most important, growing fears of social revolution among the middle classes.

CHANGING TERMS OF THE DEBATE AFTER 1918

Despite the effects of the Franco-Prussian and world wars, France remained richly endowed with 'objective' inspirations for pacifism after 1918. The Great War crippled the country's human and material resources, and anti-war feelings were widespread among those who survived the gruelling experience of the front. In the 1920s the combined membership of the two largest ex-servicemen's associations was 900,000—a far greater level of active support than could be claimed by any political party. Every year, on 11 November, hundreds of thousands of men, women, and children united in a silent tribute to the dead, and the political elite could not fail to notice the passionate sentiments which gave rise to such gatherings. The search for European peace was given a high priority by politicians such as Aristide Briand (1862–1932), the most eloquent representative of a liberal internationalist approach which sought to promote peace through the diplomatic mechanisms of the League of Nations. But this irenic quest was not the exclusive preserve of those politicians who made the search for peace their first priority. In a sense, it may be argued that the sombre memories of the immediate postwar era remained a powerful influence on the outlook of the political and military establishment throughout the interwar period. It was this mood which contributed to the Army's defensive strategy, which culminated in the drawing of the Maginot Line. It was a similar sentiment which clouded and often distorted the vision of defencists such as the Socialist Léon Blum and the Radical Edouard Daladier, who allowed their judgement to be blinded between 1933 and 1940 by their instinctive hatred of war and violence; finally, it was the same spontaneous opposition to war which inspired the actions of the small groups of 'integral' pacifists during the 1920s and 1930s.

Why did these widespread social aspirations not produce as strong a peace movement as in Britain? By far the most important factor was the relative influence of the Communist Party. As will be noted in Chapter 11, the French Communist Party (PCF) developed into a powerful social and political movement by 1936. Throughout the interwar period the PCF was at the forefront of political campaigns to promote international peace. During the 1920s the party valiantly attempted to rally public opinion in defence of the new Soviet state, and mounted a strong (albeit ineffective) campaign against the colonial policy of French governments. The PCF was never committed to an absolute pacifist stance: violence was always considered an acceptable means of bringing about its goals (even if that goal was peace). Thus the party took up the cudgels of anti-militarism and revolutionary defeatism, and urged French soldiers engaged in colonial conflicts in Africa and Asia to turn their weapons against their real enemy: the French bourgeois State. Similarly, after 1934 the party's advocacy of a 'Popular Front' to defend European peace against fascism (typified by the slogan 'bread, peace, and liberty') was constantly accompanied by stern injunctions that force might be needed to achieve this objective. Until early 1939 the PCF was the only French party which was united in opposing appeasement; Communist deputies voted *en bloc* against the Munich agreement in September 1938. In this sense the PCF could at best be described as pacificist: its opposition to war was conditional, not absolute. It often used the language of peace and co-operation to further its political objectives: domestically, to appeal to an increasingly wider social constituency (not only workers but also Catholics, the lower and middle bourgeoisie, and intellectuals); on the international front, to protect the national interests of the Soviet state.

The PCF's instrumental conception of peace did much to damage the prospects of mass mobilization on pacifist themes. Genuine pacifists could never identify fully with Communism because the party's commitment to peace was always conditional upon other priorities: the promotion of international revolution during the 1920s and the struggle against fascism in the 1930s. Neither of these goals could be achieved without violence, making any compromise between 'integral' pacifists and the party almost impossible. Furthermore, even those fellow-travellers who were prepared to accompany the PCF for at least part of the journey were rapidly disconcerted by the ease with which the party could shift its positions on key issues. Rabid anti-militarists were astonished when the PCF embraced the principle of national defence less than twenty-four hours after the signature of the Stalin-Laval pact in 1935. Anti-colonial campaigners were similarly startled when the PCF suddenly discovered the absolute merits of French civilization during the Popular Front era (although, in fairness, this rediscovery was more consistent with the benign view of colonialism articulated in the classical Marxist tradition). Anti-Fascists were completely demoralized in 1939 by the news that the Soviet Union's non-aggression pact with Hitler had been wholeheartedly endorsed by the PCF. Thus the PCF spoke the language of peace, but its actions tended to suggest that this was simply a means to another (and often less honourable) end.

The appropriation of pacifist ideas and themes by a party pursuing radically different objectives did not occur only on the Left. The problem was compounded by the fact that, for entirely different reasons, important sections of the Right also used anti-war language to further their political objectives, especially during the 1930s. There was a profound historical irony in this evolution, given that the aggressive and pessimistic brand of French nationalism which emerged after 1871 was essentially created and sustained by the Right. This tradition of inflexible nationalism did not disappear entirely after 1918. For much of the 1920s it was reflected in Poincaré's harsh policies towards Germany; in the late 1930s a very small band of right-wing nationalists (most notably Paul Reynaud, Georges Mandel, and Henri de Kerillis—the latter being the only non-Communist parliamentarian to vote against the Munich agreement in 1938) actively campaigned against the Hitlerian threat. But most of their colleagues looked away, and advocated appeasement as a means of maintaining the peace in Europe. The reasons for this widespread passiveness were varied. Pierre-Etienne Flandin (1889–1958) feared that France would certainly lose any war against Germany: the only sensible policy was therefore to remain on good terms with Hitler. Philippe Henriot (1889–1944) echoed the feelings of many of his colleagues when he maintained that the most pressing threat to French security came not from Germany but the Soviet Union. The extreme Right took this position to its logical conclusion after 1940 by supporting collaboration with Germany as the only means of preserving French society from Bolshevism. Beneath these differences in emphasis lurked the common thread of anti-communism. As the Third Republic advanced into the 1930s an increasingly large number of right-wing politicians lost their sense of identification with a regime which they regarded as dominated by 'foreign' interests (more specifically, those of Jews and Communists). As the Catholic intellectual Emmanuel Mounier wrote in late 1938, shortly after the Munich agreement, 'one cannot understand the attitude of our bourgeoisie unless one hears it muttering under its breath: "rather Hitler than Blum".'

Important though they were, these ideological and institutional realignments within both the Left and the Right are not sufficient to explain the failure of organized pacifism in France during the interwar period. The appropriation of irenic language by mainstream parties did much to damage the pacifist cause, but this problem could have been overcome if social pressures for promoting international peace and co-operation had been more powerful among the middle classes. Of course, intellectuals such as Romain Rolland and Alain (Émile Chartier) did their best to popularize pacifist ideals, and organizations such as the Association de la Paix par le Droit attempted to spread the gospel of peace to the educated strata. But the French middle classes never warmed to pacifist doctrines with the same enthusiasm as their counterparts in Britain and the United States during the interwar period. There were both institutional and sociological reasons for this relative detachment. The Radical Party, the resolute protector of the interests of the French middle classes, was always eager to assert its nationalist credentials as a means of buttressing its position in the political system. As argued earlier, the Radical brand of nationalism was relatively moderate in its expression and aspirations, and rarely assumed the bellicist overtones of the chauvinist Right. However, the saliency of the question of national defence made it imperative for the party to adopt a firm stance on the issue to avoid being outflanked by its more vociferous competitors. Perhaps even more critical to the middle classes than the issue of national defence was the question of social change. The events of 1871 reminded the middle classes in France that social revolution was no chimera, but a serious possibility which constantly had to be guarded against. France became a Republic after 1875 not because the majority of the population embraced the ideals of the republican movement, but because conservative republicans such as Thiers were able to convince the middle classes that the Republic would better protect them against social revolution than would a revived monarchy or a discredited empire. The regime which emerged was thus, to use an expression of the time, both profoundly republican and profoundly conservative. This social and political defensiveness of the French middle class was accentuated during the interwar period. During the 1920s and especially the 1930s France began to acquire a large-scale urban proletariat, and the Communist Party was able to capitalize on these underlying socio-economic transformations to develop into a mass organization. How far these emerging forms of organized class-consciousness were pushing in the direction of radical change is a question over which debate has been heated; fortunately, a ready answer is not needed for the purposes of this argument. What mattered was that the perceptions of the middle classes became increasingly clouded by the threat of a social revolution sponsored by the PCF. These fears culminated in the heady days of April–May 1936, when the wave of strikes which spread across the whole country seemed to many to herald the end of bourgeois order. The Republic no longer appeared capable of fulfilling the task which had been discharged so effectively by the first generation of republican leaders: the protection of the interests of the middle classes against the claims of the lower orders.

This growing fear of social revolution during the interwar period prevented the French middle classes from investing their political passions in the relative luxury of pacifism. Taken in conjunction with previous claims about the appropriation of irenic discourse by parties and groups whose objectives were often far from consistent with the basic premises of pacifist ideology, this argument completes the explanation of the relative failure of organized pacifism in France between 1918 and 1940. The problem was not simply that genuine pacifists lacked the organizational power to influence large sections of society, but that the primary audience became far less receptive to the sirens of pacifism than their nineteenth-century forebears. This erosion of public empathy was compounded by the selective and instrumental use of pacifist discourse by mainstream parties and groups.

PACIFISM AND THE CONSTRAINTS OF HISTORY

This historical legacy is of vital significance in assessing the limits of organized pacifistic activity in France after 1944. Despite initial appearances, the hiatus between the Third and Fourth Republics was quite modest. The political system which emerged after the resistance inherited a great deal from its immediate predecessor; thus many of the institutional factors inhibiting the growth of a unified peace movement continued to prevail. The political and ideological effects of the experiences of occupation and resistance (1940–4) were surprisingly short-lived, especially when compared to the radical transformations which affected the body politic after 1870–1 (most notably a transition to a new regime, accompanied by a complete overhaul in political and administrative personnel). Following the Liberation, furthermore, neither the Left nor the Right were affected by ideological realignments of a similar magnitude to the momentous changes of the late nineteenth century. As will be seen subsequently, the Cold War soon cut across the short-lived unity of the resistance period, and very rapidly allowed the defeated Right to re-emerge as a major force in the political system. The only significant difference was that many on the Right now wished to forget their association with the discredited experiences of collaboration, and this provided right-wing politicians with a strong impetus to drape themselves in the garb of nationalism.

The Fourth Republic did not, however, passively reproduce the ideological cleavages of the interwar period: the terms of the debate about war and peace were changed (at times quite dramatically) by domestic and international events after 1944. However, all these developments served to reinforce existing structural obstacles to the development of pacifism in France. For example, concerns about national security continued to be highlighted by political groups on both sides of the traditional ideological divide. Fears about the revival of German militarism were sufficiently strong to contribute to the rejection of the European Defence Community agreement by the French National Assembly in 1954. Furthermore, it is worth noting that France remained at war almost without interruption between 1945 and 1962. It is true that the colonial wars fought by the Fourth Republic in Indochina, Madagascar, and the Maghreb did not capture the attention and imagination of the French public until relatively late (in the Algerian case, until it became too late). None the less, the mere fact that the country was at war considerably raised the stakes of political action in favour of peace, thus making pacifist campaigners vulnerable to charges of treacherous and anti-national behaviour.

The political unity fostered by the resistance was rapidly overshadowed by the onset of the Cold War, whose ramifications in France were probably the central inhibiting factor in the development of a non-partisan peace movement. The first major consequence of the Cold War in France, as in the rest of the Western world, was to arouse fears of Soviet expansionism. In Britain and the United States this factor alone was sufficient to make widespread promotional activity in favour of peace almost impossible during the late 1940s and 1950s. In the poisonous atmosphere of the MacCarthy period any principled statement of opposition to the use of military force was regarded as 'un-American' and therefore treacherous. It was only the combined effects of the attenuation of the Cold War and the polarization of American society produced (principally) by the Vietnam war which allowed pacifist undercurrents to come out in the open in the 1960s. Similarly in Britain, it was no accident that the Campaign for Nuclear Disarmament emerged just at the point when the Cold War was beginning to give way to a tentative *rapprochement* between East and West. In other words, it was only when the fear of Soviet expansionism in Europe began to recede that the type of pacifistic activity sponsored by CND could appear legitimate in the eyes of the traditionally anti-Communist British Left. Paradoxically, it was only in the late 1940s and 1950s that France witnessed the development of a mass peace movement; and the circumstances which made this paradox possible also explain why the considerable audience enjoyed by the French Mouvement de la Paix dwindled considerably in subsequent decades. The simple explanation of this different pattern was that French Communists became the dominant force on the Left after the Liberation, and used their political, ideological, and organizational resources to build a mass peace organization which could act as a 'transmission belt' for the party. Following its withdrawal from government in 1947, the PCF became increasingly marginalized within the political system. In these circumstances the preservation of the party's links with its secondary associations became imperative. The peace movement appeared as the most promising conduit for this enterprise for several reasons. Objective circumstances were propitious: as mentioned earlier, France was at war throughout the duration of the Fourth Republic, and the party could appeal to the traditional anti-militarist feelings of left-wing activists. Furthermore, the end of the Second World War had brought home the dangers of nuclear warfare in Europe. The party was able to capitalize on these fears by launching the Stockholm Appeal against nuclear weapons in 1950, which was spearheaded by prestigious intellectuals and received 9.5 million signatures in France alone (this represented more than twice the size of the Communist electorate). To these practical considerations was added the tactical necessity of protecting the interests of the Soviet Union and its East European satellites, who were on the defensive after their illegal seizure of power in the late 1940s. Soviet propaganda throughout the Cold War alleged that the 'imperialist' camp intended to launch a military attack against the peace-loving Communist world; this message was powerfully relayed by the PCF-sponsored peace movement in France.

The PCF's direction of the peace movement's strategy and tactics, and the particular circumstances in which this leadership was exercised during the Stalinist era, severely undermined both the short- and long-term prospects of the peace movement in France. In the short term the most important negative consequence of the party's steward-ship of the Mouvement de la Paix was that the attempt to create a positive image for Soviet foreign policy was undertaken in the worst possible political context: precisely at the moment when fears of Com-munist expansionism in Europe (and beyond) were at their greatest. The Cold War context also ensured that the strategic subordination of the peace movement allowed almost minimal scope for autonomous action, and was thus more comprehensive than might arguably have been the case if the political environment had been less inimical to the PCF. The reason for the party's strong reliance on the peace movement was that its isolation in the party system was almost com-plete after 1947: hence the compelling need to use social movements as alternative conduits for the pursuit of the party's political objectives. In the longer term, the strategic alignment of the French peace move-ment on the PCF created a number of serious obstacles to the retention of a sizeable core of non-Communist pacifists within the fold. The PCF's continuing organizational control of the peace movement also prevented the development of a less overtly partisan form of pacifism during the 1950s and 1960s. During the Algerian conflict, for example, despite strong support among many party activists, the Communist leadership rejected an anti-militarist strategy and urged its members to attempt to influence the direction of events from within the Army (a hopelessly inadequate tactic, which simply resulted in Communists colluding in the perpetration of atrocities against Algerians). The result was that pacifist campaigners were forced to operate outside the party organization, and this severely weakened the thrust of the anti-war movement in France. Indeed, the symbiotic relationship between the party and the peace movement at the height of the Stalinist era made the Mouvement de la Paix vulnerable to the same accusations as were levelled against the PCF: ideological dogmatism, complete subordi-nation to the interests of a foreign power, and, perhaps most important for a movement which appealed to moral sentiments, acting in bad faith. During the Cold War pacifism in France was thus contaminated by the worst excesses of Stalinism, in stark contrast to the situation in both Britain and the United States. A good example of this type of problem was the embarrassment faced by the peace movement in trying to explain away Soviet aggressive actions. The Soviet invasions of Hungary in 1956 and Afghanistan in 1980 were noisily approved by the PCF, and the peace movement was urged to follow the Communist lead, at considerable cost to the credibility of the organization.

Another glaring inconsistency which was forced upon the French peace movement by the PCF for much of the postwar era was the selective nature of its protests against nuclear weapons. Again unlike CND, the French movement focused its campaigns exclusively on the nuclear arsenal of the West. The existence of a sizeable stockpile of tactical and strategic nuclear weapons in the Soviet Union and Eastern Europe was never presented as a problem in itself, only as a justifiable response to the aggressive intentions of the NATO alliance. The PCF's contortions over the question of the French *force de frappe* constituted a particular source of embarrassment to the peace movement. For much of the Fifth Republic the PCF was opposed to French possession of an independent nuclear deterrent, and this was consistent with its general view of Western nuclear policy. In 1977, with the same startling rapidity as in 1935 on the question of national defence, the PCF announced that it would retain a nuclear capacity if elected to office. The French peace movement was forced to adjust to this sudden change of policy with customary diligence, and shortly afterwards was made to launch a campaign against the NATO siting of Cruise and Pershing missiles in Western Europe. Again, this campaign simply echoed the apprehensions of the Soviet Union, and made little attempt to deal with the broader strategic context of the problem, notably the issue of Soviet SS-20s. A further negative consequence of the PCF's stewardship of the Mouvement de la Paix followed from the party's organizational hegemony over the Left during the 1950s and 1960s. The PCF's political and ideological dominance during this period prevented the emergence of alternative forms of mass political protest; thus a peace movement which was not strategically aligned upon the PCF could develop only at the point when Communism (in its Stalinist form) ceased to dominate the political and intellectual horizons of the French Left. From this perspective the decisive rupture occurred with the events of May 1968, which initiated the fragmentation of left-wing political culture in France. It was no accident that the anti-nuclear movement established itself as a prominent extra-parliamentary force in 1971; a number of equally significant 'new social movements' emerged during the same period. However, this flowering of issue-based politics proved to be relatively short-lived; by the late 1970s the rejuvenated Socialist Party (PS) had occupied the institutional vacuum created by the fragmentation of left-wing political culture. In so doing, however, the Socialists frustrated the further development of pacifist undercurrents. Indeed, during the 1970s the PS did little consciously to revive the pacifist tradition of the French Socialist movement. The party leader, François Mitterrand, was strongly committed to the principle of national defence and France's membership of the Atlantic alliance. Meanwhile, the left wing of the Socialist Party (led by Jean-Pierre Chevènement's CERES movement) was also deeply committed to the tradition of Jacobin nationalism. After his election to the French presidency in 1981, Mitterrand's domestic and foreign policies offered little comfort to those on the Left with pacifist or even neutralist sympathies. Part of the reason for his suspicion of French pacifism lay in his deep-seated belief that the peace movement was subordinated to the interests of the PCF (and ultimately the Soviet Union). It was this consideration which prompted the President, shortly after his election, to urge Socialists to sever all links with the PCF-sponsored Mouvement de la Paix. But Mitterrand's strategy was not simply reactive: his defence and foreign policies were derived from a vision of France's role in the world which was, in many respects, inspired by the Gaullian principle of national self-assertion.

This reference to the world-view of the General provides an opportune point of transition to another key inhibiting force in the development of pacifist ideas and values during the 1960s and 1970s: the achievements (and ideological legacy) of de Gaulle. The articulation of a distinctive nationalist ideology after 1958 was one of the essential instruments of de Gaulle's successful bid for political hegemony. His particular *idée de la France* was formulated in terms of a strategic requirement for nuclear self-sufficiency, political independence from the United States, and a powerful French presence in the developing world. De Gaulle left such a strong mark on political and governmental structures that many of these principles became welded into the institutions of the Fifth Republic: hence, for example, the overwhelming elements of continuity which characterized the defence policies of his successors. The Gaullist legacy severely damaged the prospects of a non-Communist form of pacifism in several essential respects. First, de Gaulle rapidly responded to the social and political problems which arose from the ending of French rule in Algeria after 1962. As mentioned earlier, the issue of conscientious objection was resolved; delinquent Army officers were pardoned; and Algerian *pied-noirs* were resettled in the metropolis. At the conclusion of a long war which had brought the country to the verge of civil strife, it was conceivable that strong pacifist undercurrents would emerge in French society; after all, the end of the two world wars had produced (very different but equally powerful) upsurges in pacifist sentiment. But the terms on which the Gaullist reconstruction of French political institutions was engineered excluded even the possibility of compromise with pacifist ideology. De Gaulle's highly successful coalition was cemented by a powerful nationalist ideology in which the universalist pretensions of the French republican tradition were strongly reaffirmed. In this sense, de Gaulle was successful not only in forging an effective political coalition on these terms, but also in placing claims about French grandeur at the centre of political debate. The Left could not ignore the popularity of the Gaullian vision of France's role in the world, and by the late 1970s Socialists and even Communists had accepted the basic parameters of French defence and foreign policies.

There was perhaps a more important sense in which the terms of the Gaullist reconstruction of the French Right excluded the possibility of compromise with pacifist ideology. It was argued earlier that one of the key factors which prevented the widespread dissemination of pacifism among the French middle classes during the Third Republic was the fear of social revolution. Always an astute political tactician, de Gaulle was conscious that large sections of his electorate remained fearful of the prospect of radical social change. Thus his domestic political platform during the 1960s relied heavily on the instinctive fear of the forces of 'movement' in French society. It was clear that the sentiments and values which made for empathy with pacifism were radically at odds with the fear of imminent revolutionary change. During the 1960s the French right-wing electorate continued to regard the prospect of radical social change with considerable foreboding. The decade witnessed important transformations in the French industrial infrastructure, and some of these adjustments led to an attenuation of the intensity of class conflict. Yet, despite a significant rise in standards of living, these changing material circumstances were not sufficient to offset widespread fears of social revolution. De Gaulle played on these concerns to buttress his domestic political support, and this tactic proved highly effective. This was best demonstrated by the outcome of the 1968 *élections de la peur*, which returned an absolute majority for the Gaullist party after a campaign dominated by (entirely spurious) fears of an imminent Communist revolution.

A FRUSTRATED TRADITION

The claims put forward in this chapter are both negative (with respect to many prevailing hypotheses about the absence of peace movements in France) and affirmative (in the sense of suggesting alternative explanations). From the former perspective it has been claimed that it would be unrewarding to argue that substantive inhibitions on the development of pacifist organizations were either cultural or religious. Neither the existence of powerful nationalist undercurrents nor the prevalence of a distinctive Catholic culture can be demonstrated to have precluded the growth of pacifist sentiments at different moments in the history of modern France. It is even less plausible to suggest that the ideological and institutional legacy of 1789 had any bearing on the issue: as shown earlier, the republican tradition was able to accommodate pacifist groups in its midst (particularly during the interwar period). In sum, it has been suggested that France was not significantly different from either Britain or the United States in terms of the potential for the emergence of organized pacifism. Throughout the Republican era, important sections of society either directly advocated pacifist ideas or held views which were consistent with fundamental pacifist objectives.

A number of historical, sociological, and institutional factors prevented these widespread aspirations from being translated into a unified peace movement. The first was the sheer diversity of pacifist discourse, ranging from fundamentalist expressions of absolute aversion to the use of force to the calculated and manipulative pseudo-pacifism of the Communist Party. Rather like nationalism, however, the apparent unity of irenic discourse masked significant divergences between different ideological systems over the relative ordering of pacifist concepts. A working-class anti-militarist campaigner of the late nineteenth century was completely removed from the universe inhabited by a liberal internationalist such as Léon Bourgeois, who believed that peace would naturally flow from enhanced political and economic co-operation between states. In the modern era similarly,

Communist, Christian, and environmentalist forms of pacifism operated within fundamentally different value systems, and these disparate groups remained sufficiently suspicious of each other's ulterior motives to prevent the emergence of any durable form of political collaboration. To put it slightly differently, pacifism was not an independent variable in the political system: its incidence was always connected to the expression of a primary set of ideological concerns. From a sociological perspective pacifism was not sufficiently salient as an issue to enable the transcendence of the different social identities (and interests) of peace campaigners.

Why not? At this juncture historical and institutional factors come into play. Repeated experiences of war and occupation were in many ways conducive to the emergence of pacifist sentiments; however, it was the outcomes of these campaigns for peace which often provoked a backlash against the concept of pacifism. The generation which survived the First World War was so determined to wage 'war against war' during the 1920s and 1930s that it allowed itself to be humiliated by Nazi troops in 1940. Thus, after 1944, pacifism was associated with shameful memories of defeatism and collaboration, which were expunged by a vigorous affirmation of French patriotic fervour (and the creation of the myth of *la France résistante*, entertained for different reasons both by Communists and Gaullists). From an institutional perspective the political and ideological influence of the Communist Party severely damaged prospects for the emergence of a unified peace movement. Because the Mouvement de la Paix remained under the thumb of the PCF, the most successful form of organized pacifism in France was tarred with the brush of Stalinism. In the 1960s the Gaullist resurrection of French prestige altered the terms of the political debate about questions of defence and foreign policy, forcing the French Left in particular to redefine its concepts in these areas. But pacifism could never be divorced from broader considerations of social order. Thus it has been claimed here that the importance of the Gaullian era lay less in its formulation of a coherent nationalist ideology than in the nature of its appeal to the political sentiments and values of a broad cross-section of the electorate. As in the interwar period, these social strata remained hypnotized by the fear of social change, and such a disposition was radically at odds with the necessary preconditions for empathy with pacifism.

In sum, a united pacifist movement in France required a set of catalysing circumstances, a strong internal organization, a relatively coherent vision of the world, an appeal to a clear social constituency, and an elite which was capable of exercising strategic leadership over the movement. As has been shown in this chapter, the tragedy of French pacifism was that it was never able to meet all of these conditions at any one time.

Chronology

1792   April. Declaration of war against Austria: beginning of French revolutionary wars.

1815   June. Second abdication of Napoleon after defeat at Waterloo.

1869   April. Belleville Manifesto of Radical movement advocates abolition of standing armies.

1870   September. Defeat of French troops at Sedan: end of Second Empire.

1871   May. Bloody end of the Paris Commune.
       July. Bishops urge National Assembly to help restore temporal powers of the Pope.

1882   February. Foundation of Ligue des Patriotes.

1887–9 Challenge to the Republic by General Boulanger and his supporters.

1914   August. Government of national unity formed after outbreak of First World War.

1923   January. French occupation of the Ruhr initiated by Poincaré.

1925–6 Communists denounce French suppression of Abd-el-Krim insurrection in Morocco.

1935   May. Stalin-Laval agreement converts PCF to a policy of national defence.

1936   May. Election of Popular Front government.
       October. Beginning of Spanish Civil War.

1938   September. Munich agreement.

1939   August. Nazi-Soviet pact endorsed by PCF.

1940   May–June. French military defeat by Germany; collapse of Third Republic.

1942   November. Entire French territory occupied by Axis troops.

1944   August. Liberation of Paris.

1949   April. Launching of international Communist campaign for peace and neutrality.

1950   March. Stockholm Appeal against nuclear weapons raises 9.5 million signatures in France.

1954   July. Rejection of European Defence Community by National

Assembly.

November. Outbreak of the Algerian war.

1956   November. Soviet intervention in Hungary approved by PCF.

1960   September. Intellectuals' 'manifesto of 121' advocates desertion to avoid conscription in Algeria.

1962   June. De Gaulle sponsors bill on conscientious objection.

1971   Launching of several ecological groups.

1973   August. Large environmentalist march on Larzac plateau.

1977   May. PCF endorses French possession of nuclear deterrent.

1980   January. PCF approves Soviet invasion of Afghanistan; beginning of Communist campaign against siting of Cruise and Pershing missiles in Europe.

1983   January. Mitterrand's *Bundestag* speech denounces pacifism and neutralism, and reaffirms French commitment to Alliance defence policy.

1991   January. Overwhelming public support for active French involvement in Gulf war.

CHAPTER 8

Liberalism and the Elusive Search for Consensus

Searching for liberals in France can be a trying exercise. After the advent of a stable parliamentary system in France (under the Third Republic) a mainstream Liberal Party did not emerge, as happened in Britain and in many other West European countries. As will be shown later, there were some French approximations to the Liberal paradigm, such as the Radical Party during the Third Republic and the Mouvement Républicain Populaire (MRP) during the Fourth. But the concept of liberalism was not always at the centre of their political discourse, let alone their practice. The waters were muddied even further by the appropriation of the concept by groups whose association with the traditional canons of liberal ideology was often tenuous. At the turn of the century, for instance, the Action Populaire Libérale was one of five major electoral organizations in France. It was anything but a repository of classical liberal values: most of its parliamentarians were former monarchists who had rallied to the Republic to defend the interests of the Catholic Church. The definition of liberalism was (and remains) notoriously elastic, but, throughout the nineteenth century at least, most of its exponents consistently opposed the assumption of significant political functions by the monarchy and the Church. That a French party could claim to be the inheritor of both of these *ancien régime* institutions and yet still proclaim itself 'liberal' was a telling indication of the confusion and ambiguity which surrounded the use of the concept in France.

At an ideological level the picture was equally confusing. Even those intellectuals whose views conformed strikingly to many classical liberal values seemed reluctant to identify with the concept. The publicist Alain (Émile Chartier), a member of the Radical Party, held quintessentially (classical) liberal views on a range of fundamental questions: he believed in the inalienable rights of the individual, regarded private property as the foundation of a stable political order, urged his fellow-countrymen to restrain the encroachments of public authority into their private lives, warned against the corruptibility of power, promoted the principle of secularism in education, and consistently expressed his sense of moral opposition to war. But he never stressed his ideological affinities with the European liberal tradition—partly out of intellectual parochialism, but also perhaps because, like many French political philosophers, he came to believe in the inherent originality of his thought. The real source of the problem was the absence of a legitimizing liberal discourse in France. Indeed, unlike Socialism (and later Communism), which had its scriptures, hallowed institutions, and historical memories, or even as diffuse a grouping as the counter-revolutionary tradition, which at least shared a common (if ill-defined) aspiration to restore the social and political order destroyed by the French Revolution, liberalism could never rely on a similar range of native practices and myths. As a result, the liberal tradition never acquired a clear and cohesive sense of political identity in France. As will be argued subsequently, the possibility of salvaging a liberal political project from the revolutionary experience was constantly frustrated by the ideological hegemony of the republican Left: until the late 1970s the events of 1789 were essentially appropriated by an intellectual tradition which stressed their inherently radical and revolutionary character. Furthermore, the experiences of both conservative and reformist liberal politicians in the 1830s and 1840s provided few landmarks for posterity. The July Monarchy was celebrated only for the mercenary zeal of its bourgeois elites; the Second Republic's fluttering existence was an enduring testimony to the political *naïveté* of optimistic liberalism. Thus, lacking historical benchmarks of any kind, liberal politicians were always tempted by empiricism: political practice was based not on the pursuit of clear ideological or programmatic objectives, but on the ability to adapt to the particular circumstances in which power had to be exercised. There was only a short step from empiricism of this kind to opportunism, and it was no accident that one strand of the republican movement became known as 'opportunist' during the Third Republic.

So, if French liberalism was not a unified social and ideological movement, and furthermore, many of its apparent practitioners did not even identify with the concept of liberalism, in what sense could it be described as a political tradition at all? Despite their organizational heterogeneity, liberals could be recognized by their tendency to share some of the following beliefs and pursuits: an instinctive attachment to private property, a firm (but not unconditional) confidence in representative government, a marked emphasis on the value of individual rights, a visceral sense of hostility towards strong government, a profound commitment to the principle of secularism, a concern for social justice, and, almost invariably, a tendency to stress the consensual dimension of politics, on the basis of an identification of common aspirations (and common interests) in society. But this common bedrock of principles was never translated into a unified political discourse, essentially because not all liberals agreed that they expressed their core values. Indeed, liberalism was always typified in France by the range and diversity of the undercurrents which were subsumed under its broad banner. Thus a distinction could always be drawn between the doctrinal dimension of liberalism, which was essentially the preserve of intellectuals (especially, as will be seen later, economists), and its practical dimension, which was expressed in popular identification with such quintessentially 'liberal' values as freedom of speech and secularism. At the level of practice a further distinction could be drawn between procedural and substantive conceptions of liberalism: attachment to laws, markets, and electoral mechanisms on one hand, and specific rights and entitlements (such as freedom of association) on the other. (This distinction is useful for classificatory purposes; it is accepted that a strong commitment to markets and laws expresses an attachment to these institutions which is itself substantive in character.) Another enduring dichotomy within the tradition was the contrast between socio-political and economistic conceptions of liberalism, the latter stressing that human fulfilment could be achieved essentially through unfettered entrepreneurial activity under market capitalism, the former emphasizing the redemptive attributes of a political system founded on representative government and the universality of law. This polarity was sometimes (but not always) expressed in the ideological distinction between conservative and progressive forms of liberalism. Conservative liberals tended to be only conditionally attached to the principle of democratic government, and their social programme was largely restricted to the promotion of equality of opportunity. Progressive liberals were inherently committed to the democratic heritage of the Republic, which they also associated with the promotion of greater social and economic justice. Finally, the liberal tradition witnessed an enduring division between statists and associationalists; the former tended towards the view that the various objectives of liberal ideology could be achieved primarily through State intervention, whereas the latter stressed that a true liberal polity could emerge only through an ever-increasing network of secondary associations (both religious and secular in character). These varying conceptions of the process through which liberal institutions could emerge were often articulated by different social groups: statists tended to be concentrated in urban areas and were essentially secular in their outlook, whereas a significant element of the associationalist tendency was based on rural and often religious interests.

No political group which sought to promote the values of consensus and compromise could hope for much encouragement from social and political conditions in nineteenth-century France. The Revolution destroyed traditional social and political structures and, in so doing, created deep and durable fissures which prevented the gradual reconstruction of stable institutions. Cleavages on such basic issues as the constitutional framework, religion, nationalism, and citizenship continued to divide the political community throughout the nineteenth century, and French liberals were faced with the problem of confronting their principles with the exigencies of the time. Thus the application of the principle of equality of conditions was tempered by the fear of its social and political consequences. For example, representative institutions were developed under the July Monarchy, but these were based on an explicitly restricted franchise: only citizens who annually paid at least 200 francs in taxes were allowed to vote. Similarly, the encouragement of independent associational activity in civil society was tempered by the fear of a re-emergence of the traditional social corporations of the *ancien régime* or (even worse) the development of subversive political organizations, such as the secret societies which had recourse to 'direct action' in the early 1830s. Most important, the liberal rejection of strong centralized government came into conflict with the institutional vacuum which frequently emerged at the heart of the French State during the nineteenth century. Liberals were deeply divided over how to respond to the problems posed by this particular aspect of the revolutionary legacy. Many, like Alexis de Tocqueville, pinned their hopes on the gradual development of secondary associations in civil society. This process could be helped along by the State through education and social reform, but it seemed unlikely that public authorities could perform an undertaking of this nature without undermining its original purpose. Statists criticized this approach for its excessive political passivity, and argued that liberal ideas and values could flourish only if State power was first captured and subsequently wielded to create the conditions for a liberal polity. Here lay the seeds of the contradiction which would characterize many of the policies of the Third Republic (education being the prime example): the attempt to create a consensual polity through conflictual and interventionist means.

Enough has already been said to suggest that the absence of a self-styled Liberal Party did not altogether preclude the development of liberal ideas and values in France. Distinct elements of liberal ideology and practice were articulated by a variety of groups, sometimes operating within the same institutional framework (as will be seen below in the case of the Radical Party), but more often dispersed in several parties and associations. Three such liberal strands will be identified in turn: a Radical, a conservative, and a social Catholic tendency.

THE LIBERALISM OF THE RADICAL TRADITION

In April 1869, in the *quartier populaire* of Belleville, a large gathering of electors proclaimed the political manifesto of Radicalism, and vowed to assume 'the glorious heritage of the French Revolution'. Radicalism typified the contradictory diversity of French liberalism in almost paradigmatic form. It had its positivist ideologues, such as Ferdinand Buisson (1841–1932) and Célestin Bouglé (1870–1940), who were inspired by the democratic legacy of the French Revolution (most notably the emphasis on civil equality, mass education, social solidarity, and the rights of man) and sought to infuse the placid political structures of the Third Republic with the rationalist spirit of radical social philosophy. For the ordinary party activist in the Radical *comité*, however, radicalism represented a number of simple but compelling values and practices: social order under bourgeois rule, guaranteed markets for agricultural products, and anticlericalism. The Radical Party was always divided between a progressive and a conservative wing, the latter primarily concerned with order and good government, the former continually inspired by the attempt to bring about greater social justice through institutional reform. This ideological divide in many ways reflected the temperamental difference between political and economic conceptions of liberalism. Despite their undeniable commitment to parliamentary democracy, conservative Radicals such as Edouard Herriot and Edouard Daladier tended to view the safeguard of private property and the promotion of secular education as sufficient conditions of the development of human freedom. On the other hand, their progressive colleagues, such as Léon Bourgeois (and later Pierre Mendès-France) regarded the institutions of modern capitalism as merely necessary, thus requiring the complementary action of the State to produce social outcomes which were genuinely freedom-enhancing. Finally, a further set of divisions were articulated in the contrast between statists and associationalists: most of the Radical elite (whether progressive or conservative) saw the movement's vocation as capturing State power and wielding it to implement the programmatic objectives of the party. In contrast, the associationalist tendency found a worthy advocate in the writings of Émile Chartier (Alain), a schoolteacher and philosopher who, as noted at the beginning of this chapter, advocated direct democracy and constant control of the State by the citizenry. Alain essentially rejected the positivist values which informed the world-view of the heroic generation of republicans during the second half of the nineteenth century; hence his constant denunciation of the 'specialists' and 'administrators' who came to dominate public life during the Third Republic, and his quasi-anarchic strictures against the despotic and tyrannical character of central government. His vision of a liberal polity was predicated upon the growth of intermediate associations at grass-roots level; his conception of small-scale communities governed by the *volonté générale* was a testimony to the enduring influence of Rousseau on French social thought.

These temperamental differences notwithstanding, the essential thrust of radicalism was clearly defined during the initial stages of the movement's existence. The Belleville Manifesto of 1869 was a powerful expression of opposition to political authoritarianism, and its spirit was reflected in the emerging institutional framework of the Third Republic. The document advocated freedom of association, constitutional reform, the separation of Church and State, the dismantling of standing armies, the extension of free education, and the reorganization of the State bureaucracy along meritocratic lines. Although it was founded as a national organization only in 1901, the Radical movement began to flourish during the first two decades of the Third Republic as a network of local political groupings. At first glance the Radicals appeared to have partly fulfilled classical liberal hopes for the emergence of associational activity in French society. The party was based on a loose structure of local committees, which contributed significantly to the enhancement of political participation in France in the late nineteenth and early twentieth centuries. However, this positive contribution to the development of a liberal polity was not sustained. The main reason for this loss of momentum was that the Radical Party's identity gradually became inextricably intertwined with that of the Republican regime, especially between 1902 and 1940. When in government, however, the Radicals often lost sight of the principles on which their movement was founded. This was partly a consequence of political opportunism which, as noted earlier, was a notable feature of the French liberal tradition. For example, Radical statesmen could rail against the tyranny of the State when addressing their local constituency meetings and endorse the views of their philosopher Alain on the corruptibility of political power. But the temptation to exercise such centralized power as was available to Republican governments was not rejected (nor were the lucrative side-effects which often came with political office). While in opposition the Radicals violently denounced the process of colonial expansion; after 1902 they were more than happy to act as the overlords of the newly acquired overseas territories. Two further examples of such institutional continuity were provided in the Radical governments' policies in the fields of education and agriculture, which essentially continued the *dirigiste* trends established by their predecessors after 1880. The paradox of French liberalism was starkly demonstrated in this continued use of centralized State power for the achievement of specific political and cultural ends, and this was the sense in which the Radical Party was never an entirely plausible representation of the European liberal tradition. Furthermore, the party's long association with office led to an erosion of its primary sense of purpose. By the late 1930s its associational activities were reduced to electioneering agencies; more significantly, there were many areas in which the Radicals simply no longer knew what they believed in. Thus the 1936 electoral manifesto of the party called for 'monetary stability' and an increase in the 'purchasing power of the masses'. The Radical Party had come to assume the characteristics of the proverbial radish: red on the outside, white inside, and always close to a dish of butter.

This simultaneous commitment to deflation and reflation was a clear symptom of deep differences within the party leadership over the movement's place in the political system. It was therefore not surprising that the tradition of Radical liberalism declined after 1944, and also suffered from institutional fragmentation. In the 1950s the Radicals split into two main camps. Some followed Edgar Faure

(1908–88), a sparkling opportunist of Third Republican vintage, who was keen to maintain the party's association with political office at almost any cost. Faure became Prime Minister in 1955, and in the Fifth Republic served as de Gaulle's Education Minister and President of the National Assembly. Other Radicals stayed on the centre Left, supporting the political and intellectual *démarche* of Pierre Mendès-France, who sought to modernize the Radical Party by returning to its progressive traditions. The Radical family remained divided thereafter. In the early 1970s there was a further split as the right-wing Radicals, under the charismatic leadership of Jean-Jacques Servan-Schreiber, rapidly moved into the orbit of the presidential coalition, while a breakaway group, the Radicaux de Gauche, signed the Joint Programme of Government with the Socialists and Communists. The right-wing Radicals subsequently became members of the Union pour la Démocratie Française (UDF), a federation of liberal conservative groups which coalesced to fight the 1978 legislative elections under the banner of President Valéry Giscard d'Estaing. During the 1970s and especially the 1980s, on the other hand, the left-wing Radicals were eventually transformed into satellites of the Socialist Party. Radicalism thus became one of the numerous victims of the polarization of French politics after 1958.

The greatest achievement of the radical tradition was also, in many ways, the source of its greatest weakness: the identification of the movement with the Republic itself. This symbiosis contributed significantly towards the propagation of republican values in France, and thus helped to unite large sections of society behind many of the basic principles of French liberalism: constitutional government, the separation of Churches from the State, and the principle of secularism. Radicals also rallied effectively to the defence of the Republic when it was threatened by authoritarian forces (Jean Moulin, one of the heroic figures of the French resistance after 1940, was a member of the Radical Party). But the party's association with the State was so successful and complete that it stifled the creative and dynamic dimension of its liberalism, perhaps vindicating the associationalist claim that there was an essential incompatibility between exercising centralized state power and propagating liberal values in society.

CONSERVATIVE LIBERALISM

The second strand of liberalism was far less assertive and optimistic than the Radical variant. It expressed the attitudes and values of those (essentially bourgeois) groups in French society which accepted the irreversibility of the 1789 Revolution (which distinguished them from the counter-revolutionary tradition), but none the less sought to contain and restrict the application of its principles of liberty, equality, and fraternity. Conservative liberals had no inherent love of liberty: they opposed absolutism essentially because of its wastefulness and inefficiency, and also because its frozen social hierarchies seemed to offer little scope for the upward mobility of impatient and enterprising social groups. In this sense their commitment to the principles of 1789 was strictly minimalist: for example, liberty was seen as a civil rather than political attribute, and thus not necessarily entailing any particular political procedure (such as democracy and universal suffrage); furthermore, the enhancement of social equality through redistribution was firmly disavowed. Thus the subversive connotations which the forces of 'movement' tended to associate with these concepts were always rejected by conservative liberals. Indeed, one of the essential reasons for their involvement in public life was the desire to prevent a recurrence of the social and political anarchy which had attended the radicalization of the French Revolution after 1792. Conservative liberal undercurrents were always haunted by the spectre of the Terror, and these memories of social unrest and political turbulence were resurrected during the days of the 1848 revolution, and again during the Paris Commune of 1871. This recurrent fear of social revolution partly explained the ambivalence with which conservative liberals tended to view the democratic process. It also accounted for the particular savagery with which the Commune was suppressed by the Thiers government in 1871, and the intensity with which conservative liberals feared and loathed Communism throughout the twentieth century.

The origins of the conservative liberal tradition could be traced back to the policies practised under the July Monarchy (hence the depiction of this strand as Orleanist). At its core Orleanism was an expression of the bourgeois attachment to the defence of social stability and the principle of economic freedom. In the nineteenth century the ambiguities of this conservative brand of liberalism were epitomized by the policies of François Guizot (1787–1874), a Sorbonne professor whose tenure as Prime Minister came to an abrupt end with the 1848 revolution. When in opposition Guizot's liberalism was essentially consistent with classical principles: he championed calls for greater freedom and social justice (by which he meant greater opportunities for middle-class advancement) and advocated the creation of a system of representative government. During his tenure of office he took some steps towards increasing the level of literacy in society, but turned his back on most of the principles he had hitherto advocated. He adopted a strict policy of *laissez-faire* in the economy (illustrated by his famous slogan: 'enrich yourselves'), suppressed labour unions and indeed any political activity which threatened the regime, and, as noted earlier, restricted the franchise to ensure the political supremacy of the French bourgeoisie. This package of financial orthodoxy, defence of middle-class interests, and sound management remained at the heart of the conservative liberal tradition after the advent of the Republic in the 1870s. Its practitioners during the Third and Fourth Republics included such figures as Raymond Poincaré, Georges Mandel, Paul Reynaud, and Antoine Pinay, who viewed with hostility any attempt to use the State for reflationary or redistributive purposes. In modern times this brand of conservative liberalism was reflected in Valéry Giscard d'Estaing's Independent Republicans, a grouping formed in 1962. Four years after Giscard d'Estaing became President in 1974, his Republican Party became one of the mainstays of the UDF, which, as noted earlier, came together as an electoral grouping during the legislative contest of 1978. In the 1980s and 1990s there were increasing divisions between the different components of the UDF over leadership and tactics. None the less, the members of the federation essentially shared an underlying sense of affinity with the basic principles of the conservative liberal tradition: sound economic management, commitment to the preservation of social order, and strong attachment to the principle of private enterprise. It was therefore not surprising that efforts to promote economic deregulation and greater use of market instruments by the State were championed during this period by leading UDF figures, notably François Léotard and Alain Madelin.

A subset of this strand of conservative liberalism consisted of individuals and groups whose primary concern lay in monitoring (and when possible influencing) the economic policies of the French State. It was no accident that Valéry Giscard d'Estaing described his Prime Minister Raymond Barre (without any clear sense of irony) as 'the best economist in France'. The academic discipline of economics in France was dominated by the neo-classical tradition; during the nineteenth century its major figures were the economist Michel Chevalier (1806–79) and the financial journalist Paul Leroy-Beaulieu (1843–1916), both liberal Anglophiles who enthusiastically supported the free-trade doctrine of the classical economist Richard Cobden. This neo-classical heritage was assumed by the political and administrative elites of the Third Republic. In the economic sphere the State was generally viewed as an arbiter between competing interests, rather than an actor with a clear set of priorities of its own, and this disposition was borne out in the deflationary policies followed by most governments during this period. As noted in Chapter 6, this form of supply-side economics lost its intellectual hegemony during the first three decades of the post-Liberation era, but regained some prominence in France during the 1970s and 1980s, as part of an international swing against Keynesianism in most advanced industrial societies. Monetarist economists were not the only group who were concerned with the direction of French public policy in this area after 1944. Business pressure groups such as the Conseil National du Patronat Français (CNPF) traditionally had a vested interest in developing a collaborative partnership with the State. CNPF leaders were often militant free marketeers, who sought to reduce the level of state regulation of the French economy, emphasizing the essential social and economic role performed by firms at the micro-economic level and the beneficial effects of competition and deregulation at the macro level. However, the French business community was never entirely committed to the principles of unfettered economic liberalism: there was, and remains, a strong tradition of turning towards the State for protection and assistance. For example, this *mentalité d'assistance* was always preponderant in the agricultural sector, from the days of the Méline protective tariffs of the 1890s to the neo-corporatist practices of the Fifth Republic. By the 1980s, however, many dynamic sectors of French industry had become wholly committed to the principles of economic liberalism, and these forces were given a further boost by agreements to establish a single European market after 1992.

Conservative liberals remained deeply ambivalent about the value of representative institutions for much of the modern era. In the mid-nineteenth century, Guizot typified their equivocation in the face of a democratic upsurge which seemed to threaten the social and economic interests of the bourgeoisie. After 1871 the *ralliement* of the conservative liberals to the Republic was led by Adolphe Thiers, who convinced a sizeable section of the forces of 'order' that the new regime was capable of standing up to the threat of the extreme Left. Under the Republic this strand of the liberal tradition came to occupy a strategic position in the corridors of power, in close alliance with the elites of the Radical Party; its ideological influence was reflected in the relative conservatism of the social policies of the Third Republic. But the republicanism of this conservative liberal tradition was always conditional upon the regime's capacity to deliver social peace and contain the restlessness of the working class. In the 1920s and particularly the 1930s many conservative liberals (such as André Tardieu and Pierre Laval) came to doubt that the republican system could continue to serve the social interests of *status quo* forces, and they began to drift away from the regime. The experiences of war and occupation aggravated these fissures within the conservative liberal community. A small number regarded the Vichy regime as illegitimate, and eventually fought on the side of the resistance, while the majority cowered behind Marshal Pétain until it was neither respectable nor even expedient to do so. But the conservative liberals' attachment to the Republic was again restored under the Fourth Republic, which rapidly abandoned the revolutionary objectives of the resistance after the onset of the Cold War; there was no better symbol of this realignment than the appointment as Prime Minister (in 1952) of Antoine Pinay, the epitome of the fiscal conservatism of the French forces of 'order'. With the expediency which characterized their political alignments, however, the conservative liberals abandoned the Fourth Republic when it ceased to perform its key function of preserving the social and economic *status quo*. For the first decade of the Fifth Republic conservative liberalism came under the influence of the dominant movement of the Right, the Gaullist party. At the height of its ideological and organizational power in the 1960s Gaullism effectively colonized this strand of the conservative liberal tradition under its broad banner. Its representatives in the Gaullist movement were men such as Georges Pompidou and Roger Frey, who typified the virtues of sound economic management and the protection of social order. As noted earlier, the institutional resurgence of conservative liberalism came with the election of Valéry Giscard d'Estaing to the presidency in 1974—a resurgence which also signalled the decline of the Gaullist hegemony on the Right.

Unlike the Radical strand of liberalism, which declined significantly after 1945, conservative liberals retained an important element of influence over the making of public policy in France. The enduring success of this conservative liberal strand since the mid-nineteenth century was essentially a function of three factors: its continuing ability to provide the political elite with leaders who inspired confidence in key sectors of the economy (very often because these leaders were themselves recruited from these sectors); a tendency towards agnosticism on major ideological issues (such as the constitution), which resulted in an almost infinite capacity to adapt to circumstances; finally, and perhaps most importantly, a lasting appeal to the anxieties of those groups in society which felt particularly vulnerable to the economic demands of the forces of 'movement'. In a society which remained divided (and often bitterly so) by class conflict and institutional discontinuities, there was always political space for an ideological undercurrent which appealed to the simple virtues of order, stability, and technical expertise.

THE CONCERNS OF SOCIAL CATHOLICISM

The third strand of French liberalism was expressed in the social Catholic tradition. The origins of this undercurrent stretched deep into the nineteenth century, as reflected in the efforts of Charles de Montalembert (1810–70) and Alphonse de Lamartine (1790–1869) to establish a progressive Catholic movement which could ally itself to the democratic forces of the French Revolution. Its organizational roots could be traced back to the Third Republican groups (such as Marc Sangnier's *Sillon*) which sought to distance themselves from the conservatism of the clericalist establishment. These groups emphasized the need for direct forms of Catholic activism in the political realm (an aspiration which was frowned upon by the Vatican until the late nineteenth century) and a greater sense of receptiveness to the interests of the underprivileged. The social reformism of this strand of the liberal tradition was distinct from the radicalism of the republican (and revolutionary) Left, which sought to introduce a greater measure of social equality by institutional means. (This redistributive project was one of the important legacies of the French Revolution.) It was also at variance with the establishment of the Radical Party, which was theoretically committed (in its Belleville Manifesto of 1869) to the principle of social reform, but took few practical steps in this

direction during its long association with political office after 1902.
The value system of this strand of Catholic liberalism rested on a
number of simple but forceful principles: a belief in social equality,
an attachment to the values of solidarity and co-operation, a sense of
compassion towards the victims of market inequalities, an inveterate
hostility towards all forms of materialism, a reluctance to accept the
social consequences of industrialization, a belief in local and decentralized forms of political action (expressed in the notion of subsidiarity),
and a commitment to preserve a moral dimension to political action.
Its consensualism was projected in a firm belief in the artificial character of class and constitutional divisions in French society, which it
sought to transcend by appealing to higher-order principles of social
co-operation. Throughout the nineteenth century this unitary vision
was overshadowed by the clericalist insistence on an alignment with
the counter-revolutionary Right, for which social and economic hierarchies remained the natural foundation of any political order. After
the official separation of Churches from the State in 1905, however,
social Catholic ideas and values began to gain ground. The institutional
development of these liberal Catholic undercurrents could be traced
through the progressive political groups, trade unions and youth movements of the interwar period to the Mouvement Républicain Populaire
(MRP) of the Fourth Republic, which in many ways represented the
climax of the social Catholic tradition in France. The ideological
influence of the MRP on the political culture of the French Right was
highly significant; for example, it was partly under the prompting of
social Catholic ideas that the contours of the French welfare state
were defined in France after the Liberation. An equally discreet (and
no less significant) influence later also became apparent on the Left.
Long dominated by the Marxist and Communist traditions, the French
forces of 'movement' became more ideologically pluralistic from the
1960s. An alternative to the centralizing and rather dogmatic culture
of the Jacobin Left began to emerge at this juncture, and the ideas
and values promoted by this *deuxième gauche* (an umbrella under which
could be found 'historic' figures such as Pierre Mendès-France, but
also Catholic associations and trade unions, left-wing clubs and discussion groups, and the ideologically dynamic Parti Socialiste Unifié)
were strongly inspired by social Catholic doctrines. This undercurrent
eventually merged with the newly formed Parti Socialiste in 1974, and
provided the party with several of its leading ideological revisionists,
most notably Michel Rocard and Jacques Delors. In the 1980s and

early 1990s, as the Socialists shed their Marxist and Jacobin ideological baggage, the culture of the *deuxième gauche* became a potential source for the party's ideological renewal. A particularly distinctive feature of this brand of liberalism after 1945 was its pro-European internationalism. Robert Schuman, the MRP statesman who had a distinguished career as Foreign Minister (and Prime Minister briefly in 1947–8), played a leading role in the establishment of the European Coal and Steel Community in 1951 — one of the institutional ancestors of the European Economic Community. In the campaign for the presidential elections of 1965, centrist candidate Jean Lecanuet opposed de Gaulle on a platform which was especially critical of his rabid anti-American and anti-European policies. Behind Schuman and Lecanuet loomed the imposing figure of Jean Monnet, who is rightly regarded as one of the fathers of European integration. Monnet was an optimistic liberal who believed in most of the basic values of social Catholicism. At the same time he was deeply attached to the notions of economic efficiency and technological change; in this sense he represented the reconciliation of the social Catholic tradition with the ideas and values of the modern age. He regarded the social, historical, and cultural bonds which Europeans shared as transcending the artificial cleavages created by nationalism, and devoted his life to the creation of a European political community which went beyond the narrow boundaries of existing states. At its best, Monnet's philosophy represented the positive vision of the future held by liberal internationalists throughout the world. A passage from his *Mémoires* summed up his attitude to politics. Speaking of the co-operative spirit which had developed between labour and employers' associations in the Coal and Steel Community, he argued that '[this harmony] proved that remarkable psychological transformations, which some seek by means of violent revolution, can be generated by entirely peaceful means if the minds of men are channelled towards the point at which their interests converge. *This point always exists*, even though it can be hard to find at times.'

This underlying sense of optimism went to the heart of the basic difference between competing conceptions of the liberal idea in France. On one side stood those (such as Monnet himself) who believed in the essential goodness and sociability of human nature, and took the view that the interests of different sections of society could be reconciled through consensual means. Conservative liberals, on the other hand, held a less benign view of their fellow-compatriots, and were always haunted by the spectre of social revolution and institutional chaos. Although these different liberal undercurrents were united in a common aspiration to bring together their fellow-countrymen by transcending existing ideological divisions, the core principles and values upon which this unity was to be constructed differed significantly. The Radicals offered a highly centralized State with clear social and cultural underpinnings, in which the good life was clearly and unambiguously defined around the institutions of the Republic; the social Catholic tradition looked towards local and decentralized forms of associational activity, and appealed to the solidaristic and generous instincts of the citizenry; conservative liberals, finally, focused on the eternal springs of self-interest and greed, and the panic induced in the bourgeois mind by chilling thoughts of expropriation, free love, and mob rule.

A LIBERAL RESURGENCE?

These distinct temperaments of French liberalism (Radical, conservative, and social Catholic) symbolized a political tradition which remained deeply fragmented. Despite a common aspiration to contain the effects of revolutionary change, a liberal political project failed to take root in France after 1870. Divisions between secular and religious elements, as well as different responses to the development of working-class political activism during the twentieth century, made it hard to unite these strands into a coherent political movement. The importance of historical factors also ensured that some of the articles of faith of the classical liberal tradition were never taken up by mainstream political organizations. Pacifism and pacificism, for example, were essential ingredients of English liberalism in the nineteenth century, but (as noted in the previous chapter) were rarely championed in a systematic fashion by major political organizations in modern France. Furthermore, even the institutional embodiments of these different strands failed to sustain their initial momentum. The Radical Party became fragmented during the Third Republic, and splintered after 1944; the Catholic MRP, once the largest party in France, reached such a nadir by the mid-1960s that it dissolved itself as a political organization. By the late 1960s the ideological preponderance of Gaullism on the Right seemed to signal the terminal decline of liberalism. The discourse of the Right contained few references to such classical liberal prescriptions as a balance of executive power, the promotion of individualism by the State, the encouragement of intermediate associations in society, the pursuit of European integration, and, perhaps most fundamentally, the transcendence of ideological divisions in French politics.

From the vantage point of the late 1980s and early 1990s, however, many of these liberal prescriptions appeared to have experienced a considerable revival. The election of Valéry Giscard d'Estaing as President in 1974 marked a turning-point in the fortunes of modern French liberalism. His political objectives were sketched out in *Démocratie française* (1976), in which he stressed the need to transcend the artificial social and ideological cleavages which had divided French society in modern times. In a subsequent work Giscard d'Estaing looked forward to the period when France would become an 'advanced liberal society' in which two out of every three French men and women would agree on basic social and political principles. Opinion surveys in the 1980s appeared to have vindicated Giscard d'Estaing's claims in a number of respects, revealing the existence of convergent approaches in French society on a broad range of issues. Ideological differences between Left and Right declined significantly; this agreement on essential social, economic, and political values among mainstream parties (excluding only the National Front and the Communist Party) appeared to herald a move towards the classical liberal ideal of a consensual political system. By 1989 most French men and women considered the Republic as part of France's national heritage: the 1789 Revolution was overwhelmingly regarded as a positive (and necessary) stage in the emergence of representative institutions. Furthermore, a significant proportion rejected subjective identification with a specific social class; expressed their firm attachment to the principle of state-sponsored social benefits; unreservedly endorsed the operation of market forces in the economy (but not in social affairs) and, finally, believed that traditional political categories of 'Left' and 'Right' were increasingly irrelevant. With regard to the latter, a poll conducted by SOFRES in April 1991 showed that 55 per cent of the electorate took the view that these categories no longer provided an adequate basis for understanding the French political system. Not surprisingly, many commentators took these indicators as sufficient evidence that France had assumed the basic features of a liberal polity. 'The end of French exceptionalism' was proclaimed with a great flourish by a chorus of intellectuals, academics, and mainstream politicians. Liberal thinkers from Tocqueville to Aron began to be (re)discovered; political scientists and sociologists pointed to the radical transformation of French economic and social structures since the 1960s, resulting in a significant erosion of such cleavages as class and religion; and the programmatic objectives of mainstream parties of the Left and Right began to converge significantly, after decades of ideologically and institutionally induced political conflict. Finally, the agreement of French political elites on the ineluctability of European political and economic integration appeared to offer an opportunity to define a new vision of the future, based on the consensual premises which had been championed so ardently by Monnet in the 1950s and 1960s. Liberal precepts seemed to have acquired a new prominence in the French political and ideological landscape.

None the less, several features of the French polity in the 1980s and early 1990s suggested that the triumphalist conclusions reached by these liberal political analysts were rather premature. First, a closer look at the opinion surveys during this period suggested that the consensus on political values was negative rather than positive. French citizens overwhelmingly rejected the principle of revolutionary change, for example, but were far less united over a number of other major political issues, notably European political and economic integration. Opinion polls also showed that an increasingly large proportion of the French electorate considered that politicians were incapable of addressing major social and economic problems effectively. After the presidential elections of 1988 a little more than 50 per cent of the electorate believed that François Mitterrand's re-election would have no effective consequences in their daily lives; after the formation of the Rocard government in June 1988 almost two-thirds of the electorate echoed this disenchanted view of politics. By the early 1990s this sense of frustration had become pervasive. The implications of the view that politics and politicians had become inconsequential were wide-ranging. In immediate terms this widespread sentiment was translated into increasingly high levels of volatility and electoral abstention. The different elections of 1988 and 1989 (presidential, legislative, cantonal, municipal, European, as well as the November 1988 referendum on the statute of New Caledonia) broke all previous records of abstention for each type of election. Thus more voters abstained on the second ballot of the 1988 presidential election than in any of the previous four second-ballot presidential contests; the same pattern was repeated in each of the ensuing electoral contests. Furthermore, a significant proportion of voters who did not desert the ballot-box began to cast their votes for organizations which were outside the political mainstream. Two groups reached the limelight in this way. Jean-Marie Le Pen's National Front rose to public prominence in the mid-1980s, focusing on problems of immigration and personal insecurity; however, as shown in Chapter 5, the National Front's subsequent growth was largely facilitated by a growing sense of public disenchantment with the political class as a whole. The Ecologists also emerged as a potential political force (at least in local politics) in the late 1980s and early 1990s, by exploiting widespread fears about the degradation of the environment. Both phenomena represented clear expressions of popular disenchantment with traditional patterns of partisan politics in France. While these developments should not be interpreted as a challenge to the republican character of the French political system, they clearly suggested that the apparent ideological convergence of the electorate was far more fragile than had been suggested. In particular, the emergence of the National Front, and its continuing impact on the political scene in the late 1980s and early 1990s, are difficult to reconcile with claims of growing social and political consensus. Attempts by some political observers to explain away the phenomenon as an aberration can only be regarded as a rather typical (if unfortunate) excercise in special pleading. For the sociologist Henri Mendras, for example, the rise of right-wing extremism in France in the 1980s had to be seen from a broader historical perspective. From these elevated heights, he argued, the French 'melting-pot' had been a considerable success: 'the French have on the whole become remarkably more tolerant of differences.' The anthropologist Emmanuel Todd presented the rise of racism in France in the 1980s as a 'transitional phenomenon of *anomie*' which was fundamentally inconsistent with the 'deep anthropological structures' of society. Something is clearly amiss when social scientists resort to explaining a political occurrence by appealing to transcendental historical categories or (even worse) the cavernous depths of the French mind.

The ambivalent—and in many respects illusory—character of the political consensus demonstrated the limits of the resurgence of liberalism in France during the 1970s and 1980s. These limits were compounded by the endemic historical weaknesses of the liberal tradition in France. The relative revival of liberal ideology was hardly sufficient to offset the absence of founding myths which, as noted in Chapter

1, were an essential underpinning of a durable and cohesive political tradition. Nor was this ideological renewal sufficient to provide a basis for overcoming the institutional divisions between different strands of the French liberal tradition. The UDF represented an electoral alliance of different branches of the moderate Right, but it never acquired the cohesion and sense of purpose which were the necessary conditions of the Gaullist hegemony during the 1960s. The relative autonomy of the social Catholic wing of the UDF, the Centre des Démocrates-Sociaux (CDS), after 1988 was a clear testimony to the continuing importance of the cleavage between reformist and conservative strands of liberalism. It should also be noted that the revival of liberal ideas in France did not produce a social constituency which could provide the foundations for a stable liberal politics. This was the modern expression of a traditional weakness of French liberalism: its failure to establish a distinct identity on the basis of an identification with specific social institutions and classes. In Italy, for example, Christian Democracy developed as the political wing of the Church; in Western and Central Europe social democracy was historically rooted in working-class communities; in Eastern Europe and pre-revolutionary Russia peasant parties traditionally reflected the political aspirations of rural communities. Liberalism in France always lacked firm social constituencies of this nature; the divisions between Radical, conservative, and social Catholic forms of liberalism in many ways expressed tensions between urban and rural, peasant and bourgeois, secular and Catholic forces which were constantly pitted against each other for much of the history of modern France.

From a broader perspective liberals were never able to counter the damaging effects of the weakness of intermediate associations in French society. This deficiency was typified by the low levels of membership of political organizations and especially trade unions: after the legalization of French *syndicats* in 1884 there was never more than one wage-earner in every five who was a member of a trade union in France. While other parties were relatively successful in organizing their local networks, liberal politicians consistently failed to structure their activity in this way (the Radical Party was the closest approximation to this ideal). Finally, liberal political institutions came up against what might be called the State tradition in France. The ramifications of this tradition of State power have already been described in Chapter 6, but it is worth reiterating that its appeal was so compelling that even

French liberals often yielded to the temptation to use power in ways which were inconsistent with the basic canons of classical liberal ideology. The opportunists of the Third Republic, as already mentioned, used the State to impose their conception of secular education and protect French agriculture from foreign competition. In modern times, and despite its liberal intentions, Valéry Giscard d'Estaing's presidency was marked by a further increase in political and administrative centralization, and blatant attempts to use the machinery of the state for partisan ends.

Another dimension of the frailty of the liberal resurgence could be seen in the limits of its intellectual revival. During the 1970s and early 1980s liberal intellectuals played an important role in debunking the traditional political values of the Marxist Left (the idea of radical change, the myth of Soviet Communism, and the leading role of the proletariat). Once this destructive role had been accomplished effectively, however, the new liberal ideological orthodoxies failed to secure the type of dominance enjoyed by Marxism before the 1970s. It is revealing, for example, that the 'victory' of liberal ideas and values in the French intellectual community in the 1980s did not generate a *maître à penser*. The long Marxist hegemony over French ideological life after 1945 produced several generations of leading intellectual figures, from Sartre and Merleau-Ponty in the postwar era to Althusser and Poulantzas in the 1970s. In contrast, the apparent triumph of liberal ideas in the 1980s failed to bring about a new generation of leading intellectual figures. A number of reasons may be tentatively proffered to account for this failing. First, partly as a result of the political disillusionments of the 1970s, many intellectuals retreated from partisan political activity during the 1980s. The tradition of generic political *engagement* which had prevailed during the postwar decades receded as intellectuals limited their political campaigns to specific causes, such as human rights abuses and the alleviation of poverty. In other words, intellectuals became rather more sceptical about the value of partisan commitment, and this resulted in a relative retreat from the political arena. Second, the parties of the moderate Right, which might naturally have been expected to sponsor and accommodate the theoretical enterprises of liberal intellectuals, were involved in other pressing issues for most of the 1980s: how to regain power after 1981, retain it after 1986, cope with the National Front after 1983, and transcend the bitterness and acrimony which followed the defeat of 1988. It was true that the economic policies of the Chirac government of 1986–8 were partly inspired by neo-liberal economic doctrines; yet even this corpus of ideas was not an endogenous product, but an import from the United States and Thatcherite Britain. Their Anglo-American origins did not prevent some of these ideas (most notably in the sphere of economic deregulation) from being translated into public policy between 1986 and 1988, but they certainly impeded the durable implantation of these doctrines in the French intellectual community, which remained deeply committed to its time-honoured principle of cultural insularity. Ultimately there was no better illustration of the shallowness of the liberal resurgence than its utter failure to define a clear vision of the social and political underpinnings of the new European configuration which was promised for the 1990s. The triumphalist liberal rhetoric seemed in many ways to be inversely proportional to its substance as a political and ideological force.

THE LIMITS OF THE LIBERAL REVIVAL

French liberalism was always a somewhat paradoxical political tradition, but the 1980s and early 1990s took these contradictions to new heights. On one hand there were apparent signs of political and ideological renewal: liberal economic ideas and political values were revived, and moderate politicians of the Left and Right subscribed with few reservations to the new orthodoxy of consensus politics. The Socialist government rapidly abandoned its radical social and economic ambitions, and loudly proclaimed its conversion to the liberal values of ideological consensus and political compromise. Yet, in institutional terms, the fragmentation of French liberalism remained essentially unaltered. In creating the UDF in 1978, President Giscard d'Estaing attempted to bring together the different strands of the liberal tradition. Yet its fate in the 1980s and early 1990s continued to symbolize the institutional deficiencies of French liberalism: its candidates were defeated in the 1981 and 1988 presidential elections, and its leaders fought increasingly bitter political battles to establish control of the organization. During the 1988–93 legislature the CDS broke away from the UDF parliamentary group, providing a graphic example of the endemic institutional fragility of the liberal tradition. But the most compelling evidence of the limits of the new political consensus was provided by two complementary factors: the decline of public confidence in political elites and the rising tide of popularity of the extreme

Right. Liberals seemed to have achieved their relative ideological resurgence at an extremely high political cost.

This paradoxical situation was rarely displayed in such graphic terms as in the 1980s and early 1990s, but the basic frustration of getting very close to an elusive goal is a condition which French liberals have long had to endure. The greatest and most noble French liberal of the nineteenth century, de Tocqueville, captured this sense of despair vividly in his *Souvenirs* when he exclaimed:

I don't know when this voyage will end. I am tired of thinking, time and again, that we have reached the coast, only to find that it was an illusive bank of fog. I often wonder whether the solid ground we have so long sought really exists, or whether our destiny is not rather to sail a storm-tossed sea forever.

Chronology

1789   August. Liberal legislation of French Revolution initiated, notably abolition of privileges (4 August) and Declaration of the Rights of Man (26 August).

1792   April. Declaration of war against Austria: beginning of the end of the 'liberal' phase of the French Revolution.

1830   July. Revolution ushers in constitutional monarchy of Louis-Philippe.

1833   Guizot law on primary education.

1848   February. Overthrow of Orleanist regime, proclamation of Second Republic.

1869   April. Belleville Manifesto of Radical movement.

1871   May. Brutal suppression of Paris Commune by Thiers government.

1895   November. Radical cabinet of Léon Bourgeois.

1901   June. Launching of Radical party as a national organization.

1902   May. Victory of the republican bloc in legislative elections.

1935   October. Radical congress approves common front of Left against challenge to Republic.

1944   November. Founding congress of Mouvement Républicain Populaire.

1947   November. Schuman appointed Prime Minister.

1951   April. Foundation of European Coal and Steel Community.

1952   March. Pinay government.

1954   June. Investiture of Mendès-France government.

1957   March. Rome EEC treaties ratified by National Assembly.

1962   November. Formation of Républicains Indépendents under Valéry Giscard d'Estaing.

1972   October. Creation of Mouvement de la Gauche Radicale-Socialiste (left-wing Radicals).

1974   May. Election of Giscard d'Estaing as President.

1978   February. Creation of Union pour la Démocratie Française (UDF), a federation of conservative liberals under Giscardian leadership.

1986   March. Victory of moderate Right in legislative elections.

1988   June. Centre des Démocrates Sociaux, social Catholic component of UDF, forms separate parliamentary group after legislative elections.

1993   March. Decisive victory of right-wing coalition in legislative elections.

CHAPTER 9

Resurrection and Death: the Socialist Tradition

Modern French Socialists are the inheritors of a long and complex political tradition. The complexity is best captured by the simple proposition that the Socialist Party was constituted at least three times this century: in 1905, with the coming together of the Section Française de l'Internationale Ouvrière (SFIO); in 1920, following the breakaway of a majority of the SFIO to form the Communist Party; and most recently, in 1969, when the moribund organization was dissolved and relaunched as the Parti Socialiste (PS). Quite apart from the obvious problems attending these foundational processes, the Socialist tradition was further divided over its ideological lineage. As is often the case with questions of intellectual inheritance, this legacy was the object of fierce disputes between self-styled Socialists and other left-wing political groups, most notably the Communists, whose equally complex history is examined separately in Chapter 11.

Many of the problems faced by the French socialist tradition were expressions of the basic dilemma of forging a distinct identity within the broader political community of the Left—a fractious, discursive, somewhat nebulous, yet highly ideological grouping which was born with the French Revolution. Socialism in France always situated itself firmly on the Left, and there were many aspects of this broader entity with which it identified without reservation. As with all those who considered themselves members of the Left, Socialists always recognized the French Revolution as a foundational event and upheld its general principles of liberty, equality, and fraternity. Socialism also shared many of the basic goals of the republican tradition, particularly those which appealed to the sensibilities of the Left: the creation of a political order based on the principle of popular sovereignty, the enhancement of mass participation in public life, the promotion of equality of outcome, the establishment of a secular system of education, and the moralization of public life. Socialists thus firmly believed in the intelligibility of politics: it was an essentially rational process in which the citizenry played an active role in defining the collective goals of the community. In addition, many of the Left's key ideological references throughout the nineteenth and twentieth centuries coincided with those of the Socialists: thus their thinkers welcomed Marx and Engels, but also Proudhon and Jaurès, as full members of their intellectual pantheon. Like all their fellow-comrades on the Left, furthermore, the Socialists claimed that their central political objective was to transfer resources to the underprivileged sections of the community, and create a society in which power was exercised in the interests of working people, as opposed to those who profited by the work of others. In setting out their basic objectives in this way Socialists also demonstrated their empathy with one of the salient intellectual features of left-wing politics: the tendency to define political action with reference to abstract (and universal) standards of truth, justice, and morality. To be on the Left, in sum, was an expression of a commitment to social, political, or cultural change on the basis of a preconceived vision of the future; and in their public discourse (as opposed to their practice) French Socialists consistently identified with this conception of politics.

But the Left in France was never a homogeneous community, and the Socialists always retained a distinct identity within this plurality. In the nineteenth and early twentieth centuries a socialist culture coexisted (often rather tempestuously) with liberal, anarchist and anarcho-syndicalist, and Jacobin undercurrents. After the First World War the major ideological and institutional divide within the Left opposed the Socialists to the Communists. These political conflicts within the Left helped to crystallize the identity of French Socialism, and its distinct ideological character was expressed in a specific set of core values. While they agreed with the ends of the Left, as broadly defined in the previous paragraph, Socialists inclined towards the view that the means of attaining them had to be commensurate with the moral principles they embodied. Socialists rejected the systematic use of violence as a means of furthering political ends, and essentially believed that the introduction of structural change could be achieved through gradual and evolutionary means. In contrast to the centralizing (and often authoritarian) culture of the Jacobin Left, the Socialists were deeply attached to the principles of locality and federalism. In the modern era this contrast was graphically expressed in the centralized organization wielded by the Communists, and the loose, heterogeneous, and somewhat shambolic structure which the Socialists called their party. Indeed, they were always distinctive in their emphasis on the value of individualism, which they nourished in their own movement by encouraging the flowering of ideological and intellectual diversity to an extent which was almost inconceivable in other cultures of the Left (with the exception of the liberal one).

Yet, in one respect, the Socialists were almost monolithic: the social composition of their political elite. Again in contrast to the Communists, the Socialist movement recruited its leaders from middle-class groups, and this feature remained unchanged throughout the modern era. The causes and ramifications of this element of continuity will be discussed later in this chapter, but it is worth spelling out what it meant in terms of the Socialists' relationship with the Left. It will be remembered that the Left was committed to exercising power in the interests of working people; this could be achieved either by giving political power to the workers themselves (the view taken by extreme Jacobins, anarchists, and Communists) or, alternatively, to a group of paternalist intellectuals who would safeguard their interests; not surprisingly, given the social origins of their leaders, the Socialists took the latter view. Another important dimension of Socialist particularism was its distinct conception of internationalism. Again unlike the French Communists, whose leaders showed an abiding loyalty to the Soviet Union and the international communist movement, Socialists were nationalists who operated within the political and cultural context of Western Europe. They rejected what they saw as the extreme nationalism of the Jacobins and the extreme internationalism of the Communists; they accepted that France was a member of a wider community of states, and believed that co-operation with other likeminded groups was both beneficial and necessary. Finally, in some respects like the liberal tradition, Socialists showed a considerable element of flexibility in applying the ideological principles in which they professed to believe. This elasticity often resulted in political outcomes which seemed blatantly to contradict their stated objectives: they claimed to be on the Left, but often ended up governing with the Right (or at least, adopting policies which would not have been disowned by the forces of 'order'); they proclaimed their desire to change society radically, but almost invariably tended to shore up existing social and political institutions. The most charitable way of expressing this tendency is to suggest that Socialists were the least dogmatic undercurrent of the French Left; unfortunately, as will be seen in the concluding section of this chapter, the search for compromise often took them into highly compromising situations.

As implied earlier, the concept of 'socialism' emerged in France in the early nineteenth century, as part of a wider republican movement which sought to promote greater social and political reforms. One of the first to use the term 'socialism' in a systematic fashion was the utopian thinker Charles Fourier (1772–1837), who wrote about the emergence of this new social creed in his journal *Le Phalanstère* in April 1833. During the 1840s the concept of 'socialism' was popularized by Louis Blanc (1811–82) and Pierre Leroux (1797–1871), who argued that radical social reform was possible without the type of violent upheavals which France had witnessed during the 1790s (and which the insurrectionist secret societies of the 1830s sought to revive). The basic socialist postulate that structural change could be introduced through evolutionary means was ridiculed by Marx and his followers. This, for example, is how Friedrich Engels characterized socialism in his preface to the English edition of the *Communist Manifesto* in 1888: 'By socialists were understood the most multifarious social quacks, who, by all manners of tinkering, professed to redress, without any danger to capital and profit, all sorts of social grievances.' The institutionalization of these 'social quacks' in France was initiated in the early days of the Third Republic. The most distant ancestor of the contemporary Socialist Party was the Parti Ouvrier Français, formed in 1880 under the leadership of Jules Guesde (1845–1922), an inspiring figure who was both a doctrinaire Marxist and a Jacobin nationalist. Despite the charismatic quality of its leader, Guesde's party failed to serve as a focus for rallying the Socialist movement. In fact, the early history of the French labour movement was marked by the proliferation of small groups and sects, each claiming to provide the authoritative version of the socialist ideal. Thus the Guesdists were soon competing with Possibilists (led by the pragmatic Paul Brousse in the 1880s), Alemanists (supporters of Jean Alemane in the 1890s), and an independent group, which would provide the movement with such parliamentarians as Jean Jaurès (1859–1914) and Alexandre Millerand (1859–1943).

The development of these early socialist groups was hampered by the relatively low level of industrialization in France. The period between 1870 and 1914 saw a considerable expansion of French industrial capacity, which was notably accelerated by the First World War. None the less, France remained a nation of peasants and artisans for much of the Third Republic; the proportion of the active population engaged in industrial work overtook the agricultural sector only in the 1930s. Even then, it should be remembered that more than 70 per cent of the country's manufacturing firms employed less than six workers. This had the effect of stifling the development of political consciousness among workers, as was reflected in the low level of trade-union membership. The large cohorts of industrial workers who provided the backbone of the Social Democratic Party in Germany and the trade-union movement in Britain were simply not available to French Socialist organizations in the early twentieth century, and this deficiency had a dramatic impact on their development. Thus the fragmentation of the Socialist movement during the Third Republic was in many ways a direct consequence of the tardy pace of French industrial development. But two other factors exacerbated the problem: the development of the Republican system of government, which posed the agonizing question of Socialist participation in 'bourgeois' government, and the creation of the Communist Party after 1920, which revived the ideological divisions of the Left.

THE EXERCISE OF POWER AND ITS COSTS

The modern history of French Socialism began in 1905, with the fusion of the movement's different factions and groups into a unified party, the Section Française de l'Internationale Ouvrière. Under the leadership of Jean Jaurès and Jules Guesde the SFIO soon established itself as an effective parliamentary force in French politics. In the legislative elections of 1914 the party won 1.4 million votes (and 103 seats), and in 1919 increased its support by a further 300,000 votes. Despite this growing popular appeal, the distortion of the electoral system reduced its parliamentary representation to 68. These parliamentarians were faced with a quandary in December 1920, when the party congress at Tours again split the Socialist family into two distinct branches. The majority of delegates voted to join Lenin's Third International, and later formed what became the French Communist Party (PCF). The minority elected, in the words of their leader Léon Blum, to 'watch over the old house'. Thus, only fifteen years after its creation, the SFIO was amputated, and its prospects as a political movement appeared to be seriously jeopardized. Yet the 'old house' not only survived but grew into a flourishing organization in the course of the following decades. Of the 68 parliamentarians elected in 1919, 55 decided to remain with the SFIO. The party used its electoral base to rebuild its support, survived another potentially damaging split (from a right-wing rump this time) in 1933, and by 1936 had re-established its institutional supremacy over the Left.

The Popular Front government of 1936–7 constituted a landmark in the history of French Socialism (and the French Left more generally). For the first time in republican history, the country was governed by a Socialist Prime Minister (Léon Blum); equally significant was the fact that the coalition over which he presided enjoyed the full support of the Socialist parliamentary group. Since the 1890s the Socialists had been deeply divided over the conditions under which they should hold political office. When the talented and highly ambitious parliamentarian Alexandre Millerand decided to join the republican coalition of Waldeck-Rousseau in 1899, he was accused of betraying the socialist cause—who else but a renegade could elect to join a government led by 'bourgeois' politicians? The spirit of national unity which initially attended the outbreak of the First World War helped to overcome these sectarian sentiments. The Union Sacrée brought a number of SFIO figures into government, most notably Jules Guesde, who both inspired and was carried by the wave of Jacobin nationalism which swept across the Left in the early days of the war. The institutionalization of the Republic exercised a strong appeal to some Socialist elites, offering the prospect of wielding power to implement some of the basic goals of their movement. But the war experience failed to convince the whole party of the virtues of power-sharing. When the Radical leader Édouard Herriot (1872–1957) offered the SFIO a place in his government in 1924, the party leader Léon Blum refused flatly. For the following ten years the Socialist approach was summarized in the expression 'support without participation'. The party endorsed progressive governments, such as Herriot's Cartel des Gauches (1924–6), but refused to compromise itself with ministerial office. With the formation of the Popular Front government, however, this taboo was lifted. Between the fall of the Blum ministry in June 1937 and the collapse of the Fourth Republic in May 1958, there were five governments led by Socialist Prime Ministers. Blum returned to power very briefly on two separate occasions (his total tenure of office lasted less than two months); the others were Felix Gouin (January–June 1946), Paul Ramadier (January–November 1947), and Guy Mollet (February 1956–May 1957). There were also SFIO ministers in almost all French governments between 1944 and 1951. It should also be noted that Vincent Auriol (1884–1966), one of Léon Blum's most capable disciples, became the first President of the Fourth Republic after the Liberation. The presidency of the Fourth Republic was largely a ceremonial office, but the fact that a Socialist was chosen to serve as a symbol of the Republic provided further confirmation of the close identification of the SFIO with state institutions.

The long-term result of this unrelenting quest for public office was quite predictable. The party increasingly forgot about its original purpose, which was to reform (and where possible humanize) capitalist society, and grew into an organization for which power became an end in itself, rather than a means to introduce effective social and political change in the country. The Socialists thus began to suffer from advanced sclerosis in the 1950s and 1960s; this was most visible in the haemorrhage of militants from the party. It was true that French Socialists were never a mass party by comparative European social-democratic standards. None the less, within the context of the French party system, the SFIO successfully developed its popular base during the interwar period and by 1939 could boast a membership of 260,000. The experience of the resistance brought a fresh wave of recruits, and in 1946 the party's membership had risen to 335,000. From then on, however, the organization began its inexorable decline, and by 1969 could muster only a membership of 70,000 (and, even in the unlikely event of this figure being strictly accurate, it was extremely doubtful that the party had 70,000 active members). Furthermore, this decline in party membership was accompanied by a gradual collapse of the SFIO's electoral base. There is no necessary correlation between partisan membership and electoral support: the Communists, for example, lost at least half their membership between 1947 and 1956, yet retained a relatively stable level of electoral support during this period. The Socialists, on the other hand, compounded their organizational difficulties by undergoing a steady electoral decline through the 1950s and 1960s. In the legislative elections of 1956 the Socialist Party won 3.2 million votes, and its leader Guy Mollet went on to form the next government. By the time of the presidential elections of 1969, the official Socialist candidate Gaston Defferre received a mere 1.1 million votes—not even enough to reach the runoff on the second ballot, let alone be elected.

Finally (and this was one of the underlying causes of the first and second developments) the Socialist leadership found itself under increasing attack for the party's conservatism and intellectual sclerosis. Guy Mollet's tenure of office as Prime Minister, at the height of the Algerian war in 1956–7, did little to enhance the stature and credibility of the Socialist Party. The Right accused his government of indecisiveness, while many on the Left criticized Mollet for condoning the use of torture against Algerian nationalists (both strictures were entirely justified). More generally, the SFIO was deserted by the baby-boom generation of the 1960s, for whom the party had seriously compromised the socialist ideal during the chaotic final years of the Fourth Republic. For young French men and women on the Left who could not bring themselves to join an equally discredited Communist Party, the Socialists had little to offer. Many instead joined the Parti Socialiste Unifié (PSU), a splinter group which was formed in 1960, and distinguished itself by its strong opposition to the Algerian war, its total rejection of the Gaullist Republic, and its scathing denunciation of the conservatism and intellectual inertia of mainstream left-wing parties. The PSU provided the intellectual matrix for an alternative conception of political action, and many of the student rebels of May '68 were influenced by its ideals. The PSU stigmatized the political and intellectual bankruptcy of French Socialism, and helped to bring a whole generation of non-communist left-wing intellectuals into politics. Many of its leaders later went on to achieve positions of great eminence in French politics and government. Thus it was as PSU national secretary between 1967 and 1973 that a highly intelligent and ambitious young politician by the name of Michel Rocard first made his mark on French public life.

THE REGENERATION OF FRENCH SOCIALISM

By the late 1960s, therefore, French Socialism appeared to be agonizing. It was represented by a cluster of groups and associations which had a past (during which the ideals of socialism had often been compromised) but no apparent sense of direction. Yet out of this morass emerged a new party, the Parti Socialiste (PS) which federated the different branches of the movement in the 1970s. The PS signed a political agreement with the Communists, thereby giving the movement a new lease of life. It captured the French presidency in 1981 (and retained it in 1988), and established itself as one of the dominant forces in French politics during the decade. The way in which this regeneration occurred will not be discussed here at any great length. Key factors included strong and effective leadership, under the firm direction of François Mitterrand; the decline of the working class and the corresponding rise of middle-class occupational groups, which widened the scope for the new party's electoral appeal; the artful exploitation of the tactical and strategic weaknesses of the Communists, in particular their failure to recognize the need for ideological change; a successful appeal to the post-material issues of the new Left, especially the themes of environmentalism, regionalism, feminism, and anti-racism; capitalizing on the advantages accruing to the party through the dynamics of the party system; and finally, taking advantage of the impetus of the presidential system, which turned the party into an instrument for capturing the highest prize in the political system. Rather than expand on these factors, however, the ensuing narrative will seek to contrast the changing fortunes of the Socialist Party after 1969 with the essential continuities of the French socialist tradition. When the transformations of the 1980s are set against a wider historical context, the very strong sense in which the modern Socialist Party is the heir of the French democratic socialist tradition will emerge.

In many ways the 1980s represented the most successful decade for French Socialists since the formation of the SFIO in 1905. Socialists held high office almost without interruption between 1981 and 1993. François Mitterrand became the first Socialist to be elected to the presidency of the Fifth Republic and, after his triumphant re-election in 1988, surpassed de Gaulle's previous record of longevity of tenure. Since the presidency was the main source of executive and electoral power in France, the PS was able to use its association with the President to gain an absolute majority of seats in the legislative elections of 1981, and to emerge as the single largest party after the elections of 1988. The party was, it is true, temporarily deprived of power for two years (between 1986 and 1988) when the Gaullist leader, Jacques Chirac, formed a government backed by a right-wing majority in the National Assembly. But the Socialists returned to power in 1988, and their institutional hegemony over the political and administrative system was restored. There were five Socialist prime ministers between 1981 and 1993 (Mauroy, Fabius, Rocard, Cresson, and Bérégovoy) and the scope for patronage which such a long spell in office provided was exploited to the full. Like the Gaullists, whose political domination in the 1960s was effectively used to establish a spoils system à la française, the Socialists used the advantages of incumbency to penetrate the upper reaches of the state bureaucracy (and, when necessary, plunder the coffers of the State to offset the depletion of party resources).

An important consequence of the institutional hegemony enjoyed by Socialists up to 1993 was the dramatic alteration of the party's conception of its role in the French political system. Between 1936 and 1981, as already indicated, French Socialists held office at various moments, but this never affected their *theoretical* commitment to changing the institutional system within which they operated. Léon Blum, for example, was a strict constitutionalist, who argued in 1936 that the Socialists' popular mandate was not strong enough to allow for the introduction of radical reforms in French society. But he believed that the promotion of revolutionary change should still remain the ultimate goal of French Socialists, to be implemented when circumstances made such transformations possible. Similarly, after 1958 the Socialists operated within the institutional structure of the Fifth Republic, but repeatedly claimed that their goal was to make the French executive less autocratic. After 1981, however, French Socialists ceased to complain about presidential autocracy; indeed, the PS became fully reconciled to the political and administrative institutions of the Fifth Republic. From a party which was occasionally in government the Socialists were transformed into a party *of* government after 1981. The internal implications of this transformation were momentous; as will be noted later, not all of them were positive.

Furthermore, at no other time in its history was the Socialist movement as exclusively dominated by one party as in the 1980s and early 1990s. At its origins, it will be remembered, the Socialist movement in France was marked by fragmentation and disunity. During the Third and Fourth Republics the SFIO was constantly surrounded by an array of independent parties and groups, ranging from the Parti d'Unité Prolétarienne to the Union Socialiste Républicaine. In the 1960s, the surviving SFIO was flanked by the Parti Socialiste Unifié on its left, and a stream of clubs, associations, and splinter groups, which included François Mitterrand's Convention des Institutions Républicaines. The new Socialist Party was launched at the Issy-les-Moulineaux congress of July 1969, bringing together several branches of the socialist family (including the SFIO). The real unification congress, however, took place at Epinay in June 1971, when Mitterrand's group of *Conventionels* was welcomed into the fold, and Mitterrand himself installed as First Secretary (his ascension was nothing short of meteoric: he became the leader of a party of which he had never been a member). As the new Socialist Party expanded in the 1970s and 1980s it gradually drew all other remaining non-communist parties and groups into its orbit. In 1974 the party organized the Assises du Socialisme, in which a group of PSU leaders (including Michel Rocard), ex-Gaullists, and trade-unionists joined the organization. By the mid-1980s most of the remaining non-communist groups (such as the PSU and left-wing Radicals) had come under Socialist control, even if they retained formally separate organizational structures.

In the 1980s the PS succeeded in subordinating not only the smaller range of left-wing groups and associations, but also the organization which had dominated the politics of the Left for most of the previous six decades: the French Communist Party. The decline of the PCF will be treated in Chapter 11, and will not be discussed extensively at this stage. But it must be stressed that, until the 1980s, Communists were the hegemonic force on the Left, in terms of both membership and electoral support. In the presidential elections of 1981 François Mitterrand clearly outpaced the PCF leader, Georges Marchais, on the first ballot, and by the legislative elections of 1988 the Socialists were winning three times as many votes as the Communists. In the elections to the 1981–6 legislature the PS won an absolute majority of seats, and did not even require the parliamentary support of the Communists to form a government. After the legislative elections of 1988 this situation was modified slightly, in that the Socialists no longer had an absolute majority on their own, and Socialist prime ministers had to rely on Communist support (or at least neutrality) to get much of their legislation through Parliament. But this did not give the Communists any strong leverage over their rivals, because the balance of forces between the two groups remained overwhelmingly favourable to the PS. This situation had no parallel in the postwar period; indeed, only in the early 1930s was there a similar correlation of forces between Socialists and Communists.

Finally, the Socialists' political domination gradually altered the terms of the intellectual debate on the Left concerning basic issues of institutional reform and social change. On balance, this intellectual influence of the Socialists was greater in terms of what it destroyed than in what it proposed as an alternative. The ideological bankruptcy of communism in Europe, which was compounded in France by the inflexible and dogmatic posture adopted by the PCF after 1978, finally destroyed the intellectual hegemony of communism over the Left.

The Socialists accelerated this disintegration of Communist culture by establishing their political supremacy over the PCF after 1981, then redefining the goals of socialism along less radical and more evolutionary lines. This redefinition was carried out *a posteriori*, and was derived from the experiences of Socialist governments during this period. By the mid-1980s the Socialists had abandoned many of the traditional assumptions of the French Left on such issues as state ownership, income redistribution, and constitutional change. Despite its intrinsic vagueness, the appeal of this more pragmatic conception of socialism to the intellectual strata was initially quite strong. In the presidential elections of 1988 Mitterrand's support among intellectuals was extremely high: for example, 70 per cent of teachers and social workers gave him their vote on the second ballot. Among prestigious intellectual figures in the academic, artistic, and scientific community Mitterrand and the Socialist Party fared equally well, even though many left-wing intellectuals were markedly less inclined to publicize their partisan support than in the past.

But the origins of this growing intellectual support for the Socialists went further back. There was an important sense in which the Socialists captured and fructified what remained of the political and intellectual heritage of May 1968. In some senses this proposition might seem paradoxical: the student rebels sought to destroy established order, whereas the Socialists of the 1980s became associated with that order. Part of the explanation lay in the ideological realignment of the Left after the mid-1970s. The middle-aged Socialist militants and voters of the 1980s were very often the same scruffy men and women who vandalized Paris in 1968; the difference was that many of them now owned the properties they had daubed with imaginative graffiti, and they had accordingly become rather sceptical about claims that radical socio-economic change was either possible or even desirable. But this generation continued to be inspired by some of the ideological principles of May 1968: a belief in individual rather than collective norms of action and behaviour, and a quest to transcend the social and political cleavages created by advanced industrial society. Seen from this perspective, the technocratic Socialists of the 1980s completed the work initiated by the long-haired revolutionaries of 1968. Yet the terms on which this intellectual realignment was operated generated a different set of problems. The ideological transformation of the Left was not accompanied by a breadth of vision similar to the grandiose revolutionary schemes which had mobilized the French intellectual community for much of the modern era. It proved easier to captivate the imagination of intellectuals with the promise of a new dawn than by appealing to such virtues as political pragmatism, economic interdependence, and technocratic competence. By the late 1980s and early 1990s this absence of an appealing alternative vision of the future was one of the important causes of a perceptible sense of intellectual disillusionment with the Socialists. The governments of Michel Rocard, Édith Cresson, and Pierre Bérégovoy compounded the villainy by appearing weak and indecisive, thus failing to be consistent even with their own limited objectives.

None the less, to recapitulate, the 1980s were in many ways the most successful decade enjoyed by French Socialists since the formation of the SFIO in 1905. They controlled the principal levers of political power for most of the decade; they were perceived by a sizeable proportion of the electorate as the natural party of government; they established centralized control over the traditionally disparate strands of the socialist community; they reduced the Communist Party to the status of a marginal and largely irrelevant rump in national politics; and finally, they succeeded in breaking the Marxian intellectual stranglehold on the Left, even though they failed to define precisely the contours of an alternative political project.

DEEPER CONTINUITIES: WORKERS AND INTELLECTUALS

Did all these changes signify that the Socialist movement of the 1980s was qualitatively a new phenomenon, which had broken its historical attachments to the French democratic socialist tradition? Before hasty conclusions are reached, it is worth pointing out that some of the processes described above also occurred in many West European countries. In some cases, such as the Scandinavian countries, social democracy became a hegemonic political force long before the modern French Socialist Party was even born; in others, such as Spain and Italy, the fortunes of local Socialists improved during the same period as their French counterparts. By comparative European social democratic standards, the French Socialist Party was relatively more successful in achieving and retaining political power, and exercising a dominant influence over the Left, than most other European Socialist organizations during the 1980s and early 1990s. Yet the French party was still a recognizable member of the European social democratic family, as was attested by the significant role it played in the Socialist International, and in co-ordinating the strategies of Socialist parties in the European Parliament.

But there were important senses in which the French Socialists, despite their rise to political eminence in the 1980s, also retained a considerable part of the historical legacy of their predecessors. The first strong element of continuity was sociological. The party of the 1980s was an organization whose leaders and activists were predominantly middle-class, but the PS still received a substantial proportion of working-class votes, and continued to celebrate its receptiveness to the social and political values of French workers. The transformation of French Socialism into a haven for middle-class radicals could be traced back to the interwar period. If the social origins and occupations of Socialist parliamentarians are examined, for example, a clear trend towards *embourgeoisement* is discernible. The SFIO group (68 members) elected in 1919 was predominantly proletarian, whereas the group elected in the Popular Front chamber of 1936 (147 deputies *in toto*) had just over 10 per cent of workers; the largest single professional group in the Socialist parliamentary caucus in 1936 consisted of teachers. The socio-professional backgrounds of the Socialists elected in 1981 demonstrated how little had changed in the social identity of the party leadership: 59 per cent of the Socialist parliamentary group in the 1981–6 legislature consisted of schoolteachers, a proportion which remained roughly similar in the Socialist group elected in June 1988. This over-representation of the middle classes among Socialist deputies was even more accentuated when the social origins and occupations of the party leadership were examined. Of all the leading figures in the Socialist governments of the 1980s and early 1990s, only Pierre Bérégovoy (1925–93) was a former manual worker; almost all his colleagues came from educated middle-class backgrounds. A figure such as Michel Rocard was, from this point of view, not untypical of the Socialist elite: his father was a nuclear scientist, and the young Michel was educated at one of the best *lycées* in Paris (Louis-le-Grand). Following his baccalaureate, he joined the Institut d'Études Politiques, the leading centre for the study of the social sciences in Paris, after which he entered the École Nationale d'Administration, the elite training school for French civil servants. Despite this preponderance of intellectuals in the ranks of the Socialist leadership, President Mitterrand and his party were highly successful in pitching their appeal to working-class voters. But this success continued (on a wider scale) a tradition which was firmly established throughout the century. Although the Socialists' electoral base after the 1930s was preponderantly middle-class, at least a third of their electorate consisted of manual workers throughout the modern era. In the 1980s the Socialists were by far the party with the greatest share of the blue-collar working-class vote; this was spectacularly confirmed in the second ballot of the 1988 presidential elections, when no less than three working-class voters in every four voted for François Mitterrand.

What explained the phenomenon of a party of middle-class intellectuals being supported by an overwhelming majority of French manual workers? This question raises two issues which need to be addressed separately. First, why did workers vote for the PS in such large numbers, and identify even more strongly with a Socialist president? Second, why were there so few workers in the higher echelons of the Socialist party structure? The answer to the first question could be taken from a negative and positive angle. As will be seen in Chapter 11, a relative majority of French manual workers voted for the French Communist Party until the late 1970s; the transfer of working-class allegiance to the Socialists in the 1980s was both a cause and an effect of the Communist Party's precipitate electoral decline. But these workers did not mechanically switch their allegiance: they did so because they believed that the Socialists and their president were the best guardians of their economic and social interests. Whether this belief was well founded was another matter, but what remained beyond dispute was the overwhelmingly favourable image enjoyed by Mitterrand among French manual workers for most of the 1980s. The answer to the second question—why there were so few workers in the leadership of a party whose original purpose was to exercise political and economic power in the best interests of the French working class— was more complex. Three overlapping arguments could be proffered to explain the relative absence of workers in the Socialist hierarchy. One might begin by reformulating slightly the classic argument propounded in Robert Michels's *Political Parties* (1911), where it was claimed that modern political parties were in the grip of an iron law of oligarchy. This 'law' suggested that mass political organizations invariably ended up being controlled by an elite (the oligarchy), because the practical and intellectual skills required to run an effective party machine were not available to (or even desired by) the mass membership. Although Michels based his hypothesis on the experience of a Socialist organization in Germany (the SPD), it could be argued that the French case in many senses bore out his argument. Thus, despite welcoming working-class activists in its fold in the early decades of the twentieth century, the Socialist Party ultimately became dominated by professional political figures whose social and educational skills were more attuned to the functional requirements of partisan activity.

Furthermore, the question needs to be addressed in the context of the historical relationship between Socialists and the labour movement in France. Unlike the British Labour Party and the German Social Democratic Party, French Socialists never enjoyed any organic links with the trade-union movement. The French labour movement was deeply marked by a tradition of hostility towards bourgeois politicians, which had its roots in the violent social and political conflicts of the early Third Republic. As noted in Chapter 7, this suspicion of 'intellectuals' was expressed in the anarcho-syndicalist concept of workerism (*ouvriérisme*), whose basic premise was that the political interests of the proletariat could be defended only by workers. Between 1906 and 1936 the main French labour union, the Confédération Générale du Travail (CGT), maintained a healthy distance from mainstream political organizations; after 1936 the union's leadership came under strong Communist influence, and the PCF never lost control of the organization thereafter. The Socialists thus missed the boat; this absence of institutional links between the French labour movement and the Socialist Party made it even more difficult for working-class leaders to emerge from the ranks of the party organization. Even after the regeneration of the Socialist Party in the 1970s and 1980s, relations with organized labour remained relatively cool. (François Mitterrand used to say of Edmond Maire, the former leader of the pro-Socialist union CFDT: 'Every time he speaks, I no longer understand a thing.') French trade-unionists voted overwhelmingly for the parties of the Left, but this had little impact on the socio-occupational background of the Socialist hierarchy.

Finally, no question about the historical role of workers in French politics could be answered adequately without reference to the Communist Party. The social composition of the French Communist Party leadership affected the recruitment of French Socialist elites throughout the twentieth century in one obvious way. After the early 1930s the leadership of the PCF was drawn almost exclusively from the world of manual labour. The practical consequence of this exclusion of other social groups from positions of power in the Communist Party was to drive successive generations of middle-class left-wing intellectuals towards the Socialist wing of the labour movement. In the final analysis the existence of the PCF (and its explicit commitment to the recruitment of political cadres from the working class) made even more inevitable the penetration of the Socialist Party by middle-class activists.

STRATEGY AND TACTICS

For most of the modern era the Socialist movement was faced with a strategic dilemma: given that many of its objectives (the pursuit of social justice, the promotion of economic reform, and levelling of social inequalities) overlapped to some extent with those of other political groups, to whom should the party turn to seek support for the achievement of its objectives? The Socialists came to realize by the 1930s that only under exceptional circumstances would they have a sufficiently large parliamentary majority to form a homogeneous government. This being the case, they needed to find allies in the political system, whose objectives converged sufficiently with their own to support their action in government. There were two basic options: an alliance with the forces of 'order' (in particular, the centre), or a coalition with the forces of 'movement' (most notably the Communists).

Before the Fifth Republic the Socialists experimented with both of these approaches. During the 1920s they provided parliamentary support to centrist coalition governments which excluded the Communist Party. Between 1934 and 1938 the SFIO was the leading force in the Popular Front coalition, which included both the Communists and the Radicals. They maintained this line after the Liberation, when they joined the grand coalition headed by General de Gaulle. But the advent of the Cold War in France led to a reversal of alliances, and between 1947 and 1951 the Socialists provided the essential backbone for the 'Third Force' coalition, a centrist grouping which excluded both Gaullists and Communists. It was essentially the same centrist grouping which supported the Mollet government of 1956–7. The basic problems faced by the Socialists from the late 1950s have already been identified. During the first decade of the Fifth Republic socialism appeared to be agonizing, as splinter groups broke away from the SFIO, and the old party began to suffer increasingly from intellectual and organizational sclerosis. As the Gaullists consolidated their grip on French political and administrative institutions in the 1960s Socialists were torn between two contrasting strategies to reverse their political and electoral fortunes. The first was sponsored by Gaston Defferre, the mayor of Marseilles and boss of the Bouches-du-Rhône Federation of the SFIO. In 1963 he lent his name to a political strategy which sought to unite the centre Left against the Gaullists without making any efforts to integrate the Communist Party into the new alliance. This attempt to revive the 'Third Force' strategy of the late 1940s was steadily undermined during the 1960s, as its proponents failed to make any serious headway with the electorate. Defferre tried to have himself nominated as the candidate of a united centre Left for the 1965 presidential elections, but the effort was scuttled by the Socialist leader Guy Mollet. In the presidential elections of 1969 Defferre succeeded in being chosen as the Socialist candidate but, as noted earlier, he won only a humiliating 5 per cent of the vote. The centre Left strategy did not look too promising.

An alternative strategy was advocated by François Mitterrand. One of the most perceptive and tenacious politicians of his generation, Mitterrand realized that the political and institutional structure of the Fifth Republic required a change in Socialist strategy. The fragmentation of party politics during the Third and Fourth Republics had made alliances with the centre possible; after 1958, however, the French party system was becoming increasingly bipolar. The presidency divided the political system between those who were for and against de Gaulle, and this polarization was accentuated by the majority electoral system, which forced parties into tactical alliances. In other words, Mitterrand realized that the principal electoral cleavage in the Fifth Republic was between the Right and the Left: Socialists, therefore, had to abandon their old alliance with the former, and enter into a new political partnership with the Communists. Before spelling out how this approach worked out in practice in the 1960s and 1970s, it should be emphasized that Defferre and Mitterrand were absolutely united on one basic objective: to reduce the political influence of the Communist Party. Defferre believed that this could be achieved by ignoring the PCF leadership and pitching the Socialist appeal directly at the Communist electorate. Mitterrand, on the other hand, argued that the Socialists had first to negotiate a formal alliance with the

Communists, then gradually win over their electorate to the Socialist camp. During the 1980s the PS had reached a position to accomplish precisely what Defferre was aiming at: dismissing the Communist leadership on questions of policy, but none the less relying on a full supply of Communist votes at every election.

The strategy which made such an achievement possible, however, was Mitterrand's. In the 1965 presidential elections he emerged as the candidate of the united Left against de Gaulle, and forced the General into a second ballot contest. De Gaulle was quite comfortably re-elected, but the markers of Mitterrand's victory in 1981 were already placed. The strategy of alliance between Socialists and Communists went through a phase of unity (1965–77), in which both partners struck a number of electoral agreements. This convergence culminated in the signature of the *Common Programme of Government* (1972), a detailed blueprint which sketched out the economic and social policies which the Left would implement if elected to office. In September 1977, however, the Communists broke off the alliance and put up their own candidate against Mitterrand in the 1981 presidential elections. But the dynamic movement which had been triggered by the Union of the Left was irresistible, and Mitterrand was triumphantly elected on the second ballot, after nine out of every ten first-ballot Communist voters switched their support to the Socialist candidate in the second round. (A similar proportion of Communist voters supported him on the second ballot of the 1988 presidential election.)

Thus the PS eventually achieved strategic supremacy over the PCF. The alliance had served to increase Socialist support considerably, while reducing the Communist Party's influence to under 10 per cent of the vote. But this superiority threw up another strategic dilemma. With the terminal agony of the Communists (accelerated by the collapse of Leninist regimes in the Soviet Union and Eastern Europe), the combined electoral power of the Left would not be sufficient to provide the Socialists with a stable majority in Parliament. In effect, this occurred after the legislative elections of June 1988: the Socialists emerged as the single largest party, but fell short of the absolute majority they enjoyed in the 1981–6 legislature. The logical solution was to open the presidential majority to the centre, and this was tried (without much success) by Prime Minister Michel Rocard's policy of *ouverture*. But the old dilemma resurfaced cruelly at this juncture. The centre parties refused to commit themselves fully to a political agreement with the Socialists as long as the latter continued to depend on the votes of the PCF electorate (and the tacit support of the Communist group in Parliament). The Socialists could not give up their electoral alliances with the Communists without jeopardizing many of their own parliamentary seats, and also destroying the vast network of municipal governments jointly run by the PS and PCF. The Communists had little interest in relinquishing their electoral agreement because they stood to lose even more ground without the support of the Socialists. After the party's devastating electoral defeat in the 1993 legislative elections, there was some evidence that the Socialist leadership was attempting to break out of this deadlock (for example, by considering a change to the electoral system, so as to reduce their dependence on Communist support, or in Michel Rocard's calls for a new coalition of the forces of 'movement'). It was little comfort to them that the dilemma they faced was confronted (and never fully resolved) by their forebears.

INTERNAL DIVISION

The third element of continuity in the Socialist tradition was the persistence of factional division within the party. As noted at the beginning of this chapter, socialist political culture was deeply individualistic, and the political hegemony achieved by the PS in the 1980s did not undermine this attachment to the time-honoured tradition of factional dispute, accompanied by highly publicized expressions of personal ill will between representatives of different undercurrents.

The factionalism which was inherent in the French socialist tradition stemmed from three sources. First, a relatively loose organizational structure, which provided considerable scope for the development of power centres at departmental level. In the mid-1930s the party's most fertile terrain for recruitment was the industrial North and the Mediterranean departments; throughout the Fifth Republic the departments of the Nord, Pas-de-Calais, and the Bouches-du-Rhône were the principal mainstays of party activism. These federations provided Socialists with several generations of leading figures. Guy Mollet controlled the Pas-de-Calais federation during the postwar era, and used his base in the party machine to bid successfully for the party leadership in 1946; Gaston Defferre's authoritative place in the PS in the 1970s was based on his firm and occasionally brutal leadership of the *mafioso* federation of the Bouches-du-Rhône; similarly, Pierre

Mauroy (Mitterrand's first Prime Minister after his election in 1981) was the influential leader of the federation of the Nord, one of the historical strongholds of working-class socialism. Former Prime Minister Laurent Fabius painfully discovered the importance of acquiring a regional power base in 1988: his bid to become party leader was rejected by the grass-roots, despite the full support of President Mitterrand for his candidature. Fabius was eventually chosen as First Secretary in January 1992, but only after much blood-letting between different factions. This feuding was resumed in April 1993, with the eviction of Fabius and the election of Michel Rocard as party leader.

The second source of factionalism was the personal ambition of individual leaders, which flourished in the shadow of the strong charismatic figure who dominated the PS during the 1970s and 1980s. Even in the days of the SFIO, when the party was governed by the consensual and emollient approach of Blum, ideological divisions were often artificially inflated as a means of furthering the political ambitions of Socialist leaders. After Blum's retirement Guy Mollet won control of the Socialist Party in 1946 after a rousing speech in which he declared, among other things, that the SFIO should work towards 'an economic and social revolution which will give power to the working class'. During Mollet's subsequent career, both as party leader and Prime Minister (1956–7), there was little evidence that this strategy had been pursued by the Socialists. In the 1980s the importance of personal ambition in the factional politics of the Socialist Party was enhanced by the erosion of genuine ideological differences between different groups within the party. Indeed, by the early 1990s, as strategic questions ceased to be a matter of dispute within the party, factional divisions were almost reducible to the personal ambitions of party leaders. Leaders such as Michel Rocard, Laurent Fabius, Pierre Bérégovoy, and Jacques Delors were in basic agreement on virtually all questions of political substance, yet remained deeply divided as the party prepared itself for the selection of a candidate to succeed President Mitterrand.

For much of the modern era, however, factionalism reflected essential ideological cleavages within the Socialist movement. Despite the general commitment of Socialist politicians to reformist practices when in government, there was a long tradition of ideological debate between minimalists and maximalists, who disagreed radically about the extent of social reforms and the pace at which they should be introduced. During the Popular Front era Blum was constantly under pressure from the left of the SFIO (known as *Pivertistes* after one of their leaders, Marceau Pivert) to accelerate the pace of social change; in recent times a similar role was played by the CERES faction (which changed its name to Socialisme et République in 1986). But the Marxist rhetoric used to conduct these ideological debates always had to be taken with a pinch of salt. At the Metz congress of the Socialist Party in 1979 a storm of applause greeted this wonderful flight of rhetoric by François Mitterrand: 'At the Epinay Congress Socialists chose to entrench themselves in class warfare. Without a strategy of rupture the Socialist Party would lose its identity. What use would it be for us to become a vague copy of reformist parties, which always end up as the bed-fellows of the dominant class?' As will be seen subsequently, the Socialist candidate implemented some of his promises after 1981, but it would be fair to suggest that the question posed by Mitterrand was rhetorical in more senses than one.

THE ACHIEVEMENTS OF THE SOCIALIST TRADITION

The existence of these significant elements of continuity raises the question of the Socialist contribution to French politics and government. Of course, the achievements of all political movements are worthy of scrutiny, but Socialists have a particular claim to attention. Few political parties in France have been as systematic as the Socialists in defining their goals in terms of moral and practical imperatives: the preservation of individual liberty, the encouragement of greater mass participation in public life, and the achievement of social reform. From Jaurès and Guesde to Blum and Mitterrand, Socialist politicians consistently pledged their movement's commitment to reforming and humanizing the capitalist system; in the words of Blum, to managing 'the affairs of bourgeois society in the best interests of the working class'. It is only appropriate that such lofty ambitions be treated with the respect they deserve.

The record of Socialists since the 1930s is by no means devoid of substantive achievements. The Popular Front was a strategic creation of the Communist Party, and could never have existed without the support of the Radicals; yet it was the Socialists who welded the different elements of the coalition together, and generated the momentum which made a critical contribution to the victory of April 1936. On the other hand, Blum was rightly criticized for his lack of decisiveness on key issues in 1936–7. More fundamentally, the ultimate collapse of the Popular Front in 1938 was a serious setback for the forces of 'movement', which disoriented and demobilized its activists, and ultimately cleared the way for the undermining of republican institutions by the Vichy regime. During the Fourth Republic the Socialists' record appears, at first glance, even more limited. The party failed to initiate any significant social reforms while in government in the 1940s and early 1950s, and the Mollet administration discredited itself in 1956–7 over its handling of the Algerian question. But the SFIO was entitled to claim some credit for safeguarding democratic political institutions from the combined onslaught of the Stalinist PCF and the authoritarian Gaullist movement, the Rassemblement du Peuple Français (RPF). It was clear that the PCF's commitment to political pluralism in the 1940s and 1950s was far from unconditional, even though it is difficult to surmise how far an electoral triumph of the Communists would have eventually resulted in the creation of a one-party state on the Soviet and East European model. De Gaulle's intentions on this particular question were always far more honourable than his political opponents would allow: even at the height of his campaigns against what he saw as 'party domination' in the late 1940s, he never seriously entertained the thought of abandoning the democratic heritage of the Republic. But it is arguable that the introduction of a powerful executive on the model of his Bayeux speech (1946) would have severely aggravated existing social and political tensions in France, and thus stood in the way of the outstanding achievement of the Fourth Republic: the reconstruction of the economy and the initiation of the process of modernization. Thus, in playing a critical role in obstructing revisionist challenges from both Communists and Gaullists, the SFIO helped to preserve the social fabric from strains which could have produced devastating political consequences.

What of the Fifth Republic? The transformation of the decaying SFIO into a dominant party (both within the Left and the party system more generally) in just over a decade was a remarkable achievement by any standards. Furthermore, in reconciling the Left with the political system created by de Gaulle, the Mitterrand presidency healed two equally damaging sores in the French body politic: the alienation of the Left from the public sphere, and the persistence of powerful anti-constitutional forces within the political system. But the precise achievements of the Mitterrand presidency are a matter of considerable controversy. In considering the Socialist record after 1981 a clear set of standards needs to be defined. Strikingly different pictures emerge, depending on whether one chooses to highlight the radical expectations raised by the Left in the late 1970s, the actual programmatic content of Mitterrand's '110 Proposals', or the party's impact on the broader framework of government. If the first parameter is chosen, the Socialist decade of the 1980s simply appears as a succession of failures. Many disillusioned advocates of radical change regarded the Socialists' conversion to the principles of sound finance and evolutionary change as a betrayal of the French Left's (painful) historical struggle against 'capitalism'. On the other hand, a detailed examination of the Socialist candidate's programme before 1981 would reveal that a significant proportion of Mitterrand's specific pledges were honoured under his presidency. Perhaps the most appropriate form of evaluation would be to consider the extent to which the Socialists' tenure of office substantively altered the structure of French government, which the PS always claimed needed urgent reform. From this angle the policy of decentralization was the Socialists' most ambitious attempt to transform the character of the State in France. Whatever else might be thought of Mitterrand's tenure of office, this restructuring of the relationship between centre and periphery represented one of the most significant transformations of the structure of French government since the emergence of the welfare state. The Defferre reforms reduced the excessive centralization which had been one of the durable legacies of the Jacobin state tradition in France, although their net effect was further to enhance the disparity between larger and smaller units of local government. Despite this qualification, however, President Mitterrand was right to describe these reforms as the 'leading question' (*grande affaire*) of his first seven years in office, even though the Socialists fell considerably short of the concomitant aim of expanding mass participation in public life (a point which will be returned to later).

Despite the fulfilment of many of Mitterrand's explicit promises during the 1980s, it is difficult to overlook the negative elements of the picture. What was especially significant about some of these failings was the uncanny extent to which they represented clear continuities in the socialist tradition. Some of the analogies between the problems of the 1980s and those experienced by previous generations of Socialists were compelling. As in the years of the Popular Front, the Socialist leaders of the 1980s came to office with expectations of social and political change which were so unrealistic that they had to be drastically scaled down (within a matter of months in the case of the Blum government, and a few years in that of Mitterrand). What these experiences demonstrated was a continuing failure on the part of the Socialist movement precisely to define its strategic ambitions; indeed, the same deficiency reappeared by the early 1990s, when the PS appeared unsure as to which principles and values it continued to stand for (at its 1990 Rennes congress the party promised to concentrate on the fight against 'inequalities' in French society, but did not identify what they were). This Socialist failure ultimately reflected the movement's highly instrumental conception of theory—a feature of the French Left which was also shared by the Communists. Both the SFIO and the PS tended to adopt maximalist programmes (particularly when in opposition), in which the traditional language of democratic socialism was freely blended with such Marxist notions as exploitation, class struggle, and rupture with capitalism. Why this tendency towards discursive radicalism? A number of hypotheses may be tentatively put forward. The Socialist movement in France always felt the need to justify its claim to be part of the Left; this was just as true before 1914, when the Socialists' credentials were strongly challenged by anarchists and anarcho-syndicalists, as after 1920, with the emergence of the Communist Party. Indeed, until the early 1980s the political strength of the PCF made the adoption of a radical ideological framework the only means available to the Socialists to underline their left-wing identity.

Two internal factors also contributed to this tendency towards intellectualization. As noted in this chapter, the Socialist movement was always marked by factionalism; this organizational characteristic gave an added impetus to the use of radical left-wing rhetoric by different groups, as this mode of discourse became an essential means of articulating differences between competing Socialist elites. Finally, it will be remembered that the Socialist leadership was dominated by middle-class intellectuals, who had been supremely well trained in the art of linguistic and verbal acrobatics. The literary talents of modern generations of Socialist leaders has indeed been impressive; Mitterrand's writings represent, in this respect, the faithful continuation of the socialist tradition of Louis Blanc and Jean Jaurès. But good literature is not necessarily a useful guide to the political intentions of its author; from this point of view, it is no accident that the theoretical and programmatic output of modern Socialism has tended to reveal little about its actual objectives.

The negative consequences of the Socialist predilection for abstruse theorizing became evident in the cases of both the Popular Front and the Mitterrand presidency. After promising great social and political changes, the Socialists made a hasty retreat to a pragmatic level of political and economic practice, in which any significant long-term vision was excluded (in the case of the 1980s, the vision became the daily management of public affairs). As mentioned earlier, the Socialists finally succeeded in breaking the Marxian stranglehold over the Left, but there was an important way in which this exercise remained essentially negative. The destruction of the icons of the traditional Left was not accompanied by an alternative set of aspirations and ideals. By the early 1990s, as mentioned earlier, there was no longer any clear sense of what was distinctive about Socialist ideology or political practice. This phenomenon was not restricted to France, of course, but this was hardly sufficient to exculpate the Socialists.

A third problem which the experience of the 1980s revealed was the disparity between moral principle and political practice. This was a separate issue from the question of the redefinition of strategic aims: what was at stake here was the extent to which the Socialists' practices remained consistent with their own fundamental ethical principles. Although the record was by no means entirely negative (the abolition of the death penalty in 1981, for example, was a major example of the transformation of a moral principle into public policy), the Socialists signally failed to uphold their general principles of political morality. They accused the Right of corruption and favouritism, yet their own practices throughout the 1980s and early 1990s often betrayed similar leanings. More important, perhaps, the Socialist government of Laurent Fabius did not hesitate to facilitate the rise of the National Front after 1984 on grounds of political expediency. The introduction of proportional representation in 1985 was presented by Mitterrand as a fulfilment of an earlier election pledge, but its enactment was transparently dictated by partisan considerations. Of course, all politicians exploit the trappings of public office to further their own ends. But many party members (including Michel Rocard, who resigned from the government over the issue in April 1985) were dismayed that a Socialist president could deliberately give a filip to the extreme Right in order to (attempt to) save his government from electoral defeat. Again, this unprincipled behaviour could be seen as an illustration of the basic flaw identified earlier: the yawning gap between the Socialists' theoretical pronouncements and their political practice.

By the late 1980s a fourth problem was beginning to haunt the Socialists, and this also evoked clear memories of the recent past. After a long spell in office the party had essentially ceased to exist as a vital political force. During the 1970s the PS had reconstituted its organization by grafting a host of emerging social networks (based on such issues as race, gender, and environmental concerns) onto the traditional base of the SFIO. This new generation of young militants remained loyal to the party during its first few years in office, then grew disillusioned as the organization was rapidly transformed into an electoral appendage of the government. By the late 1980s and early 1990s the collapse of the party's militant base provided clear echoes of the sclerotic condition of the SFIO in the 1960s. It is true that any party which remained in government for such a long spell could reasonably expect some erosion of its membership. The Socialists' weakness, however, was compounded by one key factor: the absence of organic links with the trade-union movement. The British Labour Party was able to maintain a comparatively strong organization in the 1960s and 1970s while in government; this was facilitated, to some extent, by the party's institutional association with the trade unions, and the preservation of a clear distinction between the parliamentary party and the Labour organization. Lacking a similar base in the working class, and surrendering all its leaders to government office after 1981, the French Socialist Party organization crumbled when its dispirited new Left militants abandoned the fold.

Finally (and this is the logical extension of the previous point) the Socialists failed to carry through their pledge to increase mass participation in public life. As noted from the outset, the French Socialist tradition consistently aimed to reduce the barriers between public institutions and civil society. The Popular Front, in this respect, encapsulated the view that 'fascism' could be defeated only if large sections of society were mobilized against the threat posed by the extreme Right. Similarly, under the Fifth Republic, the Socialist critique of political institutions strongly emphasized their perceived failure to involve the citizenry in public life. The Gaullist institutions were decried as impersonal and autocratic structures in which individuals were denied access to the State and, therefore, lacked a sense of identification with its actions (and their outcomes). Politics seemed to be reduced to the delegation of responsibility to the republican monarch, and the confirmation of his legitimacy to rule every seven years. To an important extent, the underlying rationale of decentralization was precisely to remedy this elitist conception of politics by encouraging mass participation at the lower levels of the system. It was therefore immensely ironical that it was a Socialist administration which presided over a spectacular collapse in mass identification with the political realm. The late 1980s and early 1990s saw high abstention rates in elections, falling levels of confidence in political elites, and a steep decline in political militancy. The deficiencies of the Socialists were not the sole causes of these phenomena, but their responsibility (as the governing party) for the failure of the political class to inspire and mobilize a traditionally participant society remained overwhelming. Far from increasing mass participation in public life, therefore, the net effect of the Socialist decade was (from the vantage point of the early 1990s) to have provoked a decline in public interest in politics.

Just like the Radical Party in the dying days of the Third Republic, the Socialists seemed to have lost their institutional vocation by the early 1990s. Like their Radical forebears, the Socialists became hypnotized by the attractions of ministerial office, and appeared incapable of redefining their political identity after the achievement of their primary goals. But if this narrative has shown anything, it is that Socialists have a long history of facing and, on at least three occasions, transcending death. Whether the party's traumatic defeat in the 1993 elections can be transformed into another miraculous resurrection is a matter which only the future will reveal.

Chronology

1833   April. Charles Fourier publicizes concept of 'socialism'.

1880   November. Havre Congress of Parti des Travailleurs Socialistes de France (which officially became the Parti Ouvrier Français in 1882).

1899   June. Government of republican defence under Waldeck-Rousseau; Alexandre Millerand accepts ministerial portfolio.

1905   January. Foundation of the Section Française de l'Internationale Ouvrière (SFIO).

1906   October. Amiens Charter of CGT rejects close collaboration of the trade union with SFIO.

1914 July. Assassination of Jean Jaurès.

August. Socialist ministers join Union Sacrée government.

1920 December. Tours Congress: majority of SFIO breaks away and later forms Communist Party.

1924 May. Cartel des Gauches victory; SFIO declines to participate in Herriot government.

1933 November. Déat, Marquet, and Renaudel expelled from SFIO.

1936 March. Toulouse reunification Congress of CGT.

May. Popular Front government under Léon Blum.

1946 January. Felix Gouin replaces de Gaulle as Prime Minister.

October. Guy Mollet elected First Secretary of SFIO.

1947 January. Paul Ramadier succeeds Léon Blum as Prime Minister.

Vincent Auriol elected President of Fourth Republic.

1956 February. Guy Mollet government.

1960 April. Foundation of Parti Socialiste Unifié.

1965 December. Mitterrand forces de Gaulle to contest second ballot of presidential elections.

1969 June. Nadir of French Socialism: Defferre beaten decisively in presidential elections.

July. Issy-les-Moulineaux Congress: SFIO refounded as Parti Socialiste (PS).

1971 June. Epinay Congress of PS: François Mitterrand elected First Secretary.

1972 June. Common Programme of Government signed by PS and PCF.

1974 May. Mitterrand narrowly defeated in presidential elections by Valéry Giscard d'Estaing.

1977 September. Breakdown of negotiations for updating Common Programme.

1978 March. Left loses legislative elections.

1981 May. Mitterrand elected President against Giscard d'Estaing.

June. Legislative elections give PS absolute majority; Communists invited into second Mauroy government.

1982 March. Defferre law on decentralization.

1984 July. Laurent Fabius government; PCF declines to participate.

1986 March. PS loses absolute majority in legislative elections.

1988 May. Re-election of Mitterrand for second term.

June. PS largest single party after legislative elections; government formed under Michel Rocard.

1991   May. Édith Cresson succeeds Rocard as Prime Minister.

1992   April. Pierre Bérégovoy appointed as Prime Minister.

1993   March. Decisive Socialist defeat in legislative elections.

CHAPTER 10
Gaullism and the Quest for National Unity

The variegated nature of the Gaullist tradition in French politics pre-
cludes any attempt at a schematic definition. The political scientist
Jean Charlot viewed Gaullism as a modern expression of a particular
brand of French nationalism, while his colleague René Rémond saw
Gaullism as distinctive in that it continued the 'Bonapartist' tradition
in French politics. Most left-wing commentators regarded Gaullism
as a right-wing movement, whereas Gaullists described themselves as
transcending the division between Left and Right. For many outside
observers of French politics (particularly in Britain and the United
States) Gaullism was a highly dogmatic political undercurrent, whose
domestic and external objectives were derived from a rigid set of
ideological principles; others, however, saw de Gaulle as a highly pragmatic and often opportunistic politician. For his supporters he was the
saviour of France, the man who single-handedly raised the banner of
resistance in 1940, and again rescued his country from the clutches
of extremists in 1958; his opponents belittled his role during the resistance, and accused him of manipulating events later to further his own
political ends. In an even more negative vein, two of his presidential
successors, Valéry Giscard d'Estaing and François Mitterrand,
denounced his tendency towards autocratic behaviour. The Communists censured him as an agent of monopoly capitalism. The extreme
Right branded him as a traitor, both for his role during the Second
World War and in the settlement of the Algerian question.

It is not surprising that 'the Gaullist phenomenon' should provoke
such different characterizations. De Gaulle himself was a profoundly
complex figure, whose career in public life was riddled with apparent
contradictions. His demeanour was imperial and disdainful, yet he was
adored and revered by the public. His inveterate contempt for politicians was based on a militaristic conception of the world, yet
he restored civilian power in France, and permanently eliminated
the political threat posed by the Army. He came from a family which
was deeply influenced by the writings of the Catholic monarchist

pamphleteer, Charles Maurras, but he twice rescued the Republic from the clutches of counter-revolutionary zealots. He fervently believed in the value of order, discipline, and hierarchy, but he rebelled against his superior officers during one of the darkest moments of modern French history, and later played a significant role in undermining the Fourth Republic. He was a nationalist who was deeply suspicious of Anglo-Saxon dominance, yet it was from London that he launched his famous 1940 appeal to resist German occupation. He was a passionate advocate of French territorial unity, who none the less agreed to the alienation of one of the nation's prize colonial possessions. He had a profound admiration for the continuity and stability embodied in British political institutions, yet consistently opposed British membership of the European Economic Community. He intensely disliked political parties, yet helped to found one of the dominant electoral organizations of modern France. He aspired to unite French society around a new set of institutions, but created a political system which sharply divided the community into two rival camps. Often depicted by his contemporaries as nothing more than a demagogue, de Gaulle was in fact a highly accomplished political tactician, who allowed neither his emotions nor a rigid attachment to ideology to interfere with the accomplishment of his sacred duties: the promotion of domestic unity and the defence of (his conception of) French national interests.

As noted above, de Gaulle's policies almost invariably generated opposition and controversy, despite his lofty aspirations. Yet the same figure who was reviled by the extreme Left and the extreme Right, and opposed by liberals and Socialists during most of his political career, seemed to have become part of the French national heritage by the time the centenary of his birth was celebrated in 1990. Communists nostalgically recalled their alliance with the Gaullists during the resistance, and enthused about de Gaulle's independent foreign policy. National Front leader Jean-Marie Le Pen stressed his ideological affinities with the General by highlighting their common hostility to the development of European supranationality. Liberals and technocrats remembered de Gaulle's commitment to transcending partisan and ideological divisions, and his drive to modernize the French economy; and even Socialists gave him full credit for devising the political and institutional structure of the Fifth Republic, and thus allowing their President to exercise the type of untrammelled power which François Mitterrand himself had denounced as autocratic in 1964. Thus, as with all legends, the mythical figure who emerged in 1990 revealed more about its various creators than its real historical subject. The object of this chapter will be to explore the political and ideological ramifications of the Gaullist phenomenon, so as to provide a more effective basis for evaluating the legacy of the first President of the Fifth Republic.

But Gaullism cannot be reduced to the achievements of its founder. As the originator of a new institutional system, de Gaulle lent his name and prestige to a specific political organization and, more generally, to the political and administrative structures which emerged under the Fifth Republic after 1958. Beyond the individual and the institutions he created, there also evolved a distinctive Gaullist ideology, based on a political philosophy which was deeply personal but also profoundly marked by the nationalist tradition in French politics. From a sociological perspective, furthermore, Gaullism represented the diffuse and somewhat contradictory aspirations of a considerable section of French society: the relationship between Gaullist ideology and the political perceptions, attitudes, and values of the Gaullist electorate was never simple. Finally, Gaullism did not perish with its founder: prominent political figures, associations, and parties claimed to be the rightful heirs to the throne left vacant after 1969. How has the movement come to terms with the disappearance of its founding father, and what can it mean to be a Gaullist in the France of the 1990s?

THE NECESSITIES OF STATE

From a very young age Charles de Gaulle was convinced that he was a man of destiny. At the age of 15 he wrote a school essay in which he described the French nation being saved from military humiliation by one 'General de Gaulle', the commander-in-chief of the French Army. In keeping with this vision, he joined the prestigious training school for military officers, Saint-Cyr, from which he graduated in 1912. De Gaulle received the *Légion d'Honneur* (the order created by Bonaparte in 1802 to reward distinction in public life) for bravery in action during the First World War; the general commander of his regiment was Philippe Pétain, who became a French national hero after the war. The two men would later symbolize two completely different political responses to the occupation of France in 1940. During the interwar period de Gaulle devoted himself to military strategy, and his chief concern was to modernize the Army. In 1934 he published an important work (*Vers l'Armée de métier*) in which he called for the systematic introduction of armoured divisions in the French Army. Few politicians and military strategists took this recommendation seriously until it was too late. Ironically, a similar notion found favour in the German high command, and the crushing superiority of Hitler's armoured divisions was one of the decisive factors in the defeat of the French Army in 1940.

In June 1940 the Prime Minister, Paul Reynaud, appointed de Gaulle as Under-Secretary of State in the French Ministry of War and National Defence. However, he did not remain in post for very long. A new government was formed under Marshal Philippe Pétain, who declared that France should accept the reality of defeat and cease all military resistance against the German invader. De Gaulle disagreed, and on 18 June he delivered his famous *Appel* on BBC radio, in which he called upon the French nation to continue the struggle against the enemy: 'whatever happens, the flame of the French resistance must not and will not be extinguished.' Scattered groups which had already begun to resist were heartened by the message, and gradually this movement developed into the resistance. De Gaulle eventually (although not without some difficulty) emerged as its undisputed leader; in 1944 he became the head of the French provisional government, and in November 1945 was unanimously elected Prime Minister by the Constituent Assembly. However, he resigned in January 1946, frustrated by the lack of executive power granted to the Prime Minister by the new constitution. In April 1947 he founded the Rassemblement du Peuple Français (RPF), a political organization whose main objective was to campaign for constitutional reform. Although initially successful, the RPF was rapidly sucked into the political quagmire of the Fourth Republic, and in 1953 de Gaulle announced that the organization was folding up. The General then made a dignified retreat to his country home in the sleepy village of Colombey-les-deux-Églises, and political commentators assumed that his political career was finished. As would be expected of a retiring public personality, he published his war memoirs in 1954, and in the legislative elections of 1956, 'Social-Republican' candidates, who declared their allegiance to the General, received only 4 per cent of the vote. To many, Gaullism seemed destined for the museum of political antiquities.

De Gaulle confounded these sombre predictions. In May 1958, by cleverly turning a national political crisis over Algeria to his advantage, he returned to power. By the end of the year France had a new constitution and he became the first President of the Fifth Republic. The Algerian crisis took up the first four years of the Gaullist presidency. After solving this problem by granting independence to the French territory, de Gaulle turned to his fundamental preoccupation: the modernization of the executive structure of the French State. In October 1962 he amended the French constitution by referendum, and paved the way for the direct election of the president by universal suffrage. In 1958 de Gaulle had been elected President by an electoral college consisting of local and national politicians: he could therefore not plausibly claim to be the direct representative of all French men and women. In the presidential election of 1965 de Gaulle defeated the candidate of the united Left, François Mitterrand. The modern French president was thus created: a directly elected political figure, with wide-ranging executive powers, who did not depend on other institutions for his authority, and owed his legitimacy to the people as a whole. But why did de Gaulle believe that these changes were needed?

Like most of his countrymen who lived through those troubled times, the French President was deeply marked by his experiences during the era of occupation and resistance. None the less, most of the victorious politicians of that generation (on both the Right and the Left) came out of these turbulent times with a pervasive sense of optimism. The document which vividly captured this positive outlook was the charter of the anti-Nazi resistance groups, the Conseil National de la Résistance: it vowed thoroughly to reconstruct the social and economic bases of French society after the liberation, and to reinforce the democratic foundations of the Republic. The prospects for international political co-operation seemed equally promising. Liberal political figures such as Jean Monnet believed that France's future lay in (Western) European integration, while the Communists and their allies looked to the Soviet Union and Eastern Europe for guidance. But both avenues seemed available to France as long as the grand alliance between the United States and the Soviet Union endured. De Gaulle, however, believed that such feelings of optimism were fundamentally misguided. His treatment by the Allies during the war (particularly by President Roosevelt) reinforced his view that states acted primarily out of self-interest, and that his country could expect no favours even from like-minded states such as Britain and the United States. France could not solve her problems by emulating the achievements of other nations or diluting her national identity into a wider community of European states. But, at the same time, France could not respond to the challenges of the modern age by keeping the same political and administrative machinery. After his resignation in 1946 his Bayeux speech outlined a number of proposals for the creation of a powerful executive presidency; many of these ideas were later embodied in the constitution of the Fifth Republic. De Gaulle believed that the traditional French political system (epitomized by the Third and Fourth Republics) had stifled decisive leadership and produced a generation of politicians who utterly lacked initiative and vision. De Gaulle's cutting observations about the failings of French politicians became legendary. Perhaps the remark which best summed up his attitude towards the system he inherited was his assessment of Albert Lebrun, the last President of the Third Republic, under whose leadership France surrendered to the Germans in 1940: 'He was a decent enough man. But, as head of state, he lacked two essential attributes: he was no head, and there was no state.'

France needed decisive leadership for two reasons. The first was domestic: the French were a notoriously quarrelsome people, who were capable of magnificent achievements but could produce them only if they were disciplined and directed by a strong figure. Thus Gaullism always aspired to transcend the divisions which constantly fractured French society. Rather like Bonaparte in the early nineteenth century, de Gaulle saw the goal of forging the social and political unity of the French nation as a categorical imperative. Strong leadership and national unity were the necessary prerequisites for a powerful and decisive State. This was the second necessity: a strong State was absolutely vital for the nation's survival, because France was part of an international system in which the only qualities that mattered were power and prestige. De Gaulle's tragic conception of human existence was derived from a hard-headed reading of French history: France had been repeatedly humiliated since 1789 when she was weak, and a strong State was the only way of ensuring that this indignity was never repeated. But de Gaulle's pessimistic view of life was also based on the premise that power was ephemeral and fragile, and tragedy never far removed from the statesman's horizon. In his *Mémoires d'Espoir* he observed that supreme authority in France was always dependent on the outcome of military conflict. Bonaparte fell from power after failing to conquer Europe, and Napoleon III was chased out of office after losing the battle of Sedan to the Prussians in 1870;

the Third Republic collapsed ignominiously after the allegedly impregnable Maginot Line was overrun by German troops in 1940. De Gaulle did not need to be reminded, furthermore, how the Algerian conflict had destroyed the credibility of the Fourth Republic in the eyes of the nation. Strong institutions, national unity, emphasis on the 'rank' of the French state in the world: these central concerns invariably underlay the formulation of Gaullist domestic and external policies throughout the first decade of the Fifth Republic.

THE POLITICS OF CHARISMATIC LEADERSHIP

The first important contrast which should be drawn within the Gaullist totality is the distinction between the leader and the institutions he created. De Gaulle's political philosophy, as has already been noted, stressed the centrality of decisive individual leadership. According to the Gaullist diagnosis, one of the basic problems of republican government was the excessive influence of partisan forces on the making of public policy. Michel Debré, a Gaullist constitutional expert who served as Prime Minister between 1958 and 1962, thus characterized the problem in a trenchant pamphlet entitled *Ces Princes qui nous gouvernent* (1957): 'Our trouble stems from the division among multiple parties, divided within themselves, associated with conflicting interests, and prisoners of their own ideologies.' De Gaulle was inherently distrustful of parties: at best, they were full of incompetent mediocrities whose sole ambition was to exercise power; at worst, they created artificial divisions within French society, thus destabilizing a social equilibrium which was inherently fragile. The failed experience of his own RPF movement during the Fourth Republic confirmed these prejudices, and steeled de Gaulle's determination to undermine the hold of parties on the French State.

In order to achieve this goal, de Gaulle needed to make the French president completely autonomous from the system of national parties and ideologies: hence the constitutional reform of October 1962, which provided for the election of the president by universal suffrage. But from the early days of the Fifth Republic de Gaulle developed the practice of targeting his appeal directly to the French population, without bothering with such irrelevant intermediaries as political groups or Parliament. He developed this procedure to a fine art. On important political questions he made use of the referendum: between

1958 and the end of 1962 this method was used on four occasions, each time with resounding success. He also made highly dramatic appearances on French television, where he delivered some memorable harangues against enemies of the French State. One of his most memorable performances came on the night of 23 April 1961. A military insurrection had been launched by the Army high command in Algeria and, in the mounting sense of panic, there were real fears that Paris would be overrun by insurgent troops. De Gaulle spoke in the early evening, with the entire nation glued to its radio and television sets. By invoking Article 16 of the constitution he proclaimed a state of emergency, swore that the rebels would meet with exemplary justice, and ended with a rousing appeal to the French nation to rally behind its President. But, in a way, the substance of his speech was less important than the tone in which it was delivered. He gave the appearance of ruthless determination, complete self-assurance, and referred to the leaders of the rebellion with utter contempt. The effect was overpowering, and a sizeable proportion of the rebellious troops in Algeria abandoned the insurgency immediately on hearing de Gaulle's broadcast.

The charismatic quality of the Gaullist presidency was not sufficient in itself to constitute a method of government, and de Gaulle was not foolish enough to believe (as charismatic figures sometimes tend to) that it could. So, alongside the presidential institution, de Gaulle sponsored the development of a Gaullist party, the Union pour la Nouvelle République (UNR), which was formed to contest the legislative elections of November 1958, and more generally, to provide the Gaullist government with parliamentary support. At the same time de Gaulle insisted that he was 'above party politics', and always maintained a certain distance from the Gaullist party. Election results between 1958 and 1969 gave a clear measure of the different public images of de Gaulle and his party. De Gaulle's claim that he was not merely a partisan politician was corroborated by the fact that he always commanded a sizeably greater proportion of the popular vote than the Gaullist party. The latter's best performance in the legislative elections of June 1968, when it won 10 million votes (44.7 per cent of the votes cast), was still inferior to de Gaulle's worst display, in the referendum of April 1969, when he gained the support of a 'mere' 10.5 million voters (46.8 per cent). At its peak, de Gaulle's level of popular support reached staggering heights: 17.5 million votes in the 1958 referendum on the new constitution (79.2 per cent of the vote), 15 million in the

1961 referendum on Algerian self-determination (75.2 per cent), and 13 million (61.7 per cent) in the October 1962 referendum on the direct election of the president. Part of the discrepancy might be explained by the fact that a referendum focused on a single issue, and that those who supported de Gaulle on that specific issue did not necessarily agree with his policies more generally. This was to some extent true, but it should also be remembered that de Gaulle made a habit of turning each referendum into a vote of confidence in his own leadership. His resignation from the presidency in April 1969 followed directly after his defeat in a referendum on senatorial reform.

The French electorate clearly believed that de Gaulle's appeal in some senses transcended traditional partisan cleavages, but his carefully cultivated image of being 'above politics' was not swallowed uncritically. An opinion poll conducted in March 1967 found that only 17 per cent of the electorate believed that de Gaulle had conducted himself as a genuine arbiter; almost two-thirds of the voters thought that he acted primarily as the leader of the majority Gaullist party. The myth of an elevated presidential institution, thriving in quasi-spiritual communion with the French nation without the need for any political intermediaries, rapidly wore thin as de Gaulle realized that an effective presidency had to be buttressed by an array of political and administrative institutions. The Gaullist party was, in effect, manipulated from the Elysée Palace: its leadership was chosen personally by de Gaulle, its material and intellectual infrastructure was provided from government sources, and its political programme was based on priorities defined by de Gaulle himself. This dependence on the presidency proved to be extremely beneficial for the Gaullist party throughout the 1960s, as it enabled the organization to develop into the first truly 'modern' French political party. The Gaullists were the first to import such American electioneering techniques as the systematic use of opinion polls, canvassing voters by telephone, and heavy reliance on advertising to cultivate the party's public image. These devices were well beyond the imagination and resources of most other political parties in France. The French Communist Party could match (and arguably surpass) the Gaullists in terms of centralization and mass membership, but, even with the considerable help of their Soviet comrades, the Communists could not hope to compete with the Gaullists' financial resources.

Yet there remained an important sense in which de Gaulle was 'above' the system of party politics, and this was by virtue of the functional attributes of the presidential system itself. In fact, the strength of the executive system created by de Gaulle had few competitors in other advanced industrial societies. The constitution of the Fifth Republic gave the president strong leverage over all other political and administrative institutions. Some of the president's powers required the counter-signature of the prime minister: these 'traditional' powers included the negotiation and ratification of treaties, appointment of ministers, civil servants, and heads of nationalized industries. But the real source of the French president's power lay in his 'prerogative' entitlements, which did not need to be sanctioned by any other institution. The president appointed the prime minister, had the right to have messages read out in Parliament, to organize a referendum, to dissolve Parliament (not more than once a year), to appoint three members (including the president) of the Constitutional Council (whose remit was to ensure the constitutionality of laws promulgated by Parliament), and, last but not least, to declare a state of emergency if the integrity of the Republic was compromised (as was deemed by de Gaulle to have occurred in April 1961). More important than these formal prerogatives, however, was de Gaulle's interpretation of the spirit of the constitution. The framers of the 1958 constitution had intended a distribution of power between the different offices of the new State. In a press conference he gave in January 1964, however, the President declared that 'it is clearly the President *alone* who holds and delegates the authority of the state.' For most of the duration of his presidency the power exercised by de Gaulle was unrestrained simply because it was accepted, including (and perhaps especially) by those who might have had some constitutional ground to challenge him. He sacked his Prime Ministers Debré and Pompidou when he decided that the country (by which he meant himself) had had enough of them. They were under no constitutional obligation to resign, and did so because they were loyal presidential subordinates. The Council of Ministers fared no better. During the first years of the Fifth Republic, any attempt to discuss critically the basic orientations of presidential policy in cabinet was regarded as an intolerable act of insubordination. When, for example, Finance Minister Antoine Pinay ventured to criticize de Gaulle's anti-American foreign policy, he was icily informed that it was not the business of the Finance Minister to have (let alone express) views on foreign policy. De Gaulle regarded any issue pertaining to defence, foreign, and colonial matters as his 'reserved domain'. But, as he demonstrated repeatedly throughout his presidency, there were no areas of government activity in which he did not intervene when he felt that such action was warranted. He never (publicly) proclaimed 'L'État c'est moi,' but this was an entirely fitting description of his monarchical conception of the State.

Ultimately, the Gaullist Republic was a system in which none of the traditional institutional counterweights to executive power could be said to function effectively. The Prime Minister and his Council of Ministers, as already noted, were pliant executors of the presidential will. Parliament was not treated with excessive deference either. The constitution set clear (and, in effect drastic) limits upon the power of the French National Assembly: these were set out in Articles 24–51, and included control of Parliament's agenda by the government, severe limits on the legislating authority of individual members, and a variety of means of ensuring that government legislation was adopted without discussion. But, as if these restrictions were not sufficiently compelling, de Gaulle also never missed an opportunity to humiliate French parliamentarians. When his Prime Minister, Georges Pompidou, was defeated in a vote of confidence in the National Assembly in early October 1962 over the issue of constitutional reform, de Gaulle took this as a personal affront. He first mortally offended Parliament by immediately reappointing Pompidou as Prime Minister (according to Article 50 of the constitution, a Prime Minister who lost a vote of confidence had to tender his resignation). Furthermore, a successful vote of censure meant that Parliament had to be dissolved and fresh elections organized. De Gaulle was bound, again by the constitution, to 'consult' the presidents of both the lower and upper houses before announcing the dissolution. He duly received the President of the Senate, Gaston Monnerville, but their meeting lasted just long enough for Monnerville to be icily informed of the President's decision and shown the way out of the Elysée Palace. Monnerville had found out, in no uncertain terms, that the will of the General was the general will.

GAULLISM AS A POLITICAL TRADITION

The Gaullist institutions conceived after 1958, and the political and social philosophy which underlay their creation, did not emerge from an intellectual vacuum. Identifying the ideological distinctiveness of Gaullism is necessarily a comparative exercise: it involves trying to assess the extent to which Gaullist philosophy was derived from earlier traditions of political thought in France.

The judgement of de Gaulle's contemporaries is not a promising place to begin such an enquiry. As noted at the beginning of this chapter, Gaullists tended to stress the exceptional character of their political philosophy, while their opponents often reduced the institutional system created by the General to a form of pure authoritarianism. This view was common to most non-Gaullists, and was expressed by two politicians who themselves subsequently went on to assume the presidential mantle. In 1964 François Mitterrand described the political system created by de Gaulle as a *coup d'état permanent*: in other words, an authoritarian power structure in which legality was always circumscribed by *raison d'état*, and the interests of the people always subordinated to the desires of the ruler. In 1967 Valéry Giscard d'Estaing similarly warned against the Gaullist tendency towards 'the solitary exercise of power'. But Gaullism could never be reduced to the exercise of strong leadership for its own sake. De Gaulle may sometimes have confused his desires with the pursuit of the common good, but his justification of the principle of centralized leadership was always couched in terms of the national interest. As already argued, de Gaulle believed that the State was the source and guarantee of national unity: its strength was necessary to allow the French *génie* to flourish, and its prestige had to be maintained to prevent the enemies of France from taking advantage of her. But although de Gaulle was obsessed with the concepts of State and nation, it is hard to identify him as the inheritor of an exclusive ideological tradition. As argued in Chapter 5, French nationalism was never intellectually or politically homogeneous. The Jacobins, for example, were fervent nationalists, who believed in centralized state power and national unity, and were firmly opposed to the existence of autonomous intermediate institutions at regional or local levels. Was Gaullism the modern expression of the Jacobin tradition? In many respects the intellectual lineage is clear; at the same time, there was another tradition of French nationalism, which was typified in the late nineteenth century in the writings of Maurice Barrès and Charles Maurras. This 'integral' form of French nationalism was positivistic, anti-democratic and populist, doctrinaire, and informed by a deeply pessimistic view of history. As noted earlier, de Gaulle was educated in a milieu in which the writings of Maurras were regarded as authoritative, and his own defensive form of nationalism in some ways mirrored the concerns of the Action Française pamphleteer. At the same time de Gaulle placed his own imprint on the traditions he inherited. He rejected the aggressive expansionism which was an essential component of classical Jacobinism and also refused to exclude any group from French society on racial or cultural grounds, as was commonly advocated by the adversarial nationalist tradition. His universalism was expressed in cultural rather than militaristic forms. His nationalism, although it fell somewhat short of the generous and inclusive conception which typified the republican tradition, was fundamentally opposed to the sectarian excesses which were condoned throughout the twentieth century by Charles Maurras and his true disciples.

This ambivalent heritage is further demonstrated if Gaullism is assessed in the light of traditional notions of 'Left' and 'Right' (or, in French political terminology, 'movement' and 'order'). Was Gaullism a philosophy of order? As already noted, René Rémond saw the Gaullist experience as the modern manifestation of the Bonapartist tradition of the French Right: a political philosophy which was derived from the practices of Napoleon (and his nephew), and stressed the imperatives of state-building, authority and hierarchy, technical competence, administrative centralization, and, above all, decisive individual leadership. Was Gaullism a continuation of the Bonapartist spirit? The answer can only be affirmative if one takes de Gaulle's constant emphasis on firm leadership at face value; notes the prominent position afforded to financial interests in the Gaullist movement; and, perhaps most significantly, remembers that an essential element of the electoral appeal of Gaullism (of both de Gaulle and the Gaullist party) rested on the fear of anarchy. As noted in Chapter 7, de Gaulle's famous *après moi le déluge* struck a profound chord in a society which was still deeply marked by the psychological traumas of war and occupation in the 1940s, and the threat of civil war in the late 1950s. In the legislative elections of June 1968, furthermore, the Gaullists unashamedly exploited provincial fears triggered by the May events in Paris. They were so successful in generating this collective anti-Communist psychosis that the Gaullist party swept back into office with an absolute majority of seats in the National Assembly.

But it would be churlish to present Gaullism as simply representing the virtues of order and good government. From the early days of the resistance, de Gaulle and the Gaullist movement were full of contempt for the reactionary and cowardly French conservative forces which provided the bulk of Marshal Pétain's support after 1940. De Gaulle himself was never philosophically or temperamentally inclined towards conservatism. This was already implicit in his defiance of the political and military establishment during the occupation; it was further underlined by his support for progressive social and economic legislation during his brief spell as Prime Minister after the liberation (the most notable element of which was perhaps his decree granting women the right to vote). His close companions during the resistance and the Fourth Republic, who subsequently occupied the highest positions in the Gaullist State, were men of progressive political origins and affiliations: André Malraux was a former Communist adventurer, who became de Gaulle's Minister of Culture; Michel Debré was a Radical who identified with the Jacobin tradition; Edmond Michelet was a progressive social Catholic; Jacques Chaban-Delmas was a secular modernizer, and René Capitant was an old-fashioned social reformer. De Gaulle never ceased to denounce the 'forces of capital' which, he believed, had always been his main political adversaries. During both the Fourth and Fifth Republics, he proclaimed his desire to sponsor participatory and profit-sharing schemes which would give workers a greater stake in the productive process, and many of his ideas in this field were borrowed from the conceptual armoury of social Catholicism.

Despite these worthy intentions, however, de Gaulle's practical achievements in the social field were rather lacklustre. The political and administrative elite which was propelled into high office during the 1960s was basically technocratic in its outlook: it firmly believed in the need to modernize the French economy, and recognized that social and economic reforms were necessary to this effect. But radical measures were rarely proposed, and those that were (for example, a scheme for worker participation) failed to be implemented effectively. Left-wing Gaullists, such as René Capitant and Edgar Pisani, often complained bitterly about the lack of reforming zeal of their colleagues in government. But real responsibility must be placed squarely on the shoulders of the supreme leader. As has been made clear, de Gaulle was sufficiently in control of the levers of political and administrative command to ensure that his political priorities were fully respected by his governments. Even in the early years of his presidency he was always able to impose his preferences on his political associates. That he chose to devote more of his time to questions of foreign and defence policy provides some indication of where his relative political priorities lay. It may also be added that de Gaulle was too fine a tactician to forget that a sizeable contingent of his personal electorate, and the overwhelming majority of those who voted for Gaullist candidates, were precisely those French men and women who preferred order and good government to progressive notions of redistribution and social change.

Gaullism, therefore, was exclusively an ideology neither of order nor movement: it contained elements of each, and these elements always cohabited with some unease. But, however uncomfortably, they *did* cohabit, and this proved to be one of the bases of Gaullist hegemony in French politics during the 1960s. In a sense this was probably the most significant way in which de Gaulle perpetuated the Bonapartist spirit. By forcing the Right to abandon its emphasis on tradition and conservatism, he adapted its political objectives to the needs of a modern society. Like Bonaparte, who domesticated the spirit of the French Revolution in order to reconstruct the social and political order, de Gaulle secured the political hegemony of the Right by blending many of the principles of 'movement' into his own programmatic vision. But de Gaulle's ideological eclecticism was not purely opportunistic. He certainly realized that the Right could not aspire to govern durably if it remained rooted in its traditionalist vision of society, and this appreciation provided a powerful impetus for ideological change. However, much of the drive also came from de Gaulle's intrinsically strong commitment to the notions of modernization and social justice, without which France could not, in his view, occupy its rightful position in the international arena.

GAULLIST FOREIGN POLICY

An additional complicating factor in attempting to define the political philosophy of Gaullism was foreign policy. Here again, the course charted by de Gaulle contained elements which could not be attributed to an exclusive ideological approach. The great divide in postwar European politics, both between and within nations, was generated by the Cold War. After 1945 France sided resolutely with her Western allies against the Soviet bloc, and the internal political cleavages created by this alignment produced two competing conceptions of foreign policy. On one hand there were those (conservatives, liberals, and Socialists) who argued that France's destiny was anchored in a West European political and military alliance against the Communist bloc. This alignment involved membership of the North Atlantic Treaty Organization

(NATO), the economic integration of West European states, and a common recognition of the political leadership of the United States in the defence of the democratic world. On the other hand there were those (Communists and their *progressiste* allies; members of peace movements) who claimed that France should align herself with the Soviet camp in order to protect the nation's political, economic, and cultural interests from the evil designs of American imperialism. European integration, according to this view, was simply a capitalist conspiracy to enhance the exploitation of French workers.

De Gaulle's underlying approach to foreign affairs rejected the centrality of the ideological conflict between capitalism and communism. As a hard-headed realist, he believed that all states were primarily motivated by interests, and that grand ideologies such as communism or capitalism simply provided the language in which these conflicting interests were articulated. These interests were relatively constant, and were determined by national identity and character, geography, cultural attributes, and the legacy of past political experiences. De Gaulle believed that French national interests could be secured only if she moved away from the artificial ideological cleavages created by the Cold War. So where did he stand in relation to the two conceptions of foreign policy previously outlined? He accepted the prevailing view that France's destiny lay in Europe, but agreed with the Communists that further economic and political integration was harmful. His reasons for rejecting European integration overlapped to some extent with those of the Communists: like the Jacobin leadership of the PCF, de Gaulle believed that the nation-state was an indispensable tool for achieving social and economic progress. At the same time de Gaulle accepted the need for a common political stand against Soviet Communism, but rejected the view that Americans should play any significant role in the matter. The Gaullist world-view was therefore distinctive from that of other French political groups: it accepted Europe, but as a cultural rather than a socio-economic concept; it took the Russian threat seriously, but claimed that France could handle it without a military alliance with like-minded states; it was deeply hostile to Communism, but often appeared to suggest that France was equally (if not more) threatened by the United States.

When de Gaulle returned to power in 1958 he set about implementing his vision of the new role France should play in the international system. Although he was kept busy with the Algerian problem until 1962, he rapidly confirmed France's nuclear capacity: the first French nuclear explosion was conducted in February 1960. At the same time he initiated moves to pull away from NATO, and in March 1966 withdrew from the military structure of the Western alliance. Armed with a nuclear deterrent which purported to symbolize French independence from East and West, de Gaulle proceeded to lead his country towards her destiny as a great nation. Thus European co-operation across ideological boundaries was initiated. De Gaulle's idea of constructing a European community 'stretching from the Atlantic to the Urals' never achieved its high objectives, mainly because of the scepticism with which the project was received by the Russians and their allies. The Soviet invasion of Czechoslovakia in August 1968 ended the dream of an independent form of Communism in Eastern Europe, and also put paid to the Gaullist notion of an independent European alliance against the superpowers. But it sounded good, and also gave de Gaulle the opportunity to put down the Americans and their lackeys, the British. De Gaulle was sharply critical of American imperialism in the developing world, and urged President Lyndon Johnson to withdraw his troops from Vietnam. In January 1964, at a time when China was still regarded as one of America's greatest enemies, de Gaulle established diplomatic relations with the People's Republic. Meanwhile, British efforts to gain entry into the European Economic Community were consistently opposed by de Gaulle, who used his veto powers to deny Community membership to the country which he contemptuously described as the 'Trojan horse of the United States in Europe'. De Gaulle still remembered his cavalier treatment by the Allies during the war, and his dealings with the British and the Americans in the 1960s were still informed by these painful memories. But his hostile pronouncements against Western imperialism, and his highly sympathetic approach to the Communist powers of the East, should not be misconstrued as an attempt to reverse French alliances. When East–West confrontation reached its climactic point in October 1962 during the Cuban missile crisis, de Gaulle was one of the first Western statesmen to proclaim his unqualified support for the position taken by President Kennedy. In other words, when it really mattered, France remained a loyal member of the Atlantic alliance, and firmly opposed any attempt by the Soviet Union to gain strategic advantages over the West.

De Gaulle may not have succeeded in many of his foreign policy ventures, but in one field (arguably the most important) his achievement was indisputable: he rekindled the French sense of national pride. He washed away the stigma which had accompanied two decades of national humiliation, institutional instability, and colonial conflict, and convinced a sizeable proportion of the electorate that France had become a great nation again. Once more, this reflected his demonic ability to appeal to voters across the traditional frontiers of partisan politics. As in domestic politics, there was something for everyone in de Gaulle's foreign policy. Conservatives approved his hawkish nuclear policy, his paternalistic approach to Africa, and his military and diplomatic ties with such dictatorial regimes as South Africa and Portugal. Liberals warmed to his efforts at Franco-German reconciliation, which yielded the treaty of co-operation of January 1963; and the Left paid tribute to his anti-American policies, and his readiness to initiate a dialogue with the Soviet and Chinese leaderships. The French public was not slow to express its appreciation of this artistic collage. An opinion poll taken in March 1968 indicated that almost two-thirds of the electorate was 'satisfied with France's role in the world'. This was a true measure of de Gaulle's accomplishment. Ten years earlier, when he assumed power in the dramatic circumstances of the Algerian crisis, the mere suggestion that France had any role to play in international affairs would have been greeted with derision.

GAULLISM AFTER DE GAULLE

After his defeat in the referendum of April 1969 de Gaulle promptly resigned from office, and retired to his beloved village of Colombey-les-deux-Églises, where he died in November 1970. The Gaullist tradition did not, however, pass away with its founder: its legacy continued to mark the French political and institutional system, although the fortunes of the Gaullist movement swung quite dramatically in the years which followed the death of the General. A number of important areas of change may be identified.

First, Gaullists lost what many came to see as their principal vocation as a political institution: holding high office. De Gaulle was succeeded by Georges Pompidou as President in 1969, but after his demise the Gaullists repeatedly failed to capture what they saw as *their* presidency. In 1974 and 1981 the official Gaullist candidates, Chaban-Delmas and Chirac, did not even perform well enough in the first round to contest the run-off between the two best-placed candidates. In 1988

Jacques Chirac was present on the second ballot, but lost by more than 2 million votes to the incumbent President, François Mitterrand. Chirac, it is true, held the position of Prime Minister twice after de Gaulle's death (1974–6 and 1986–8), but on both occasions the experience came to an abrupt and premature end. Chirac's (admittedly glittering) consolation prize was to capture the municipality of Paris in 1977, and transform it into an impregnable fortress of municipal Gaullism (he was triumphantly re-elected in 1983 and 1989). Indeed, the leadership of the Gaullist Rassemblement pour la République (RPR) became dominated by Parisian elites, brought into positions of high office through the municipal networks of Paris and its surrounding areas. This process of elite recruitment differed significantly from that of the 1960s, when the overwhelming majority of Gaullist 'barons' came to local politics through exercising national power. The RPR's enforced spell in opposition after 1976 had the effect of inverting the relationship between centre and periphery within the party, and paved the way for the emergence of a new generation groomed in local politics. There remained a fundamental irony in this situation: the privileged recruiting terrain for Gaullist elites, and one of the most valuable electoral show-pieces of modern Gaullism, represented a form of politics (local government) for which its founder had nothing but contempt.

A clear consequence of the Gaullists' failure to retain the presidency was the erosion of their hegemony over the coalition of right-wing and centre parties. During the first two decades of the Fifth Republic the French party system was dominated by two blocs, each of which was organized around a hegemonic political and ideological force. Throughout the 1960s the Gaullists occupied an unassailable position within the right-wing coalition. In the legislative elections of 1968 Gaullists accounted for almost 80 per cent of the total right-wing vote; ten years later, however, the rise of the liberal Giscardian wing of the Right had brought this proportion down to just under 50 per cent. In the 1980s the fragmentation of the forces of 'order' was accentuated by the emergence of the National Front. Jean-Marie Le Pen's party was denied fair representation in Parliament in the 1988 and 1993 legislative elections, but a good indication of the electoral strength of his movement was provided in the presidential election of 1988. In the first round the Gaullist candidate Chirac won 6 million votes, the liberal Raymond Barre 5 million, and Jean-Marie Le Pen 4 million. Gaullism now stood for only around one-third of the total right-wing vote. The golden days of unconditional Gaullist supremacy over the other parties of the Right appeared to have ended, at least for the foreseeable future. In addition, the RPR became deeply divided over a range of fundamental issues, including leadership, relations with other forces of 'order', and political strategy. Five basic cleavages emerged in the 1980s: an organizational struggle between the Parisian leadership of the RPR and the representatives of the provinces (both departmental and municipal); a generational conflict between the old guard (led by Chirac and his barons) and the new wave of Gaullist young turks (typified by Philippe Séguin); a temperamental difference between the technocratic wing of the party (led by Edouard Balladur, appointed Prime Minister after the 1993 legislative elections), which was keen to stress the managerial and administrative competence of the Gaullist elites, and the populists (embodied in the abrasive and truculent personality of Charles Pasqua), who wanted the party to revert to the pugnacious traditions of popular Gaullism; a cultural divide between advocates and opponents of European political and economic integration, which caused intense acrimony during the 1992 referendum campaign for the ratification of the Maastricht treaty (RPR leader Chirac supported the agreement, while two of its leading opponents were Pasqua and Séguin, who normally belonged to different wings of the party, but whose interests converged over this issue); and finally, an ideological cleavage between right- and left-wing Gaullists, continuing the battle over whether the movement should define itself as primarily a party of 'order' or 'movement'. These internal divisions do not set the Gaullists apart from most other mainstream parties, which have witnessed the emergence of similar internal fault lines in the 1980s and early 1990s. But they undoubtedly represent a significant change from the unity and cohesiveness which the Gaullists proudly presented to the political world in the 1960s.

Third, the social profile of the Gaullist movement changed considerably after 1970. De Gaulle, it will be remembered, was able to pitch his electoral appeal across party lines, and this meant (given the class-based structure of partisanship) that his movement acquired an interclass character which clearly distinguished it from traditional conservative organizations. De Gaulle's personal following among the working class remained very high throughout the 1960s; in the first ballot of the 1988 presidential election, however, Jacques Chirac won the support of only 9.5 per cent of the working class. More generally, the Gaullist presidential electorate began to contract: by the late 1980s it had become much more regionalized than ever before (Chirac's showing in 1988 was poor in the north, the east, and the south-east), and it increasingly assumed the socio-occupational profile of a conservative electorate. The Gaullist vote became predominantly older and more female, and primarily rested on social forces which were static and even declining: the older age groups, the rural world, and the Catholic community. Thus the Gaullist movement could no longer aspire to transcend the social divide between forces of 'order' and 'movement'. Indeed, despite the genuine hostility of most of its leaders to the ideas and values projected by the National Front, there were increasing areas of ideological convergence between the electorates of the two movements. Gaullist and National Front voters shared overlapping concerns over such issues as immigration, order and insecurity, and the protection of French national identity. In the heyday of its hegemony over the Right, Gaullism was able to appeal to conservative constituencies of this kind without allowing their objectives and values to dominate its thinking. By the 1990s, however, the shrinking social base of the Gaullist party had somewhat undermined the ability of its leaders effectively to transcend the division between 'order' and 'movement'.

In addition, the basic economic philosophy of the Gaullist elites underwent a significant change in the 1980s. De Gaulle, it will be remembered, believed that the State had an essential role to perform in society, and he naturally practised a high level of State intervention in the economy. As noted in Chapter 6, this *étatiste* conception was first displayed in the immediate aftermath of the Liberation, when de Gaulle personally presided over the nationalization of several key industrial sectors, including banking and transport. In the 1960s and early 1970s both de Gaulle and Pompidou were actively involved in handing out enormous state subsidies and tax incentives to French industrial conglomerates to assist in the battle against foreign competition. This *dirigiste* conception of economic management was abandoned by the Gaullists in the 1980s, and in some ways reversed during Chirac's brief tenure as Prime Minister between 1986 and 1988. The Gaullist Prime Minister, rather uncharacteristically, set about rolling back the frontiers of the French State by announcing an ambitious programme of privatizations. By the time of the 1988 presidential elections, the Chirac government had transferred a total of thirty companies to the private sector (the aim of the 1986 privatization Act was to transfer 65 companies away from public control by 1991). The privatization programme was halted after the re-election of President Mitterrand in 1988, and the Gaullists' conversion to neo-liberalism had its limits: there was never any attempt to privatize public-sector monopolies of gas, electricity, and coal between 1986 and 1988. None the less, the change in the economic philosophy of the Gaullists was sufficiently marked to constitute a perceptible departure from the General's *étatiste* conception of the role of the State in economic matters. This ideological transformation was confirmed by the announcement of the Balladur government's economic programme in April 1993, which included a commitment to further privatizations and economic deregulation.

Finally, significant changes in the international political and economic environment in the late 1980s and early 1990s threatened some of the key features of Gaullian diplomacy with redundancy. French foreign policy in the 1970s and 1980s remained essentially faithful to the principles and priorities defined by de Gaulle: an independent nuclear deterrent, a policy of relative equidistance towards the superpowers, a measured involvement in European affairs, an active role in North–South economic debates, and somewhat contradictorily, a high level of arms sales to developing countries. With the signature of the Single European Act in 1986, however, France's traditional attachment to a state-centred conception of European unity was abandoned. It was a testimony to the scale of the domestic political realignments that many Gaullists enthusiastically endorsed an agreement whose character the General would have denounced as rabidly supranationalistic. As noted earlier, the Gaullist elite was divided over the issue of the ratification of the Maastricht agreement in the 1992 referendum, but it is worth noting that even leading RPR opponents of the treaty (such as Séguin) accepted the ineluctable character of European economic unity. Finally, the principle of equidistance between superpowers, the other major pillar of Gaullist foreign policy in the 1960s and 1970s, was also swept away in the late 1980s by the collapse of Leninist regimes in Eastern Europe. With only one superpower left in the international arena, France's position as the arbiter of the East–West conflict in Europe was no longer tenable. Indeed, the participation of French troops alongside American and British forces in the 1991 Gulf war marked a subtle but significant realignment of French diplomacy—for some this change was deemed to be so significant as to constitute a throwback to the pre-Gaullist days of French military intervention in Suez. International events thus appeared to have overtaken the thrust of de Gaulle's ideas concerning France's vocation in Europe and the wider world.

THE GAULLIST CONTRIBUTION TO FRENCH POLITICS

Despite these changes in the physiognomy of Gaullism during the decades which followed the death of its founder, the legacy of the General became a subject of widespread political consensus. In 1990, as the French political elite rallied to commemorate the centenary of his birth, de Gaulle's domestic and external policies were overwhelmingly endorsed. The Gaullist presidency, which had so bitterly divided political opinion in the early days of the Fifth Republic, had become an institution venerated not only by the electorate, but also by mainstream parties across the political spectrum. The election of a Socialist, François Mitterrand, to the French presidency in 1981 reconciled the Left to the presidential institution, and Mitterrand himself often referred to the 'Gaullian' dimension of his foreign policy. Yet, precisely at the moment when the French nation was finally united around many features of the Gaullist world-view, the wheels of international fortune moved France away from the position so carefully mapped out by de Gaulle in the 1960s. Thus, as France entered an era of uncertainty in the 1990s, it was no longer possible to define precisely in what respect Gaullian principles could continue to inspire the conduct of French foreign policy. In the domestic political arena the RPR continued to proclaim itself as the continuation of the Gaullian tradition; however, as has been seen in the previous section, there were many important areas in which this claim was difficult to sustain. At the height of its political and ideological influence over French society Gaullism stood for a distinct type of nationalism, the principle of centralized government, a highly interventionist economic philosophy, the strict subordination of its party elites to the leader, and a strong emphasis on the need to transcend the division between 'order' and 'movement'. By the 1990s the RPR was either unable or unwilling to uphold many of these principles, thus making it hard to vindicate its claim to be the inheritor of classical 'Gaullism'.

But even if the true character of its contemporaneous manifestation is a matter of some dispute, the extent of the classical Gaullist contribution to French politics is incontrovertible. From the perspective of

French politics in the twentieth century many of de Gaulle's achievements were unparalleled. Although the victory of the resistance in
1944 was made possible by the contributions of a wide range of political
groups (most notably the Communists, as will be noted in the following
chapter), no individual played a greater role than de Gaulle. It was his
example which encouraged many ordinary French citizens to reject
the rampant defeatism which spread across the country after 1940; it
was under his authoritative leadership that the disparate resistance
groups formed a coalition which eventually helped to expel the German
occupant, and bring down the collaborationist Vichy regime. For this
contribution alone de Gaulle's name will deservedly be honoured by
every new generation of French men and women. But, as noted
throughout this chapter, the aspiration to transcend existing divisions
in French politics and society was always at the heart of the Gaullist
project, and there were many areas in which this ambition met with
great success. After his return to power in 1958 de Gaulle rekindled
a sense of national pride among his compatriots, and succeeded (somewhat in the face of objective indicators) in disseminating the view that
France was a great nation once more, and that her recent experiences
of political strife and institutional instability would never again be
repeated. But the unity which de Gaulle created was not based only
on the illusion of greatness. The founder of the Fifth Republic ended
a number of conflicts which his predecessors had found singularly
intractable. After the 1960s the Army ceased to be a disruptive force
in French politics; political elites no longer bickered over the question
of State subsidies to private schools; and the executive was given all
the powers it needed to govern effectively. Perhaps his greatest political
achievement was the creation of a hegemonic party which (in the
1960s) united the different strands of the Right in a way which was
almost unique in modern French history. Since the French Revolution
the characteristic condition of the French Right was division and disunity; only in extremely rare circumstances did its different
components forge durable alliances. Not only did de Gaulle unify the
forces of 'order', he also modernized their conception of government
and society, thus creating the basis for the political domination exercised by the French Right during the 1960s and 1970s. It was no
accident that the decline of the modern Right as a governing force
came precisely at the time when Gaullism lost its capacity to maintain
its strong ideological and institutional influence over the forces of
'order'.

There were, of course, a number of grey areas in the Gaullist legacy, and it would be unseemly not to point out some of the darker shades. De Gaulle's obsession with shoring up the powers of the executive often led him consciously to place the interests of the State above those of its citizens. The most invidious consequence of this tendency was to relegate law to a subordinate position in the Gaullist hierarchy of institutional values—something of a paradox for a leader who twice rescued his country from the lawlessness of occupation and impending civil war. At the same time the almost imperial grandeur of the Gaullist State also had the effect of creating a wide gulf between the citizenry and their public institutions—again, a rather contradictory legacy, given that de Gaulle's greatest constitutional innovation (the direct election of the president) was based on the desire to strengthen the popular legitimacy of French government. Finally, the founder of the Fifth Republic sought to transcend the social and political divisions with which France was afflicted, but the constitutional framework he devised in many ways reinforced the ideological division between Left and Right. De Gaulle was not sectarian in choosing his associates; as has been made clear in this narrative, his close colleagues were men of widely different cultural and ideological temperaments. But, from the moment they joined him, they were expected to show absolute and unconditional obedience; there was never any place at his side for independent-minded politicians. One was either for or against de Gaulle (hence his fondness for referendums); once this choice was made, everything else fell into its appointed place. But this mechanism for unity itself became a source of political division—another enduring paradox of the Gaullian Republic.

But paradoxes were, after all, at the very heart of de Gaulle's own personality, and it is both a testimony and a tribute to the charismatic quality of this exceptional statesman that, several decades after his passing, French politicians were still negotiating their way through his contradictory political legacy.

Chronology

1890   November. Birth of Charles-André-Joseph-Marie de Gaulle at Lille.

1912   September. Graduation from St Cyr military academy with rank of sub-lieutenant.

1916   March. De Gaulle captured after fierce battle near Verdun; presumed dead, and awarded Légion d'Honneur.

1925   July. Captain de Gaulle invited to join staff of Marshal Pétain.

1934   Publication of *Vers l'Armée de Métier*, highly critical of French military doctrine.

1940   January. De Gaulle pamphlet denounces Army high command for incompetence.

   5 June. Appointed under-secretary of state in Ministry of War and National Defence by Paul Reynaud.

   18 June. De Gaulle calls for continued resistance from London.

1943   June. Committee of National Liberation formed in Algiers under de Gaulle and Giraud.

1944   September. Provisional government established under de Gaulle.

1945   November. Constituent Assembly elects de Gaulle as Prime Minister.

1946   January. Resignation of de Gaulle.

1947   April. Formation of Gaullist Rassemblement du Peuple Français.

1953   January. Folding up of RPF.

1954   Publication of de Gaulle's *Mémoires de Guerre*.

1958   June. De Gaulle government voted in by National Assembly.

   September. Referendum on constitution of Fifth Republic.

   December. De Gaulle elected President.

1960   February. French nuclear device exploded.

1961   April. Attempted coup by rebellious officers in Algeria defeated by de Gaulle.

1962   July. Independence of Algeria proclaimed.

   October. Referendum approves election of President by universal suffrage.

1963   January. Treaty of friendship and co-operation signed with Germany.

1965   December. De Gaulle re-elected President in second ballot contest against François Mitterrand.

1966   March. France withdraws from NATO military command.

1968   May. 'May events' in Paris; de Gaulle briefly appears to lose control of situation.

   June. *Élections de la peur*: Gaullists returned with absolute majority.

1969   April. Referendum on senatorial and regional reforms rejected; de Gaulle resigns.

   June. Georges Pompidou elected President.

1970   November. Death of de Gaulle at Colombey-les-deux-Églises.

1974   April. Death of Pompidou; Gaullists lose ensuing presidential election.

   June. Jacques Chirac becomes Prime Minister under new President Giscard d'Estaing.

1976   December. After Chirac resignation, creation of neo-Gaullist Rassemblement pour la République.

1977   March. Chirac elected Mayor of Paris.

1981   April. Chirac defeated on first ballot of presidential elections.

1986   March. After electoral victory of the Right in legislative elections, Chirac appointed Prime Minister.

1988   May. Mitterrand re-elected President; second successive defeat for Chirac in presidential election.

1990   November. Commemoration of the centenary of de Gaulle's birth: tributes from all political parties.

1993   March. After the victory of the Right in legislative elections, Edouard Balladur appointed Prime Minister.

CHAPTER 11

The Implosion of the Communist Tradition

In the last week of April 1958 a letter addressed to President of the Republic René Coty arrived at the Elysée Palace. Its author was a young conscript who was about to be posted to Algeria, where the French Army was involved in a protracted and brutal war against the Algerian independence movement, the Front de Libération Nationale (FLN). The letter read as follows:

> I have been drafted to go to Algeria. I have decided to refuse to participate in the war which France is now waging against Algeria, and which threatens to spread to the whole of north Africa. My conscience cannot accept that I should fight against a people whom I regard as the friends and allies of France. I wish to promote friendship between the French and Algerian peoples, and remain true to the French traditions of justice and freedom which are invoked in the preamble of the constitution ... I am ready to bear arms to defend my country, which I love above all else, if she is attacked. But I categorically refuse to commit acts which I would later have cause to regret. Please accept, Mr President, the expression of my attachment and highest esteem for the French Republic and its constitution.

This brief note was written by Étienne Boulanger, an active member of the French Communist Party (PCF), and the contents of his letter provided a good illustration of the social and political values of a committed party activist. Here was a militant with a high level of political awareness, who took very seriously the view that political action had to be consistent with moral principles; a patriot who was ready to die for his country, but also believed in the internationalist precept of friendship between peoples; a citizen of the French Republic, who believed in the value of order and constitutional government, and fully recognized that the due process of law had to be respected, yet could not bring himself to obey an injunction which contradicted his own principles of natural justice; a man of great physical courage, who was prepared to face up to the consequences of his beliefs (and was in fact imprisoned, then sent back to serve in Algeria for a further twenty-eight months). Perhaps most important of all, this letter showed that active party membership was quite compatible with the exercise of autonomous political judgement. In 1958 the PCF was firmly opposed to conscientious objection, arguing that the Army could not be allowed to become a preserve for militarists and colonialists. Despite a continuing commitment to his party, however, Boulanger took the view that there were circumstances in which Communists had a duty to refuse to serve in the French Army. His willingness to defy the State while retaining a critical distance from his own political community was an enduring testimony to the qualities which were exemplified by several generations of Communist militants: a sense of discipline, courage, determination, and self-abnegation in their commitment to political activity. Yet, at the same time, these activists retained a lingering sense of moral and political autonomy, which was never entirely submerged by the party leadership's efforts to create a fully cohesive and monolithic force.

The point behind the narration of this little episode is not simply to introduce the subject of this chapter from the perspective of an individual's experience, but also to show that Communism in France was a highly complex political tradition. The Communist movement developed into a centralized political community which consciously sought to create (and perpetuate) a specific way of life, and this aspiration was in many ways captured in Annie Kriegel's classic depiction of the Communist community as a counter-society. Part of the reason why the PCF acquired a justified reputation for social and political cohesiveness was because it (almost literally) created its own distinctive political tradition. This construct was based on an appeal to a social community (the working class), a specific brand of Marxist ideology, a hierarchical organizational structure, an expressive set of political rituals, and a broad range of historical references. Many of these were borrowed from domestic and external political experiences, both historical and contemporaneous. The French revolutionary tradition (especially its Jacobin variant), the republican experience, and the impact of Soviet practices all provided the basic material with which the party constructed its identity. But the final product was unique, both from the perspective of the French political tradition and also from that of the European Communist movement. At the height of its power and influence, the PCF prided itself in being a party unlike any other (*un parti pas comme les autres*), and this was true in more senses than one, as will be demonstrated subsequently in this narrative.

But what was also true, as the case of conscript Étienne Boulanger showed only too well, was that the undeniable unity of the PCF was never monolithic in character, despite the strident claims of the party leadership (and many outside observers). Indeed, the literature on the PCF has tended to neglect the tens of thousands of Communist militants like Boulanger, who chose to remain inside their party despite their (often grave) disagreements with its strategies and tactics. The stories of those generations of Communists who left the PCF have been comprehensively narrated, and the underlying grounds for their disaffiliation from the party closely examined. But the prominence given to the narratives of ex-Communists has contributed to the production of an excessively monochromatic portrait of the Communist community. Even, and perhaps especially when the PCF presented a united front to the outside world, it still accommodated a broad range of social and political undercurrents in its midst. This is not to suggest that the party was fundamentally divided, but rather diverse. A Parisian Communist did not have quite the same perspective on the world as a provincial party member, and there were further temperamental nuances between urban and rural Communists, working-class and intellectual members, those holding elective offices and those who worked as full-time party functionaries (*permanents*), and, last but not least, between these permanent cadres and the wider mass of ordinary party members. These differences will not be discussed systematically in this chapter, but their significance is worth stating at the outset. Communism survived and prospered in France for much of the century because of its capacity to tap into diverse popular traditions, respond creatively to social and political challenges, and thus transform itself to confront the imperatives it faced. In other words, like all the other traditions discussed in this book, the Communist tradition was based on social dynamism and a high degree of political inventiveness; conversely, it was the erosion of these qualities which precipitated the decline of the party in the 1970s and 1980s.

Indeed, by the early 1990s the Communist tradition appeared to have lost much of its dynamism. Despite its strength as a political organization, the PCF was always inherently more vulnerable than other political forces in France, because its fate could be directly affected not only by domestic social and political trends, but also the consequences of events in the Soviet Union and Eastern Europe. As the decade came to an end the outlook for the PCF seemed bleak on both fronts. The party's return to government in the early 1980s had come to an abrupt and inglorious end, its leadership was utterly discredited, its official ideology was derided even by the Left, its electoral audience had dwindled, its social constituency among workers had shrunk, and its organization had collapsed as Communist militants (generally the most dependable of left-wing activists) had deserted the fold. Most humiliating, the rationale for the PCF's very existence had been called into question by the collapse of Leninist regimes in the Soviet Union and Eastern Europe. The PCF was formed in the aftermath of the Tours congress of the French Socialist Party (SFIO) in 1920, shortly after the October Revolution in Russia; the political and ideological collapse of Soviet Communism in 1991 seemed to suggest, not only that the PCF was outmoded, but that its very creation had been based on false premises. There were indeed many ironies about the Tours congress, which later generations of Communist leaders celebrated as a decisive moment in the history of the labour movement in France. For one thing, the Communist Party was not actually born at the Tours congress but in May 1921, when its statutes were adopted by its first national congress. Furthermore, the federations of the Socialist Party which decided to affiliate to the new organization were overwhelmingly non-proletarian in character—a rather quaint beginning for a party which would come to proclaim itself as the vanguard of the working class.

Two further comments can be made about the PCF's celebration of 1920 as its founding year. The party was formed on a strong wave of hostility against the Socialist parliamentary *notables*, elected officials whose social origins and cultural inclinations were far removed from the experiences of the working class. Yet the PCF would later acquire a large parliamentary force of its own, and relations between this group and the party rank and file would often be fraught with similar elements of tension. However, what was most incongruous about the PCF's subsequent canonization of the Tours congress was the contrast between the fundamental nature of the party which was created in 1920, and the values it later sought to embody. Most of the new leaders of the party were middle-class activists; the party later made the formation of a working-class leadership the cornerstone of its recruitment policy. Furthermore, the driving force behind the new political organization was Lenin's Third International; until 1941 at least (and arguably until much later) the basic strategic directives of the party were formulated in Moscow. Indeed, only in 1938 did the organization become known as the French Communist Party (instead of various other appellations which underlined its subordination to the

Communist International). Thus the PCF stressed its internationalist and revolutionary character in its early years; by the late 1930s, however, nationalism and republicanism were at the forefront of Communist discourse. Finally, the new organization started by adopting an aggressive and highly confrontational attitude towards the Socialists. By 1935 the SFIO was being assiduously courted by the Communist leadership, and a year later a Socialist prime minister was voted into office with the full support of the Communist parliamentary group.

In sum, there were considerable elements of ambiguity in the PCF's subsequent celebration of the foundational character of the Tours gathering. The organization which struggled to survive in the harsh political climate of the 1920s in many respects bore little resemblance to the strong and often dominant political force which the PCF later became. As will be shown in this narrative, the party's political successes were achieved because it gave a lower priority to many of the principles which it had espoused in its infant years. But it should always be remembered that these founding principles were never completely excised from Communist political culture, even at times when the PCF's policies seemed to be following entirely different strategic routes. The party's identity was thus based on a complex set of practices, experiences, and influences, which often pulled its leaders in contradictory directions. These different components of the PCF's identity will become clearer after a closer examination of the Communist counter-society at the height of its political and ideological influence.

THE COMMUNIST COUNTER-SOCIETY IN ITS PRIME

The elections of November 1946 marked the zenith of the PCF's electoral fortunes. With almost 29 per cent of votes cast, the Communists emerged as the largest single party, just ahead of the Christian democratic Mouvement Républicain Populaire (MRP), and quite a long way in front of the Socialist SFIO. This electoral preponderance of the PCF in the aftermath of the Liberation was one of numerous illustrations of the organization's commanding position in the political system.

First, the PCF was beyond any question the largest and most cohesive political force in France during this period. Between 1945 and 1947 party membership rose continuously to reach an all-time peak of around 900,000 towards the end of 1947. Although this figure should be reduced by at least a quarter to correct deviations produced by the party's accounting methods, it still put the Communists a long way ahead of other mainstream political organizations. The only party which seriously challenged the Communists' hegemony as a mass movement during this period was the Gaullist Rassemblement du Peuple Français (RPF), founded in April 1947 to support the revisionist aspirations of General de Gaulle. By 1948 the RPF claimed a rather extravagant membership of 1.5 million; most political analysts agree, however, that the Gaullists never had more than 500,000 members. This was a considerable figure (especially by French standards), but it still left the Communists as the dominant organizational force in French politics after the Liberation.

Furthermore, this powerful and centralized political movement was the nerve centre of an organism which was present in almost every conceivable aspect of public and private life in France. The PCF was justified in defining itself as a *parti pas comme les autres* because, as mentioned earlier, it was a complete and almost self-sufficient political community in itself. This distinctiveness of the PCF was reflected in numerous properties which the organization shared with a State. The central institutions of the party machine were its government; party members and sympathizers were its citizens; Communist-controlled commercial enterprises formed the backbone of its economy; and an elaborate substructure of organizations, ranging from recreational groups to research institutes, were its intermediate associations, drawing together different sections of the citizenry into the social and political life of the Communist community. Between 1945 and 1947 this community appeared to be spreading throughout French society. Communist ministers in government recruited party activists into public administration; the largest trade union, the Confédération Générale du Travail (CGT), was controlled by Communists; associations of Communist writers, historians, biologists, women, ex-servicemen, and youth sprouted in every corner of French territory. Some even estimated that up to 75 per cent of the recruits in the newly formed riot unit, the Compagnie Républicaine de Sécurité (CRS), were former Communist members of the party's paramilitary resistance organization, the Francs-Tireurs et Partisans (FTP). Rarely in the modern history of the French polity had a party's reach extended so deep into society.

Part of the explanation for the commanding position assumed by the organization lay in the PCF's role during the resistance. Communists were held in immense respect for the decisive role they played in organizing the internal resistance against German occupying forces (and their allies in the Vichy regime). There had been some murky aspects in the party's early attitude towards the war. The Communist leadership had supported the Nazi-Soviet pact in September 1939, and accordingly refrained from calling for full-scale military resistance against the German invasion of France in 1940. Only when the Nazis invaded the Soviet Union in June 1941 did the PCF formally declare war on the German invaders and their French collaborators in the Vichy régime. (It is true that there were individual acts of resistance by party members, but these were not openly encouraged by the Communist hierarchy.) But these uncomfortable facts were forgotten (or deliberately suppressed) in the euphoric aftermath of the Liberation. Communist partisans had fought gallantly between 1941 and 1944, and the party leadership basked in the posthumous glory of its heroic militants. Although the party's claim that 70,000 Communist *résistants* had been executed during the occupation was rather extravagant, the courage of party activists who had risked their lives to liberate their country from foreign occupation was almost universally celebrated. Unlike his valiant troops, the Communist leader Maurice Thorez (1900–64) had spent the war years in the relative comfort and security of a Soviet city. None the less, he was considered as a hero by the Communist rank-and-file; as a Minister of State in postwar French governments he was also regarded as a competent and capable administrator by many of his colleagues, including General de Gaulle.

The prestige of the Communist Party in the French intellectual community was also at its zenith in the postwar era. The appeal of the PCF to French intellectuals was a function of several factors: the effectiveness of its organizational role in the resistance, the powerful attraction of Marxism, and the widespread aspiration to fraternize with the working class. The Communists had taken the lead in organizing networks of intellectual resistance after 1941: a typical example was the clandestine journal *Les Lettres françaises*, which published contributions from committed anti-Fascist writers across the political spectrum. Even more spectacularly, and this was an enduring tribute to the PCF's organizational abilities, the Communists set up two clandestine printing-houses in the very centre of Paris, which published a total of twenty-five works during the occupation. After the Liberation the intellectual audience of the Communist party extended far and wide. In 1946 there were seventeen daily Communist newspapers; the circulation of the Paris-based *l'Humanité* was greater even than that of such established conservative newspapers as *Le Figaro*. More generally, the revolutionary ideology which was central to the PCF's Marxism appealed to many intellectuals, who often regarded membership of the Communist Party as the logical extension of the battles they had fought (or, in some cases, failed to conduct) against the German invader. As Jean-Paul Sartre remarked, Marxian Communism was firmly ensconced in the horizon of the French intellectual community, to such an extent that (for the first and last time in French history) anti-Communists were on the defensive—an awesome testimony to the party's intellectual hegemony at the time.

There was another, yet unmentioned, reason for the political and intellectual domination of the PCF, and this constituted the fifth dimension of Communist preponderance in the postwar years. Like the Catholic Church, the French Communist Party was a transnational institution, whose operational centre was based in Moscow. The religious analogy was consciously adopted by the Communist hierarchy, which sometimes described the PCF as 'the eldest daughter of the Communist Church'. French Communists had always regarded themselves as one of the leading forces in the Communist International during the interwar period, and they had often paid a heavy price for their loyalty to the Soviet Union and to Stalin. After its approval of the Nazi-Soviet pact in September 1939, for example, the PCF was proscribed by the French government, and its parliamentarians arrested. In 1945, however, with the heightened prestige of the Soviet Union in the eyes of the international community, the PCF benefited hugely from its association with the Stalinist system. The Soviet Union had lost 20 million citizens, but had expelled the Germans from Russian territory; this had turned the tide of the Second World War, and ultimately made the Allied victory possible. More generally, the optimistic vision of the future projected in classical Marxism seemed to be close to fulfilment after 1945, as Communist parties were swept to power across the European continent. As Maurice Thorez declared in an interview in the London *Times* in November 1946, advanced industrial societies were rapidly evolving towards communism, and no longer even needed to follow the Bolshevik route of violent revolution. Even the adversaries of the Communists believed that history was on the PCF's side: the Gaullist intellectual, André Malraux, believed that French politics would soon be reduced to a titanic confrontation between Gaullism and Communism.

WHY NO REVOLUTION?

Given the hegemonic position occupied by the PCF in France in the immediate aftermath of the Liberation, it might have been expected that its leaders, as good Leninists, would advocate the storming of the Elysée Palace. But the PCF made no attempt to seize power through violent and insurrectionary means. Why did it refrain from such a course of action? As noted earlier, the immediate and uncompromising pursuit of radical social and political change had been the defining attribute of French Communism from its very birth. In accepting the stringent membership terms of Lenin's Third International, French Communists had become committed, as stated in the First Condition of entry into the International, to demonstrate their 'loyalty to the cause of the Proletarian revolution'. During much of the interwar period the PCF had followed this injunction to the letter. Between 1920 and 1934 French Communists had selflessly devoted themselves to the cause of the revolution, often at high personal cost to both party leaders and activists. The party's advocacy of anti-militarism and anti-colonialism had triggered repressive action by French governments against Communists. Its categorical refusal to form any alliance with Socialists (who were amiably described as 'social Fascists' by the late 1920s) had brought political isolation and material deprivation. Party leaders had operated in conditions of quasi-clandestinity, and had been constantly threatened by the State: in June 1929, Maurice Thorez was arrested at a secret meeting of the Central Committee, whose whereabouts were obligingly conveyed to the Sureté by a police informer.

By 1945, however, all these trials, tribulations, and humiliations were well behind the party. The Communists were now a respectable party of government, and enjoyed a large electoral audience, an efficient and cohesive political organization, a broad range of links with social and economic groups, and a high level of prestige among French intellectuals. If ever there was a propitious moment to move into revolutionary gear, this was surely it. Yet the PCF did little between 1944 and 1947 to seize the revolutionary moment. Not only did the party not even try to achieve what had always been defined as its ultimate goal, it even asked its supporters in Communist paramilitary organizations to surrender their weapons, told French workers that their overriding concern was to 'win the battle of production', and generally adopted a highly responsible and pragmatic approach to public affairs. How was this attitude to be explained? Did the French Communists, as many on the extreme Left subsequently alleged, betray the revolutionary cause by propping up 'capitalist' institutions precisely at the moment when they were most vulnerable?

The reasons which made the French Communist leadership shy away from an insurrectionary strategy after 1944 were complex, and went much deeper than simplistic arguments of class betrayal and political treachery. The political identity of the PCF was transformed by an important process which occurred between the party's revolutionary phase (between 1920 and 1934) and its accession to political prominence during the resistance: the Popular Front. The latter political strategy, which was imagined by the Communist International as a means of countering the rise of fascism and right-wing authoritarianism in Europe, was first successfully implemented in France by the PCF, in alliance with Socialists and Radicals. The Popular Front's overall achievements were limited, but from the Communist point of view the experience had a number of durable consequences. It transformed the PCF into an established parliamentary force, with 72 elected members in 1936; a mass political organization, whose membership rose from around 28,000 in 1933 to more than 300,000 in late 1937; a working-class party, with strong support in urban industrial areas such as the Parisian crescent, and organic links with the largest trade union in France, the CGT; and finally, a nationalist party, which celebrated its ancestry in the radical revolutionary experiences of the late eighteenth and nineteenth centuries, but also regarded itself as the inheritor of French republican traditions. As the Communist journalist Paul Vaillant-Couturier (1892–1937) noted in *l'Humanité* a year before his death: 'We are people with solid roots in the soil of France . . . Our party, through its attachment to the moral and cultural traditions of the land, is a necessary expression of eternal France.' This acknowledgement of the unity of French historical experience overturned the PCF's initial sectarian distinction between bourgeois and proletarian cultures, and constituted a turning-point in the definition of the modern identity of French Communism.

It was this republican party which revived during the resistance and became the leading force of the land after 1944. It was no longer a small rump of fractious conspirators, but a large, efficient, and popular organization; its leaders had influenced this transformation of the party's identity, but were also bound by it. The Communist leadership also remembered with distaste the PCF's recent experience of political marginalization: before 1934, and between 1939 and 1941, Communists had deliberately alienated themselves from the national political community. The results, on each occasion, had been disastrous: the PCF had almost disappeared from the political scene. Despite the radical instincts of the party grass-roots (which were also shared by some members of the Politburo), Maurice Thorez and his close associates were not at all inclined to jeopardize their party's hard-fought respectability and prominence by trying to seize power by insurrectionary means after 1944. Thus the republican experiences of the party had made its leadership especially attentive to the potential costs of operating outside the political mainstream, and also, by the same token, the undeniable benefits that could accrue to the organization if it remained within it. Indeed, any attempt to seize power through insurrectionary means after 1944 would have been extremely risky. Despite their commanding positions in the administration and in society, the Communists would have encountered fierce opposition from their allies in the resistance if they had tried to force their way into office. This would have unleashed a civil war in France, and the Communists would certainly not have retained their high level of popular support if they had initiated a conflict of this nature so soon after the end of hostilities in 1944. The country was weary after four years of foreign occupation and civil strife; few wished for a return to the violent conflicts which had torn French society apart between 1940 and 1944. From an operational point of view, furthermore, any Communist insurgency would have brought into action American troops stationed in France, and it would have been foolhardy to think that the Communists could have surmounted this obstacle without severe difficulties. Unlike Soviet-occupied Eastern Europe, where indigenous Communists were able gradually to grasp the levers of power by relying on the operational support of the Red Army and the KGB, Communists were totally deprived of any Soviet logistical backing in France. As the case of the Greek Communist insurrection demonstrated subsequently, a rebellion engineered under such circumstances was doomed to failure.

This led directly to the third consideration underlying the PCF's reluctance to follow the revolutionary path after 1944: the preferences of the Kremlin. In October 1944 Churchill and Stalin had defined the ideological contours of postwar Europe: the Soviet Union was granted its sphere of influence in Eastern Europe, in exchange for which Communists were to refrain from seizing power in West European countries. Stalin initially adhered rigidly to this division of power, and formally instructed the French Communist leader, Maurice Thorez, to avoid pursuing 'adventurist' tactics after the Liberation. Since the PCF's general political strategy was strongly influenced by the interests of the Soviet Union throughout this period, the French Communist leadership followed the Soviet undertaking to respect the ideological division of Europe between capitalism and communism. But it must be stressed that Thorez and the Communist leadership were more than happy to follow this injunction. Indeed, to refrain from revolutionary activity meant that the PCF would continue its resistance policy of forming wide alliances with other democratic and socialist groups. These broad alliances would increase the party's popularity. Increased popularity would bring further electoral support, and with high levels of electoral support would come political influence at national and local levels, and the institutionalization of Communist power in France. The identity and political objectives of French Communism were thus established on the basis of a conflation of the PCF's perceived interests with the strategic imperatives of the USSR. This chain of reasoning would remain central to the political strategy of the PCF in the 1950s and 1960s, and would be even more strongly emphasized when the party subsequently loosened its strategic subordination to the Soviet Union.

At its apogee in the Liberation era, therefore, the French Communist Party had already developed a distinct political strategy, which incorporated the pursuit of radical change into a gradual process of institutional development. This did not imply that the party was no longer revolutionary; it meant, rather, that it would seek to achieve its revolutionary objectives by consolidating and building upon the advances it had made during the postwar era. The problem, however, was that the different components of the PCF's identity pulled the party in conflicting directions. The retention of the PCF's social identity as the party of the proletariat, for example, was completely at variance with a broad-based electoral strategy, which required the development of cross-class support. Fidelity to the Leninist heritage demanded the preservation of a heavily centralized and often authoritarian party machine, whereas local groups of Communist militants expressed a strong yearning for greater internal democracy. Finally, the cultivation of the PCF's image as a republican party of government implied an adhesion to the values of order and pragmatism, whereas a revolutionary party represented (at least in the short run) the negation of these values. The consequences of the party's failure to reconcile these conflicting imperatives will be examined in the following section.

THE IMPLOSION OF FRENCH COMMUNISM

By the early 1990s the parlous condition of the French Communist Party was no longer a matter of debate. The party which prided itself on being the first political force of the land in 1946 was reduced to the level of support it enjoyed in the bleakest period of its electoral history, in the early 1930s. The PCF suffered a marked electoral decline after the late 1970s, but the origins of the party's setbacks could be traced to the late 1950s, more precisely to the elections of November 1958, which decimated the Communists' parliamentary representation and brought down the PCF's share of votes from around 25 to 20 per cent. The second shock-wave was experienced in the elections of June 1968: the party kept its total share of the vote, but irretrievably lost ground in some of its urban strongholds (such as the Parisian region). In 1981, finally, the Socialist victory reduced the party's share of the vote by a further 5 per cent, and this was followed by an accelerated decline throughout the 1980s. In the legislative elections of March 1993 the PCF polled 9.2 per cent of the votes cast: this took the party back to its level of support in the late 1920s. The party organization was also in tatters. Official sources claimed a membership of approximately 600,000 in the late 1980s, but this was such a wild exaggeration that it had to be divided by at least ten to obtain a realistic estimate of the number of party members (and it was far from clear how many of these were active in any meaningful sense of the term).

The party which could make its presence felt in almost every aspect of public and private life in France after the Liberation had become a marginalized and decaying institution. The analogy between the PCF and a State was increasingly difficult to maintain. The party headquarters at the Place du Colonel Fabien still presented a formidable outward appearance, but the reality was starkly different. The PCF's network of economic institutions was severely hit by the party's decline; for example, the survival of many Communist-owned enterprises depended on a steady stream of orders from Communist-controlled municipalities. After the municipal elections of 1977, however, the PCF's municipal base began to contract, and the financial (as well as political) implications of this development were extremely serious. In so far as intermediate associations were concerned, the PCF's empire also began to disintegrate during this period. Some of the causes promoted by these institutions declined in saliency. Ex-servicemen, for example, diminished as a proportion of the active population in the 1970s and 1980s, and this naturally altered the political and social importance of the *anciens combattants*. The peace movement, which was one of the PCF's most significant satellite organizations in the late 1940s and 1950s, subsequently lost much of its appeal, and the Communists' attempts to revive the enterprise in the 1980s were frustrated by a variety of factors, not least the firm position adopted on defence issues by the Socialist government. The Confédération Générale du Travail remained the party's most dependable institutional asset in society, but what was once by far the country's largest trade union was also affected by decline and internal dissension. In 1966 the CGT won 50 per cent of the vote in elections to enterprise councils; by 1985 the figure had fallen to 29 per cent. This collapse had numerous implications for the PCF, but perhaps the most central was the loss of a key source of recruitment for its political cadres. Many of the party's historic figures, such as Benoit Frachon (1893–1975), came to Communist politics through trade-union activity, and the decline of the CGT after the 1960s made this link increasingly precarious.

These various manifestations of institutional decline were accompanied (and partly caused) by a remarkable collapse in the credibility of the PCF as a political force. At the Liberation, it will be remembered, the prestige of the party and its leadership had reached unparalleled heights. In the 1980s opinion surveys pointed to a profound rejection of the institution by French society. Between 1944 and 1947 Maurice Thorez and his Communist colleagues in successive French governments firmly established the PCF's identity as a party of government. In 1986, two years after Communist ministers had withdrawn from the Socialist government, a poll found that less than 20 per cent of the electorate endorsed the PCF's credentials as a party which was fit to hold office. The party's general credibility in the eyes of the public declined steadily throughout the 1980s. This negative image of French Communism had many sources, but one particular factor is worth singling out: the public perception of the party leader, Georges Marchais. The robust and forceful personality of this former metallurgist, who became the PCF's General Secretary in 1970, was not always a source of public disapproval. For most of the 1970s Marchais's earthy qualities were in fact regarded as a refreshing change from the smooth, cultivated, and rather impersonal style favoured by the political elites of the Fifth Republic. But the Communist leader overstepped the clear line between simplicity and vulgarity, and thus rapidly switched from public favour to popular disgrace. By the early 1980s Marchais's public image had suffered a serious decline not only among wider sectors of opinion but also, most damagingly, within the Communist community itself. The rise of internal dissent in the party in the 1980s and early 1990s (borne out by the emergence of such recognized undercurrents as the *rénovateurs*, *reconstructeurs*, and *refondateurs*) provided a stark illustration of the declining authority of the Communist leadership.

The final dimension of the decline of French Communism in the 1980s, as noted earlier, was a direct consequence of the collapse of Communism in the Soviet Union and Eastern Europe. In the postwar era Communism appeared to be spreading across the international system with an almost inexorable logic. Between 1945 and 1950 new Marxist-Leninist states emerged in Central and Eastern Europe, and in 1949 China, the world's most thickly populated country, also moved into the Communist orbit. Communists all over the world (including France) maintained that capitalism was under siege, and that its eventual demise was inevitable. Throughout the Cold War French Communists accepted the post-Stalinist Soviet view that, although the two systems could coexist in relative peace, capitalism would inevitably be superseded by communism in the long run. The disappearance of the Soviet Union in 1991, after a decade of painful agony, finally put paid to these aspirations. Whereas in the postwar era European Communists could rely on their association with the Soviet Union to enhance their domestic prestige, by the late 1980s and early 1990s any such substantive connection was regarded as highly embarrassing. For example, a great stir was caused when documents leaked to the Russian press in 1992 revealed that the PCF had received substantial financial assistance from the Soviet Communist Party *until as late as 1988*. The Italian Communist Party acknowledged that the failure of Soviet-style Communism required a fundamental reassessment of its identity as a political movement, and in March 1991 renamed itself the Democratic

Party of the Left. The PCF not only refused to acknowledge that the demise of the Leninist tradition had any internal significance for French Communism; it even refused to accept growing evidence throughout the 1980s that the Soviet system was on the brink of collapse. As late as December 1987, the PCF was still publicly committed to the view that Soviet-style Communism was inherently superior to capitalist democracy. By the early 1990s French Communists thus increasingly appeared as relics of a bygone age, clinging tenaciously to political values and world-historical references which were both outmoded and utterly discredited.

THE DISINTEGRATION OF A TRADITION

The decline of Communism in France provides a good illustration of the circumstances under which political traditions disintegrate. It is not easy to trace the beginning of this process to a specific moment in time; for one thing, the different indicators of Communist decline operated on different time-scales. For example, the party's membership fell consistently throughout the Fourth Republic, but its level of electoral support remained relatively stable. During the first decade of the Fifth Republic the party's electoral performances fluctuated considerably, while party membership stabilized (albeit at a lower level than that of the late 1940s). During much of the 1970s the level of party membership rose again, but the PCF's electoral fortunes continued to decline steadily. Underlying these apparently conflicting trends was a gradual process of social and political change in France, which undermined many of the underlying foundations of the Communist tradition. Three particular factors are worthy of mention: the transformation of the class structure, the modifications of the political system, and the evolution of left-wing ideology.

Ever since the Popular Front the party's political fortunes depended critically on the support of the working class. In the 1950s the PCF received the votes of approximately 50 per cent of French workers; by the 1988 presidential election, however, a mere 17 per cent of French workers gave their support to the official Communist candidate. Almost as many workers voted for the National Front candidate, Jean-Marie Le Pen, and a relative majority supported the Socialist candidate, François Mitterrand. In other words, Communists could no longer claim a monopoly of working-class identification. This realignment was partly a function of the absolute decline of the working class as a proportion of the active population in France: in 1975, 40 per cent of the work-force consisted of industrial workers; by 1987 the overall proportion had fallen to 33 per cent. In certain sectors the loss was considerably greater: in the steel industry, for example, around a quarter of the work-force was made redundant between 1976 and 1983 alone. The modernization of French industry also altered the condition of the working class. Living standards increased, old patterns of social solidarity were undermined, and the degree of subjective identification with the very notion of class declined significantly.

In sum, there were fewer manual workers, and those who remained shared few of the beliefs, attitudes, and values of earlier generations of French industrial workers. The problem was compounded by the PCF's inadequate political response to this process of quantitative decline and qualitative change. The party tried to broaden its appeal to other social groups in the 1960s and 1970s, and the growth of its membership in the 1970s attested the success of this strategy. Yet it continued to underline its attachment to the proletarian identity of the organization. The party may still have retained much of its support among French workers if (like its Italian counterpart in the 1960s and 1970s) it had shown some willingness to recognize the significance of socio-cultural changes in working-class lifestyles. But the PCF leadership followed exactly the opposite route, preaching its classic homilies about nasty bosses and humiliated workers (these refrains were especially marked in the election campaigns of 1978 and 1981). As noted in Chapter 7, the PCF inherited a tradition of workerism (*ouvriérisme*) which was widely disseminated in the French labour movement in the late nineteenth century. The Communist leadership's continuing articulation of workerist themes almost a century later had predictable consequences: from the late 1960s large sections of the working class ceased to recognize themselves in the crude stereotypes conveyed by Communist propaganda. Paradoxically, by the early 1990s the French Communists had come to represent exactly the opposite of the vanguard of the working class: the party now achieved its best electoral performances in areas of industrial decay, rural stagnation, and demographic decline (such as the department of the Allier). The vanguard appeared to have turned into the rearguard.

Almost as important a factor as the changing roles of the working class were the negative institutional effects of the Fifth Republic on the PCF. The move from a political system in which Parliament was the central institution (in the Third and Fourth Republics) to the presidentialism of the Fifth Republic pushed the PCF away from the centre of gravity of French politics after 1958. The direct election of the president, introduced after the referendum of October 1962, made it impossible for a party with a narrow and sectional appeal, such as the PCF, to contend for the supreme prize in French politics. Furthermore, the presidential system of the Fifth Republic altered the nature of political competition among parties by introducing the notion of a 'presidential majority'. Since the Communists could never control the presidency, they were denied the beneficial political effects of association with the policies and personality of the incumbent at the Elysée Palace. The Gaullists in the 1960s, the Giscardian UDF in the 1970s, and the Socialists in the 1980s were all able successfully to play the presidential card in legislative elections. This tactic was unavailable to the PCF, and it suffered consequently. It should also be added that non-presidential organizations such as the PCF were inherently more vulnerable to the effects of parliamentary dissolution. Thus Communists were often caught off-balance by the president's decision to call fresh elections to the National Assembly: in 1968 they were blamed for the student disturbances of May, and in 1981 and 1988 they were at a severe disadvantage because of the election (and subsequent re-election) of a Socialist president.

Finally, the electoral system was also unkind to the Communists. An examination of the relationship between votes and seats in the Parliament elected in 1988 provides an immediate insight into the distorting effects of the French electoral system. In the legislative elections of June 1988 it took an average of about 33,000 votes to elect a Socialist deputy, 36,000 to elect a right-wing deputy, but 100,000 to elect a Communist. (These figures were based on the total number of votes received by each party on the first ballot, divided by the number of seats eventually won by each party.) The main cause of this distortion was the two-ballot system, which again made it harder for a sectionally based party to win enough support on the first round to survive to the run-off. After 1962 Communists agreed to endorse Socialist candidates on the second ballot of legislative elections, but this had the effect of blurring the party's specific identity and encouraging, in the long run, a tendency for left-wing voters to regard the Communist Party as an irrelevant feature of the political landscape — and this ultimately became a self-fulfilling prophecy. Thus the institutional dynamics of the Fifth Republic prevented the Communists from competing on equal terms with their Socialist rivals.

The ideological transformation of left-wing politics after the 1960s also contributed to the PCF's decline. In the golden era of Communist hegemony over the French Left, the political centrality of notions of party, class, and revolution was firmly entrenched in the intellectual landscape. The core ideological principles of the Left included absolute empathy with the working class, and a firm belief in the desirability of radical change; furthermore, it was an article of faith of the French Left (and a source of despair to many) that these changes could not be brought about without the Communist Party. After the 1960s, however, these principles ceased to dominate the political horizon of the French Left. With the decline of the proletariat, the very notion of class ceased to be considered as the principal basis for political action, and was replaced by a plurality of concerns such as gender, race, and ecology. Revolutionary change was no longer considered either necessary or desirable; and left-wing activists and voters became more healthily sceptical of the value of uncritical commitment to political activity. In the 1980s these essential transformations in left-wing political values were reflected in the dominant position achieved by the Socialists, who regarded themselves as interclass rather than working-class, reformist rather than revolutionary, and the bearers of a practical rather than metaphysical conception of political activity. The Communists failed to adapt to these changes in the core political values of the Left, and thus appeared to be swimming against the current of history. Their predicament (and lack of intellectual flexibility) was only too well underscored by their feeble response to the collapse of Soviet-style Communism in the late 1980s and early 1990s.

WAS 1920 A MISTAKE?

At this point the question raised in the early part of this chapter may be reopened: what contribution did the Communist Party make to the practice of politics in France? With the collapse of the Soviet Union in 1991, it was increasingly suggested that the very creation of the PCF in 1920 was a historical error or (even worse) an aberration forced upon the French labour movement by the intervention of an unscrupulous foreign power. Indeed, few voices have been heard to lament the decline of the PCF. Most of the academic studies of the party were written by ex-Communists, who were rarely inclined to take a sympathetic view of the organization to which they once belonged. Hardened anti-Communists, on both the Left and the Right, expressed unbridled pleasure at witnessing the agony of a party they regarded as the embodiment of evil. However, right-wing politicians had cause to regret the party's weakening, since it deprived them of a highly effective propaganda weapon against the Left at election times. A strong Communist Party was always an embarrassing ally for the Socialists; as noted in the previous chapter, the Right proved extremely skilful at exploiting the Left's vulnerability on this count. For the Socialists, the decline of the PCF was seen as a vindication of the position taken by a Blumist minority at the Tours congress in 1920. The existence of the PCF, in other words, had divided the labour movement, and unnecessarily delayed the development of a dominant social democratic force on the Left. As for the extreme Left, whose relations with the PCF were always those of detestation, the crumbling of the PCF merely confirmed the judiciousness of Trotsky's theses about the bureaucratic degeneration of the Soviet revolution in the 1930s. In their eyes the 'Stalinism' of the PCF, once the source of its towering strength, had ultimately corrupted the organization and precipitated its demise.

There is no denying that, in the seven decades of its existence, the PCF's contribution to French politics was often purely negative in character, even in those areas where it achieved the targets it had set itself. It created a highly centralized party machine, which surpassed in effectiveness and cohesion anything the forces of 'movement' in France had ever been able to produce. This was achieved, however, by creating (or rather, importing from the Soviet Union) the organizational principle known as democratic centralism. In theory this Leninist system provided a method of combining accountability (the election of higher echelons of the party by the lower levels) with effectiveness (the endorsement and implementation of decisions reached collectively by all members). In practice, however, the Communist leadership used this mechanism to control the organization from above, and systematically root out all forms of internal opposition to its policies. Generations of devoted Communist militants were thus expelled from the party for daring to question the collective wisdom of its leadership. The PCF also succeeded in constructing its political identity around the working class, but often misled the French labour movement by subordinating its interests to the strategic designs of the

USSR. It is true that the party began to loosen some of its ties to the land of the October Revolution during the 1970s, and this process eventually culminated in the policy of 'Eurocommunism'. The party affirmed its desire to build a 'socialism in French colours', abandoned its commitment to the Leninist principle of the dictatorship of the proletariat, and criticized the Soviet system for failing to uphold its own constitutional principles of free speech and political account-ability. After 1978, however, the party turned its back on this approach, and indeed appeared to revert to the policy of proletarian international-ism—an unconditional attachment to the strategic objectives of the Soviet Union. Even though the Communist leadership did not revert fully to the practices of the Stalinist era, when the Soviet system was presented as a model society for mankind, its realignment on Soviet positions was unmistakable. The PCF endorsed the Soviet invasion of Afghanistan in early 1980 (in contrast, the party had criticized the Soviet suppression of the Prague Spring in 1968), supported the crushing of the Polish trade union, Solidarity, by General Jaruszelski in late 1981, and remained profoundly committed to defending the foreign policy of the Soviet Union. As already noted, the collapse of Leninist regimes in Eastern Europe after 1989 provided a further illustration of the PCF's commitments. Throughout the revolutionary period which saw the collapse of Communist rule, Georges Marchais maintained that the balance sheet of these countries was globally posi-tive, and that the problems faced by local Communist parties were conjunctural rather than structural. As in 1956, when the Thorezian leadership chose to deny the very existence of Kruschev's secret speech (rather than confront the painful implications of de-Stalinization), the PCF observed what was happening in Eastern Europe and simply preferred to bury its head in the sand.

But, just as it would be improper to gloss over the negative aspects of the PCF's activities, it would be unseemly to overlook the party's undeniable contributions to political and social life in France. Two elements are particularly worthy of attention. First, the existence of a strong Communist Party in France did much to enhance the pro-letariat's sense of confidence and self-awareness. Of course, the PCF could not have become a dominant political force without the working class, and there were many ways in which the party was merely an institutional expression of the class dynamics in French society. But this sociological reductionism should not be carried too far. At the height of its organizational power the PCF was able to contribute to the formation of working-class identity, and significantly expand the political horizons of the proletariat. The party organization promoted generations of working-class militants to positions of power and responsibility, and thus helped to give French workers a greater sense of confidence in their own abilities. The symbolic value of Communist participation in French governments (both in 1944–7 and 1981–4) was particularly powerful in this respect. The presence of men like Maurice Thorez and Charles Fiterman alongside their 'bourgeois' counterparts helped to vindicate the PCF's claim that workers could legitimately aspire to positions of power in society and remain within their class. This was always the distinctive feature of the PCF's conception of working-class fulfilment. Communists sought to achieve this end by celebrating the collective virtues of the proletariat, whereas other political forces did so by encouraging workers (in the final analysis) to escape from their class. In this context it is also worth remembering the positive role played by local Communist Party organizations in the integration of European immigrants into French society after the 1930s. Here again the PCF provided an institutional focus for groups which felt excluded or marginalized from the rest of society, and performed a valuable service in the cause of social integration.

The other great Communist contribution to French public life during the twentieth century was its key role during the Second World War. It is important to tread carefully here; the resistance remains one of the hallowed terrains of modern French political mythology. But however much Communist historiography may have inflated the role of the PCF between 1940 and 1944, a number of basic points remain incontrovertible. First, the PCF was the only party in France which consistently warned against the dangers of appeasing Hitler. When the Munich agreement was endorsed by the French National Assembly in September 1938, only the Communist parliamentary group voted against it. Second, not too much should be made of the Communists' reluctance to engage in battle with the German occupying forces between 1940 and 1941. It is true that the PCF behaved extremely cynically during this period, and sometimes came close to active collusion with the occupant. But the Communists were hardly the only political group against which the charge of cynicism could be levelled. Most French people lost their moral and political bearings during the first year of the occupation; this was to a large extent why Marshal Pétain's appeal proved so great in the immediate aftermath of 1940. However, the vigorous role the Communists played in the resistance after June 1941 more than amply compensated for earlier errors of judgement. It is sometimes suggested that the PCF only played such a role at the behest of Stalin, and that its overall subordination to the interests of the Soviet Union during this period deprived it of any entitlement to public respect and gratitude. But this would be a misleading representation of the world-view of the average Communist militant. The Communist resistance was one of the mainstays of French patriotism during the occupation; even de Gaulle readily admitted that the PCF had unfalteringly served French national interests at the time. Communists played their part in helping France restore its republican institutions after the indignities of military defeat, occupation, and collaboration. They did so overwhelmingly because they hoped that the struggle against the Germans would be the first step towards building a fairer and more humane society. That events did not quite take such a turn is no cause to forget that Communists defended (and died for) the cause of freedom during one of France's darkest hours.

But political forces cannot live merely in the past. The PCF's steady decline from the late 1950s provided a graphic illustration of the fate suffered by political currents which failed to redefine their objectives in such a way as to make them accessible to new generations. Rather like the clericalists of the Third Republic, the PCF remained doggedly attached to a conception of its identity which appeared increasingly archaic in the face of changing social and political trends. As will be remembered, the development of the PCF into a mass organization in the 1930s had been accompanied (indeed, made possible) by a radical transformation of its identity as a political force. By the late 1940s the Communist tradition had evolved into a unique blend of republicanism, Jacobinism, working-class sectarianism, and Soviet internationalism. This package was held together by the recent political experiences of the party, especially the heroism of its militants during the resistance. By the 1960s and 1970s, however, the PCF continued to bank on memories of its glorious past, precisely at the moment when Georges Pompidou's remark that France was tired of heroism struck a resonant chord in society. These changing social and political conditions required an imaginative leap similar to that performed by the Italian Communists during the same period. Such an intellectual change would by no means have guaranteed the political survival of the PCF, but it would at least have made possible the transmission of the core values of French Communism from the postwar generation to its successors. Instead the PCF reaffirmed its traditional identity, maintaining its attachment to principles and values which had been a source of great strength to the party in the immediate aftermath of the war. Nowhere was the party's agony more plainly revealed in the 1980s than in its growing inability to appeal to the young. In the first ballot of the 1988 presidential elections, less than 6 per cent of voters aged between 18 and 24 voted for the Communist candidate; his best performance was among the age groups which had experienced the resistance. The party had become a retirement home for old men and women, basking in fond memories of the glorious past. It had little to offer to younger generations, for whom the battles of the resistance and the Cold War represented nothing more than echoes of a distant past.

In other words, the party was exhausted. It could no longer inspire young men like Étienne Boulanger to risk their lives for the sake of a heroic institution, the promise of a better world, or simply the pursuit of a moral ideal. Before his untimely death on the eve of the Second World War, the Communist journalist Paul Vaillant-Couturier used to repeat that *le communisme est la jeunesse de ce monde*—Communism is the youth of the world. By the 1990s the decline of the movement in France (and across Europe) had painfully demonstrated that youth is never eternal.

Chronology

1920   December. Tours congress of the SFIO splits over membership of Third International.

1921   May. First national congress of the Communist Party.

1923   January. Resignation of General Secretary, Oscar Louis Frossard.

1925   May. PCF launches campaign against colonial war in Morocco.

1927   November. Adoption of 'class against class' tactic by Central Committee.

1934   October. Thorez speech invites creation of Popular Front against fascism.

1936   May. Election of Popular Front government; Communists decline to participate.

1938   October. Munich agreement ratified by French National Assembly by 535 votes against 73 (of which 72 were Communist).

1939   September. After PCF approval of Nazi-Soviet agreement, French government announces dissolution of Communist Party.

1940   June. Defeat and capitulation of French Army; PCF defines war as imperialist, and refuses to join de Gaulle in advocating resistance against Germans.

1941   June. Nazi invasion of Soviet Union; launching of French Communist campaign for resistance against Vichy and German occupation.

1942   September. First issue of clandestine Communist literary journal *Les Lettres françaises*.

1944   September. Communist ministers join provisional government headed by de Gaulle.

1946   November. PCF wins largest share of votes in legislative elections (28.6 per cent).

1947   May. Communist ministers sacked by Socialist premier Ramadier.

1953   March. Death of Joseph Stalin.

1954   November. PCF condemns nationalist insurrection in Algeria.

1956   November. Soviet invasion of Hungary approved by PCF.

1958   November. Severe defeat of Communists in legislative elections.

1964   May. Waldeck Rochet becomes General Secretary.

1965   December. PCF supports Mitterrand as common candidate of Left against de Gaulle in presidential elections.

1968   August. Communist leadership condemns Soviet invasion of Czechoslovakia.

1970   February. Georges Marchais emerges as new leader.

1972   June. Joint programme of government signed by PCF and Socialist Party.

1978   March. Defeat of Left in legislative elections.

        April. Beginning of internal rebellion against party leadership.

1980   January. PCF supports Soviet invasion of Afghanistan.

1981   May. Election of François Mitterrand to presidency, with Communist support on second ballot.

        June. Communists invited to join Socialist government.

1984   July. Communists leave government.

1987   December. Former Communist ministers marginalized; reaffirmation of superiority of Soviet-style Communism over capitalism.

1988   April. Poor performance of Communist candidate Lajoinie in presidential election.

May. François Mitterrand re-elected for second term as President.

1991   March. Birth of Democratic Party of the Left after Rimini congress of Italian Communist Party.

1992   January. Resignation of Mikhail Gorbachev, last President of the Soviet Union.

BIBLIOGRAPHIES

Bibliographical references in Chapter 1 will be found in the footnotes.

CHAPTER 2   THE POLITICAL ROLES
OF INTELLECTUALS

Primary Texts

ARON, RAYMOND, *The Opium of the Intellectuals* (London: Secker and Warburg, 1957).
—— *Mémoires* (Paris: Julliard, 1983).
BENDA, JULIEN, *La Trahison des clercs* (Paris: J. J. Pauvert, 1937).
DEBRAY, RÉGIS, *Le Pouvoir intellectuel en France* (Paris: Ramsay, 1979).
FINKIELKRAUT, ALAIN, *La Défaite de la pensée* (Paris: Gallimard, 1977).
GLUCKSMANN, ANDRÉ, *Les Maîtres penseurs* (Paris: Grasset, 1977).
KANAPA, JEAN, *Critique de la Culture*. 2 vols (Paris: Éditions Sociales, 1957).
LÉVY, BERNARD-HENRI, *Éloge des Intellectuels* (Paris: Grasset, 1987).
QUINET, EDGAR, *La République: conditions de la régénération de la France* (Paris: Dentu, 1873).
SARTRE, JEAN-PAUL, *Plaidoyer pour les Intellectuels* (Paris: Gallimard, 1972).

Studies of Particular Periods or Intellectual Communities

BELLESORT, ANDRÉ, *Les Intellectuels et l'avènement de la troisième république 1871–1875* (Paris: Grasset, 1931).
BOURDIEU, PIERRE, *Homo academicus* (Paris: Minuit, 1984).
—— *La Noblesse d'état: grandes écoles et esprit de corps* (Paris: Minuit, 1990).
CAUTE, DAVID, *Communism and the French Intellectuals 1914–1960* (London: André Deutsch, 1964).
CHARLE, CHRISTOPHE, *La Naissance des 'intellectuels'* (Paris: Minuit, 1990).
DIGEON, CLAUDE, *La Crise allemande de la pensée française* (Paris: Presses Universitaires de la France, 1959).
GAGNION, ALAIN (ed.), *Intellectuals in Liberal Democracies* (New York: Praeger, 1987).
HAZAREESINGH, SUDHIR, *Intellectuals and the French Communist Party: Disillusion and Decline* (Oxford: Oxford University Press, 1991).
JUDT, TONY, *Un Passé imparfait: les intellectuels en France 1944–1956* (Paris: Fayard, 1992).

MACLEAN, I., WINCH, P., and MONTEFIORE, A., *The Political Responsibility of Intellectuals* (Cambridge: Cambridge University Press, 1990).

ORY, PASCAL, and SIRINELLI, JEAN-FRANÇOIS, *Les Intellectuels en France, de l'Affaire Dreyfus à nos jours* (Paris: Armand Colin, 1986).

SIRINELLI, JEAN-FRANÇOIS, *Génération intellectuelle: khâgneux et normaliens dans l'entre-deux-guerres* (Paris: Fayard, 1992).

SULEIMAN, EZRA, *Private Power and Centralization in France: The Notaires and the French State* (Princeton, NJ: Princeton University Press, 1987).

CHAPTER 3   THE REPUBLICAN TRADITION

Primary Sources

BARNI, JULES, *Manuel républicain* (Paris: Librairie Germer Baillière, 1872).

BARRAL, PIERRE, *Les Fondateurs de la troisième république* (Paris: Armand Colin, 1968).

BOURGEOIS, LÉON, *La Solidarité* (Paris: Armand Colin, 1896).

CONDORCET, MARIE DE, *Esquisse d'un Tableau historique des Progrès de l'esprit humain* (Paris: Flammarion, 1988; first published in 1793).

DEBRAY, RÉGIS, *Qui vive la république!* (Paris: Jacob, 1988).

MAUBLANC, RENÉ, *Esquisse d'une Morale républicaine* (Paris: Bibliothèque Française, 1945).

MENDÈS-FRANCE, PIERRE, *La République moderne* (Paris: Gallimard, 1962).

ROBESPIERRE, MAXIMILIEN, *Textes choisis*. 3 vols (Paris: Éditions Sociales, 1974).

SIEYÈS, EMMANUEL, *Qu'est-ce que le tiers état?* (Paris: Presses Universitaires de France, 1982).

TARDIEU, ANDRÉ, *La République à refaire* (Paris: Gallimard, 1932).

Studies of Republicanism

AGULHON, MAURICE, *La République au village* (Paris: Seuil, 1979).

—— *Les Quarante-Huitards* (Paris: Gallimard-Julliard, 1975).

AZÉMA, JEAN-PIERRE, and WINOCK, MICHEL, *La Troisième République: naissance et mort* (Paris: Calmann-Lévy, 1976).

BERSTEIN, SERGE, and RUDELLE, ODILE, *Le Modèle républicain* (Paris: Presses Universitaires de France, 1992).

ELGEY, GEORGETTE, *La Quatrième République*. 3 vols (Paris: Fayard, 1965–92).

ESTÈBE, JEAN, *Les Ministres de la république* (Paris: Presses de la Fondation Nationale des Sciences Politiques, 1982).

GUILHAUMOU, JACQUES, *Marseilles républicaine 1791–1793* (Paris: Presses de la Fondation Nationale des Sciences Politiques, 1992).

HALÉVY, DANIEL, *La République des ducs* (Paris: Grasset, 1937; reprint, Livre de Poche, 1972).

HAMON, LÉO (ed.), *Les Opportunistes: les débuts de la république aux républicains* (Paris: Éditions de la Maison des Sciences de l'Homme, 1991).

HAYWARD, JACK, 'The official social philosophy of the French Third Republic: Léon Bourgeois and solidarism', *International Review of Social History* 6 (1961), 19–48.

NICOLET, CLAUDE, *L'Idée républicaine en France* (Paris: Gallimard, 1982).

—— *La République en France: état des lieux* (Paris: Seuil, 1992).

NORA, PIERRE (ed.), *Les Lieux de mémoire*, vol. 1, *La République* (Paris: Gallimard, 1984).

PETOT, JEAN, 'La tradition républicaine en France', *Jahrbuch des Öffentlichen Rechts der Gegenwart* 38 (1989), 77–108.

WILLIAMS, PHILIP, *Crisis and Compromise: Politics in the Fourth Republic* (London: Longman, 1964).

ZELDIN, THEODORE, *France 1848–1945*. 4 vols (Oxford: Clarendon Press, 1979–81).

CHAPTER 4 RELIGION, CLERICALISM, AND THE REPUBLICAN STATE

Primary Sources

BONALD, LOUIS DE, *Théorie du Pouvoir politique et religieux* (Paris: UGE, 1965).

DRUMONT, EDOUARD, *La France juive* (Paris: Marpon et Flammarion, 1885).

GAMBETTA, LÉON, *Le Cléricalisme* [speech given at the National Assembly in May 1877] (Paris: Société d'Instruction Républicaine, 1877).

JOLY, ALBERT, *L'Enseignement clérical et la société civile* (Paris: Société d'Instruction Républicaine, 1873).

MAISTRE, JOSEPH DE, *Considérations sur la France* (Paris: Garnier, 1980).

VALSERRES, F. DE, *Foi et Patrie, ou la France chrétienne* (Limoges: Barbou, 1872).

VEUILLOT, LOUIS, *Paris pendant les deux sièges* (Paris: Victor Palmé, 1871).

Studies of Religious and Anticlerical Groups

GIBSON, RALPH, *A Social History of French Catholicism 1789–1914* (London: Routledge, 1989).

LAUNAY, MARCEL, *Le Bon Prêtre: le clergé rural au XIXème siècle* (Paris: Aubier, 1986).

LEVALLAIN, PHILIPPE, *Albert de Mun: catholicisme français et catholicisme romain du Syllabus au Ralliement* (Rome: École Française de Rome, 1982).

LOCKE, ROBERT R., *French Legitimists and the Politics of Moral Order in the Early Third Republic* (Princeton, NJ: Princeton University Press, 1974).

MAYEUR, JEAN-MARIE, *Catholicisme et Démocratie chrétienne* (Paris: Le Cerf, 1986).

PIERRARD, PIERRE, *La Vie quotidienne du prêtre français au XIXème siècle 1801–1905* (Paris: Hachette, 1986).

POULAT, EMILE, *Église contre bourgeoisie* (Tournai: Casterman, 1977).

RÉMOND, RENÉ, *L'Anticlericalisme en France* (Brussels: Complexe, 1985).

SIRINELLI, JEAN-FRANÇOIS, *Histoire des Droites en France*, vol. 3, *Sensibilités* (Paris: Gallimard, 1992).

CHAPTER 5   THE TWO FACES OF FRENCH NATIONALISM

Nationalist Writings

BARRÈS, MAURICE, *Scènes et Doctrines du nationalisme*. 2 vols (Paris: Plon, 1925).

GAULLE, CHARLES DE, *Mémoires d'Espoir*. 2 vols (Paris: Plon, 1970–1).

GIRARDET, RAOUL, *Le Nationalisme français 1871–1914* [an anthology] (Paris: Armand Colin, 1966).

LE PEN, JEAN-MARIE, *Les Français d'abord* (Paris: Carrère/Lafon, 1984).

MAURRAS, CHARLES, *Mes Idées politiques* (Paris: Albatros, 1986).

RENAN, ERNEST, *Qu'est-ce une nation?* (Paris: Calmann-Levy, 1882).

Studies of French Nationalism

AZÉMA, JEAN-PIERRE, and BÉDARIDA, FRANÇOIS, *Vichy et les français* (Paris: Fayard, 1992).

BRUNET, JEAN PAUL, *Jacques Doriot: du communisme au fascisme* (Paris: Balland, 1986).

CAMUS, JEAN-YVES, and MONZAT, RENÉ, *Les Droites nationales et radicales en France* (Lyons: Presses Universitaires de Lyon, 1992).

DREYFUS, FRANÇOIS-GEORGES, *Histoire de Vichy* (Paris: Perrin, 1990).

GUILLEMIN, HENRI, *Nationalistes et Nationaux 1870–1940* (Paris: Gallimard, 1974).

HOFFMANN, STANLEY, *Le Mouvement Poujade* (Paris: Armand Colin, 1956).

JENKINS, BRIAN, *Nationalism in France: Class and Nation since 1789* (London: Routledge, 1990).

LACOUTURE, JEAN, *De Gaulle*. 3 vols (Paris: Seuil, 1984–6).

NGUYEN, VICTOR, *Aux Origines de l'Action Française* (Paris: Fayard, 1991).

PERRINEAU, PASCAL, and MAYER, NONNA (eds), *Le Front National à découvert* (Paris: Presses de la Fondation Nationale des Sciences Politiques, 1989).

RÉMOND, RENÉ, *Les Droites en France* (Paris: Armand Colin, 1982).

STERNHELL, ZEEV, *Ni droite ni gauche: l'idéologie fasciste en France* (Paris: Complexe, 1987).

TOMBS, ROBERT (ed.), *Nationhood and Nationalism in France: From Boulangism to the Great War 1889–1918* (London: HarperCollins Academic, 1991).

WINOCK, MICHEL, *Nationalisme, antisémitisme, et fascisme en France* (Paris: Seuil, 1990).
ZELDIN, THEODORE, *France 1848–1945* (Oxford: Clarendon Press, 1987).

CHAPTER 6   THE STRENGTHS AND LIMITS OF THE ÉTATISTE TRADITION

Historical Perspectives of the State

BRAUDEL, FERNAND, *The Identity of France* (London: Collins, 1988).
CHARLE, CHRISTOPHE, *Les Hauts Fonctionnaires en France au XIXème siècle* (Paris: Gallimard-Julliard, 1980).
ESTÈBE, JEAN, *Les Ministres de la République 1871–1914* (Paris: Presses de la Fondation Nationale des Sciences Politiques, 1982).
GIRARDET, RAOUL, *L'Idée coloniale en France* (Paris: Table Ronde, 1972).
LEROY-BEAULIEU, PAUL, *L'État moderne et ses fonctions* (Paris: Guillaumin, 1900).
TOCQUEVILLE, ALEXIS DE, *L'Ancien Régime et la révolution* [first published in 1856] (Paris: Gallimard, 1967).
WRIGHT, VINCENT, *Le Conseil d'État sous le second empire* (Paris: Armand Colin, 1972).

Aspects of the Modern State

BIRNBAUM, PIERRE, *Les Sommets de l'État: essai sur l'élite du pouvoir en France* (Paris: Seuil, 1977).
CROZIER, MICHEL, *La Société bloquée* (Paris: Seuil, 1970).
HALL, PETER, *Governing the Economy: The Politics of State Intervention in Britain and France* (Cambridge: Polity, 1986).
HAYWARD, JACK, *The State and the Market Economy: Industrial Patriotism and Economic Intervention in France* (Brighton: Harvester, 1986).
HOFFMANN, STANLEY, *France: Change and Tradition* (London: Gollancz, 1963).
JOBERT, BRUNO, and MULLER, PIERRE, *L'État en action: politiques publiques et corporatismes* (Paris: Presses Universitaires de France, 1987).
KESSLER, MARIE-CHRISTINE, *Les Grands Corps de l'État* (Paris: Berger-Levrault, 1985).
POULANTZAS, NICOS (ed.), *La Crise de l'État* (Paris: Presse Universitaires de France, 1976).
ROSANVALLON, PIERRE, *L'État en France* (Paris: Seuil, 1990).
WRIGHT, VINCENT, *The Government and Politics of France*. 3rd ed. (London: Unwin Hyman, 1989).

CHAPTER 7   WHY NO PEACE MOVEMENT IN FRANCE?

Pacifist Writings

ALAIN [Chartier, Émile], *Mars ou la guerre jugée* (Paris: Gallimard, 1950).

BONZON, THIERRY (ed.), *Nous crions grâce: 154 lettres de pacifistes* (Paris: Éditions Ouvrières, 1989).

BRIAND, ARISTIDE, *Paroles de paix* (Paris: Figuière, 1927).

GIONO, JEAN, *Écrits pacifiques* (Paris: Gallimard, 1978).

LECOIN, LOUIS, *Écrits 1948–1971* (Boulogne: Union Pacifique, 1974).

Studies of Pacifism

ARON, RAYMOND, *Paix et guerre entre les nations* (Paris: Calmann-Lévy, 1962).

BILIS, M., *Socialistes et pacifistes 1933–1939* (Paris: Syros, 1979).

CARTER, APRIL, *Peace Movements: International Protest and World Politics since 1945* (London: Longman, 1992).

CEADEL, MARTIN, *Thinking about Peace and War* (Oxford: Oxford University Press, 1987).

COOPER, SANDI, *Patriotic Pacifism: Waging War on War in Europe 1815–1914* (Oxford: Oxford University Press, 1991).

COURTOIS, STÉPHANE, *Le PCF dans la guerre* (Paris: Ramsay, 1980).

FAUCIER, NICOLAS, *Pacifisme et antimilitarisme dans l'entre-deux-guerres 1919–1939* (Paris: Spartacus, 1983).

INGRAM, NORMAN, *The Politics of Dissent: Pacifism in France 1919–1939* (Oxford: Oxford University Press, 1990).

ROCHON, THOMAS, *Mobilizing for Peace: The Anti-Nuclear Movements in Western Europe* (Princeton, NJ: Princeton University Press, 1988).

SABIANI, JULIE (ed.), *Le Pacifisme dans les lettres françaises de la belle époque aux années trente* (Orléans: Centre Charles Péguy, 1985).

WINOCK, MICHEL, 'Le pacifisme à la française 1789–1991', *L'Histoire* 144 (May 1991), 34–45.

CHAPTER 8   LIBERALISM AND THE ELUSIVE SEARCH FOR CONSENSUS

Writings of Nineteenth- and Twentieth-Century Liberals

ALAIN [CHARTIER, ÉMILE], *Éléments d'une doctrine radicale* (Paris: Gallimard, 1925).

BAYET, ALBERT, *Le Radicalisme* (Paris: Valois, 1932).

BOURGEOIS, LÉON, *La Solidarité* (Paris: Armand Colin, 1896).

CONSTANT, BENJAMIN, *Principes de politique* (Geneva: Droz, 1980).

GISCARD d'ESTAING, VALÉRY, *Démocratie française* (Paris: Fayard, 1976).

GUIZOT, FRANÇOIS, *Des Conspirations et de la justice politique* [first published in 1822] (Paris: Fayard, 1984).

MANENT, PIERRE, *Les Libéraux, de Milton à Raymond Aron* [a collection of texts] (Paris: Hachette, 1986).

MENDÈS-FRANCE, PIERRE, *La République moderne* (Paris: Gallimard, 1962).

MINC, ALAIN, *La Machine égalitaire* (Paris: Grasset, 1987).

PRÉVOST-PARADOL, LUCIEN, *La France nouvelle* (Paris: Garnier, 1868).

SORMAN, GUY, *La Solution libérale* (Paris: Fayard, 1984).

TOCQUEVILLE, ALEXIS DE, *Souvenirs* (Paris: Calmann-Lévy, 1893).

Studies of Liberalism

BERSTEIN, SERGE, *Histoire du Parti radical*. 2 vols (Paris: Presses de la Fondation Nationale des Sciences Politiques, 1980–2).

CAILLOT, E. FRANÇOIS, *La Pensée libérale au 19ème siècle* [On Constant, Tocqueville, and Prévost-Paradol] (Lyons: Hermès, 1987).

DREYFUS, F. GEORGES, *Histoire de la Démocratie-Chrétienne en France* (Paris: Albin Michel, 1988).

GIRARD, LOUIS, *Les Libéraux français 1814–1875* (Paris: Aubier, 1985).

MANENT, PIERRE, *Histoire intellectuelle du libéralisme: dix leçons* (Paris: Calmann-Lévy, 1987).

MEYSONNIER, SIMONE, *La Balance et l'horloge: la genèse de la pensée libérale en France au 18ème siècle* (Montreuil: Éditions de la Passion, 1989).

NORDMANN, J. THOMAS, *Histoire des Radicaux 1820–1973* (Paris: La Table Ronde, 1974).

PRELOT, MARCEL, and GALLOUÉDEC-GENUYS, F., *Le libéralisme catholique* (Paris: Armand Colin, 1969).

RÉMOND, RENÉ, *Les Droites en France* (Paris: Armand Colin, 1982).

SIRINELLI, JEAN-FRANÇOIS, *Histoire des Droites en France*. 3 vols (Paris: Gallimard, 1992).

WARSHAW, DAN, *Paul Leroy-Beaulieu and Established Liberalism in France* (Dekalb, Ill.: Northern Illinois University Press, 1991).

CHAPTER 9 RESURRECTION AND DEATH: THE SOCIALIST TRADITION

Writings of Socialist Thinkers and Leaders

BLANC, LOUIS, *Organisation du Travail* (Paris: Prévot, 1840).

BLUM, LÉON, *A l'Échelle humaine* [Includes the speech 'Pour la vieille maison', given at the 1920 Tours congress] (Paris: Gallimard, 1971).

CHEVÈNEMENT, JEAN-PIERRE, *Le Pari sur l'intelligence* (Paris: Flammarion, 1985).

FABIUS, LAURENT, *C'est en allant vers la mer* (Paris: Seuil, 1990).

FOURIER, CHARLES, *Oeuvres complètes* (Paris: Anthropos, 1971).
GUESDE, JULES, *État, politiques, et morale de classe* (Paris: Giard et Brière, 1901).
JAURÈS, JEAN, *Études socialistes* (Paris: Ollendorf, 1902).
LEROUX, PIERRE, *Oeuvres 1825–1850* (Geneva: Slatkin, 1978).
MAUROY, PIERRE, *A gauche* (Paris: Albin Michel, 1985).
MITTERRAND, FRANÇOIS, *Politique (1938–1981)* (Paris: Marabout, 1984).
PROUDHON, PIERRE-JOSEPH, *Textes et Débats* (Paris: Livre de Poche, 1984).
ROCARD, MICHEL, *Le Coeur à l'ouvrage* (Paris: Seuil/Jacob, 1987).

Studies of French Socialism

BELL, DAVID SCOTT, and CRIDDLE, BYRON, *The French Socialist Party: The Emergence of a Party of Government* (Oxford: Oxford University Press, 1988).
BERGOUNIOUX, ALAIN, and GRUNBERG, GÉRARD, *Le Long Remords du pouvoir: le parti Socialiste français 1905–1992* (Paris: Fayard, 1992).
BRUNET, JEAN-PAUL, *Histoire du Socialisme en France de 1871 à nos jours* (Paris: Presses Universitaires de France, 1989).
DANIEL, JEAN, *Les Religions d'un président* (Paris: Grasset, 1988).
JUDT, TONY, *Marxism and the French Left* (Oxford: Oxford University Press, 1986).
LEFRANC, GEORGES, *Le Mouvement socialiste sous la troisième république*. 2 vols (Paris: Payot, 1977).
LIGOU, DANIEL, *Histoire du Socialisme en France 1871–1961* (Paris: Presses Universitaires de France, 1962).
MARET, JEAN, and HOULOU, ALAIN (eds), *Histoire des socialistes: l'identité socialiste des utopistes à nos jours* (Paris: PRO-EDI, 1990).
SAMUEL, ALBERT, *Le Socialisme: histoire, courants, pratiques* (Lyons: Chronique Sociale, 1981).
WILLARD, CLAUDE, *Socialisme et Communisme français* (Paris: Armand Colin, 1978).

CHAPTER 10   GAULLISM AND THE QUEST FOR NATIONAL UNITY

Gaullist Writings

CHABAN-DELMAS, JACQUES, *L'Ardeur* (Paris: Stock, 1975).
DEBRÉ, MICHEL, *Ces Princes qui nous gouvernent* (Paris: Plon, 1957).
——— *Trois républiques pour une France*. 4 vols (Paris: Albin Michel, 1984–8).
GAULLE, CHARLES DE, *Vers l'Armée de métier* (Paris: Berger-Levrault, 1934).
——— *Mémoires de guerre*. 3 vols (Paris: Plon, 1954–9).
——— *Mémoires d'espoir*. 2 vols (Paris: Plon, 1970–1).

MALRAUX, ANDRÉ, *Antimémoires* (Paris: Gallimard, 1967).
—— *Les Chênes qu'on abat* (Paris: Gallimard, 1971).
MICHELET, EDMOND, *Le Gaullisme, passionante aventure* (Paris: Fayard, 1962).
PALEWSKI, GASTON, *Mémoires d'action 1924–1974* (Paris: Plon, 1988).
POMPIDOU, GEORGES, *Le Noeud gordien* (Paris: Plon, 1974).
SOUSTELLE, JACQUES, *Vingt-huit ans de gaullisme* (Paris: J'ai Lu, 1971).

Studies of de Gaulle and Gaullism

CHARLOT, JEAN, *Le Gaullisme d'opposition 1946–1958* (Paris: Fayard, 1983).
—— *The Gaullist Phenomenon* (London: Allen and Unwin, 1971).
DREFUS, FRANÇOIS-GEORGES, *De Gaulle et le gaullisme* (Paris: Presses Universitaires de France, 1982).
GIESBERT, FRANZ-OLIVIER, *Jacques Chirac* (Paris: Seuil, 1987).
LACOUTURE, JEAN, *De Gaulle*. 3 vols (Paris: Seuil, 1984–6).
PONCEYRI, ROBERT, *Gaullisme électoral et 5ème république*. 2 vols (Toulouse: Presses de L'IEP de Toulouse, 1985–6).
RÉMOND, RENÉ, *Les Droites en France* (Paris: Aubier, 1982).
RUDELLE, ODILE, *Mai 58, de Gaulle et la république* (Paris: Plon, 1988).
SIRINELLI, JEAN-FRANÇOIS, *Histoire des Droites en France*. 3 vols (Paris: Gallimard, 1992).
WILLIAMS, PHILIP, and HARRISON, MARTIN, *Politics and Society in de Gaulle's Republic* (New York: Anchor, 1973).

CHAPTER 11 THE IMPLOSION OF THE COMMUNIST TRADITION

Writings of Party Members (and Ex-Communists)

ALTHUSSER, LOUIS, *Ce qui ne peut plus durer dans le PC* (Paris: Maspéro, 1978).
DUCLOS, JACQUES, *Mémoires*. 7 vols (Paris: Fayard, 1967–73).
HINCKER, FRANÇOIS, *Le Parti communiste au carrefour: essai sur quinze ans de son histoire 1965–1981* (Paris: Albin Michel, 1981).
KRIEGEL, ANNIE, *Ce que j'ai cru comprendre* (Paris: Laffont, 1991).
LE ROY LADURIE, EMMANUEL, *Paris-Montpellier: PC-PSU 1945–1963* (Paris: Gallimard, 1962).
MARCHAIS, GEORGES, *Le défi démocratique* (Paris: Grasset, 1973).
MORIN, EDGAR, *Autocritique* (Paris: Julliard, 1959; reprint, Éditions du Seuil, 1975).
SPIRE, ANTOINE, *Profession permanent* (Paris: Seuil, 1980).
THOREZ, MAURICE, *Fils du peuple* (Paris: Éditions Sociales, 1949).
TILLON, CHARLES, *On chantait rouge* (Paris: Laffont, 1977).

Studies of the PCF

COURTOIS, STÉPHANE, *Le PCF dans la guerre* (Paris: Ramsay, 1980).

HAZAREESINGH, SUDHIR, *Intellectuals and the French Communist Party: Disillusion and Decline* (Oxford: Oxford University Press, 1991).

KRIEGEL, ANNIE, *Les Communistes* (Paris: Seuil, 1968).

LAVAU, GEORGES, *A quoi sert le parti communiste français?* (Paris: Fayard, 1981).

LAZAR, MARC, *Maisons rouges: les partis communistes français et italiens de la Libération à nos jours* (Paris: Aubier, 1992).

PUDAL, BERNARD, *Prendre parti: pour une sociologie historique du PCF* (Paris: Presses de la Fondation Nationale des Sciences Politiques, 1989).

RACINE, NICOLE, and BODIN, LOUIS, *Le PC pendant l'entre-deux-guerres* (Paris: Armand Colin, 1972).

RIOUX, J. P., PROST, A., and AZÉMA, JEAN-PIERRE (ed.), *Les Communistes français, de Munich à Chateaubriant* (Paris: Presses de la Fondation Nationale des Sciences Politiques, 1987).

ROBRIEUX, PHILIPPE, *Histoire intérieure du parti communiste*. 4 vols (Paris: Fayard, 1980–4).

VERDÈS-LEROUX, JEANNINE, *Au Service du parti: le PC, les intellectuels, et la culture 1944–1956* (Paris: Fayard, 1983).

—— *Le Réveil des somnambules: le PC, les intellectuels, et la culture 1956–1985* (Paris: Fayard, 1987).

INDEX